THE ART OF THEOLOGY

STUDIES IN PHILOSOPHICAL THEOLOGY, 25

Series editors:
Lieven Boeve (Leuven), Willem B. Drees (Leiden), Douglas Hedley (Cambridge)
Advisory Board: H.J. Adriaanse (Leiden), V. Brümmer (Utrecht), P. Byrne (London), J. Clayton (Boston), I.R. Dalferth (Zürich), J. Greisch (Paris), E. Herrmann (Uppsala), M.M. Olivetti (Rome), C. Schwöbel (Heidelberg), J. Soskice (Cambridge)

Editorial Profile:
Philosophical theology is the study of philosophical problems which arise in reflection upon religious beliefs and theological doctrines.

1   H. de Vries, *Theologie im Pianissimo & zwischen Rationalität und Dekonstruktion*, Kampen, 1989
2   S. Breton, *La pensée du rien*, Kampen, 1992
3   Ch. Schwöbel, *God: Action and Revelation*, Kampen, 1992
4   V. Brümmer (ed.), *Interpreting the Universe as Creation*, Kampen, 1991
5   L.J. van den Brom, *Divine Presence in the World*, Kampen, 1993
6   M. Sarot, *God, Passibility and Corporeality*, Kampen, 1992
7   G. van den Brink, *Almighty God*, Kampen 1993
8   P.-C. Lai, *Towards a Trinitarian Theology of Religions: A Study of Paul Tillich's Thought*, Kampen, 1994
9   L. Velecky, *Aquinas' Five Arguments in the* Summa Theologiae *Ia 2, 3*, Kampen, 1994
10 W. Dupré, *Patterns in Meaning. Reflections on meaning and truth in cultural reality, religious traditions, and dialogical encounters*, Kampen, 1994
11 P.T. Erne, *Lebenskunst. Aneignung ästhetischer Erfahrung*, Kampen, 1994
12 U. Perone, *Trotz/dem Subjekt*, Leuven, 1998
13 H.J. Adriaanse, *Vom Christentum aus: Aufsätze und Vorträge zur Religionsphilosophie*, Kampen, 1995
14 D.A. Pailin, *Probing the Foundations: A Study in Theistic Reconstruction*, Kampen, 1994
15 M. Potepa, *Schleiermachers hermeneutische Dialektik*, Kampen, 1996
16 E. Herrmann, *Scientific Theory and Religious Belief, An Essay on the Rationality of Views of Life*, Kampen, 1995
17 V. Brümmer & M. Sarot, *Happiness, Well-Being and the Meaning of Life, a Dialogue of Social Science and Religion*, Kampen, 1996
18 T.L. Hettema, *Reading for Good. Narrative Theology and Ethics in the Joseph Story from the Perspective of Ricœur's Hermeneutics*, Kampen, 1996
19 H. Düringer, *Universale Vernunft und partikularer Glaube. Eine theologische Auswertung des Werkes von Jürgen Habermas*, Leuven, 1999
20 E. Dekker, *Middle Knowledge*, Leuven, 2000
21 T. Ekstrand, *Max Weber in a Theological Perspective*, Leuven, 2000
22 C. Helmer & K. de Troyer (eds), *Truth: Interdisciplinary Dialogues in a Pluralistic Age*, Leuven, 2003
23 L. Boeve & L.P. Hemming (eds), *Divinising Experience. Essays in the History of Religious Experience from Origens to Ricœur*, Leuven, 2004
24 P.D. Murray, *Reason, Truth and Theology in Pragmatist Perspective*, Leuven, 2004

THE ART OF THEOLOGY

HANS URS VON BALTHASAR'S THEOLOGICAL AESTHETICS AND THE FOUNDATIONS OF FAITH

by

STEPHAN VAN ERP

PEETERS
LEUVEN – PARIS – DUDLEY, MA
2004

Library of Congress Cataloging-in-Publication Data

Erp, Stephan van, 1966-
  The art of theology: Hans Urs von Balthasar's theological aesthetics and the foundations of faith / by Stephan van Erp.
    p. cm. -- (Studies in philosophical theology ; 25)
  Includes bibliographical references and index.
  ISBN 90-429-1467-X (alk. paper)
    1. Balthasar, Hans Urs von, 1905 – I. Title. II. Series.

BX4705.B163E77 2004
230'.2'092--dc22

2004043794

© 2004 - Peeters, Bondgenotenlaan 153, 3000 Leuven, Belgium.

ISBN 90-429-1467-X
D. 2004/0602/73

All rights reserved. No part of this book may be reproduced or transmitted in any form or by any means, electronic or mechanical, including photocopying, recording, or by any information storage and retrieval system, without permission in writing from the publisher.

ACKNOWLEDGEMENTS

When I started doing the research which resulted in this book, I thought it would be a lonely enterprise. The opposite has proven true. Along the way and especially in the past few months, I have discovered that performing the art of theology is a fertile ground for friendship, and encouraging and inspiring conversations.

First of all, I owe a debt of gratitude to Frans Maas and Nico Schreurs who supervised this research. With great interest and involvement, they patiently followed my explorations in the new field of theological aesthetics and the intricate theology of Hans Urs von Balthasar. I also would like to thank many others who contributed to this book, by engaging in discussions on theology and aesthetics or on specific topics about which they knew much more. Among them, I would especially like to mention Inigo Bocken, Erik Borgman, Georges De Schrijver, Rob van Gerwen, Robert Jan Peeters, Derk Stegeman, Rudi Te Velde, Holger Zaborowski and the members of the TOOG research group of the Theological Faculty of Tilburg, the Netherlands.

It would have been much more difficult to write this book in the English language if I had not received an invitation of John Webster and the Master of St Benet's Hall, Dom Henry Wansborough o.s.b., to study at the University of Oxford for two years. Despite our radical differences, John Webster has become a major influence on my thought, and not only by persistently encouraging me to articulate those differences. In Oxford, I met many friends and colleagues, among whom Jennifer Cooper, Bernard Green o.s.b., Chris Harding, Philip Kennedy, Diarmaid MacCulloch and the late George Schner s.j., who all showed me new perspectives on the study of religion and taught me how to express my thoughts in English. However, without the language skills of Joe Halliwell, Peter Huddlestone and Huub Stegeman, this book could not have reached its present form and expression. Although any errors that remain are my own, Sigrid Schumacher saved me from the worst embarrassments by correcting the text. I gladly dedicate the book to her as one of a younger generation of students of theology who accept the challenge of understanding faith and religious traditions, which will become increasingly difficult in the twenty-first century.

Finally but not least importantly, I am grateful to the Netherlands Organisation for Scientific Research (NWO), the Theological Faculty of Tilburg, and the Radboud Foundation for their financial support and to the editors of Studies in Philosophical Theology for accepting this book in their series.

Tilburg, November 2003
Stephan van Erp

TABLE OF CONTENTS

Acknowledgements V

Table of contents VII

Abbreviations XIII

Introduction 1

A. FUNDAMENTAL THEOLOGY AND AESTHETICS 9

1. Fundamental theology 11

   1.1. What is theology? A short answer 11
      a. Reasoning about God 11
      b. Communicating faith 13
   1.2. Fundamental theology: history and criticisms. . . . 15
      a. A short history of fundamental theology 16
      b. Criticisms of fundamental theology 20
      c. Maintaining the field 23
   1.3. Three challenges for fundamental theology 25
      a. Possibility in diversity 26
      b. Particularity in expression 27
      c. Freedom in responsibility 28
   1.4. In search of method 30
      a. The limitations of meta-theories 31
      b. The limitations of current methods 34
   1.5. Demonstratio aesthetica? 37

2. Theology and aesthetics 41

   2.1. The return of aesthetics in theology 42

   2.2. Towards a theological aesthetics 45
      a. The ambivalent history of theology and the arts . . 45

b. The emergence of modern philosophical aesthetics
Alexander Baumgarten: aesthetics as the science of
sensory knowledge 46
Immanuel Kant: aesthetics of taste and the sublime. . 47
2.3. Foundations of theological aesthetics. 49
a. Gerardus van der Leeuw: imagination as a
consequence of the imago Dei 50
b. Paul Tillich: the work of art as the human expression
of ultimate meaning 53
c. Hans Urs von Balthasar: beauty as form and analogy
of the divine 54
2.4. Four types of contemporary theological aesthetics . . 57
a. Theologies of art 58
b. Aesthetics in philosophical theology 59
c. Transcendental-theological aesthetics 62
d. Theological aesthetics and redemption 64

B. HANS URS VON BALTHASAR'S THEOLOGICAL AESTHETICS . . 69

3. Hans Urs von Balthasar: a life in theology 71

3.1. Key dates in the life of Hans Urs von Balthasar . . . 71
3.2. Introducing Hans Urs von Balthasar. 73
a. A change in theological style. 74
b. A cultural education. 76
3.3. Finding the sources 79
a. Entering the Jesuit order 79
b. Catholic philosophy. 80
3.4. Strange meetings 81
a. Adrienne von Speyr 81
b. Karl Barth 82
3.5. Magnum opus 85

4. Theological hermeneutics and metaphysics 87

4.1. Theological context: history and method 88
4.2. Theological hermeneutics: incarnation as the alpha
and omega of theology 91

      a. The formal structure of theology 91
      b. The material realm of theology 94
          Revelation and history 94
          Revelation and mission 96
          Revelation and tradition 97
  4.3. Theological metaphysics I: the doctrine of the transcendentals 98
      a. Amending the philosophical doctrine of the transcendentals 99
      b. The transcendental and triune structure of the trilogy . 102
      c. The theological doctrine of the transcendentals . . . 104
          The triangular structure of theology 105
          A trinitarian interpretation of the transcendentals . . 105
  4.4. Theological metaphysics II: analogy of being 108
      a. Analogy of being and imago Dei 109
          Analogy and analogy of being 109
          Real distinction as the theological foundation of the analogy of being 111
      b. Analogy of being: the Catholic form of thought . . . 112
          Joseph Maréchal's epistemological foundation of knowledge of God 112
          Erich Przywara's ontological foundation of knowledge of God 113
          The influence of Przywara's concept of analogy on Balthasar 114
      c. Analogy of being within analogy of faith: in dialogue with Karl Barth 116
  4.5. Theology of the Trinity: katalogia trinitatis 117
      a. Trinitarian presuppositions of human logic 118
      b. Kenotic ontology 120

5. Theological aesthetics 125

  5.1. Towards a theology of beauty 126
      a. The beauty of revelation 127
      b. Perceiving the divine form 129
  5.2. Theological aesthetics I: foundations 131
      a. Structure: seeing the form 132
      b. Key concepts: form and glory 133

	Form	133
	Beauty and glory.	137
c.	Aesthetic evidences	139
	Subjective evidences	139
	Objective evidences	143
5.3.	**Theological aesthetics II: a guide through Herrlichkeit**	153
a.	Studies in theological styles	153
b.	The realm of metaphysics	148
c.	Old covenant and new covenant	151
5.4.	**Aesthetics as fundamental theology**	153
a.	Aesthetics as a theological criticism	153
	Against modern aesthetics	153
	Against the Protestant elimination of aesthetics . . .	154
	Against Catholic hermeneutics and historical-critical method	156
b.	The reciprocity of fundamental theology and dogmatic theology	157
c.	After the form of revelation	160

6. Nicholas of Cusa. The catalogical imagination 163

6.1.	**The Renaissance: passage to modernity?**	163
a.	The history of philosophy discontinued.	164
b.	The history of philosophy continued.	166
6.2.	**The history of metaphysics: before and after Cusanus**	169
a.	Metaphysical developments before Cusanus	170
b.	Metaphysical developments after Cusanus	172
6.3.	**Cusanus and Renaissance aesthetics**	174
a.	Aesthetics from the Middle Ages to modernity . . .	174
b.	A reconstruction of Cusanus's aesthetics	177
6.4.	**Human vision as analogy: a philosophical appraisal** .	180
a.	Cusanus and the analogy of being	180
b.	Glory and analogy	182
c.	Analogy as negative theology.	184
6.5.	**Seeing the present God: a theological critique** . . .	185
a.	Analogy as positive theology	186
b.	Created in the image of the possibility-to-be	188
6.6.	**Balthasar's primacy of catalogical vision**	191
a.	Seeing non-otherness in otherness	191

  b. The catalogical imagination 193

7. Friedrich Wilhelm Joseph Schelling. The Absolute in art . . 195

 7.1. The advancement of modernity 196
  a. Three modern developments 196
  b. Second god or modern Prometheus? 199
 7.2. Schelling and the aesthetics of German idealism . . 201
  a. German Idealism 201
   The age of revolution 201
   The aesthetics of Romanticism and Idealism 203
  b. Friedrich Wilhelm Joseph von Schelling 205
   Life and works 205
   Schelling's works on art and aesthetics 206
   Schelling's philosophy of art 208
 7.3. Absolute beauty: a philosophical appraisal 211
  a. The Ego and the sublime 211
   Fichte and the evolution of modernity 211
   The sublime nothingness of absolute freedom . . . 212
  b. The Absolute in art 213
   Nature and spirit 213
   Beauty, the sublime and the glory of God 214
 7.4. Being and God: a theological critique 215
  a. Freedom between the Absolute and the Ego 216
  b. Identity and analog 218
   Cusanus revisited 218
   A tritheistic God 219
  c. Mythology and theology 220
   Mythology 220
   Revelation 222
 7.5. Prometheus rebound 223

C. THEOLOGICAL AESTHETICS AS FUNDAMENTAL THEOLOGY . . 229

8. The art of theology 231

 8.1. Perceiving glory 231
  a. The legacy of modernity: appearance, production, charis 232

      b. Analogical foundation: love beyond expression . . . 235
      c. Catalogical foundation: trinitarian kenosis 237
      d. Theology: revelation and form 239

8.2. Fides quaerens imagines: faith seeking forms. . . . 242
      a. Perception: sense and sensibilities 245
      b. Imagination: playing the field 248
      c. Construction: building a theory 251

8.3. Understanding the sublime 254
      a. Doctrinal aesthetics 255
      b. Sublime redemption 258
      c. Kenotic reasoning 262

Bibliography 269

Index of names 293

ABBREVIATIONS

Analogie I	Analogie und Dialektik. Zur Klärung der theologischen Prinzipienlehre Karl Barths, in: *Divus Thomas* 22 (1944), 171-216.
Analogie II	Analogie und Natur. Zur Klärung der theologischen Prinzipienlehre Karl Barths, in: *Divus Thomas* 23 (1945), 3-56.
AddS	*Apokalypse der deutschen Seele. Studien zu einer Lehre von letzten Haltungen*: Bd. 1: *Der deutsche Idealismus*; Bd. 2: *Im Zeichen Nietsches*; Bd. 3: *Die Vergöttlichung des Todes*, Einsiedeln 1998² (1937-1939).
Bibliographie	*Hans Urs von Balthasar. Bibliographie 1925-1990*, [Bearbeitet von Cornelia Capol], Einsiedeln 1990.
EdmI	*Die Entwicklung der musikalishen Idee. Versuch einer Synthese der Musik*, Einsiedeln 1998 (Braunschweig 1925).
Epilog	*Epilog*, Einsiedeln 1987.
GdhM	*Die Gottesfrage des heutigen Menschen*, Wien/München 1956.
GiF	*Das Ganze im Fragment. Aspekte der Geschichtstheologie*, Einsiedeln 1990² (Einsiedeln 1963).
GinL	*Glaubhaft is nur Liebe*, Einsiedeln 1985⁵ (Einsiedeln 1963).
H I	*Herrlichkeit. Eine theologische Ästhetik I. Schau der Gestalt*, Einsiedeln 1961.
H II	*Herrlichkeit. Eine theologische Ästhetik II. Fächer der Stile*, [2 Bände: *1. Klerikale Stile, 2. Laikale Stile*], Einsiedeln 1962.
H III,1	*Herrlichkeit. Eine theologische Ästhetik III,1. Im Raum der Metaphysik*, [2 Bände: *1. Altertum, 2. Neuzeit*], Einsiedeln 1965.
H III,2,1	*Herrlichkeit. Eine theologische Ästhetik III,2. Theologie, 1. Alter Bund*, Einsiedeln 1966.
H III,2,2	*Herrlichkeit. Eine theologische Ästhetik III,2. Theologie, 2. Neuer Bund*, Einsiedeln 1969.

Katholisch	*Katholisch*, [Kriterien 36], Einsiedeln 1993³ (Einsiedeln 1975).
KB	*Karl Barth. Darstellung und Deutung seiner Theologie*, Einsiedeln 1976⁴ (Köln 1951).
MW	*Mein Werk—Durchblicke*, Einsiedeln 1990.
PI	*Pneuma und Institution*, [Skizzen zur Theologie IV], Einsiedeln 1974.
SC	*Spiritus Creator*, [Skizzen zur Theologie III], Einsiedeln 1967.
TD I	*Theodramatik I. Prolegomena*, Einsiedeln 1973.
TD II,1	*Theodramatik II. Die Personen des Spiels: II,1 Der Mensch in Gott*, Einsiedeln 1976.
TD II,2	*Theodramatik II. Die Personen des Spiels: II,2 Die Personen in Christus*, Einsiedeln 1978.
TD III	*Theodramatik III. Die Handlung*, Einsiedeln 1980.
TD IV	*Theodramatik IV. Das Endspiel*, Einsiedeln 1983.
TddT	*Theologie der drei Tage (Mysterium Paschale)*, Einsiedeln 1990 (Einsiedeln 1970).
TdG	*Theologie der Geschichte. Neue Fassung*, [Christ Heute, 8. Heft], Einsiedeln 1979⁶ (Einsiedeln 1959).
TL I	*Theologik I. Wahrheit der Welt*, Einsiedeln 1985.
TL II	*Theologik II. Wahrheit Gottes*, Einsiedeln 1985.
TL III	*Theologik III. Der Geist der Wahrheit*, Einsiedeln 1987.
UA	*Unser Auftrag. Bericht und Entwurf. Einführung in die von Adrienne von Speyr gegründete Johannesgemeinschaft*, Einsiedeln 1984.
VC	*Verbum Caro*, [Skizzen zur Theologie I], Einsiedeln 1990³ (Einsiedeln 1960).
Wis	*Die Wahrheit ist symphonisch. Aspekte des christlichen Pluralismus*, [Kriterien 29], Einsiedeln 1972.

INTRODUCTION

> Either the Maker
> Conceiving a holier revision
> Of what he had already created
> Sculpted man from his own ectoplasm,
> Or earth
> Being such a new precipitate
> Of the etheric heaven
> Cradled in dust unearthly crystals.
>
> Then Prometheus
> Gathered that fiery dust and slaked it
> With the pure spring water
> And rolled it under his hands,
> Pounded it, thumbed it, moulded it
> Into a body shaped like that of a god.
>
> From: Ted Hughes, *Tales from Ovid.*[1]

Creation evokes the language of art. It is a story of making and meaning: brought forth by a poetic spirit and generating a play of possibilities. These possibilities must mediate truth, to construct new stories of meaning. And if these new stories are to reflect their inspiration, they should mediate the truth of creation, which is the reality of their becoming. The mediating continuity between divine creation and human creativity lies at the heart of the *Book of Genesis* and other creation stories that tell of the intimate relationship between gods and men, a relationship constituted by a mode of reciprocity. As in the quotation above, human beings are made either from the Maker's 'ectoplasm', or from the earth in an unearthly fashion. As images, though removed from their origin, they nevertheless reflect it, and must be creators in their own right.

Human creativity, expressed in a work of art, is considered to be a matter of inspiration and intuition. It needs neither standards, nor guidelines. It does not follow predictable patterns, nor is it determined by any specific goal. It is meaning in the making and therefore susceptible to appreciation and evaluation. Theology sets itself these tasks but also participates in the process of making meaning. It explores the continuity and

---

[1] T. Hughes, *Tales from Ovid. Twenty-four passages from the Metamorphoses*, London 1997, 7-8.

discontinuity between divine and human creations by generating images and poetic constructions. Yet, unlike art, it is primarily a matter of reason. It follows patterns of consistency and coherence, and is shaped by the will to clarify and explain. Unlike Prometheus, who shaped a godlike body of man from the waste of creation, the theologian desires to form a body of letters and understanding that reflects the divine spirit as its origin.

The relationship between theology and art has been the subject matter of many theological studies of the past few decades. These studies investigate how works of art mediate the meaning of religious beliefs and how faith is expressed in the language of art. The possibility of mediation and expression is explained by the similarities between faith and art. Both refer to reality symbolically and affect people in a way that seems to be ultimately inexpressible. The present book will not attempt to explore how art can be called 'religious' or how faith can be called 'artistic', because art and faith are different in manner and method. Instead, the present book turns to the study of art and beauty in order to understand better the subject matter of theology.

Like philosophical aesthetics, theological aesthetics is a study of making and meaning. In both disciplines, the event of making is considered a combination of human skills and production, with the ungraspable moments of talent, inspiration and intuition, be they divine or not. As study of meaning, each discipline explores subjective responses to the givenness of reality. Though touching on these similarities, the present study will emphasise that theological aesthetics differs from philosophical aesthetics and that it is a discipline intrinsic to theology. For in Christian theology, the subjective responses to the givenness of reality are not only regarded as generating meaning, but also as participating in the meaning of divine creation. Theological aesthetics therefore relates to the themes of perception, imagination and beauty in personal and relational terms. The result is a view on the human ability to be a creator in one's own right as a given possibility to respond to the Creator. To actualise this possibility means becoming a co-creator who mediates the truth of creation.

This view has consequences for the nature of theology. Theology participates in both the life of creation and the artistic process of making meaning, entailing that it is co-creative. But what does it mean to reason co-creatively? How do the spirits of invention and discovery in modern science relate to the spirit of creation in theology? In other words, what is theological understanding if it seeks to mirror the divine spirit? Where does it find that spirit and how can that discovery be explained to others? These questions lie at the heart of this book. By introducing aesthetics as a way of doing theology, I seek to answer these questions in order to understand the art of theology.

Schematically, this book consists of three parts. Part A, *Fundamental theology and aesthetics* (chapters one and two), presents the main question "What is theology?", together with fundamental questions concerning the nature of theology and aesthetics, as they are discussed by representative contemporary theologians. Part B, *Hans Urs von Balthasar's theological aesthetics* (chapters three to seven), is a systematic study of the theology of Hans Urs von Balthasar and his theological aesthetics in particular. Besides offering an introduction to his life and theology, it also presents a close analysis of his interpretation of modern metaphysics, exemplified by the ideas of Nicholas of Cusa and Friedrich Wilhelm Joseph Schelling. Finally, part C, *Theological aesthetics as fundamental theology* (chapter eight), returns to the main question, developing a new response based on the evaluation of Balthasar's aesthetics and the recapitulation of the questions about the nature of theology.

Having given a broad overview of this book's structure, I now turn to a detailed inventory of its contents.

Chapter one, *Fundamental theology*, introduces the main question of this study: "What is theology?" There are two problems with giving an immediate answer to that question. First, it seems impossible to reason about faith in an invisible and transcendent God. Second, if such an attempt is to be made, one has to account for the truth claims of theology in conversation with the prevailing attitude of scientific rationality and an increasingly secular culture. Therefore, to answer the question about theology, one must search for a better understanding of faith and new ways of communicating faith to others. In modern theology, this has been the task of fundamental theology. Recent literature however has denounced fundamental theology as intrinsically apologetic, or mistakenly trying to prove the existence of God by means of natural reason. This present book advocates maintaining the field of fundamental theology, especially in an age of secularism and religious diversity. It is therefore important to find a way of doing theology that performs its tasks of reasoning about God and communicating faith without isolating itself from the culture to which it belongs. At the end of this chapter it is suggested that aesthetics could be a way of doing theology that meets these demands. In doing so, it will offer an explanation of the nature of theology.

Chapter two, *Theology and aesthetics*, gives an overview of the recent history of theology and aesthetics. Gerardus van der Leeuw, Paul Tillich and Hans Urs von Balthasar are presented as the founders of theological aesthetics. Each shedding light on a different aspect: van der Leeuw on imagination, Tillich on expression and Balthasar on beauty. Thus, through long forgotten themes, they laid the foundations of a new subdiscipline. Thanks to these founders, contemporary theology shows a great interest in aesthetics and the arts. Therefore, a typology is given in this chapter, which distinguishes four directions in the theological study of art and aesthetics: first, theologies using works of art as sources; second, theologies based on philosophical-aesthetic theories; third, theologies that are grounded in an aesthetic transcendental category; and fourth, theologies that interpret aesthetics as a theory of redemption. Throughout this chapter, a preference for the fourth type of theological aesthetics as a theory of redemption is defended. But to understand the importance of this type of theological aesthetics for the fundamental theological questions raised in chapter one, I suggest that a closer examination of Balthasar's theology is required.

Chapter three, *Hans Urs von Balthasar: A life in theology*, presents a brief overview of the life and works of Balthasar opening with a timetable of the key dates in his life. Alongside a chronological account of his life, from his youth, through his education to the maturity of his magnum opus, I formulate a description of his theological style. It is important to understand the motives behind this style against the background of the theology of his age. Balthasar's interest in aesthetics explains what he thought was needed for the theology of his time. This chapter also investigates the influences of such diverse thinkers as Erich Przywara, Henri de Lubac, Karl Barth and Adrienne von Speyr on his work.

Chapter four, *Theological hermeneutics and metaphysics*, offers an overview of Balthasar's theological ideas. Although he is regarded as one of the great theologians of the twentieth century, an introduction to his work is still needed. The vast amount of his books and articles—some of which are as yet not translated into English—and his conservative standpoint in church politics have made him one of the most unread, yet most controversial theologians of this age. Therefore, it is important to study his work without prejudice and to focus on the metaphysical and hermeneutical foundations of his theology, instead of on his church political writings. First, Balthasar's own account of his position in the theological context of his time is recapitulated by means of the incarnational foundation of his theology. Next, the three tasks for theology that he identified, are described as understanding the relationships between revelation and history, mission and tradition. After this formal and material description of his theology, a full analysis is presented of the key doctrines that constitute his metaphysics: the doctrine of the transcendentals and the doctrine of the analogy of being. At the end of this chapter, Balthasar's incarnational foundation of theology is reiterated within the framework of his trinitarian theology that determines his thought as a kenotic ontology.

Chapter five, *Theological aesthetics*, presents Balthasar's theological aesthetics in three ways. First, it systematically introduces the motives and key concepts of the first part of his trilogy: *Herrlichkeit. Eine theologische Ästhetik*. The ideas of 'beauty' and 'glory', and of 'perception' and 'form' are understood within the context of theology in general, and of Balthasar's metaphysics in particular. Second, a guide is given through this seven-volume work that consists of more than 4000 pages. Despite their scope and diversity, his systematic introduction, the twelve theological styles that he has chosen to illustrate his views, his account of the history of ideas from Homer to Heidegger, and his two-volume biblical theology, exhibit a dazzling coherence of vision. Finally, this chapter explains the importance of this achievement for fundamental theology and for the main question of this present book in particular. At the end of this survey, it becomes clear that in order to answer the question of theology in contemporary culture in dialogue with Balthasar's aesthetics, it is necessary to investigate his evaluation of the theological and metaphysical developments of modernity.

Chapter six, *Nicholas of Cusa: The catalogical imagination*, presents a close reading of Balthasar's monograph on Nicholas of Cusa in *Herrlichkeit III,1*. Cusa has a special position in Balthasar's account of the history of metaphysics. Balthasar calls his thought the 'knot' at the beginning of modernity, in which the ancient and biblical foundations of human thought are held together with a modern conception of human freedom. This chapter therefore engages with the contemporary debate on whether the Renaissance is the beginning of modernity or not, suggesting that the debate would benefit from a focus on aesthetics. According to Balthasar,

Cusa's 'aesthetics' is the best expression of the analogy of being in the history of philosophy, because it seeks the relationship between the biblical interpretation of divine revelation and the modern idea of a free explorative and creative human being. Thus, the result of analysing his reading of Cusa offers a further refinement of the characterisation of Balthasar's theology as being premodern. Furthermore, it underlines the importance of the concept of analogy in his work, because he endorses Cusa's idea of the human subject as a second god, which describes how the human mind desires the vision of God by means of the creation of forms that mediate divine revelation.

Chapter seven, *Friedrich Wilhelm Joseph Schelling: The Absolute in art*, investigates Balthasar's assessment of scientific and philosophical developments in modernity that led to the ideas of German Idealism. This chapter centres the attention on the philosophy of Friedrich Wilhelm Joseph Schelling, who called art the organ of philosophy and considered it capable of expressing the Absolute. After an introduction to Schelling's philosophy within the context of the Romantic Movement and German Idealism, his idea of art as the concurrence of nature and freedom is closely investigated. For Schelling, like nature, true art is divine, which prompts Balthasar to interpret his philosophy as being tritheistic: Schelling's aesthetics might too readily identify the work of art with the Absolute. For this reason, because it risks replacing a revealing God with the mind of the Romantic genius, Balthasar characterises Schelling's thought as 'promethean'. It will become clear though that the problem is not the replacement but rather the denial of revelation, which Balthasar characterises as 'the eclipse of glory'.

Chapter eight bears the title of this book: The art of theology. It begins with a critical evaluation of Balthasar's theological aesthetics and his analysis of modernity. He argues that the promethean theme in modernity resulted in the eclipse of glory. His aesthetic alternative is the description of faith as 'seeing the form' and the subjective act of faith as 'purely receptive'. But, these descriptions do not suffice to perform Balthasar's tasks for theology to understand the relation between revelation and history, mission, and tradition. It appears to be especially difficult to apply them to the dynamics of a living tradition in a secular and religiously diverse culture. After some critical evaluation, this final chapter returns to the main question of this book: "What is theology?" The introduction of aesthetics in order to answer that question results in a proposal for developing theological aesthetics. This proposed programme for contemporary theology consists of three movements: perceiving glory, seeking forms of faith, and understanding the sublime. The assumption is made that if the creative forms of faith and theology can become points of revelation, they should in some sense mirror the divine spirit that reveals itself in the world. In short, thinking about faith and theology aesthetically and thinking theologically about aesthetics, results in the discovery that theology is a kenotic style of reasoning in two movements: it seeks to communicate with others, without being apologetic, and it anticipates the life of redemption.

A.

FUNDAMENTAL THEOLOGY AND AESTHETICS

1. FUNDAMENTAL THEOLOGY

In this chapter, I will describe some questions concerning the nature of theology. First, I will explain the insufficiency of a short answer to the question "What is theology?" (1.1). After that, I will provide a longer answer and sketch a short history of fundamental theology, the subdiscipline of modern theology that deals with questions concerning the nature and subject matter of theology (1.2). Next, I will sketch the challenges of fundamental theology today and reformulate its tasks (1.3) and method (1.4), and explain the methodological difficulties that arise once these tasks need to be combined into one theological system and communicated to others. Finally, I will present the reasons for an aesthetic approach in theology, which might solve some of the described methodological problems (1.5).

1.1. What is theology? A short answer

What is theology? It may concern the reader that a theological book questions its own theological status. Moreover, one might wonder whether a book that begins at the beginnings, will ever manage to find its end. Theology is notorious for reconsidering its own nature and searching for a justification of its existence. The danger is a theological meta-discourse on method that never actually does what it discusses. The theologian Hans Frei once quoted someone saying, "A person either has character or he invents a method" and complained that for years, he himself tried to trade method for character, but never really managed.[1] The same is probably true of this present book, and although I agree with Frei that theory is dependent on practice, the following may not leave the level of methodological considerations at all.

a. Reasoning about God

There are good reasons for the continual and persistent disputes about the nature of theology. The short answer to the question "What is theology?"

---

[1] H.W. Frei, *Types of Christian theology*, New Haven 1992, 19.

would be: Theology is reasoned discourse about God.[2] Although that answer is quite adequate, it immediately raises several other questions concerning the possibilities of reasoning about an invisible and ultimately unknowable being. In an academic context, it might be an embarrassment for theologians that the core subject matter of theology seems only to be accessible for believers or might not exist at all. However, no theologian would claim that his or her method is irrational or a matter of mere faith. Therefore, to be treated with more than affable compassion by other academics, the theologian will want to account for the possibility of reasoning about this extraordinary subject matter.

A rational account of theology and its subject matter is susceptible to three notorious pitfalls. The first is an overly apologetic theology that safeguards its content by defending it against philosophical and scientific criticisms. The result is a closed system that, instead of entering into dialogue with other academic disciplines, justifies its idiosyncratic method with a certainty that seems as eternal as its own subject. The second danger is an excessive systematisation in an attempt to avoid vagueness or esotericism by copying the rigour of scientific analysis. The third and perhaps most dangerous trap for a rational justification of theology is the assumption that the existence of God can be proven by means of natural reason alone, without the illumination of divine grace.[3]

Despite these pitfalls of giving a rational account of theology, the question "What is theology?" still needs an answer for the straightforward reason that it seeks to avoid a fideist or unacademic theology. There are several possible types of answers to this question that have been practised in the history of modern theology. One could *map* the field of theology, by describing the history of human activities that were involved in the development of what is called 'theology', or by mentioning all the sub-disciplines that together form the academic subject as it is taught at universities. However, this would ignore the question of the possibility of accessing the theological object. One could *model* theology after other types of knowledge, by creating a schematic prototype of an academic discipline and trying to find a definition of theology based on similarities and differences with other disciplines.[4] Yet, that would only clarify

---

[2] Cf. M. Wiles, *What is theology?*, Oxford 1976; D. Ford, *Theology. A very short introduction*, Oxford 1999.
[3] A. Dulles, s.j., *The craft of theology. From symbol to system*, New York 2000², 55. Cf. Ph. Blond, Introduction. Theology before philosophy, in: Id. [ed.], *Post-secular philosophy. Between philosophy and theology*, London 1998, 1-66.
[4] A. Dulles, s.j., *Models of revelation*, Dublin 1992³, 32.

theology as an academic discipline among other disciplines. Or, one could appeal to a *metaphor* and concretise a general definition of theology by means of an image, like 'communication', 'imitation' or 'construction'.[5] But that would only define theology by means of comparison with what it is not. Further in this chapter, I will recapitulate these types of describing the nature of theology.

b. Communicating faith

The chosen type of answer, mapping, modelling or appealing to a metaphor, to the question "What is theology?" not only depends on the style or opinion of the theologian, or the questions that need to be addressed, but also on the audience the answer is addressed to. The theologian David Tracy is renowned for distinguishing three audiences of theology: society, the academy and the church.[6] This distinction also expresses the unfortunate divide, albeit one not made by Tracy himself, between orthodox and liberal or correlation theologies. The division suggests that roughly speaking orthodox theologies would address a church audience exclusively, while correlation theologies would address society as a whole.[7] Theologians relating to the academy deal with the variety of audiences in different ways, making a distinction between theory and practice, or between philosophical, historical and literary methods and theological method. In the latter case, theological method would distinguish itself by choosing the hermeneutical practice of a specific religious community as its main source.

Tracy also uses the three audiences of theology to differentiate three theological disciplines: fundamental, systematic and practical. Fundamental theologies then, would address the demands of the academy. Systematic theologies would relate to the public of the church, while practical theologies would deal with the concerns of society as a whole.[8] It is possible to think of many examples that would refute the feasibility of this theological organisation based on the variety of theological audiences.[9]

---

[5] G.P. Schner, s.j., Metaphors for theology, in: J. Webster, Id. [eds], *Theology after liberalism. A reader*, Oxford 2000, 3-51, 3.

[6] D. Tracy, *The analogical imagination. Christian theology and the culture of pluralism*, London 1981, 3-46.

[7] Cf. D.G. Kamitsuka, *Theology and contemporary culture. Liberation, postliberal and revisionary perspectives*, Cambridge 1999.

[8] Ibid., 56-57.

[9] For example, would the practice of the church not also be of concern to practical theologians? Would the demands of the academy not also be of concern to the church and therefore to systematic theologians, etc.?

However, my main argument against Tracy's distinctions is the presupposition that the question "What is theology?" could only be answered in either a personal or a social way, because the answer would depend on the audience it is addressed to. Although it is important to account for the context in which that question is asked and for who it is asked by, the answer always suggests a prior theological self-understanding. That self-understanding is not only constituted by its relation to a certain audience, but also to the reality that it refers to and the way it understands itself as a discourse per se. In other words, prior to the question of the nature of theology, the subject matter and method of theology have already constituted its very nature. Consequently, that question, although asked by a certain audience, should at least be accompanied by the questions of God and faith.

The focus on what constitutes theology internally does not immediately dispense with the audience however. As soon as theologians have established the nature of their field, they will want to communicate the outcome of their debates to others. And if they are hesitant to do so, they will, as Tracy has pointed out correctly, "risk ignoring the actual complexity of different selves related to the distinct social relations and therefore to the distinct plausibility structures present in each theologian".[10] How, then, would theologians communicate these plausibility structures to others? This is not only a question of 'publicness', but also of method. Paradoxically, the most common way of communicating what it means to reason theologically is through philosophy. Even more paradoxically, there are philosophical rather than theological reasons for rejecting philosophical reasoning in defence of theology, because the plausibility of theological statements might only be meaningful for the believing community that they are derived from. In a secularised culture, a strict interpretation of the radical otherness of different language games seems more vital than ever before. Still, believers and non-believers do communicate and their communication, although perhaps insufficient and a fertile ground for misunderstandings, is reasonable in some sense. Besides this observation, the fact that theologians themselves want to present their field as reasonable, a suggestion supported by a long history of philosophy of religion, shows the inextricable relation of philosophy and theology.

If a brief definition of theology is accepted as "reasoned discourse about God", several questions remain to be answered. These questions are

---

[10] D. Tracy, *The analogical imagination*, 5.

concerned with the sources, methods and the audiences of theology. To account for all these questions at once, the Swiss theologian Ingolf Dalferth has defined theological rationality as *ars combinatoria*: a method that integrates several systems of reference, like faith, knowledge, life experience, politics, religion, law and economics.[11] Still, although Dalferth's description of theological method might be helpful, theology cannot be reduced to any of these systems of reference and should especially not surrender to a standardisation of academic discourse or give way completely to other than theological considerations.[12] That brings us back to the original question "What is theology?", and it has become clear that a longer answer is needed.

1.2. Fundamental theology: history and criticisms

The theological subdiscipline that usually deals with questions concerning the nature of theology is called 'fundamental theology'. However, this name is not commonly used and any theologian who uses it uncritically is most likely a Roman Catholic whose theology is influenced by continental philosophy.[13] English speaking theologians, with some notable exceptions, rarely use the term.[14] Francis Schüssler Fiorenza has explicitly rejected the term in favour of 'foundational theology'.[15] Others believe that the question of the nature of theology could be treated by a philosophy of religion or a philosophical theology.[16] It would not be very

---

[11] I. Dalferth, *Kombinatorische Theologie. Probleme theologischer Rationalität*, [Quaestiones Disputatae 130], Freiburg im Breisgau, etc. 1991, 19-20.

[12] J. Webster, *Theological theology*, [An inaugural lecture delivered before the University of Oxford on 27 October 1997], Oxford 1998, 11-12.

[13] The most well-known are: H. Fries, *Fundamentaltheologie*, Graz, etc. 1985²; H. Waldenfels, *Kontextuelle Fundamentaltheologie*, Paderborn 1988²; H. Verweyen, *Gottes letztes Wort. Grundriss der Fundamentaltheologie*, Düsseldorf 1991².

[14] G. O'Collins, s.j., *Fundamental theology*, New York, etc. 1981; Id., *Retrieving fundamental theology. Three styles of contemporary theology*, London 1993; F.J. van Beeck, *God encountered. A contemporary Catholic systematic theology 2/1. The revelation of the glory*, [Part 1, "Fundamental theology"], Collegeville 1993.

[15] F. Schüssler Fiorenza, *Foundational theology. Jesus and the church*, New York 1986, xiii.

[16] This has been a subject of debate since Schleiermacher defined the nature of theology in the introduction of: F.D.E. Schleiermacher, *Der christliche Glaube nach den Grundsätzen der evangelischen Kirche im Zusammenhange dargestellt*, [Kritische Gesamtausgabe I. Abt, Bd. 7,1, Hrsg. v. H. Peiter], Berlin 1980 (Berlin 1821-1822). Cf. N. Schreurs, J.S. Drey en F. Schleiermacher aan het begin van de fundamentele theologie. Oorsprongen en ontwikkelingen, in: *Bijdragen. Tijdschrift voor filosofie en theologie* 43 (1982), 251-288.

fruitful to linger over the details concerning the very enterprise itself, rather than focussing on its main issues. However, before it can become clear why the issues of fundamental theology are indeed fundamental to the whole of theology, it is important to describe in short its history and mention its critics.[17] After that, I will discuss the reasons for maintaining the term 'fundamental theology'.

a. A short history of fundamental theology

The first theologian to use the term 'fundamental theology' explicitly was Johann Nepomuk Ehrlich (1810-1864), a pupil of Anton Günther (1783-1863), who was the founder of the *Wiener Schule* and interested in speculative philosophy and positive theology. Ehrlich coined the phrase 'fundamental theology' in his theological handbook, and it was clearly his intention to found a new theological discipline concerning the theoretical principles of theology.[18] He was the first to structure his justification of theology around its goal, purpose and method, thereby treating it as a science and establishing its inner unity.

However, the original use of the term does not necessarily mark the beginning of the field's history. If fundamental theology is regarded as apologetics, one needs to go back further in time, for example to the theology of Johann Sebastian Drey (1777-1853), the founder of the *Tübinger Schule*, who wrote an apology of faith.[19] Confronted by the philosophy of the Enlightenment, he tried to justify Christian faith by means of the philosophy of German idealism. Drey not only defended certain Christian

---

[17] Cf. next to the abovementioned introductions and handbooks of fundamental theology: W. Joest, *Fundamentaltheologie. Theologische Grundlagen- und Methodenprobleme*, Stuttgart 1974; R. Latourelle, G. O'Collins [eds.], *Probleme und Aspekte der Fundamentaltheologie*, [Hrsg. d. dt. Ausg., Endred. d. Übers., Bearb. d. Apparats Johannes Bernard], Innsbruck, etc. 1985 (Transl. of: *Problemi e prospettivi di Teologia Fondamentale*); R. Latourelle, R. Fisichella [eds], *Dictionary of fundamental theology*, [Orig. Dizionario di teologia fondamentale], New York 1995; P. Knauer, *Der Glaube kommt vom Hören. Ökumenische Fundamentaltheologie*, Freiburg im Breisgau 1991[6]; H. Ott, *Apologetik des Glaubens. Grundprobleme einer dialogischen Fundamentaltheologie*, Darmstadt 1994; H. Wagner, *Einführung in die Fundamentaltheologie*, Darmstadt 1996[2]; K. Müller [Hrsg.], *Fundamentaltheologie. Fluchtlinien und gegenwärtige Herausforderungen*, Regensburg 1998; J. Werbick, *Den Glauben verantworten. Eine Fundamentaltheologie*, Freiburg im Breisgau 2000.

[18] J.N. Ehrlich, *Leitfaden für Vorlesungen über die allgemeine Einleitung in die theologische Wissenschaft und die Theorie der Religion und Offenbarung als I. Theil der Fundamental-Theologie*, Prag 1859; Id., *Leitfaden für Vorlesungen über die Offenbarung Gottes als Thatsache der Geschichte. II. Theil der Fundamental-Theologie*, Prag 1862.

[19] J.S. von Drey, *Die Apologetik als wissenschaftliche Nachweisung der Göttlichkeit des Christentums in seiner Erscheinung*, Mainz 1844-1847.

beliefs in particular, but also tried to provide the ultimate foundation of theology. Thus, he developed a division in his apologetics, distinguishing three treatises: on revelation, on the specific Christian revelation with the resurrection as its highest manifestation, and on the Catholic Church. This threefold organisation would become, in more or less amended forms, a standard in the study of the foundations of theology until the second half of the twentieth century.[20]

One could even go back further, locating the origins of fundamental theology in the sixteenth century. However, others have written that early history and I will not attempt to repeat their work.[21] Even so, I would like to mention the work of a Spanish Dominican friar and bishop in the sixteenth century, Melchior Cano (1509-1560). He is renowned for mapping the field of theology, mirroring the work of John Damascene and Peter Lombard in the Middle Ages. Cano distinguished ten sources of theology: seven proper sources, which are constitutive of revelation and the church: scripture, tradition, the Catholic church, councils, the papacy, the Fathers and scholastic theologians; and three important but non-constitutive sources: human reason, philosophy and history.[22] By establishing a hierarchy in the authority of these *loci theologici*, Cano was the first to express explicitly a theological self-awareness, thereby starting a new direction in theological teaching.

Mapping the field of theology has the advantage of opening the debates on what belongs to theology and what does not, and on the gradual differences in the authority of sources. Moreover, it is a theological method, which does not need the approval of other disciplines or tries to model its own method after other methods, like science or transcendental philosophy. However, this method of mapping was hardly paradigmatic for nineteenth and twentieth century fundamental theology, which was essentially apologetic. Of course, apologetics is as old as theology itself, but in the nineteenth century, it became a theological subdiscipline in its own right with a clear and distinct method.

'Traditional' or 'classical' apologetics was divided into three courses, called *demonstrationes*, based on the insight of Thomas Aquinas that

---

[20] Cf. G. Ebeling, Erwägungen zu einer evangelischen Fundamentaltheologie, in: *Zeitschrift für Theologie und Kirche,* 67 (1970), 479-524.

[21] Cf. H. Verweyen, *Gottes letztes Wort,* 13-35; F. Schüssler Fiorenza, *Foundational theology,* 251-264; H. Wagner, *Einführung in die Fundamentaltheologie,* 1-14.

[22] Melchior Cano, *De locis theologicis libri XII,* Salamanca 1563; H.-J. Sander, Das Außen des Glaubens—eine Autorität der Theologie. Das Differenzprinzip in den loci theologici des Melchior Cano, in: Id., H. Keul, [Hrsg.], *Das Volk Gottes. Ein Ort der Befreiung,* Würzburg 1998, 240-258

"from effects evident to us, we can demonstrate what in itself is not evident to us, namely, that God exists".[23] These demonstrations were meant to provide a rational justification of first, religion and man's ability to experience and confirm religious truth; second, the possibility and the truth of the concrete historical revelation in Jesus Christ; and third, the church as the place of truth in this world.[24] In the neoscholastic manuals of the late nineteenth and early twentieth centuries, answers to the question as to how divine revelation and human reason are related were called *praeambula fidei*. These centered on the religious and moral truths that can be known by human reason and whereby faith is justified as a free human act in the presence of the demands of reason.[25] Fundamental theology as *analysis fidei* became increasingly focused on the search for infallible certainty of the subject of faith.[26]

Since the First Vatican Council, the method of Roman Catholic fundamental theology has been dominated by neoscholastic systematic philosophy. However, the church's response to the modernist and rationalist influence on theology also generated new directions in fundamental theology, especially in the work of Maurice Blondel (1861-1949), Pierre Rousselot (1846-1924) and Dominique De Petter (1905-1971).[27]

---

[23] Thomas Aquinas, *Summa Theologiae*, I, q1-13 (Ia,2,2).

[24] This became known as the 'German form' of fundamental theology, contrasted with the 'Roman form', which relegated the demonstration of religion to a philosophy of religion and replaced it with a demonstration of revelation. Cf. H. Wagner, *Einführung in die Fundamentaltheologie*, 15; H. Waldenfels, *Kontextuelle Fundamentaltheologie*, 82; F. Schüssler Fiorenza, *Foundational theology*, 267.

[25] There were other proposed methods for analysing the possibility to reason about faith, for example: 1. *Motivum fidei*, concerning the reasons or *motives* for one's believes, whereby faith is given by the authority of God's self-revelation in a true and infallible form. 2. *Motivum credibilitatis*, analysing the motives by which it is *possible* to believe, i.e. the signs of revelation, like the church, miracles and prophecies, whereby the certainty of a revealed fact allows one to conclude that the contents of revelation are believable. 3. *Motivum credenditatis*, concerning the reasons why one *should* believe, and seeing the connection between the act of faith and the salvation made evident by God and trying to solve the problem of divine and human freedom. Cf. R. Latourelle, R. Fisichella [eds], *Dictionary of fundamental theology*, 195-196, 324-336.

[26] Cf. G. Essen, "Und diese Zeit ist unsere Zeit, immer noch". Neuzeit als Thema katholischer Fundamentaltheologie, in: K. Müller [Hrsg.], *Fundamentaltheologie*, 23-44, 27.

[27] The philosophy of the dominican friar Dominique De Petter never became widely known, presumably because it was written in Dutch. As a metaphysician, he did not problematise the nature of theology as such, but, being the philosophy teacher of Edward Schillebeeckx, his anti-Kantian theory of the 'implicit intuition' influenced an important branch of hermeneutical theology in the second half of the twentieth century: D.M. De Petter, Impliciete intuïtie, in: *Tijdschrift voor philosophie* 1 (1939), 84-105. Cf. S. van Erp, *Intentionaliteit en Intuïtie. De Petters formulering van de realistische metafysica tegen de achtergrond van de 'traditionele' metafysica en de husserliaanse fenomenologie*, [unpublished thesis], Tilburg 1995.

Especially Blondel redefined fundamental theology, by establishing human interiority as the new foundation of apologetic theology. His 'method of immanence' searched for human needs and tendencies that point to divine revelation.[28] It was a reaction against the extrinsecist method of neoscholastic theology, which tried to find a justification of faith by means of signs, like prophecies and miracles, applying external criteria to the field of theology.

In the second half of the twentieth century, the character of fundamental theology evolved into an introduction to theology. These *prolegomena* finally developed into fundamental theologies from a certain methodological perspective, which tried to establish the main principles of theology. At this time, the transcendental method of Karl Rahner and Bernard Lonergan, seeking anthropological grounds for the openness to the self-disclosure of Being and subsequently to the divine self-revelation in Jesus Christ, became dominant.[29] In the 1970s and 1980s, other tasks and methods were emphasised in fundamental theology, e.g. the hermeneutical theologies of Eugen Biser and Francis Schüssler Fiorenza, the ecumenical theology of Peter Knauer, the dialogical theology of David Tracy or the dramatic theology of Raymund Schwager. The confrontation of theology with a variety of literal and historical methods of late- and postmodern thought caused an increase in the number of fundamental theologies, and for a while it seemed that the world of theology had become obsessed with method.[30] It prompted William Placher to complain that contemporary theologians should "abandon their preoccupation with methodology and get on with the business of really doing theology".[31]

In the relatively short history of fundamental theology, its definition, tasks and method have often changed. Throughout this history though, its development was conditioned by three factors. First, by the polemic spirit of theology since the Reformation, which led to its apologetic nature. Second, by the reflection on the academic status of theology, which

---

[28] M. Blondel, *Lettre sur les exigences de la pensée contemporaine en matière d'apologétique et sur la méthode de la philosophie dans l'étude du problème religieux*, Paris 1956 (1896).

[29] K. Rahner, *Hörer des Wortes. Zur Grundlegung einer Religionsphilosophie*, [Neu bearbeitet von J.B. Metz], München 1963²; Id., *Grundkurs des Glaubens. Einführung in den Begriff des Christentums*, Freiburg im Breisgau, etc. 1976; B. Lonergan, *Method in theology*, London 1971.

[30] Cf. K. Tanner, How I changed my mind, in: D.C. Marks [ed.], *Shaping a theological mind. Theological context and methodology*, Aldershot 2002, 115-122, 115.

[31] W. Placher, *Unapologetic theology. A Christian voice in a pluralistic conversation*, Louisville 1989, 7.

resulted in the encyclopaedia or *prolegomena* of theology. Third, by the shift from a general dogmatics to a doctrine of principles and foundations of theology. Fundamental theology is clearly a responsive discipline that is either in dialogue with the culture it participates in, or with academics from other disciplines. But despite this responsive character, it has never managed to silence its critics.

b. Criticisms of fundamental theology

Diverse in its forms, fundamental theology has attracted many critics. This in itself may not be surprising. Everyone who tries to provide a foundation for all of Christian faith or theology, will immediately find several opponents who suggest another, competing foundation or argue that such an enterprise could never succeed. A first set of criticisms is directed against the foundational claim of fundamental theology per se.[32] From a logical perspective 'foundationalism' could be defined as the view that mediately justified beliefs require rational support for their validity in immediately justified beliefs. From a disciplinary perspective, it could be regarded as the view that systems of knowledge, in content and method, require first principles.[33]

Nonfoundationalists have approached the fundamental or foundationalist view in theology negatively.[34] The argument of nonfoundationalist philosophers such as Willard Van Orman Quine, Richard Rorty and Donald Davidson against foundationalism in general, exposes the objectivist expectations of modern knowledge. The criticism by nonfoundationalists usually begins with a pejorative assessment of Cartesian epistemology. Descartes's theory of knowledge, based on the metaphor of knowledge as a building, requires all beliefs to be justified by tracing them back to a special category of beliefs that cannot be called into question.[35] Thus, according to its critics, foundational thought wrongly justifies claims to knowledge, and even the discipline of philosophy itself, by an illegitimate appeal to the authority of universal principles of understanding. According to the nonfoundationalists, the foundationalist arbitrarily draws a limit

---

[32] Cf. P. Helm, *Faith with reason*, Oxford 2000, 21-42.
[33] Cf. L. Dupré, *Religious mystery and rational reflection. Excursions in the phenomenology and philosophy of religion*, Grand Rapids 1998, 1-40.
[34] Cf. J. Thiel, *Nonfoundationalism*, Minneapolis 1994; S. Hauerwas, N. Murphy, M. Nation [eds], *Theology without foundations. Religious practice and the future of theological truth*, Nashville 1994.
[35] Cf. N.C. Murphy, *Beyond liberalism and fundamentalism: how modern and postmodern philosophy set the theological agenda*, Valley Forge 1996.

where none could possibly exist and then designates that limit as the true foundation for all knowledge.[36] Moreover, to claim that theological knowledge has such an ultimate foundation, implies a privileged or basic class of beliefs that are intrinsically credible.[37] Thus, remarking the ever-receding horizon of an infinite regress of justification, the nonfoundationalist argument is especially valid for the very existence of a field like fundamental theology. In the light of the nonfoundationalist critique, establishing a rational foundation for divine revelation seems an impossible goal.[38]

One way to escape this dispute is to argue that the rationality of theology is constituted by coherence and consistence, because theology is "a self-correcting enterprise that examines all claims [and] all relevant background theories".[39] Although this might save theology the embarrassment of being irrational, it does not fully account for its definition as reasoned discourse about God. For, though God might be theology's nonfoundational foundation and its discourse might be regarded as rational, these arguments do not secure the possibility of making claims about God. Thus, neither external logical criteria for rationality, nor an internal set of credible beliefs would justify the project of fundamental theology, which seeks the intelligibility of faith and theology and thus the possibility of these human enterprises.

The nonfoundationalist critique applies particularly to the transcendental method that, through the strong influences of Rahner and Lonergan, has come to dominate fundamental theology in the second half of the twentieth century. Transcendental theology seeks fundamental philosophical principles that could form the first and definitive principles for theological knowledge as well. Yet, the nonfoundationalist critique might as well be valid for the entire project of fundamental theology as apologetics, since it is impossible to defend the rationality of a position that is ultimately nonfoundational, i.e. the standpoint of revelation. But this is only true if being rational means having and applying knowledge that is based upon firm and definitive foundations.

A second set of criticisms is directed against the claim that fundamental theology is a theological discipline, rather than a philosophical or an

---

[36] J. Wentzel van Huyssteen, Book review of J. Thiel, Nonfoundationalism, in: *Theology today* 52 (1996) 4, 521-524, 522.
[37] Id., *Essays in postfoundationalist theology*, Grand Rapids 1997, 226.
[38] Cf. S.J. Grenz, J.R. Franke, *Beyond foundationalism. Shaping theology in a postmodern context*, Louisville 2001, 28-37.
[39] F. Schüssler Fiorenza, *Foundational theology*, 287.

introductory one. The motivation of this critique is the thought that it is impossible to demonstrate the possibility of divine revelation by means of human reason. Karl Barth is without doubt the main advocate of this position, which is best described as a radical dichotomous dualism of revelation and reason. The theological *prolegomena* to his *Church Dogmatics* do not form a philosophical introduction to theology, but a Christian doctrine of the Trinity.[40] This is a significant theological choice, because it reflects Barth's opinion that the one and only true justification of faith is the sovereignty of God and not the intellectual categories of Enlightenment philosophy.[41] That in turn brings Barth to the paradoxical claim that theologians ought to speak of God and at the same time cannot speak of God. For Barth, the problem of theology is that humanity is separated from God. Therefore, he thinks that "(...) as an academic discipline in the sense of the other disciplines, theology has no right to exist in the university; it exists beyond the boundary of scientific possibilities as a reminder of something that needs to be said by all disciplines but which, things being as they are, can only be said by such an emergency measure as the presence of theology in the university".[42] However, for Barth, theology is already highly limited in its very essence, since it can only be a witness to something, which it cannot justify. Moreover, it has to defeat speaking about God once God speaks.[43]

On the assumption that fundamental theology and natural theology are identical, Barth's criticism of natural theology, i.e. the study of what can be known about God apart from revelation, also became a criticism of fundamental theology. This identification is understandable, because the objects of natural theology were the *praeambula fidei*, i.e. the religious truths that can be known by human reason, contrary to the truth that can be known through revelation alone. However, believing in God is not the same as believing in a matter of fact, and therefore it is according to some inaccessible to natural reason altogether.[44] Some extreme proponents of this view have concluded that faith and reason are incommensurable, but others have declared that faith and reason are identical and that it is impossible to justify faith by something other than by the sheer fact of

---

[40] K. Barth, *Kirchliche Dogmatik, I,1. Prolegomena*, München 1932.
[41] Cf. J.P. Mackey, *The critique of theological reason*, Cambridge 2000, 275; C. Schwöbel, Theology, in: J. Webster [ed.], *The Cambridge companion to Karl Barth*, Cambridge 2000, 17-36.
[42] C. Schwöbel, Theology, 22.
[43] Cf. P. Avis, Karl Barth. The reluctant virtuoso, in: Id., *The methods of modern theology. The dream of reason*, Basingstoke 1986, 35-69.
[44] D.Z. Phillips, *Faith and philosophical enquiry*, London 1970, 3.

faith itself, which then would be adequately reasonable. And that would turn fundamental theology into a meaningless tautological act, which would make it completely redundant.

Yet, if fundamental theology after all these criticisms is still stubbornly searching for the intelligibility of faith, then it must account for the ability of human reason to understand the articles of faith, which are said to be revealed. According to the abovementioned critics, a hermeneutical approach in fundamental theology, as many have suggested, would not solve this problem, for it would confuse meaning with truth. Following their arguments, fundamental theology could be nothing more than either a philosophical introduction to theology or a hermeneutical exposition of beliefs, interpretations and opinions and therefore in essence not theological, because neither would be able to address the one and only truth of theology: the revelation of God. Nonetheless, it remains to be seen whether, if a fundamental theological approach were to be regarded theological, it would have to cross the limits of its own presupposition, undoubtedly shared by all, by addressing the knowability of the Unknowable.

c. *Maintaining the field*

Francis Schüssler Fiorenza has suggested redesignating the term 'fundamental theology' as 'foundational theology'. In his book that bears that title, he still uses 'fundamental theology' for all the traditional conceptions of the field as a distinct and independent discipline from doctrinal theology.[45] However, to avoid all the misunderstandings that could emerge by using the 'old' name, which is strongly associated with apologetics, natural theology or philosophical questions of religion as *prolegomena* to theology, he proposes to use the term 'foundational theology'. He also expresses an awareness of the foundational fallacies and rejects the possibility of finding a single and independent criterion or foundation for either theology or faith.[46] Instead, he mentions the resurrection and the church as the foundations of theology, thereby showing the inevitable theological nature of the field. To describe the foundational character of resurrection and church, he chooses to use the metaphor of a raft upon the sea, rather than the firm fundaments of a building or a pyramid. Despite these amendments, the term 'foundational theology' may prompt other, but still incorrect conceptions of the discipline in question, and

---

[45] F. Schüssler Fiorenza, *Foundational theology*, xiii.
[46] Ibid., 285-289.

perhaps even more so. Besides rationalist or apologetic associations as a product of modern philosophy, it also has to defend itself against foundational implications, as Schüssler Fiorenza himself has had to do.

My suggestion would be to maintain the term 'fundamental theology', which at least avoids the suggestion that it is trying to establish a single or independent foundation for theology. Nevertheless, it is still a fundamental discipline, because it asks for the very essence of theology. As such, fundamental theology is a discipline that expresses theological self-understanding, which in the case of theology cannot be self-evident because its subject matter is not immediately available. Therefore, a justification of the authority of sources and the way they are applied in theology is indispensable. Thus, fundamental theology is the methodological self-reflection of theology. It is the study of the validity and authority of sources and methods of the various subdisciplines, like historical, literal, dogmatic and practical theology. Its task is to critically judge the presuppositions and argumentations of theological standpoints.[47] Consequently, fundamental theology is intrinsic to all theology, and hence not just to systematic theology. Theological self-understanding is implied in every theological statement and made explicit in fundamental theology. Hence, fundamental theology is a theological discipline per se that might be used as an introduction to theology, but theoretically comes after theology. It is a theological meta-discourse without which theology might become fideist or repetitious.[48]

Moreover, the association of fundamental theology with apologetics does not necessarily have to be repudiated. It is important to justify the tasks and methods of theology in a changing cultural and academic context. But that would entail a type of apologetics that, instead of merely defending the articles of faith, wants to account for its views on God, the world and humanity. Theologians are taking part in academic and public debates and it will continue to be a challenge for them to defend their standpoints without presenting their beliefs as being closed for debate.

Aside from maintaining the term 'fundamental theology', I would argue for maintaining the field as a theological subdiscipline, because it explicitly expresses the theological self-understanding that is implied in all other

---

[47] Cf. 1 Peter 3,15: "But sanctify the Lord God in your hearts: and be ready always to give an answer to every man that asketh you a reason of the hope that is in you with meekness and fear."

[48] A similar definition of the field can be found in G. O'Collins, *Retrieving fundamental theology*, 40-47; and in A. Dulles, *The craft of theology*, 53-68.

theological subdisciplines. As such, it is a necessary and an intrinsically theological field. But, 'maintaining the field' could also be used as a metaphor for fundamental theology. As in an agricultural context, it refers to a foundation that can hardly be called firm. It sometimes needs to be broken up and ploughed to be fertile again. It needs sowing, manuring and irrigation. This 'maintenance of the field' particularly is the task of fundamental theology. It has to question and reformulate theology's fundamental presuppositions, like the authority of sources and methods, so that these will prove to be fertile for theology as a whole.

1.3. Three challenges for fundamental theology

Defining fundamental theology as theological self-understanding does not release it from its apologetic character. On the contrary, in that process of self-understanding, Christian theologians will make use of the information and language of the culture they partake in.[49] Influenced and at the same time confronted by that culture, they will want to describe at least the particularity of Christian faith and theology and distinguish these from other faiths and world views.[50] A theology that seeks some kind of justification by demonstrating the credibility of its subject matter must nowadays reconcile itself to a contemporary context in which the object of theology is not just heavily debated and far from being self-evident, but is also inconceivable to many and because of this, even unknown. The absence of God and the impossibility of identifying theology as a well-defined discipline are facts that should be taken into account in every attempt at a justification of faith and theology, if the aim is not merely to preach to the converted. In addition, the theologian in search of a better understanding of his own faith must realise that he or she is part of a culture that emphasises the absence rather than the presence of God. This culture is not only religiously diverse but also sometimes indifferent to religion because for many people even the absence of God does not match any experience anymore. Theologians do not have to surrender to contemporary culture; they should realise, however, that a changing and radically different cultural context leaves its traces in any theology that wants to be part of this context rather than to be alienated from it or merely

---

[49] G. Ward, The beauty of God, in: J. Milbank, G. Ward, E. Wyschogrod, *Theological perspectives on God and beauty*, Harrisburg 2003, 35-65, 35.
[50] *Gaudium et spes*, 4.

countercultural.[51] Therefore, this current cultural context is unavoidably a new challenge for the tasks and methods of fundamental theology because faith and theology are confronted by a changing audience to which theologians themselves also belong.

Being part of contemporary culture and a credible partner in the current diversity of postmodern conversations, fundamental theology will have to continue to describe the particularity of Christian faith and theology. Mirroring the three demonstrations of classical apologetics by distinguishing three different but interwoven challenges, I will reformulate the task of fundamental theology today without suggesting that it is an exhaustive programme.

a. Possibility in diversity

To start with, fundamental theology should try to account for current religious diversity, because this diversity challenges the concept of truth that each separate religion has.[52] David Tracy suggests the model of conversation to be the "central hope for recognising the possibilities which any serious conversation with the claim to attention of the other and the different yields".[53] His concept of the 'analogical imagination' then, would offer new possibilities to see similarities in experienced differences and otherness, without retreating into principles like harmony, convergence or sameness. Therefore, conversation would be the appropriate method for a renewal of theological self-understanding, which in this case would be based on the possibilities opened up by other conversation partners.

---

[51] Cf. R. Schreiter, c.pp.s., *The new catholicity. Theology between the global and the local*, Maryknoll 1997.

[52] Cf. K.E. Yandell, *Philosophy of religion. A contemporary introduction*, London 1999, 65-80; K. Ward, *Religion and revelation. A theology of revelation in the world's religions*, Oxford 1994, 3-49. Note however, that religious diversity is not just a problem for philosophy of religion, nor is it only a matter of comparing different uses of religious concepts (Ward). A philosophy of religion will only be able to account for the fact of religious pluralism itself, while Ward's comparative theology can only list the dissimilarities and similarities of specific religious concepts. Christian fundamental theology has its own task establishing the truth concept used in Christian theology in confrontation with other concepts of truth.

[53] D. Tracy, The uneasy alliance reconceived. Theological method, modernity and postmodernity, in: J. Webster, G.P. Schner, s.j., *Theology after liberalism*, 335-360, 345 (originally published in: *Theological studies* 59 (1989), 548-570). See also: R. Schreiter, c.pp.s., Possibilities (and limitations) for an intercultural dialogue on God, in: I. Bocken et al. [eds], *On cultural ontology. Religion, philosophy and culture*, [Essays in honor of Wilhelm Dupré], Maastricht 2002, 149-164.

Tracy presents three new criteria for fundamental theology to fulfil this conversational task in the new postmodern situation. First, fundamental theology should be receptive to the hermeneutical notion of truth as manifestation. Second, it should critically evaluate how a given claim to manifestation coheres or not with what is otherwise regarded as reasonable. Third, it should consider the ethical and political implications of these claims and become aware of how fundamental theology itself participates in the process of transformation of religion and society.[54] The key word here is 'manifestation', which occurs when otherness and dialogue lead to religious participation.[55] Fundamental theology should be hermeneutically receptive to the truth notion of manifestation in a context of diversity and consequently, its task would be to critically evaluate and reason about the claims that are based on the possibility of a hermeneutical appropriation of a manifestation as truth.

b. *Particularity in expression*

Next, fundamental theology will have to provide insights into the images and the words that are used in Christian theology to express its dogmas and beliefs, and make them plausible. This task is even more urgent in a world in which this plausibility is being questioned, ignored or even denied. Tracy calls this theological task 'proclamation', by which he means the classic religious expression that in essence is the consequence of radical non-participation.[56] Fundamental theology can only reach a sufficient self-understanding in confrontation with other religious claims if it expresses a consciousness of both manifestation and proclamation without surrendering to the temptation of exclusivity. It should stress the particularity of Christian faith without ceasing to be open to manifestations of otherness. However, Christianity is a system of symbols "grounded in the radical Christian faith that Jesus Christ is both the decisive word and the decisive manifestation of God and ourselves".[57] Therefore, the particularity of Christian faith proclaimed in Christian theology is both a limit to the diversity that people are confronted by today and an openness to the otherness of the surrounding world. It is the task of fundamental theology to express this concurrence, without which theology would become a mere proclamation of faith that excludes others.

---

[54] D. Tracy, The uneasy alliance reconceived, 344.
[55] Id., *The analogical imagination*, 203.
[56] Ibid.
[57] Ibid., 215.

Expressing the concurrence of manifestation and proclamation might not be as easy as Tracy suggests. If manifestation has the consequence of religious participation and proclamation of non-participation, it is difficult to imagine what the consequence of a balance between manifestation and proclamation would be. The problem is that the proposed dichotomy for example does not leave any room for a form of religious non-participation that is chosen by the subject. In other words, contemporary unbelief is Tracy's problem and his model of conversation only deals with other religions, but not with atheistic contemporaries. This is the reason why his position is called 'fideist': either he practices openness to the possibilities presented by other religious standpoints, or he confirms his own beliefs. In neither case is he able to rationally justify his own standpoint and presuppositions when confronted by others, especially non-believers.[58] This criticism however would also be valid when Tracy, and any other theologian for that matter, would want to account for the truth claims of their own religious doctrines to fellow theologians and people of their own religious community. In that community, the debate on tradition and authority continues, especially in a culture where the boundaries of a religious community are not as well-defined as they used to be. The utilisation of fideist arguments in that internal debate might even be more harmful than in the discussion with others.

c. Freedom in responsibility

If one wants to avoid the fideist position, it is crucial to give a rational account of one's religious standpoint and beliefs. However, to avoid a rationalist reduction of faith, one must explain the choices and engagements that are involved in being a Christian. Therefore, to complement Tracy's dichotomy of manifestation and proclamation, I would like to suggest that the third task of fundamental theology is to justify the freedom of faith and the responsibility that comes with it. Theological inquiry arises from the Christian community's freedom and responsibility to search for an understanding of its faith.[59] Such a reasonable justification of one's own religion is part of the challenge and the ability to imagine shapes for faith, which can be experienced and exchanged within the church community but also in dialogue with those without. Fundamental

---

[58] S. Wendel, Postmoderne Theologie? Zum Verhältnis von christlicher Theologie und postmoderner Philosophie, in: K. Müller [Hrsg.], *Fundamentaltheologie*, 193-214, 212.

[59] D.L. Migliore, *Faith seeking understanding. An introduction to Christian theology*, Grand Rapids 1991, 1.

theology then, is the rational evaluation of personal and communal convictions that will make Christian faith a credible and intelligible conversation partner in contemporary society.[60]

In the dominant streams of modern philosophy, especially the Cartesian and Kantian variants, the autonomous subject became a free agent that is capable of founding all knowledge. The subject itself is regarded as the securing body of certainty and truth. This prominent place of the subject in modernity affirmed individual human dignity but at the same time led to an amoral and asocial hyperindividualism.[61] In dialogue with this philosophical standpoint and its consequences, fundamental theology should search for the conditions of the possibility of human freedom as part of the constitution of faith.[62] During the twentieth century, Karl Rahner reformulated the task of fundamental theology based on this anthropological turn in modern philosophy. In doing so he presupposed that the essence of Christianity would straightforwardly appear in an anthropological worldview.[63] But does the modern concept of freedom as autonomy also offer possibilities for rethinking theological self-understanding in the current socio-cultural context? Were that the case, it would have an enormous impact on the Christian understanding of revelation, scripture and authority in tradition. The modern subject might become a fourth power over and against these three guiding principles of Christian theology, thereby questioning or even violating their sovereignty.

However, this is not the only problem presented by the anthropological turn in fundamental theology and its concentration on human freedom. One may wonder whether theology should be theocentric or christocentric, instead of anthropocentric. An anthropocentric theology that focuses too much on religion as an aspect of the inner self, instead of history or society, may affirm the modern idea that religion is a private matter. Yet, this might also be the consequence of the original intention of fundamental theology that, because it searches for the rational appropriation of faith, it inevitably loses sight of its subject matter, i.e. God and His self-revelation in the world. Furthermore, the application of human freedom as a philosophical principle of theological hermeneutics may lead to a theology that merely "(..) has to search for ways to a practical

---

[60] J. Wentzel van Huyssteen, *Essays in postfoundationalist theology*, Grand Rapids 1997, 14.
[61] Cf. R. Bauckham, *God and the crisis of freedom. Biblical and contemporary perspectives*, Louisville 2002, 178-209, 197.
[62] G. Essen, "Und diese Zeit ist unsere Zeit, immer noch", 44.
[63] K. Rahner, Theologie und Anthropologie, in: *Schriften zur Theologie VIII*, Einsiedeln 1967, 43-65.

testimony of faith, which encourages people to a committed assumption of their freedom and lets them discover themselves as autonomous hearers of the gospel".[64]

However, theological self-understanding would also want to seek the intelligibility of both the components of the short answer to the question "What is theology?", i.e. human reason and God, instead of reconstructing human autonomy for the purpose of the practical witness of faith. Fundamental theology follows the opposite movement and tries to understand the freedom of Christian witness as the expression of faith, which is a reciprocal and communicative, rather than autonomous act. A philosophical concept of freedom, especially in its modern meaning of autonomy, could only be of use to a justification of reason alone and not of faith. Nevertheless, to avoid theological esotericism, it should be acknowledged that the philosophical and the theological concepts of reason must not differ. Therefore, as a hearer of the gospel that establishes human freedom as a God-given and covenanted type of freedom, the fundamental theologian should criticise and argue against the modern philosophical concept of freedom as autonomy. This, however, does not entail a theological critique of modern philosophy altogether abandoning the concept of freedom. On the contrary, in dialogue with modern philosophy, the challenge of fundamental theology today is to describe faith as a free act, and to present the freedom to witness as a responsive and responsible choice.[65]

1.4. In search of method

Having established the tasks of contemporary fundamental theology, the question of how to perform these tasks evidently follows. Theology must not only be aware of the current situation in the church, the academy and society, but also self-conscious of how it deals with this situation. In this process of self-awareness, the problems of diversity, particularity and freedom will not only reveal the tasks of fundamental theology, but also the specificity of its method. Indeed, fundamental theology is not merely

---

[64] Th. Pröpper, Freiheit als philosophisches Prinzip theologischer Hermeneutik, in: Id., *Evangelium und freie Vernunft. Konturen einer theologischen Hermeneutik*, Freiburg im Breisgau 2001, 5-22, 21.
[65] Cf. S. Hauerwas, *With the grain of the universe. The church's witness and natural theology*, [The Gifford Lectures 2001], London 2002, 205-241; J. Wentzel van Huyssteen, *Essays in postfoundationalist theology*, 11-39.

the description of theological method, but accounts for the methods used in the various disciplines of theology as well. But fundamental theology must do more than provide a meta-theory. It has its own method that, because it is intertwined with other theological subdisciplines, cannot be completely dissimilar from them. Conversely, all subdisciplines should be open to this search for accountability performed by fundamental theology. For example, the literary method in theology is never purely literary, for it has to account for its choice of text and the *Sitz im Leben* of both text and reader, which undoubtedly influence the approach to that text.[66] Likewise, empirical theology cannot completely rely on its empirical research techniques alone for the justification of a rational or systematic approach in theology.[67] Fundamental theology therefore should search for common characteristics in the variety of theological methods and explain their accountability and functionality. In this section, I will show that neither meta-theories, nor certain influential methods in contemporary theology, liberal, postliberal, and correlation or revisionary theologies, address adequately all the different tasks of fundamental theology. Although they are presented as fundamental or foundational theologies, they do not search for commonalities in theological methods, but instead they stress one or two of the theological tasks I mentioned, thereby misrepresenting fundamental theology as a detached discipline.[68]

a. The limitations of meta-theories

Bernard Lonergan's definition of theological method, although thirty years old, remains pertinent to the abovementioned considerations:

> Method is not a set of rules to be followed meticulously by a dolt. It is a framework for collaborative creativity. It would outline the various clusters of operations to be performed by theologians when they go about their various tasks. A contemporary method would conceive of those tasks in the context of modern science, modern scholarship, modern philosophy, of historicity, collective practicality and co-responsibility.[69]

---

[66] Cf. E. van Wolde, The limits of linearity. Linear and non-linear causal thinking in biblical exegesis, philosophy and theology, in: *Bijdragen. Tijdschrift voor filosofie en theologie* 62 (2001), 371-392, 390-392.
[67] H. Schilderman, Blazing the trail of empirical theology, in: H.-G. Ziebertz, F. Schweitzer, H. Häring, D. Browning [eds], *The human image of God*, [on the occasion of Johannes A. van der Ven's 60th birthday], Leiden 2001, 405-433, 425.
[68] Cf. F.J. van Beeck, s.j., *God encountered. A contemporary systematic theology 2/1/1*, 264-273.
[69] B. Lonergan, *Method in theology*, xi.

Lonergan's definition, stressing collaboration and modernisation, is directed against the scholastic method in which he was educated. The Jesuit theologian Avery Dulles also recognises certain limitations of scholastic method, but not until after he has enumerated the advantages of it: respect for authority of predecessors and church teaching; the importance of proceeding systematically by ordering the questions logically and avoiding unnecessary repetition; systematic responsibility by looking upon each treatise as part of an all-embracing whole and distinguishing standpoints, arguments and counterarguments, even against one's own standpoint; and finally, the recognition that not all conclusions were equally certain by referring to the sources of arguments.[70] However, according to Dulles, scholasticism did not leave room for a confrontation of systems as connected wholes, nor did the systematic objections raised actually lead to dialogue between adversaries.[71]

Lonergan's definition of theological method is not merely critical of its previous scholastic history but also contains a positive proposal for creative collaboration. Indeed, theological method should be open to cooperate with other disciplines. To meet the three challenges for fundamental theology today, theologians cannot ignore the results of other fields of research. However, this may not be as easy as Lonergan suggests. As a transcendental theologian he assumes that there will be an underlying unity of all academic disciplines, a unity best described epistemologically by the different faculties of human cognition that all disciplines have in common.[72] Fundamental theology then, would have to describe the foundations of faith in concordance with the foundations of other disciplines. The differences between religions are considered to be the result of different decisions, or conversions as Lonergan puts it, while the pluralism of expressions within a single religious system depends on varieties in the presence or absence of differentiated consciousness. Although Lonergan appreciates this religious diversity and differentiation "both for the understanding of the development of religious traditions, and for an understanding of the impasses that may result from such development", he believes that the different views and expressions have a common origin, which needs to be approached epistemologically.[73] This epistemological approach of individual experience and conversion however not only ignores the communal experience in the church, which nowadays is partly

---

[70] A. Dulles, The problem of method. From scholasticism to models, in: Id., *The craft of theology*, 41-52, 42-43.
[71] Ibid., 45-46.
[72] B. Lonergan, *Method in theology*, 3-25.
[73] Ibid., 271-281, 271.

based on a communication about the differences in religious experiences but leaves no room for the specificity of revelation or religious experience, which may not adequately be described by or methodologically rooted in epistemological categories.[74]

To avoid an epistemological or historical reduction in fundamental theology and to make space for an evaluation of different and even contradictory systems in theology, one could map the differences to get an overview of the field. And yet, as experience teaches, "the map is not the territory" because it merely describes what is there, without explaining the why and wherefore.[75] Avery Dulles therefore advocated the utilisation of models or typologies to describe the particularity of the subject matter of theology. With reference to Reinhold Niebuhr's *Christ and Culture* he argues that typologies have the advantages of scholasticism, by "pointing out the issues and choices to be made and the theoretical implications of pure positions" whilst avoiding its limitations.[76] Dulles maintains that typologies focus on the structural features of systems and stress the dissimilarities between them, without giving any definitive status to any given typology. Indeed, he even considers that a typological approach is incapable of preferring any one system within a typology. However, the latter is not necessarily the case. Hans Frei for example, who is renowned for the application of a typology to theology, expresses his preference for a specific type of theology based on the criteria that are constitutive of his typology.[77] Although a typology is never a definitive or closed system, and is still able to signify the great themes of Christian theology, it can only account for the diversity of theological positions. A typology will not however, be able to account for the theological character shared by all positions, nor will it be able for example to explain why faith is a free, personal act in response to revelation. For the present research, and with respect to the challenging tasks of contemporary fundamental theology, a typology alone will therefore not suffice.[78]

George Schner weighs several metaphors for theology in a recent collection of essays on postliberalism.[79] According to him, a metaphor is an

---

[74] Cf. Ch. Taylor, *Varieties of religion today. William James revisited*, Cambridge 2002.

[75] Cf. the title of J.Z. Smith, *Map is not territory. Studies in the history of religions*, Chicago 1978.

[76] A. Dulles, *Models of revelation*, 25.

[77] H. Frei, *Types of Christian theology*, 5-6.

[78] In chapter two, I will however practice the art of typology to describe the similarities and dissimilarities between different theologies that deal with aesthetics and the arts.

[79] G.P. Schner, s.j., Metaphors for theology, in: J. Webster, Id. [eds], *Theology after liberalism*, 3-51.

image that makes concrete a general definition in a different manner and, when applied to theology, it also functions as a methodological proposal. Because metaphors for theology "aim at providing a kind of unity, and imply an order and purposefulness to the web of convictions", they seem an appropriate tool to describe the nature of theology, since fundamental theology must seek to find the commonalities within the variety of theological methods.[80] The several functions of a metaphor, as explanation, creative inspiration and focus, seem highly appropriate to the challenges of fundamental theology, because they also reflect the nature of religious language.[81] Yet the question arises: can a metaphor be more than just the reflection of the language of faith? A metaphorical theology will only be a way of doing fundamental theology if it accounts for the rationality of the application of metaphors to the subject matter and the nature of theology. Although one can only express one's faith and understanding of God and revelation in analogies and metaphors, a merely metaphorical approach in describing the nature of theology will replace one particularity with another, with the danger of falling into the fallacy of fideism.

b. The limitations of current methods

As noted before, fundamental theology is neither a philosophical introduction nor a generic meta-theory. Instead, being an integral part of every aspect of the whole of the theological enterprise, it evaluates and proposes what makes theology theological. In dialogue with the current situation in the church, the academy and society, fundamental theology is the discipline in which theological differences are assessed, the uniqueness of faith is emphasised and the responsible freedom towards revelation and tradition is explained. Neither maps, nor models, nor metaphors, are able to perform all these tasks at the same time. More importantly, none of these meta-theoretical ways will be able to account for the theological character of theological methods.

The most appropriate among the current influential theological methods to meet these terms seems to be correlation method, because it stresses the interdependence of faith and culture. Attempting to avoid the fideist fallacy, correlation method integrates various discourses and refers to theology and culture in terms of dialogue, mutual criticism or

---

[80] Ibid., 3.
[81] Cf. K. Feyaerts, L. Boeve, Introduction, in: *Metaphor and God-talk*, [Religions and discourse, ed. by J Francis], Bern, etc. 1999, 7-14, 9.

confrontation.[82] As such, it necessarily deals with diversity, particularity and freedom. The advantage is a type of theology which acknowledges that faith communities are part of the public realm, which will only find their identity in relation to other cultural systems. The question, however, remains how the interdependence between faith and culture will lead to either the discovery of the particularity of faith or to a criticism of a specific religious belief. Correlation method would rather look for cultural continuities instead of historical changes and discontinuities in faith and theology itself. Correlation method has been severely criticised by postliberals such as George Lindbeck who, referring to Schleiermacher, criticised correlationists like Paul Tillich for making "religion experientially intelligible to the cultured and uncultured among both its despisers and appreciators" to defend particular Christian claims by mistakenly appealing to experience in general. Correlation method, Lindbeck continues, turns out to be only significant to theologians themselves and does not impress other academics whatsoever.[83] Instead, he suggests, the "grammar of religion" should be explained by the analysis of practice, which will open theological research for dialogue with other academic disciplines.

Liberation theologians have also stressed practice within a specific context as a starting point for theology. Although they share with correlation theologians the need for an analysis of experience, they refer to the specific experience of socio-political oppression and human suffering, rather than to experience as a general epistemological category. The liberationist appeal to practice therefore differs from the postliberal one, which focuses on communal reading practices instead of on the political practice of violence, exclusion and oppression. Despite their differences and although they account for cultural diversities and the particular convictions of faith, both liberationist and postliberal theologies fail to explain the theological character of their methods. Defending itself against becoming a general theory, postliberalism consciously presents itself as strictly self-descriptive.[84] Liberation theology unintentionally falls into that same category when it ideologically and often atheoretically proclaims its convictions and intentions.[85] To perform the task of

---

[82] Cf. F. Schüssler Fiorenza, Systematic theology: tasks and methods, in: Id., J.P. Galvin [eds], *Systematic theology. Roman Catholic perspectives, Vol. I*, Minneapolis 1991, 1-87, 55-61.

[83] G. Lindbeck, *The nature of doctrine. Religion and theology in a postliberal age*, Philadelphia 1984, 129-130.

[84] J. Webster, Theology after liberalism?, in: Id., G. Schner, s.j. [eds], *Theology after liberalism*, 52-61, 57-58.

[85] Cf. D.G. Kamitsuka, *Theology and contemporary culture*, 26-38.

theological self-understanding in a changing society and in dialogue with conflicting notions of rationality, fundamental theology needs a method which freely explores the possibilities of communicating Christian self-description to all conceivable audiences.

In summary, fundamental theology is a purely theological discipline and not a meta-theory or philosophical *prolegomena*. Materially, it may be a separate discipline in a theological curriculum but formally, it cannot be separated from any other subdiscipline in theology, since it evaluates the theological character of each of them by proposing what theology should be. The double movement of evaluation and proposal shows that fundamental theology and with it, the answer to the question of the nature of theology should be open to correction and change. It also shows indirectly that fundamental theology is intrinsic to all subdisciplines because they influence its evaluation by means of dialogue with other academic disciplines and society, just as a proposal of what theology should be will influence the respective approaches and confrontations of theological subdisciplines with the academy and society. In Christian theology, this type of correlation is grounded in the belief in God and His revelation in Christ and the world. As such, the ground of Christian theology, which argues for the legitimacy of one's theological method in the face of society's needs and the contemporary notions of rationality established by non-theological academic disciplines, is itself grounded in Christian faith.

This double focus of theology is the problem of fundamental theology. A contemporary theological self-understanding must always also be an expression of the awareness that theological doctrines *sub ratione Dei* are confronted with dissimilar notions of rationality. Thus, the current tasks of fundamental theology originate in this dissimilarity, and every answer as to what theology is, should articulate it, rather than seek possible correlations between different views on the world and humanity. Merely proclaiming the particularity of Christian faith will not suffice either. If Christian doctrines are grounded in conversions and convictions alone, an idiosyncratic and non-communicable method will be the result. Therefore, to find a balance between faith and reason, theologians need to move between the two freely. In that process, they will find themselves confronted with basic beliefs and a prevailing notion of rationality that hopefully serve them in their freedom to reason and believe, just as it serves to clarify and modify what it means to reason and believe responsibly. In doing so, the theologian expresses the hope that divine revelation is not merely a matter of faith or metaphysical opinion, but that it is also possible to communicate it to others, and to show believers and non-believers alike at least the joy of faith, which inspires the community of believers to which theologians belong.[86]

1.5. Demonstratio aesthetica?

Fundamental theology tries to solve the problem of how to communicate its religious inspiration, not only because of its double focus on faith and reason but also because it might be able to reconstruct this inspiration in such a way that the light of divine revelation shines through its rational discourse. Only thus will theology do justice to its foundation in faith. It must be said however that revelation and therefore theological inspiration are not reconstructable. Nevertheless, it is possible to describe and explain the ways believers perceive and respond to divine revelation. Theology itself is one of these ways as it is the ongoing attempt to reflect revelation in its reflections and to communicate how believers communicate with God, as they believe God communicates with them. In this present book, I will defend the position that art and beauty are appropriate concepts to describe the communication of faith and that therefore fundamental theology can be defined aesthetically.[87]

In the last few decades many theologians have already proposed a close connection between theology and the arts.[88] The first and perhaps most obvious reason for establishing such a connection is the fact that art and beauty are essential features of religion and religious communities. It is a theological miscalculation that verbal theology stands on its own in explaining what faith is. The expressions of faith in symbols, images and

---

[86] Cf. A. Shanks, *'What is truth?' Towards a theological poetics*, London 2001, 3-7.
[87] I acknowledge that my description of the tasks of fundamental theology is similar to F. LeRon Shults's description of the task of postfoundationalist theology: "to engage in interdisciplinary dialogue within our postmodern culture while *both* maintaining a commitment to intersubjective, transcommunal theological argumentation for the truth of Christian faith, *and* recognizing the provisionality of our historically embedded understandings and culturally conditioned explanations of the Christian tradition and religious experience." F. LeRon Shults, *The postfoundationalist task of theology. Wolfhart Pannenberg and the new theological rationality*, Grand Rapids 1999, 237. Postfoundationalism's most distinctive goal however, is the linking of theological hermeneutics with epistemology instead of with aesthetics.
[88] Cf. G. Howes, Theology and the arts. Visual arts, in: D. Ford [ed.], *The modern theologians. An introduction to Christian theology in the twentieth century*, London 1997², 669-685. See also chapter two.

songs have their own explanatory force. These religious acts have the aesthetic dimension in common. The Hispanic-American theologian Alejandro García-Rivera calls this 'living theology' and says that art and aesthetics animate it, just as rationality gives substance to textbook theology.[89] One could even go further by saying that living theology is the practice that textbook theology should expound theoretically. Since art and beauty are essential characteristics of religious behaviour and experience, textbook theology must incorporate aesthetics. Such a theology could, for example, subsequently lament what has happened to the beautiful in the church or ask how to ensure that beauty and good art will return.

A second reason for having a theological interest in aesthetics is the traditional claim that art and beauty are ways to gain knowledge about God, because of God's self-revelation in the beauty of the world. To explore this would be a field expansion for performing the task of classic fundamental theology, which apologetically sought proofs for religion, revelation and the church. However, the idea behind a *demonstratio aesthetica*, which would be the demonstration of the truth of faith by referring to worldly beauty or by means of (artistic) images, has been problematised from the Iconoclast controversy, through the Reformation, to the postmodern emphasis on negative theology. Nevertheless, these fierce debates, which served and still serve to protect Christian worship either against verbal reduction or idolatry, prove that an aesthetic awareness in theology is needed, if only to establish a definitive separation of theology and art.[90]

Questioning the nature of theology may lead to a third reason for making the relationship between theology and the arts explicit. If theology is regarded as, in the words of Karl Rahner "man's reflexive self-expression about himself in the light of divine revelation", then the arts might prove to be intrinsic to theology itself, because theological expressions may not be restricted to words and arguments alone, but also involve man's creative power expressed in architecture, images and sounds.[91] This motive to construct a theology of the arts also addresses the idea of God's self-revelation in scripture and tradition in a beautiful and artistic way, in poems, psalms and prophecies and the sacramental beauty of the

---

[89] A. García-Rivera, *A wounded innocence. Sketches for a theology of art*, Collegeville 2003, viii.

[90] Cf. J. Dillenberger, *A theology of artistic sensibilities. The visual arts and the church*, New York 1986, 217f.

[91] K. Rahner, Theology and the arts, in: *Thought* 57 (1982), 24.

liturgy.[92] The presentation of the contemporary debate on the nature of theology in this chapter is an indication that I will focus on this third reason.

However, an all too easily established connection between theology and the arts may forget the fact that they have their own methods independent of each other. Any proposal towards a unity of art and theology may not only 'desecrate' theology's own iconoclastic awareness, but also ignore the pluralistic sensibilities of contemporary culture. In this book therefore, no such proposal for a correlation between theology and the arts can be found. However, I am conscious of the needs of society and the church to recover a shared spiritual dimension through the arts, and thus, as a theologian, I hope to help find ways that art can engage theology and vice versa. Nevertheless, to meet the challenge of fundamental theology to express the particularity of Christian faith in a context of diversity, my starting point will be pluralistic. I believe that by taking a pluralistic methodological stance, assuming that art and theology do something differently even when they centre on the same reality, I will show that they have more to offer to one another than when it is too self-evidently suggested that all art is essentially of a religious nature or that theology should be 'artful'.

Yet, I propose that the study of aesthetics will be helpful in answering the question "What is theology?" and explore further the possibilities of understanding both the concept of faith and fundamental theology aesthetically. I defend the view that an aesthetic approach will solve the problem of fundamental theology, i.e. how to understand faith and communicate it to others theologically. I start with the assumption that aesthetics is an appropriate way of understanding the interwovenness of divine and human communication. It is a field that explores the reciprocity of reception and construction that defines both faith and theology's communication with a diversity of audiences. Aesthetics is the theory that searches for universal and communicable values and meaning based on the particularities of works of art and beauty. Similarly, theology is grounded in the practical life of faith and seeks the conversation with church and society. However, to answer the question "What is theology?", I think it will not be sufficient to find the similarities between theology and aesthetics, but it will be possible to suggest an answer after

---

[92] Cf. W.A. Dyrness, *Visual faith. Art, theology, and worship in dialogue*, Grand Rapids 2001.

having established the commonalities between the two disciplines and by proposing aesthetics as a way of doing theology. That proposal for a theological aesthetics will put forward how to perform the art of theology, by doing justice to seeing the ground of theology as a given freedom to create forms of faith that express a responsive and responsible desire to communicate with both God and others.

2. THEOLOGY AND AESTHETICS

> Glory be to God for dappled things
> For skies of couple-colour as a brinded cow;
> For rose-moles all in stipple upon trout that swim;
> Fresh-firecoal chestnut-falls; finches' wings;
> Landscape plotted and pieced—fold, fallow, and plough;
> And áll trádes, their gear and tackle and trim.
>
> All things counter, original, spare, strange;
> Whatever is fickle, freckled (who knows how?)
> With swift, slow; sweet, sour; adazzle, dim;
> He fathers-forth whose beauty is past change:
> Praise him.[1]

Gerard Manley Hopkins's (1844-1889) playfully rhythmic poem *Pied Beauty* shows the close connection of faith and beauty. In this poem, Hopkins does not consider the aesthetic experience to be religious, but describes an experience of the beauty of ever-changing nature that alerts one to the divine presence in creation, which makes people want to praise God. Yet, as Augustine had already said, paradoxically natural beauty both does and does not embody the beauty of God:

> But what do I love when I love my God? Not material beauty or beauty of a temporal order; not the brilliance of earthy light, so welcome to our eyes; not the sweet melody of harmony and song; not the fragrance of flowers, perfumes and spices; not manna or honey; not limbs such as the body delights to embrace. It is not these that I love when I love my God. And yet, when I love Him, it is true that I love a light of a certain kind, a voice, a perfume, a food, an embrace.[2]

As shown in the previous chapter, the theologian cannot ignore the role of art and beauty in understanding the specific experiences, actions and truth claims of faith. It is important to understand the differences between the beautiful and the religious, so that they are not too easily identified nor reduced to one or the other. Consequently, by clarifying the dialogue between theology and aesthetics, it will become clear what their specific and mutual tasks are. In this chapter, I present recent theological interest

---

[1] G. M. Hopkins, Pied Beauty, in: *Poems of Gerard Manley Hopkins*, [Edited with notes by Robert Bridges], London 1918.
[2] Augustine, *De civitate Dei*, xxii, 24.

in art and aesthetics. By confronting theology with aesthetics, I will define the task of theological aesthetics.

2.1. The return of aesthetics in theology

Aesthetics has long been a forgotten chapter in the history of theology. However, in the last two decades, many theologians have focussed on the significance of the arts for theology.[3] The ideas of 'beauty' and 'imagination' have also returned to the conceptual framework of theology.[4] However, the subject matter of theological aesthetics is not always clearly defined. Sometimes the emphasis is on works of art, because art objects mediate religion and so can be regarded as sources for theology. In other cases, the stress is on beauty and imagination, understood as important characteristics of theological rationality itself. It is remarkable that not only correlation theology, but also critical and post-critical, liberal and neo-orthodox theologies show a great interest in aesthetics. The possibility of theological representation and construction is at the centre of the debate between modern and postmodern theologies. This is a debate about the nature of theology, its sources and its method. Therefore, the main

---

[3] These are some of the most important recent publications on theology and the arts: R. Harries, *Art and the beauty of God*, London 1993; W. Lesch [Hrsg.], *Theologie und ästhetische Erfahrung. Beiträge zur Begegnung von Religion und Kunst*, Darmstadt 1994; G. Larcher [Hrsg.], *Gott-Bild. Gebrochen durch die Moderne*, [Für K.M. Woschitz], Graz, etc. 1997; G. Pattison, *Art, modernity and faith. Restoring the image*, London 1998²; W.E. Müller, J. Heumann [Hrsg.], *Kunst-positionen. Kunst als Thema gegenwärtiger evangelischer und katholischer Theologie*, Stuttgart, etc. 1998; J. Begbie [ed.], *Beholding the glory. Incarnation through the arts*, London 2000; P. Schmidt, *In de handen van mensen. 2000 jaar Christus in kunst en cultuur*, Kampen 2000; W.A. Dyrness, *Visual faith. Art, theology and worship in dialogue*, Grand Rapids 2001; P. Sherry, *Images of redemption. Art, literature and salvation*, London 2003.

[4] These are some recent publications on theology and imagination or beauty, which will not be explicitly discussed in this chapter: J. Mackey [ed.], *Religious imagination*, Edinburgh 1986; R. Hoeps, *Das Gefühl des Erhabenen und die Herrlichkeit Gottes. Studien zur Beziehung von philosophischer und theologischer Ästhetik*, Würzburg 1989; F.B. Brown, *Religious aesthetics. A theological study of making and meaning*, Princeton 1993²; P. Avis, *God and the creative imagination. Metaphor, symbol and myth in religion and theology*, London 1999; D. Brown, *Tradition & imagination. Revelation & change*, Oxford 1999; Id., *Discipleship & imagination. Christian tradition & truth*, Oxford 2000; F.A. Maas, Beauty and religion. Being touched by a sense of openness and underlying unity of all things, in: W. Derkse et al. [red.], *In Quest of humanity in a globalising world. Dutch contributions to the jubilee of universities in Rome 2000*, Leende 2000, 275-292; J. Mackey, *The critique of theological reason*, Cambridge 2000; C. Crockett, *A theology of the sublime*, [With a foreword by Charles Winquist], London 2001; E. Farley, *Faith and beauty. A theological aesthetic*, Aldershot 2001. See also section two of the bibliography.

function of the reintroduction of aesthetics in theology seems to be its contribution to a new theological self-understanding.

The aesthetic approach in theology, however, remains suspect. The long history of iconoclasm resounds in the reproach aimed at neo-Catholic[5] orthodoxy that it adorns the Christian faith with too much beauty and is only interested in the outward appearance of the liturgy, for example, rather than its content.[6] This aestheticism of faith would supposedly cover the Christian message rather than create room for its revelation. Another criticism is that an aesthetic approach in theology does not find its sources in scripture or revelation, but in philosophical aesthetics or art. The idea behind this criticism is that theology should not try to find its foundations in dialogue with other disciplines, or that it should not even seek ultimate foundations for theological reflection at all.[7] After all, theological truth cannot be founded. Any attempt to do so compromises the sovereignty of its origin, which does not submit itself to any form of human reason, including the aesthetical.

Are there are any good reasons to applaud the return of aesthetics in theology, or should this tendency be regarded with suspicion? In this chapter, I will guide the reader through the rapidly increasing amount of literature on the subject of theology and aesthetics. It will become clear that, because of the different applications of aesthetics in theology, it is not obvious what the subject matter of aesthetics is. Once a forgotten aspect of theology, aesthetics has now become a misapprehended one. Moreover, during the short history of theological aesthetics, the emphasis has shifted radically from the doctrine of the *imago Dei* to the doctrine of salvation. In the first part of this chapter (1.1), I will discuss three theologians who explicitly developed a theological aesthetics in the twentieth century (Gerardus van der Leeuw, Paul Tillich and Hans Urs von Balthasar). Their different conceptions of the field formed the foundations of theological aesthetics, although they mainly focused on the relation between divine creation and human imagination.

---

[5] The term 'neo-Catholic' can be confusing, because it is used in a different and sometimes even contradictory sense. By 'neo-Catholicism', I mean the revival of Roman Catholic orthodoxy and traditionalism since the 1990s.
[6] For the history of iconoclasm, cf.: J. Pelikan, *Imago Dei. The Byzantine apologia for icons* [A.W.Mellon Lectures in the Fine Arts, 1987], Princeton 1990; E. Nordhofen, *Der Engel der Bestreitung. Über das Verhältnis von Kunst und negativer Theologie*, Würzburg 1993.
[7] See previous chapter, especially section two.

In the last few decades, theological analysis of art and aesthetics has shifted to the autonomous capacity of the artist to express good and evil, or truth and falsehood in art (among others theologians such as Alex Stock, Hans Küng and Eberhard Jüngel have directed this movement). This has brought the work of art itself to the centre of theological aesthetics. Other theologians are looking into the analogous relation between a creative God and creative creatures. Others even see art and beauty as means of liberation and salvation. To organise this diversity in current theological aesthetics, I will present a typology of the various aesthetic positions in the last section of this chapter (2.4). From this typology, I will express my preference for an aesthetic approach in theology, which focuses on theological (protological, soteriological, eschatological) subjects, rather than on the work of art or on preceding philosophical considerations.

I hope that by giving an overview of contemporary theological aesthetics, it will become clear that an aesthetic approach in theology concerns the method, sources and tasks of theology. I will argue that theological aesthetics should offer much more than merely a phenomenological comparison between the aesthetic and the religious experience. It should also offer more than artistic illustrations to a given theological content. The premise of this chapter is that theological aesthetics constitutes a broadening of theological rationality. Therefore, it might complement conceptual analysis and hermeneutics in theology. Theological aesthetics points to a faithful receptivity to beauty (and ugliness!), without ignoring the creative and often difficult work of constructing images of faith. On the contrary, an aesthetic approach in theology will demonstrate the inextricable connection between receptivity and construction in faith.

Before I continue, I would like to express an awareness of the iconoclastic suspicion directed toward this subject. Many neo-orthodox or postliberal theologians might claim that theologians who apply other sources in theology than revelation, scripture or the church, trivialise the subject of theology or unnecessarily widen the field of its activity.[8] I acknowledge that to a theologian, both the aesthetic perception and the religious imagination necessarily stand in a tradition of revelation. Of all disciplines, theological aesthetics will show that theology can and perhaps even must begin with a doxology. After that, the theologian will search for cogent reasons to end with one as well, like Hopkins has shown in his poem *Pied Beauty*.

---

[8] For example, J. Webster, Theology after liberalism?, in: Id., G. Schner, s.j. [eds], *Theology after liberalism. A reader*, Oxford 2000, 52-64; A. van de Beek, *Ontmaskering. Christelijk geloof en cultuur*, Zoetermeer 2001.

2.2. Towards a theological aesthetics

a. The ambivalent history of theology and the arts

Christian theology and aesthetics share a common history of twenty centuries. Christianity seems to be a tradition of the Word and indeed, at certain points in its history it tried to banish beauty and the arts. However dreadful this may sound, it was a prudent attempt to guarantee the integrity of holiness and the sovereignty of the divine. But Christianity should regard its own tradition of art and beauty as a possibility to anticipate redemption, a way to imagine a future life in the Kingdom of God. The history of this ambivalent relationship between theology and the arts is much older than Christianity itself. Here are some of its landmarks.[9] It begins with Plato's (428-347 BC) fulmination against the pernicious influence of poets in the Greek city-state, and Aristotle's (384-322 BC) systematic analyses of Greek theatre and continues through Augustine's (354-430) expositions about music and the allotment of a regular place for the concept of beauty in philosophy by Plotinus (204-270) and Pseudo-Dionysius (ca. 500).[10] Thomas Aquinas (1225-1274) and Cajetan (1468-1534) define 'the beautiful' as one of the transcendental concepts. Francisco Suarez (1548-1617) rejects it as such.

The iconoclastic controversy of the Second Council of Nicea in 787 and the Reformation are moments in this history when its discussion of the relation between art and faith became problematic or even impossible.[11] The iconoclastic controversy revolved around whether the divine could be represented pictorially and whether such representations, icons, should be venerated. The iconoclasts based their stance on the second commandment and since it was held that icons were images of the divine, they were forbidden and to worship them was idolatrous. The suspicion of art that erupted in the iconoclast controversies was carried forward to the Reformation. Although the attitude of reformers like Erasmus, Luther and Calvin towards art and especially towards statues and images in

---

[9] Cf. P. Sherry, *Spirit and beauty. An introduction to theological aesthetics*, London 2002² (1992), 4-17.

[10] Cf. G. Jantzen, Beauty for ashes. Notes on the displacement of beauty, in: *Literature & theology* 16 (2002) 4, 427-449.

[11] This premodern history is up for renewal after Hans Urs von Balthasars attempt in *Herrlichkeit. Eine theologische Ästhetik*, [7 Bde.], Einsiedeln 1962-1969. Some initial impetus can be found in J.W. de Gruchy, *Christianity, art and transformation. Theological aesthetics in the struggle for justice*, Cambridge 2001, 9-52.

churches was complex—and they would certainly not have condoned all the image-smashing that was done in the name of their reforms—their books contain plenty of passages which could be used to charge the Roman church with the worship of idols.

In the history of theology and the arts, the works of art themselves must not be forgotten. After all, the arts could be seen as either sources or rivals of theology in this context. That would take us back even further in time, starting with Homer and going from there to the Greek tragedians, the Byzantine icon painters, the cathedral builders of the Middle Ages, Grünewald's and Van Eyck's altarpieces, and Hildegard von Bingen's and Johan Sebastian Bach's sacred music, to mention but some, right into the modern age. Moreover, let us not forget the iconographical history of objects, representations, poetry and music used in liturgy and catechesis.[12] All these works of art were not only illustrations or explanations of religious content, but also expressions of religious experience and as such shaped the experiences of their audiences. These are only a few of the milestones in the history of theology and that which later would be called aesthetics.[13]

b. The emergence of modern philosophical aesthetics

Alexander Baumgarten: aesthetics as the science of sensory knowledge
In the modern age, art acquired an autonomous position towards the church and its authority, while philosophy and theology were parting to some extent. Within that cultural and academic context, aesthetics became a philosophical discipline in its own right. Alexander Gottlieb Baumgarten (1714-1762) invented the term and defined philosophical aesthetics as a science of cognition by the senses.[14] In doing so, he invoked the Greek meaning of the word *aisthèsis*, which means 'perception', and to the connected noun *aisthètika*, which denotes the objects perceived. By this definition, he regarded aesthetics as the lower part of epistemology (*gnoseologia inferior*). However, Baumgarten considered sensory

---

[12] For a history of Christian art up to the Renaissance, I gladly refer to the excellent overview in: H. Belting, *Bild und Kult. Eine Geschichte des Bildes vor dem Zeitalter der Kunst*, München 1991². See also J. van Laarhoven, *De beeldtaal van de christelijke kunst. Geschiedenis van de iconografie*, Nijmegen 1992.

[13] Overviews of the history of philosophical aesthetics can be found in W. Tatarkiewicz, *Geschichte der Ästhetik*, Basel 1987; Th. Baumeister, *De filosofie en de kunsten. Van Plato tot Beuys*, Best 1999; H. Bredin, L. Santoro-Brienza, *Philosophies of art and beauty. Introducing aesthetics*, Edinburgh 2000.

[14] A.G. Baumgarten, *Aesthetica*, Hildesheim 1961 (1750-1758).

knowledge autonomous in relation to logical knowledge. He called aesthetics the art of thinking beautifully (*ars pulchrae cogitandi*) and the art of forming taste (*ars formandi gustum*). The attainment of beauty, construed as the perfect form of sensory knowledge, is the subject of this type of aesthetics. By emphasising human faculties such as perception, imagination and intuition, Baumgarten sought to correct the rationalist epistemology of his age, which considered these faculties to be inferior and therefore not suitable for scientific analysis.[15]

Immanuel Kant: aesthetics of taste and the sublime
A few decades later, at the end of the eighteenth century, romantic philosophers had come to regard aesthetics as the philosophy of art. Around that time, Immanuel Kant (1724-1804) developed his aesthetic theory of beauty and since his *Critique of judgment* (1790), many philosophers understand the concept of 'beauty' as a subjective judgement.[16] According to Kant, beauty is disinterested, by which he means that it has no other goal than to be beautiful, and the creative imagination serves no other purpose than to bring about human joy and pleasure or at most to create some confusion in a seemingly clear-cut reality.[17]

To be able to understand Kant's aesthetics, one needs to interpret the third critique in relation to its two predecessors. This is necessary not only to demonstrate the systematic unity of this trilogy, but also to understand that the final critique was written to bridge between the first two. After the first two critiques, Kant found himself faced with a chasm between objective knowledge and moral actions, in other words between theoretical laws and practical freedom. As analysed in the two first critiques, human beings find themselves subject on the one hand to the categories of reason, which describe the laws of the (phenomenal) world as it appears to us, and to the laws of reason, which presuppose a moral obligation and therefore a certain freedom in relation to the (noumenal) world as it is, on the other. The reflective judgement, which can mediate between the a priori laws of reason and the a priori principles of freedom should also be based on an a priori principle that cannot be a given, as that would confront us with a new chasm that again would need to be bridged.

---

[15] Cf. R. Viladesau, *Theological aesthetics. God in imagination, beauty and art*, Oxford 1999, 6.
[16] I. Kant, *Kritik der Urteilskraft und Schriften zur Naturphilosophie*, [Hrsg. von W. Weischedel], Darmstadt 1983⁵.
[17] Cf. H.E. Allison, *Kant's theory of taste, A reading of the critique of aesthetic judgment*, Cambridge 2001.

According to Kant, beauty grants us access to the noumenal world. Therefore, he attributes the formal representation of beauty to the *Ding an sich* and not to reason. Beauty may reveal the objective material of the subjectivity of the artist, but it does not confirm the world in itself, as it is essentially disinterested. Francesca Murphy criticises this Kantian analysis of aesthetical judgements for creating an existential vacuum, because understood in this way they neither confirm the external world, nor lead to any meaning outside the subject. However, beauty should refer to a reality that can be beheld in the work of art or in nature, and as such, the beautiful is dependent upon an objectivity that shows itself and therefore becomes accessible to the subjective beholder.

The disinterested pleasure of Kant's concept of beauty is an involvement of the beholder in the reality of the work of art, which gives itself as beauty. As such, beauty is dependent upon both a subjective and an objective given. It is dependent upon a judgement and on being judged, on seeing and being seen. Nevertheless, it has no goal and serves no purpose, according to Kant. He thinks that the subjective pleasurable feeling that is mediated by a judgement of taste presupposes that everyone else will agree with that judgement, as is often the case (*sensus communis*). Although this may not have the status of an objective judgement, there is a certain subjective generality.

The judgement of sublimity or exaltedness is similar to that of the beautiful.[18] Like the judgement of beauty, it is a reflective judgement, disinterested and in itself imperative.[19] Yet, there are important differences. The beautiful is judged for its form. In contrast, the sublime is judged for its formlessness and its boundlessness. The judgement of beauty associates imagination with the phenomenal world; the sublime, on the other hand, is associated with the noumenal world. A second difference is that the beautiful gives us a pleasurable feeling, whereas the sublime overwhelms us, breaks us away from our established patterns and fills us with an enormous vitality that enthrals us.[20] It is this characteristic of the sublime that connects humanity to the supersensory, and that is why it is of equal if not greater interest than Kant's analysis of the beautiful for theology. Where the beautiful has a suitable form, enabling its presentation and imagination, the sublime is formless. Because of this third difference between the beautiful and the sublime, the latter has often

---

[18] Cf. C. Crockett, *A theology of the sublime*, 67-84.
[19] I. Kant, *Kritik der Urteilskraft*, A73-77.
[20] Ibid., A120.

been associated with the idea of God: It resists any attempt at demarcation or representation. It violates our imagination but the more the sublime fights our imaginative powers and our attempts to grasp it, the more it is experienced as the sublime.

In conclusion, one might say that though modern aesthetics often means 'philosophy of art', philosophy of art is usually clearly distinguished from aesthetics. Aesthetics does not limit itself to the work of art. After all, the judgement of beauty and the aesthetical experience and imagination refer to more than just the work of art and can be applied to the experience of nature, the sciences or to everyday life. The problem with the definition of aesthetics is its double focus, i.e. on beauty and on the work of art. That is why aesthetics cannot be reduced to one single, clear question, like epistemology or ontology. So far, aesthetics has consisted of a set of questions that have different foci. Around these questions is a debate about whether they form a separate philosophical discipline at all, or whether they are part of metaphysics, ethics or epistemology. However, one can establish that the aesthetic operates in a field that is demarcated by the judgement of beauty and human creativity. Beauty is disinterested, as Kant emphasised, and creative imagination has no other purpose than the pleasure of man and the furtherance of enjoyment, or at least creates some confusion in a seemingly clear-cut reality. Aesthetics observes this, describes it and tries to explain it, and like any other than descriptive disciplines, it will have to come to normative judgements about its subject.

2.3. Foundations of theological aesthetics

After the development of aesthetics as an independent philosophical discipline, theologians did not cease to engage with art and beauty on their own terms. An early example of a theologian who explicitly dealt with aesthetics was Jonathan Edwards (1703-1758). Aesthetics forms the heart of his Trinitarian theology, in which God's beauty is pre-eminent among his attributes.[21] Other theologians, like Matthias Scheeben in his theology of grace and glory (1835-1888), commented theologically on the new philosophical aesthetics of Kant, Hegel and Nietzsche. Finally, Jacques Maritain (1882-1973) brings the consideration of art and beauty to Roman

---

[21] Cf. R. Delattre, *Beauty and sensibility in the thought of Jonathan Edwards*, New Haven 1968; P. Sherry, *The spirit of beauty*, 12.

Catholic neoscholastic philosophy.[22] He attempt to design a neoscholastic theory of aesthetics, but does not consider modern developments in philosophical aesthetics. In particular, he ignores the Kantian concept of beauty as disinterestedness, by interpreting the work of art teleologically. Being part of ethics the work of the artist is regarded as a good act that strives for perfection.

By the early twentieth century there still was no separate discipline of theological aesthetics but that was set to change as three renowned theologians had a decisive influence on the development of theological aesthetics, each emphasising a specific aspect: imagination (Gerardus van der Leeuw), the work of art (Paul Tillich), and beauty (Hans Urs von Balthasar). First I will summarize these aspects, then I will examine closely each aesthetic theory separately.

Gerardus van der Leeuw was the first theologian to explicitly deal with the relation between art and religion. His central question was about the relation between divine and human imagination: To what extent can the creative artist answer to divine creation? Paul Tillich was not interested in that specific question. He did not want to regard the creative act of the artist as an act of faith. Rather, he asked how faith could be expressed in a work of art, concentrating on its style and expression. Finally, Hans Urs von Balthasar wrote a theological aesthetics, in which he hardly paid any attention to actual works of art. For him 'beauty' is the first and last word of theology. According to Balthasar, faith is the perception of divine glory in worldly beauty. Thus, these three theologians have defined a new theological field by stressing different aspects of philosophical aesthetics.

a. Gerardus van der Leeuw: imagination as a consequence of the imago Dei

Gerardus van der Leeuw's monumental work, *Wegen en grenzen* (1932¹), has remained an international standard for theological aesthetics right up to this day.[23] Van der Leeuw constructed a phenomenology of religion based on a philosophy of art. He provides lengthy phenomenological considerations of dance, drama, literature, the plastic arts, architecture and

---

[22] J. Maritain, *Art et scholastique*, Paris 1920.
[23] G. van der Leeuw, *Wegen en grenzen. Een studie over de verhouding van religie en kunst*, Amsterdam 1955³ (1932). English translation: *Sacred and profane beauty. The holy in art*, New York 1963.

music. Each chapter concludes with a systematic theological aesthetic consideration: theological aesthetics of the image, of music, of dance, etc. In his preface, he says that Christians who write about art are driven by resentment. Theologians do not allow the arts to play a role in relation to that which transcends this world. Artists, on the other hand, deny religion this role, and instead claim that by means of worldly beauty they are able to "glorify themselves into heaven".[24]

What art and religion have in common, van der Leeuw argues, is that in the creation of the artist, one can see the outlines of divine creation. The same point has been made by pope John Paul II.[25] However, according to van der Leeuw, their difference is that religion is the answer to divine revelation whereas art does not have its own faith or dogma. Still, human imagination is a response as well, and according to van der Leeuw, it might well be, although not explicitly, the answer to that same religious revelation. If so, then he believes it should also be possible to see something of the divine glory in the beauty of the world and in works of art. The background to this argument is van der Leeuw's following discussion with Karl Barth.

In his *Church Dogmatics* (*Kirchliche Dogmatik*) Karl Barth never explicitly mentions theological aesthetics, nor does he provide a systematic discussion of the importance of art and beauty for theology. Van der Leeuw, however, picks up Barth's treatment of the concept of human beings as the images of God.[26] The idea that man is created after the image of God arises from an interpretation of Genesis 1,26-27, in which man is said to be created after the image of God, and therefore made steward of creation. Barth emphasises the fact that although human beings are images of God, they cannot avail themselves of this image character. Human beings are created rather than developed or evolved. This createdness entails that there is an analogy between God and man, which is a similarity within an even greater dissimilarity. This type of analogy is the only model in which man can be regarded as an image of God. Barth does not mean an analogy here that could also articulate the material

---

[24] Ibid., xi-xiii.
[25] John Paul II, *Apostolic letter to the artists*, 1: "None can sense more deeply than you artists, ingenious creators of beauty that you are, something of the pathos with which God at the dawn of creation looked upon the work of his hands. A glimmer of that feeling has shone so often in your eyes when—like the artists of every age—captivated by the hidden power of sounds and words, colours and shapes, you have admired the work of your inspiration, sensing in it some echo of the mystery of creation with which God, the sole creator of all things, has wished in some way to associate you."
[26] K. Barth, *Kirchliche Dogmatik I,1*, München 1932, 250f.

similarities between God and man. However, by using the word 'image' he suggests a forming principle, which achieves its form in the human reality of body and mind in faith.[27]

Van der Leeuw determines the subject of theological aesthetics as image rather than as movement, word or sound. The image always coincides with a different reality than the image itself. This coincidence is an essential relation of both realities, since it is the manifestation of one in the other. In that sense, the artist's imagination is like the creative force of God. The artistic act of creation leads to a concrete form, just like creation itself. This means that ultimately the image of God is also a concrete form and something that takes place in this world. This concrete form of the image of God is the subject of the relation between God and man as His creation. If God is like man, man should be like God, according to van der Leeuw. This makes human imagination a consequence of the Old Testament concept of the *imago Dei*.

According to van der Leeuw, Paul differs radically from the authors of Genesis. In Genesis, human beings have already been reached by God because of creation but Paul says that God needs to give himself personally in order to communicate with human beings again. Thus, van der Leeuw argues that a theological aesthetics is always a theology of the Fall, standing between creation and resurrection. After all, something has happened to human beings. They are no longer like God in the same way that Adam was.[28] Little remains of the image of God, but there is still the createdness of man. Created in the image of God, this can only be understood through the image of a man in Christ.

The idea of the *imago Dei* means that a likeness to God can be found in man. With this, God has given man a possibility to be like Him, albeit a possibility man cannot appropriate fully. However, he can live and perform it, not as a personally achieved possibility but as a given possibility of faith. Van der Leeuw may have derived these theological nuances from Barth's theology, but at the same time, he reproaches Barth for his incorrect interpretation of the image of God. He argues that Barth interpreted the difference of Creator and creation as a radical separation so that there cannot be any personal creative force in human imagination to faithfully answer to the givenness of the *imago Dei*.

---

[27] G. van der Leeuw, *Wegen en grenzen*, 338-339.
[28] Ibid., 345.

b. *Paul Tillich: the work of art as the human expression of ultimate meaning*

Paul Tillich ignored the possible mediating function of the work of art, which was questioned or even deemed impossible by Barth and van der Leeuw.[29] Instead, he considered the work of art to be the medium par excellence for religious man to express ultimate meaning. Tillich does not so much emphasise human beings as images of God, but the function and meaning of the work of art itself.

When a work of art is associated with holiness, it is often all too quickly seen as 'religious art', according to Tillich. He believes the reference to the holy in art should not be limited to religious art or theological interpretations of the meaning of a work of art. To clarify the various relations of art and religion, he distinguishes between four types of association: 1. art with no explicitly religious subject; 2. art with no religious subject, but which nevertheless subconsciously answers questions for the meaning of its own context and existence; 3. art with an explicitly religious subject, yet unable to answer questions for ultimate meaning; 4. art with an explicitly religious subject that has its own religious style. Tillich prefers the second and the fourth, because he is interested in the expression, explicit or implicit, of ultimate meaning.[30]

Tillich posits that the style in which a religious idea was formed, rather than the explicit subject of the work of art, is decisive for the appearance and the expression of ultimate meaning. That is why he links art and religion through their concept of style and distinguishes between five different artistic styles of religious experiences and expressions.[31]

He starts with an ugly and frightful style he believes should also be part of the category of the holy. The artistic style that accompanies it, is what he calls *numinous realism*. This is a realistic style, which depicts things and people in such a way that they obtain an estranging and ambivalent aura in which the fearful and awe-inspiring (*tremendens*) is given shape. If religious imagination expresses ultimate meaning without the intervention of or a reference to a specific reality, then it adopts an *abstract* style. The religious form, which sees history itself as a manifestation of ultimate meaning, comes with a *scientific descriptive* realistic style. The realism, which accepts no holiness without justice, is connected to an

---

[29] P. Tillich, *Theology of culture*, New York 1959; Id., *On art and architecture*, New York 1987.
[30] Cf. L. Dupré, *De symboliek van het heilige*, Kampen 1991, 90-108.
[31] P. Tillich, *On art and architecture*, 139-158, esp. 142-152.

ethical-critical style. Critical realism devoid of any distinct artistic form will degenerate into a mere presentation of a distorted reality, in which ultimate meaning cannot appear and which only manifests hopeless pseudo-intellectual criticism. If one wants to express hope, it is best to use an *idealistic* style. Ultimate meaning can only manifest itself in this style when the highest possibilities of being are anticipated. However, the idealistic style can degenerate into a sentimental or kitschy style, as is often the case in religious and political art.

Tillich's distinction between style and expression of the work of art and the associations he makes with different religious forms have elicited a particularly strong response from theologians who use works of art as starting points for their theology. Although he is one of the very few theologians of the twentieth century who has shown an interest in the arts, he is of little consequence for the later development of theological aesthetics. I believe this is because the association between concrete works of art and a general ultimate meaning remains indeterminate. After all, is it not the power of a work of art that it can express an experience of ultimate meaning in such a way that it achieves a form or a face, and becomes a story or a history? Tillich may have understood that the symbolic form of expression of the work of art makes it suitable as a religious form of expression, but he has not fully considered the possibilities of a work of art to give ultimate meaning a concrete or historical content. As a result, he was not faced with the question as to whether the work of art is an appropriate representation of either ultimate meaning or of human expression. His emphasis on the symbolic and expressive effects of the work of art meant that he paid little attention to the contextual, theological-ethical implication of the work of art.

c. Hans Urs von Balthasar: beauty as form and analogy of the divine

Hans Urs von Balthasar has always emphasised the close connection between ethics and aesthetics in his theology. In his article Revelation and beauty (*Offenbarung und Schönheit*), he criticises Kierkegaard's *Either-Or* for distinguishing too strongly between the aesthetic and the ethical-religious (VC 100-134). Like van der Leeuw, he enters into a debate with what he calls a Protestant theology, which 'eliminates aesthetics from theology' (H I 53-66). Where van der Leeuw is interested in human imagination, Balthasar is interested in (divine) beauty. More than any other theologian before him, he focuses on the aesthetic perception of beauty, which is why he is generally referred to as the 'theologian of beauty'.

According to Balthasar, revelation and beauty are not two radically different variables which can be clearly distinguished. His entire theological work tries to answer the question of how worldly beauty can be regarded in the light of divine beauty without being identified with it. Considering the field of theological aesthetics merely as a theological application of philosophical epistemology or ethics will not suffice for him (VC 100). Instead, he thinks that the concept of beauty should have its own central place in theology.

If aesthetics is to occupy a central place in philosophy and theology, one must recognise that the philosophical concept of the beautiful as distinct from the true and the good, is not merely a methodological choice but expresses certain prior metaphysical conceptions of the world. A philosophy of the beautiful immediately calls to mind Antiquity, the Renaissance and the Romantic Age. In the age of the Enlightenment (Kant) and in the philosophy of the German idealists (Schleiermacher, Schelling, Hegel, Schopenhauer) beauty held a place of honour. It is ironic that the theologian of beauty argues that those who treat beauty as an independent concept and separate it from truth and goodness, with which it forms the transcendental centre of reality from which the light of being shines into the world, are at risk of aestheticising beauty (VC 101).

Balthasar's monument in the short history of theological aesthetics, *Herrlichkeit. Eine theologische Ästhetik* (1961-1969), should be interpreted in its theological context. The rigid systematic method of neoscholastic philosophy left no room for aesthetics.[32] According to Balthasar, the historical-critical exegesis of scripture also had the effect of eliminating aesthetics from dogmatic and therefore eventually all theology (VC 103). Any theology that renounces its non-exact, aesthetic inspiration delivers contemplation and intellectual vision to pure logic and, in doing so, will separate itself from the tradition of the church fathers, to whom the relation between revelation and beauty was still self-evident. However, he believes that aesthetics also describes the connection between the immanent experience of reality researched by science and the transcendent experience of reality of Christian faith (VC 102).

According to Balthasar, 'beauty' is the first and final word of theology. It clarifies the double focus of theology—on truth and goodness—because it expresses its evidence or even its visible and objective proof. As such, it cannot be grasped directly, however, because beauty is simultaneously

---

[32] A notable exception is J. Maritain's *Art et scholastique*, but Balthasar considered a scholastic approach in theological aesthetics a contradiction in terms.

the splendour of the mystery about which theology speaks. He argues that beauty has become mere semblance in the modern world, and is no longer seen for itself but for something else, and is often only mistrusted. He calls 'beauty' the primal phenomenon of all experience, of all communication and of all understanding.

According to Balthasar, beauty is experienced when a sovereign and free essence, which gives itself disinterestedly, is seen in an appearing form (H I 16f.). The primal phenomenon of beauty is not a spirit without body, a pure experience, nor is it a body without spirit, pure matter. Instead, it is at the crossing point of form and perception, where the perceiving gaze becomes enraptured with that which is perceived. This configuration of rapture and perception is analogous to the configuration of grace and faith. Grace is part of the essence of the form of revelation that the faithful perceives in the world. This is possible because the faithful has already been enraptured by grace.

The idea of man as image of God in Balthasar's theology has its basis in this original experience of beauty too. Man is able to experience himself as a primal phenomenon, insofar as he sees himself as a communication, i.e. as an appearance among other appearances. Therefore, man is a reappearance, appearing even before he has taken the initiative, one who answers, a mirror, an image. If man really is an image of God, Balthasar argues, it must be a form of creation that does not limit the spiritual and physical freedom of man, but one that is analogous to divine freedom (H I 20). In his theological aesthetics, ethics and aesthetics are one, because the perception of divine beauty is the ground of human freedom.

Balthasar's insights have been decisive for current theological aesthetics. This is not due merely to his monumental contribution to the discipline but also to the vast scope of his work. He dealt not only with the concept of beauty but also with perception and with the idea of the image of God. Moreover, through aesthetics, he succeeded in giving classical dogmatic doctrines a new relevance for the theology of his time. Nevertheless, the lack of concrete and current examples from the arts has made his work inaccessible and difficult to apply in a contemporary theological context. Furthermore, for contemporary tastes his work has an unacceptable exalted character since it pays no attention to ugliness. In his *Wegen en grenzen*, van der Leeuw characterises certain theologians "so used to kneeling that they pull everything down with them to kneel. They have forgotten how to get up, and they can only kneel on the backs of others."[33] Balthasar might well be criticised on the same grounds.

---

[33] G. van der Leeuw, *Wegen en grenzen*, xii.

Van der Leeuw, Tillich and Balthasar have laid the foundations of modern theological aesthetics. Their emphasis on certain aspects of aesthetics, like imagination, the work of art or beauty, has largely structured the field for theology. Like philosophical aesthetics, theology has a threefold focus on different aesthetic aspects. In theology, these aspects come with their own problems and questions. The theologians discussed above have put these questions on the theological agenda: What is the consequence of the biblical *imago Dei* for the independence of human imagination? How does a work of art communicate a specific religious view on life? How does worldly beauty mirror divine grace? With these questions, they have brought aesthetics to the attention of the theologians of the twentieth century. They have extended the theological set of concepts and have enriched the epistemological and ethical rationality of theology with an aesthetic one. In doing so, they have shown that an aesthetic approach does justice to the particularity of experiences of faith and religious imagination. For theological aesthetics, this means that it has been a fully-fledged discipline right from its inception, and that the theologian did not have to borrow anything from philosophy, literature or the plastic arts. On the contrary, theology has a number of unique questions that no other academic discipline has, which are not part of theological ethics or epistemology, and can rightly be called 'aesthetical'.

2.4. Four types of contemporary theological aesthetics

From the variety of its foundations the field of contemporary theological aesthetics has become even more diverse. There is the variety in focus: imagination, beauty and the work of art, but this diversity is multiplied by the choice of method and theological subject. For example, its method may be art critical, postmodern, transcendental or systematic theological. Similarly, it may take certain theological doctrines, such as creation or salvation, as its subject. Current theological aesthetics can roughly be divided into two categories: an aesthetics which takes the work of art as its starting point and an aesthetics that has beauty and imagination as its central subjects. In my opinion, a theology of art limits the systematic possibilities aesthetics offers to theology as a whole. The aesthetics of beauty and imagination offers little more than a theological application of philosophical concepts in most cases. However, it could also be a new approach in theology that offers both a different view on theological doctrine and a new field in theology, as the pioneers of theological aesthetics have shown.

In my search for the theological character of aesthetics, I will discuss the current state of affairs from four types of approaches: 1. Theology of art; 2. Philosophical-theological aesthetics; 3. Transcendental-theological aesthetics; 4. Theological aesthetics and redemption. I will show that theologians can conceptualise aesthetics within their own hermeneutical framework. The experience of beauty or the creative imagination applied to a doctrine of creation, soteriology or eschatology will require separate theological approaches. The typology I will expound below is an arrangement of the diversity of positions in aesthetics, but at the same time, it is an overture to what theological aesthetics should be, without repudiating the value of other positions. In what follows, I will express my preference for the final type I describe: a theology of beauty as a theology of redemption.

a. Theologies of art

Theological iconography points out the religious content or presence in modern works of art. A theology of art describes the religious or Christian theme of works of art, recognizing the current autonomous position of the artists. Based on these descriptions, a theology of art will find what art and faith have in common. Narrowing down theological art criticism to works of art with a religious theme usually leads to a vision exclusively aimed at its functionality in the church. Tillich's position that art without a religious theme can still be interpreted religiously is often forgotten.[34]

Functionality in the church is not the primary concern of theologies of art. On the contrary, current initiatives like the *Bildtheologische Arbeitsstelle* of Alex Stock at the University of Cologne, the *Arbeitsstelle für christliche Bildtheorie, theologische Ästhetik und Bilddidaktik* at the University of Münster under the direction of Reinhard Hoeps, and Jeremy Begbie's and Trevor Hart's *Theology through the Arts* in St Andrew's are looking for new religious expressions in the arts.[35] A German online journal has the religious approach of and in art as its primary focus.[36] These projects try to practice theology by choosing modern, often abstract and

---

[34] A misunderstanding that is exposed in text and image in: A. Kölbl et al. [Hrsg.], *ENTGEGEN. ReligionGedächtnisKörper in Gegenwartskunst*, [Ausstellung anlässlich der II. Europäischen Ökumenischen Versammlung in Graz, 23. Mai – 6. Juli 1997], Ostfildern-Ruit 1997. Cf. M. Delrue, Kunst & liturgie als epifanie, in: R. Quaghebeur, D. Verbiest [red.], *Epifanie. Actuele kunst en religie*, Antwerpen 2000, 117-160.
[35] J. Begbie [ed.], *Beholding the glory;* Id., *Sounding the depths. Theology through the arts*, London 2002.
[36] A. Mertin, K. Wendt [Hrsg.], *Magazin für Theologie und Ästhetik* (http://www.theomag.de/).

conceptual art as its primary source and, in the case of *Theology through the Arts*, contemporary music and literature.

In *Bildsinn und religiöse Erfahrung* (1984), Hoeps formulates theological foundations for understanding modern abstract art. The relation between art and theology is by no means regarded by him self-evident however. First of all, any theological appreciation of art must account for the Old Testament iconoclast commandment. The question remains whether the function and content of imagery have a place in the history of salvation and whether they are in direct competition with the meaning of faith itself or not. This leads Hoeps to consider the possibility of using images for the preaching of the gospel.[37]

The catechetical efforts of Alex Stock's theology of art, which is mainly inspired by Tillich's theology of art, have led to a dogmatics founded on aesthetic categories. He wonders whether the current marginal position of Christianity in western culture is a problem or rather a new possibility for the relation between art and religion? In *Zwischen Tempel und Museum*, Stock presents an extensive survey of the current theological attention for art but does not draw any systematic conclusions.[38] This, however, is the objective in *Poetische Dogmatik*, of which the first two volumes form a poetic Christology.[39] Here he calls for a new, aesthetic union between the practice of liturgy and the theory of dogma. However, Stock's attempt to reinterpret dogmatics through the arts does not amount to much more than an appreciation of art based on an already existing and more or less explicitly argued theological content. That content itself is not subject to discussion and indeed cannot be discussed if it is not confronted by the experience and rationality that forms the foundation of both art and theology.

b. Aesthetics in philosophical theology

The diverse positions of theological aesthetics can partly be explained by the choice of philosophical conversation partners or the period that

---

[37] R. Hoeps, *Bildsinn und religiöse Erfahrung: Hermeneutische Grundlagen für einen Weg der Theologie zum Verständnis gegenstandsloser Malerei*, [Disputationes Theologicae; Bd. 16], Frankfurt am Main 1984, 174-175.

[38] A. Stock, *Zwischen Tempel und Museum. Theologische Kunstkritik. Positionen der Moderne*, Paderborn, etc. 1991.

[39] Id., *Poetische Dogmatik. 1. Namen; 2. Schrift und Gesicht; 3. Leib und Leben; 4. Figuren*, Paderborn, etc. 1995-2001; Id., *Keine Kunst, Aspekte der Bildtheologie*, Paderborn, etc. 1996; Id., Über die Idee einer poetischen Dogmatik, in: G. Larcher [Hrsg.], *Gott-Bild. Gebrochen durch die Moderne?*, 118-128.

influenced the aesthetic theologian. Classic philosophy interpreted the beautiful as that which precedes all human perception. It does not coincide with the body, as Plotinus remarked, but it is present in the body. This beauty is a transcendental concept: a characteristic of everything that is. Christian theologians have mainly applied this aesthetic ontology to the doctrine of creation, as exemplified by van der Leeuw. Current transcendental theology no longer claims that beauty precedes all perception.[40] Albrecht Grözinger argues that, in a postmodern era, one must no longer speak ontologically about art and beauty.[41] But in spite of his criticism, current theology is still very much involved in ontologically founded aesthetics.

Modern philosophy with its emphasis on the subjective experience, has highly influenced theological aesthetics. However, Walter Benjamin has contradicted a self-evident relation between aesthetic and religious experience in his famous essay *Das Kunstwerk im Zeitalter seiner technischen Reproduzierbarkeit*.[42] By pointing to the changing cultic context of art, he suggests that religion and art have grown apart in the modern age. In his essay he explains that the modern experience of art is no longer embedded in religion and has lost its cultic value. Instead, it has become part of the public domain. By displaying the work of art in the museum, it becomes painfully obvious that the cultic value of a religious work of art consisted of its inaccessibility and hiddenness. According to Benjamin, this causes the religious and the modern aesthetic experience of the work of art to be fundamentally different. Although originally intimately related, they have grown apart, with the consequence of art losing an essential quality: to present the unrepresentable.

Walter Lesch also regards the aesthetic experience problematic for theology, if only because experiences themselves should always be seen as a problem in the light of revelation. This is not so much because the aesthetic experience cannot provide access to a higher reality but because the aesthetic experience is not more and nothing less than the outcome of a

---

[40] Vgl. F.A. Maas, Beauty and religion. Being touched by a sense of openness and underlying unity of all things, in: W. Derkse et al. [red.], *In Quest of humanity in a globalising world*, 275-292.

[41] A. Grözinger, Gibt es eine theologische Ästhetik?, in: W.E. Müller, J. Heumann [Hrsg.], *Kunst-positionen*, 35-43.

[42] W. Benjamin, Das Kunstwerk im Zeitalter seiner technischen Reproduzierbarkeit, in: Id., *Gesammelte Schriften*, [Bd. 1,2, Unter Mitwirkung von Th.W. Adorno und G. Scholem; hrsg. von R. Tiedemann und H. Schweppenhäuser], Frankfurt am Main 1974, 471-508, par IV.

playful and postmodern experiment with possibilities.[43] He emphasises the constructive aspect of the aesthetical, without directly ascribing a mediating function between God and the world to human creativity.

The postmodern theme of the necessarily unbridgeable chasm between the human and the divine is central in the clearest example of postmodern theological aesthetics, that of Mark C. Taylor.[44] In his theology the work of art becomes an image of the absence of that which is presented instead of a representation of it. Thus, art is the expression of the fact that there is nothing outside the image, or of the conclusion that the image as a mimetic representation has become impossible.[45] What remains are the images themselves as appearances of truth or transcendence, which are not representable themselves. Taylor interprets postmodernism as a late version of modernism because there is still a longing for transcendence. According to him, there can only be real hope if the expectation of a fulfilment of this longing is abandoned. Until this happens, every imaginative act will be idolatrous.

Viewed in the wake of the history of iconoclasm, the postmodern 'rediscovery' of the impossibility of the representation of God is an important theo-political and self-correcting theme. If works of art and aesthetic experiences are expected to be sources for theology, then more caution is needed. Theologians will have to think about what it means to relate theologically to art and beauty. A theology of art cannot answer this question sufficiently because the validity of theological argumentation and rationality themselves are not at stake. A theology that closely associates itself with the modern concept of experience cannot answer this question either because it fails to clearly distinguish between the aesthetic and the

---

[43] W. Lesch, Autonomie der Kunst und Theologie der Kultur. Zugänge zum theologischen Interesse an Kunst und Kultur, in: Id., *Theologie und ästhetische Erfahrung*, 1-24, 10-12.

[44] M.C. Taylor, *Disfiguring. Art, architecture, religion*, Chicago 1992. Cf. H. van den Bosch, Bis der Schein der Wirklichkeit...überwindet, in: H. Lombaerts, J. Maas, J. Wissink [red.], *Beeld & gelijkenis. Inwijding, kunst en religie*, Zoetermeer 2001, 42-56; Id., *Een apologie van het onmogelijke. Een kritische analyse van Mark C. Taylors a/theologie aan de hand van Jacques Derrida en John D. Caputo*, Den Haag 2002, 35-45.

[45] Cf. J.-F. Lyotard, *Le postmoderne expliqué aux enfants. Correspondance 1982-1985*, Paris 1986. Lyotard believes the beautiful cannot be represented and can only be seen as absence *vis-à-vis* the work of art. In modern aesthetics, only the form of the work of art can comfort and delight the observer, thanks to its recognizable consistency. Postmodern aesthetics will have to do without the comfort of good forms however, Lyotard argues. It can only keep searching for new presentations, not for the enjoyment of their beauty but just to feel even better that there is something that cannot be represented.

religious, let alone Christian experience. That is why postmodernism had to reduce theology to human desire and in doing so stressed the impossibility rather than the possibility of a theological aesthetics. In contrast, the following two types of contemporary theological aesthetics described below have nevertheless continued searching for the conditions of such a theological exercise.

c. Transcendental-theological aesthetics

As befits an heir to the tradition of transcendental theology, Hansjürgen Verweyen attempts to consider the rationality of theology. In that attempt to find a philosophical foundation for theology he hit a barrier that forced him to amend the strictly epistemological and ethical rationality of philosophy for theology. Aesthetics provided him with the way out.

In his outline of fundamental theology *Gottes letztes Wort* (1991), Verweyen formulates fundamental philosophical criteria that should make it possible to recognize a historical event as a definitive self-revelation of God.[46] Within this rational model for theology, in which he searches for a philosophical concept of fundamental and ultimate (*letztgültige*) meaning, he introduces the concept of 'beauty'.[47] Verweyen claims that it is (natural) beauty that is the determination of being, which mediates between the true and the good. There is beauty in the appearance of a rose that shows itself as a being: an exemplary identity with the ground of being, which is God. Asking for the cause of this beauty is impossible, because the ground itself appears in being. In his dissertation *Ontologische Voraussetzungen des Glaubensaktes* (1969), Verweyen tried to combine this metaphysics of beauty, which uses the medieval concept of the transcendentals, with the transcendental philosophy of Kant.[48]

Verweyen wants to broaden the subject of fundamental theology by making the formation of judgement dependent upon astonishment about the wondrous. According to Verweyen, any object is limited by the intentionality of the human subject as predicated in Karl Rahner's transcendental

---

[46] H. Verweyen, *Gottes letztes Wort. Grundriss der Fundamentaltheologie*, Düsseldorf 1991.

[47] In the latest edition of *Gottes letztes Wort* (Düsseldorf 2000³) the idea of 'ultimacy' (*letztgültigkeit*) is abandoned. Cf. H. Verweyen, *Theologie im Zeichen der schwachen Vernunft*, Dusseldorf 2000³; Id., *Ontologische Voraussetzungen des Glaubensaktes. Zur transzendentalen Frage nach der Möglichkeit von Offenbarung*, Düsseldorf 1969, 173 177; Id., *Botschaft eines Toten? Den Glauben rational verantworten*, Regensburg 1997, 96-118.

[48] H. Verweyen, *Ontologische Voraussetzungen des Glaubensaktes*, 99.

theology. In the act of astonishment, the ground of being is effected in beings in such a way that all transcendental categories of reason are questioned from the start. The subject will only come to the fore when the astonishment wanes and one starts to wonder how the ground of being can be grasped. For that, one needs to adopt a different perspective instead of fixing one's gaze on the moment in which the ground of being appeared unsolicited—and therefore independent from the subject.

The phenomenological priority of astonishment and wonder gives Verweyen the opportunity to rationally account for the historical revelation of Jesus Christ. If it is really a revelation of indeterminate being, man cannot have determined this event, which could be perceived by the senses. Here, the ground of being does not appear in the judgement of being, but in the astonishment that precedes judgement. Thus, Verweyen gives aesthetics a prominent place in a rationalist theology. Gerhard Larcher, who discusses aesthetics as the central undertaking of fundamental theology, develops Verweyen's primacy of aesthetics in theology further. According to Larcher, a theological study of aesthetics is necessary to investigate the limits of the modern concept of autonomy. The *demonstratio religiosa* of fundamental theology should be based on aesthetics to emphasise the gift-character of faith. As such, it is at the same time a critique of an all too rational, empirical or scientific method in theology.[49]

Another recent example of transcendental theological aesthetics is that of Richard Viladesau.[50] Contrary to Verweyen, he believes that a transcendental theology does not have to be grounded rationalistically or philosophically. It does however offer a broader perspective than the systematic theological and, with that, the possibility of entering into dialogue with other academic disciplines. A systematic theological aesthetics provides the necessary concreteness and thus complements the necessary heuristic and relatively indeterminate structure of the transcendental method.[51]

---

[49] Cf. G. Larcher, Vom Hörer des Wortes als "homo aestheticus". Thesen zu einem vernachlässigten Thema heutiger Fundamentaltheologie, in: Id., K. Müller, Th. Pröpper [Hrsg.], *Hoffnung die Gründe nennt. Zu Hansjürgen Verweyens Projekt einer erstphilosophischen Glaubensverantwortung*, Regensburg 1996, 99-111; Id., Bruch und Innovation. Thesen und Fragen zum hermeneutischen Problem, in: Id. [Hrsg.], *Gott-Bild. Gebrochen durch die Moderne?*, Graz, etc. 1997, 47-56; Id., Fundamentaltheologie und Kunst im Kontext der Mediengesellschaft. Neue Herausforderungen für eine alte Beziehung, in: J. Valentin, S. Wendel [Hrsg.], *Unbedingtes Verstehen?! Fundamentaltheologie zwischen Erstphilosophie und Hermeneutik*, Regensburg 2001, 161-176.

[50] R. Viladesau, *Theological aesthetics*; Id., *Theology and the arts. Encountering God through music, art and rhetoric*, New York 2000.

[51] Id., *Theological aesthetics*, 38.

Viladesau argues that, if it is true that all proofs of God's existence are expressions of the transcendental experience of man, and if it is at the same time true that an aesthetic experience is more than a purely sensory experience, it should be possible to formulate a transcendental approach of God's existence. This will have the aesthetic experience as its starting point, and by means of this experience, God is found as the necessary condition of such an experience.[52] The conditions for the experience of beauty as a joyful confirmation of existence—even in its finite limitedness—is an implicit and inevitable confirmation of God, according to Viladesau. Beauty is not a name for God here, but it refers to being, which is seen as essentially joyful.

d. Theological aesthetics and redemption

Beauty is not a name for God, according to the transcendental theologians Verweyen and Viladesau. Instead, beauty is a quality of our experience of reality. Human imagination can try to refer to the divine in reality based on that experience. Is there nothing else art and imagination could do apart from searching for analogies of divine glory? Or to put it differently, should not a theological aesthetics also look for the content and the meaning of the image, in addition to the image that mediates between God and man? A theological aesthetics should not just point to the creational character of imagination, but also to the redemptive character.[53] Below, I will mention some authors who have emphasised the soteriological importance of aesthetics.

According to Hans Küng, art in our time has become an expression of human estrangement and abandonment rather than a reference to the divine reality.[54] It stands to reason that art reflects the current crisis of meaning. In the context of that crisis, art gets its redemptive character. With a positive confirmation of reality, the artist implicitly confirms a meaning, a primal ground for this reality. In this way he or she can take root again in a basic trust without losing autonomy or independence.[55]

---

[52] For a history of 'beauty' as a transcendental concept, see: Ibid., 124-134. It would be too much of a diversion to go into the history of 'beauty' as a transcendental concept here, but in general, it is said that beauty no longer has its own content, but is either a characteristic or the binding principle of the other transcendentals 'truth' and 'goodness'. Beauty is usually not regarded as independent transcendental concept, but is rewarded a transcendental status.

[53] Cf. P. Sherry, *Images of redemption*.

[54] H. Küng, *Kunst und Sinnfrage*, Zürich, etc. 1980.

[55] Ibid., 39-40.

According to Küng, it is the task of the work of art itself to serve humanity; a humanity that is grounded and protected by a concealed divinity. The work of art is more than a mere appearance of the idea and more than just play. It is either an implicit or explicit reference (*Hinweis und Vorgriff*) to a world, which has not yet been completed, but nevertheless appears in the work of art (*Vorschein und Abglanz*).[56]

The Protestant philosopher-theologian Nicholas Wolterstorff formulates a similar point of view but emphasises the artist's responsibility to do justice to his or her convictions.[57] This is what the artist has in common with the Christian: artistic calling is analogous to the calling of a believer. Wolterstorff criticizes the authors of theological theories of art like Tillich for omitting this element of action. He believes theologians may have adopted the modern image of the artist as someone who renders our consciousness and our emotions in a new creation and have failed to see this new creation as an act of faith.[58] Wolterstorff's reproach to the theologians is that they have only awarded aesthetics a contemplative and mediating rather than an active function.

Alejandro García-Rivera and John de Gruchy are recent examples of theologians who have considered aesthetics from the perspective of liberation and action. They have embedded their aesthetics in the Spanish language and the communities of the United States and modern South Africa respectively.[59] Like Wolterstorff, García-Rivera is of the opinion that theological aesthetics should be about the theo-political consequences of human imagination for culture and society. De Gruchy calls for a cooperation between the artist and the church with the common purpose of transforming society.

These theologians are not just interested in beauty. For them, a work of art can also show how the human heart is disturbed and tortured. Ugliness in a work of art can show oppression or the memory of oppression. Thus, the work of art is able to change our perception and show us a dimension of divine beauty by presenting its opposite. This can only be done in the form of a foreshadowing, the promise of salvation and eternal life.[60]

Eberhard Jüngel's article *Auch das Schöne muss sterben* (1984) is a good example of the soteriological and eschatological perspectives an

---

[56] Ibid., 57-58.
[57] N. Wolterstorff, *Art in action. Toward a Christian aesthetic*, Grand Rapids 1980.
[58] Ibid., 68-69.
[59] A. García-Rivera, *The community of the beautiful. A theological aesthetics*, Collegeville 1999; Id., *A wounded innocence. Sketches for a theology of art*, Collegeville 2003.
[60] J. de Gruchy, *Christianity, art and transformation*, 200.

aesthetic approach in theology offers.[61] In a variation on the doctrine of the transcendentals he concludes that the aesthetic relationships man has—with other people, the world or God—can be characterised by the difference between beautiful and ugly. The essence of this aesthetic relation is the impossibility to make exact the judgement of taste.[62] Paradoxically, beauty focuses the attention on other perceptions as on something that is no longer necessary for the beauty of that which is perceived as beautiful. That is why beauty is said to be 'disinterested'. According to Jüngel, beauty breaks the bounds of reality by encompassing it in its own disinterested way. By breaking the normal bounds, beauty anticipates a healing future.[63] Ugliness too is capable of this, he believes. Ugliness captivates the beholder for the sake of a freedom that liberates the beholder from all his natural and moral bounds. Jüngel calls this the 'elementary removal of boundaries' which concerns not just the realm of causality, nor that of the morality of the purposeful action, but also what he describes as the essence of aesthetic pleasure. This boundary-removing effect of gloss is the criterion of beauty and he calls it religious.[64]

Truth is mediated in beauty but according to Jüngel it is nothing but a promise, a foretaste of the truth which never appears in the light of its own being. At best, it formulates the entirety of a finite and transient, historical world.[65] This entirety however, is put into perspective by the Creator, without whom the wholeness of the world would be an immense overestimation of the sum of the parts. According to Jüngel, an immediate presence of undivided existence is only possible when the Creator reveals Himself entirely. Only when the Creator Himself appears, will being as such be entirely present and lucid to itself. As a single point in a separate whole, to which it refers *pars pro toto*, beauty is essentially finite and transient. Consequently, unlike other theologians, Jüngel distinguishes radically between beauty and God. Beauty has to perish and cannot be made absolute. On the contrary, beauty has to 'die' to make truth itself appear.[66] One can see the danger here of a return to an iconoclastic attitude toward art and beauty.

---

[61] E. Jüngel, Auch das Schöne muss sterben—Schönheit im Lichte der Wahrheit. Theologische Bemerkungen zum ästhetischen Verhältnis, in: *Zeitschrift für Theologie und Kirche* 81 (1984), 106-127.
[62] Ibid., 108.
[63] Ibid., 110.
[64] Ibid., 114-115.
[65] Ibid., 124.
[66] Ibid., 125.

Today, postmodern theologians question the representative function of art and beauty, which cannot any longer be naturally seen as representations of the divine or the holy. The arts are expected to represent injustice, finitude and even ugliness and in doing so, to redirect the human gaze toward holiness and beauty. Currently, beauty is often awarded an anticipative and eschatological quality, which as a consequence has given it a relative independence from the divine and the holy. This independence however, is not merely a direct result of modern philosophy, which places the subject in the foreground. Rather, aesthetic themes like image, representation and beauty have refocused the attention on the iconoclasm of the bible and the eschatological character of revelation. Therefore, one can conclude that in the twentieth century theological aesthetics has developed from a participative reconstruction to an anticipative construction of divine beauty.

In the preceding typology of contemporary theological aesthetics, I have tried to emphasise theology's own unique task *vis-à-vis* aesthetics and in its dialogue with aesthetics. It should do more than consider the work of art as a source of faith but it will not suffice to utilize merely philosophical aesthetic concepts. Twentieth century transcendental theologians, seeking a rational foundation of faith, have pointed towards the limits of rationality and considered art and aesthetics ways of depicting and describing these limits. However, they have not sufficiently considered the redemptive meaning of art for theology. If they had done so, instead of marking the limits of theological rationality they would have been able to redefine it by its liberating or redemptive qualities by means of aesthetics. The confrontation of theology with art and aesthetics has shown that theological rationality is distinct from a scientific or a philosophical one. Not because theology would be less rational or essentially irrational but because it is inspired by and responds to divine revelation. This is the reason why neither a philosophical concept of art and beauty nor a theological reference to worldly beauty alone is sufficient.

This chapter opened with two quotations. The first was Hopkins's poem *Pied Beauty*, which described the constant changes in nature that make people aware of the divine presence in the world, for which they praise God. The second quotation came from the *Confessions* of Augustine, the patron saint of theologians, who warned against an identification of worldly beauty with God. This warning led to the neglect of beauty in the history of theology but in the second half of the twentieth century many theologians have restored beauty to the heart of theology.[67] Art and aesthetics have returned to the attention of theologians. Works of art and experiences of beauty were recognised as sources for theology again and in some cases even regarded as sources of faith.

The most significant among these theologians was undoubtedly Hans Urs von Balthasar, who became known as 'the theologian of beauty'. As mentioned before, he wrote a literary monument that has become a landmark in theological aesthetics. Not only was he persistently aware of Augustine's warning against the worship of beauty, consciously banishing both worldly beauty and the creation and expression of the artist from his theological aesthetics, he also argued against any transcendental or philosophical approach. Instead, he described divine revelation in aesthetic terms without forgetting the ethical and truth claims of faith. He considered an aesthetic approach the most appropriate way to describe the concrete and historical events in which the love of God is perceived, thus being the foundation of faith. Most importantly for this present research, Balthasar introduced aesthetics as fundamental theology. His work will offer an answer to the question of why aesthetics is a good way of doing theology. His emphasis on a theological treatment of art and beauty will also answer the question "What is theology?" by means of aesthetics. To find these answers, I will closely analyse his theological aesthetics in the following chapters.

---

[67] Cf. G. Jantzen, Beauty for ashes, 437.

B.

HANS URS VON BALTHASAR'S THEOLOGICAL AESTHETICS

3. HANS URS VON BALTHASAR: A LIFE IN THEOLOGY

3.1. Key dates in the life of Hans Urs von Balthasar

1905	12 August, Hans Urs von Balthasar is born in Lucerne
1917-24	Attends grammar school in Engelberg (o.s.b.) and Feldkirch (s.j.)
1924-28	Studies germanic philology in Zürich, Vienna, Berlin
1925	*Die Entwicklung der musikalischen Idee*
1927	Summer, 30-day vocational proceedings near Basel
1928	Doctoral degree in Germanic Philology (Zürich)
1929-31	Acceptance into the Jesuit order, noviciate
1931	Studies philosophy in Pullach near Munich
1933	Studies theology in Fouvrière near Lyon
1936	26 July, receives holy orders at St Michael, Munich
1937-39	*Apokalypse der Deutschen Seele*; editor of *Stimmen der Zeit*
1938	Publishes collected texts of Origen in *Geist und Feuer*
1939	Translates Paul Claudel's *Le soulier de satin* (*Der Seidene Schuh*), performed in Zürich in 1944
1940-48	University chaplain in Basel
1940	Meets Adrienne von Speyr
1941	*Kosmische Liturgie* (Maximus Confessor)
1941	Foundation of *Studentische Schulungsgemeinschaft*
1944	Starts taking dictations for Adrienne von Speyr
1945	Foundation of the *Johannesgemeinschaft*
1947	Foundation of the *Johannesverlag*
1947	Foundation of the *Akademische Arbeitsgemeinschaft*
1948	Exercises to cooperate with Adrienne von Speyr
1948	*Der Laie und der Ordensstand*
1950	January, leaves the Jesuit order
1951	*Karl Barth. Deutung und Darstellung seiner Theologie*
1952	*Schleifung der Bastionen*
1956	Moves to Basel
1956	Incardination in the diocese of Chur
1956	*Die Gottesfrage des heutigen Menschen*
1956-67	Leader of the *Johannesgemeinschaft*

1959	Seriously ill
1961-69	*Herrlichkeit. Eine theologische Ästhetik*
1963	*Glaubhaft ist nur Liebe*
1965	Golden cross from Mount Athos
	Honorary doctorates from the universities of Edinburgh and Münster
1966	*Cordula oder der Ernstfall*
1967	17 September, Adrienne von Speyr dies
	Honorary doctorate from the university of Fribourg, Switzerland
1968	*Erster Blick auf Adrienne van Speyr*
1969	*Theologie der drei Tage*
	Member of the *International Theological Commission*
1971	*Guardini Award* of the Catholic Academy of Bavaria
1972	Foundation of *Communio: International Catholic Review*
1973	Corresponding Fellow of the British Academy, London
1973-83	*Theodramatik*
1975	*Katholisch*
1975	Associé étranger de l'Institut de France
1976	*Henri de Lubac. Sein organisches Lebenswerk*
1977	*Christlicher Stand*
	Balthasar symposium at the Catholic University of America, Washington
1980	Honorary doctorate from the Catholic University of America, Washington
1983	Foundation of the priestly branch of the *Johannesgemeinschaft*
1984	*Premio internazionale Paolo VI*, Rome
	Unser Auftrag
1985	International colloquium on Adrienne von Speyr, Milan
1985-87	*Theologik*
1986	*Was dürfen wir hoffen?*
1987	*Epilog*
1987	*Wolfgang Amadeus Mozart Award,* Basel
1987	*Kleiner Diskurs über die Hölle*
1988	Balthasar symposium in Madrid
	28 May, appointed a Cardinal
	26 June, dies
	1 July, funeral in Lucerne, conducted by Joseph Cardinal Ratzinger

3.2. Introducing Hans Urs von Balthasar

It is possible to introduce a theologian in several ways, depending on the interest one has in the theologian concerned. One might be purely interested in the theology, the starting points, the concepts used, the main arguments and the conclusions as a result of all this. One could explore the historical, social and cultural context in which this theological work takes place, what it is influenced by or which elements of its context it has its influence on. One may want to get to know the person behind the work and try to understand a theological style and content by means of an exploration of someone's personal education and encounters in life or even try to unravel someone's personal character itself.

Theologians are usually involved in a variety of contacts and communities. They are usually not and should not be mere academics. Nor are they or should they work entirely in service of the church. Especially in the twentieth century, when they played an important role in a rapidly changing culture, theologians were involved in different contexts. Apart from working in the church, continuing its search for self-understanding and self-expression, in which they participate necessarily, be it either as lay people or as priests and bishops, theologians have been teachers and researchers at universities and schools, journalists and politicians; they have been involved in cultural debates on ethical matters, the arts and inter-religious communication. But most of them have been working in a local context, dealing with pastoral, personal and communal matters. Theologians usually operate in several of the aforementioned contexts at the same time. Biographies of theologians therefore usually require the description of a theological life on several levels concurrently: theological, socio-cultural and personal. That is why the story of the theologian's life is quite often most compelling for someone interested in people who lived and worked at the centre of a certain socio-cultural context in a certain age.

Such is especially the case for the story of Hans Urs von Balthasar's theological life. Born in 1905 and dying in 1988, his life covers nearly the whole of the twentieth century, and as a consequence, his theology was confronted by the major changes in the church and society of those days.

a. A change in theological style

In the history of twentieth century theology, Balthasar has a unique position. Although regarded by many as one of the most significant theologians of the century, Balthasar's theology is not widely known. One could say that his theology has been very important to a small group of mainly Roman Catholic theologians but not very influential on most contemporary theologians.[1] Consequently, one might draw the conclusion that at the time Balthasar published his work it was already out of date, but that does not explain the fact that after his death the number of publications on his theology is increasing exponentially. There are several explanations for this late reception. For example, Balthasar's theological style can hardly be described as conventional. Although educated and working in the context of a rational neothomist theology, Balthasar engaged with the spiritual style of the church fathers. Later, in the 1960s and 1970s, when theological method was very much influenced by the metaphysics and epistemology of existential phenomenology, he based his systematic theology on the concepts of 'beauty' and 'drama', introducing the arts such as literature and theatre into theology.

Besides his unconventional methods in theology, some events in Balthasar's personal life possibly gave cause to the neglect of his theology in academic circles. The fact that he left the Jesuit order rather early in his career might have denied him the possibility to work at a university during the rest of his life, since the Jesuits were very much involved in the teaching of philosophy and theology at German and French universities in the first half of the twentieth century. It might even have led to the Roman and diocesan curia ignoring him as a theological adviser during the Second Vatican Council. After the council, Balthasar got involved in the theological journal *Communio*, the conservative counterpart of *Concilium*. These two theological journals were covering the whole of the Roman Catholic theological-political spectrum after the council, and Balthasar's involvement—in the beginning being an editor for both—would at least change his theological style, writing shorter articles concerning ecclesiological matters. Another reason for the neglect of

---

[1] Although one might say that Balthasar's theology has influenced the 'Radical Orthodoxy' movement, whose members are not exclusively Roman Catholic, there has been little substantial research on his work in that context. Some people who have been cooperating with projects of 'Radical Orthodoxy', have published a collection of essays on Balthasar: L. Gardner, D. Moss, B. Quash, G. Ward, *Balthasar at the end of modernity*, [Foreword by F. Kerr and Afterword by R. Williams], Edinburgh 1999.

his theology in academic circles could be his theologically intimate relationship with Adrienne von Speyr. Some might have thought that his defence of her mystical visions and his adaptation of her spiritual scriptural readings changed his theology into a more speculative or even obscure style. Finally, the English translation of his works is still in progress.

Introducing Hans Urs von Balthasar is still a necessary task in contemporary theology. Many may have heard of him, very few know his theological work. Even those that do are still in need of an overview of his work. It consists of more than one hundred books and even more articles, translations, speeches, sermons, reviews and introductions.[2] Considering the unique position of Balthasar in twentieth century theology and being aware of the personal, ecclesiastical and political tensions that all played an important role in his life and undoubtedly marked his theology, a first glance at Balthasar's theology will astonish everyone. Not just his unusual theological method but especially his voluminous oeuvre and the richness and wide variety of the subjects he deals with, will leave everyone at least with admiration and respect. Although Balthasar invented a new theological style, tapping new sources like literature and theatre, confronting them with theological content and interpreting them to answer theological questions, his main achievement is his engagement with nearly everyone in the history of ideas of western culture. For this reason, Henri de Lubac called Balthasar "the most cultured man of his time".[3]

In this chapter, I will present Balthasar's life chronologically, emphasising his most important encounters with artists, theologians, philosophers and others who had a significant influence on his theology. At the same time, his main publications and their subjects will be mentioned, so in the end the reader will have an overview of the man and his work, within the framework of their theological and socio-cultural context. In chapter four, Balthasar's key concepts and key ideas that are essential for understanding his work and its importance for contemporary theological debates, will be analysed more systematically.

---

[2] *Hans Urs von Balthasar. Bibliographie 1925-1990*, [Neu bearbeitet und ergänzt von Cornelia Capol], Einsiedeln 1990.

[3] H. de Lubac, Ein Zeuge Christi in der Kirche. Hans Urs von Balthasar, in: *Communio* 4 (1975), 39-49.

b. A cultural education

Hans Urs von Balthasar was born 12 August 1905 in Lucerne, Switzerland.[4] He was the first son of Gabrielle Pietzcker and Oskar Ludwig von Balthasar, both members of aristocratic and influential Catholic families in Lucerne. Gabrielle wrote articles for a women's journal called *Die Schweizerin* and was the author of a history of the Swiss Women's Federation. Hans Urs's father, Oskar was a well-known architect and an active member of the Swiss conservative party.[5] Hans had a younger brother and sister and grew up, according to his own memories, in an extremely happy, warm, and comforting environment. His mother wrote in her family chronicles: "Hans is a devotee of anything beautiful and has a weakness for girls". His parents made him learn French and Latin at a very young age. Balthasar himself referred to his childhood as a period in which he especially enjoyed playing the piano (Schubert's Mass in e-flat major when he was five, Tchaikovsky's Pathétique when he was eight).[6] It should therefore not surprise us that before his twenties he wrote his first book on the topic of music, called *Die Entwicklung der musikalischen Idee. Versuch einer Synthese der Musik* (*The development of the musical idea. An essay on the synthesis of music*), in which he tries to synthesise the properties of music like rhythm, melody and harmony.[7] Already here, some key ideas of Balthasar's later work are present, especially those of analogy and form:

> Music is the form that brings us closest to the spirit. It is the thinnest veil that separates us from it. But it shares the tragic fate of all art: It has to remain a desire and therefore tentative. And precisely because it is closest to the spirit, without being able to grasp it completely, the desire in it is strongest.

---

[4] For an extensive biography, see: E. Guerriero, *Hans Urs von Balthasar. Eine Biographie*, Einsiedeln 1993. The following books and articles also contain biographical information: P. Henrici s.j., Erster Blick auf Hans Urs von Balthasar, in: K. Lehmann, W. Kasper [Hrsg.], *Hans Urs von Balthasar. Gestalt und Werk*, Köln 1989, 18-61; Id., Hans Urs von Balthasar: A sketch of his life, in: D.L. Schindler [ed.], *Hans Urs von Balthasar. His life and work*, San Fransisco 1991, 7-44; Id., Hans Urs von Balthasar. His cultural and theological education, in: B. McGregor, o.p., Th. Norris [eds], *The beauty of Christ. An introduction in the theology of Hans Urs von Balthasar*, Edinburgh 1994, 10-22; Th. Krenski, *Hans Urs von Balthasar. Das Gottesdrama*, [Theologische Profile], Mainz 1995; M. Schulz, *Hans Urs von Balthasar begegnen*, Augsburg 2002.

[5] For more information on Balthasar's family and ancestors, among whom many Jesuit missionaries, politicians and librarians, see E. Guerriero, *Hans Urs von Balthasar*, 19-30.

[6] *Unser Auftrag. Bericht und Entwurf. Einführung in die von Adrienne von Speyr gegründete Johannesgemeinschaft*, 31.

[7] *Die Entwicklung der musikalischen Idee. Versuch einer Synthese der Musik*, Einsiedeln 1998² (1925).

Music is most like immanent meaning, because it also is development. Both are dynamic, unspeakable and beyond words. It is, like all art, logical, probably even more than other forms of art. It is a human limit, and beyond this limit starts the divine. It is an infinite monument for the fact that people can have a premonition of what God is: eternal and simple, multifarious and dynamically flowing in Himself and in the world as Logos.[8]

Interested in literature and music, Balthasar distinguished himself in Germanic studies (philology and literature) in Vienna and Berlin, although he originally studied philosophy. Some of the people he was acquainted with and the philosophers and writers they introduced him to would be of crucial importance for his later work. In Vienna he was most impressed by Hans Eibls lectures on Plotinus but he also developed a deep friendship with the psychoanalyst Rudolf Allers, who introduced him to theology as a continuation of psychology because it would read the people's hearts more profoundly than any other field of study. However, Balthasar followed his own interests as well, studying music and literature, and especially reading Goethe, to whom he is indebted for his concept of form (*Gestalt*) that would be at the centre of his theology for the rest of his life. This taught him:

> (…) to be able to perceive, assess, and interpret a form, meaning: the synthetic vision (in contrast to the critical of Kant or the analytical of the natural sciences) and I owe this seeing of the form to someone who, rising from the chaos of *Sturm und Drang*, didn't cease to see, create and value the living form: Goethe.[9]

When Balthasar moved to Berlin, he started attending lectures of Romano Guardini. Guardini, who lectured on the interface between philosophy and theology, which would introduce him to his own dissertation subject: the thought of Bonaventura and to the literary work of Dante, Pascal, Hölderlin and Dostoievsky, who were going to have the honoured places in Balthasar's gallery of portraits in part two of *Herrlichkeit* (*The Glory of the Lord*).

As was to be expected, Balthasar's dissertation would cover literary, as well as philosophical and theological subjects. It dealt with the eschatological problem in modern German literature.[10] A few years later, Balthasar would publish his studies on German literature in a more extensive form,

---

[8] Ibid., 57.
[9] Dank des Preisträgers an der Verleihung des Wolfgang Amadeus Mozart-Preises am 22. Mai 1987 in Innsbruck, in E. Guerriero, *Hans Urs von Balthasar*, 419-424, 420.
[10] *Geschichte des eschatologischen Problems in der modernen Deutschen Literatur*, [Abhandlung zur Erlangung der Doktorwürde der philosophischen Fakultät der Universität], Zürich, 1998² (1930).

covering three volumes in which he discussed the writers and philosophers separately, so it could actually count as a literary-historical handbook for German literature and philosophy of the last two centuries, while his dissertation was a more systematic work.[11] Already in these early works Balthasar displayed an enormous energy and he showed that he was able to understand his encyclopaedic knowledge within the framework of one great synthetic vision. His aim was to offer a history of last things as a mythological history of ideas, expressed in philosophy, theology and the natural sciences. It is a lament for the loss of transcendence since the Middle Ages, leaving us with nothing but the modern ideas of progress and foundation.

Balthasar reworked and extended his dissertation in *Apokalypse der deutschen Seele* (*Apocalypse of the German Soul*). It comprises three tomes. In the first part he discusses and criticises *in extenso* the philosophy and literature of the Enlightenment (Lessing, Herder) and of German Idealism and Romanticism (Baumgarten, Goethe, Schiller, Schlegel, Kant, Hegel, Jean Paul, Schelling, Novalis, Hölderlin, Fichte, Schopenhauer, et al.). This also shows Balthasar's partiality for Greek culture, idealist and romantic philosophy and themes from music, literature and the visual arts. In the second part, he elaborately analyses Nietzsche's philosophy of tragedy, confronting it with Dostoievki's literary work. In the final part he deals with the young Heidegger's philosophy of being after surveying the poetry of Rilke and the thought of Scheler and Husserl. His final discussion partner is Karl Barth. Balthasar gives a rather critical account of Barth's early work, entering into an on-going debate with this great Protestant theologian. This would, after fifteen years of friendship, during which they both would modify their theological positions, lead to Balthasar's highly acclaimed monograph on Barth.[12] In Balthasar's conclusions in *Apokalypse der deutschen Seele*, in which he extrapolates three structural eschatological concepts, 'myth', 'utopia' and 'kairos' from his historical analyses, Barth would, together with Heidegger, appear to be the promise of twentieth century thought. At that moment in time, that was a rather perceptive prophesy.

---

[11] *Apokalypse der deutschen Seele. Studien zu einer Lehre von letzten Haltungen*: Bd. 1: *Der deutsche Idealismus;* Bd. 2: *Im Zeichen Nietsches;* Bd. 3: *Die Vergöttlichung des Todes*, Einsiedeln 1998² (1937-1939). The first volume was republished under the title *Prometheus* in 1947.

[12] *Karl Barth. Darstellung und Deutung seiner Theologie*, Köln 1951 (Einsiedeln 1976⁴).

3.3. Finding the sources

a. Entering the Jesuit order

While completing his Germanic studies, he decided to join the Jesuit order and continued to study philosophy and theology for some years. During this time with the Jesuits, he was introduced to Ignatian spirituality, based on a religious attitude that can be characterised by 'indifference', a concept he would later find in the works of the mystics Eckhart and Ruusbroeck as well.[13] Despite his leaving the order in 1950, the Ignatian exercises remained a lifelong source of inspiration,[14] long after having left the order, he would publish the Ignatian exercises with a detailed commentary.[15] At the end of his life he wrote a biography of Ignatius of Loyola.[16]

After entering the Jesuit order in 1929, he studied philosophy in Pullach, near Munich, and theology in Lyon from 1933 to 1937. Here he was introduced to Henri de Lubac's *Nouvelle Théologie* and his influential work *Catholicisme*,[17] and to E. Przywara's doctrine of the *analogia entis* which would become, in a theologically amended form, the main structural principle of Balthasar's theology.[18] The influence of de Lubac and his idea of the *ressourcement* of theology, i.e. reading and interpreting the work of the church fathers and adapting their spiritual reading of scripture as a way of doing theology instead of taking the 'perennial' neothomist philosophy as a starting point, was so strong that Balthasar was mainly engaged in their translation and study. As a result, his earliest publications are mainly translations and studies of Origen,[19] Maximus Confessor[20]

---

[13] 'Indifference' here has the meaning of disinterestedness and gratuitousness, instead of unconcernedness, detachment or apathy.

[14] "For me, in the spiritual realm between John and Ignatius all that is decisive takes place". *Mein Werk*, 18.

[15] *Ignatius von Loyola, Die Exerzitien* (*Exercitia Spiritualia*), Luzern 1946 (Einsiedeln 1990^{10}).

[16] *Ignatius von Loyola*, Einsiedeln 1996.

[17] Translated into German with an introduction by Balthasar: *Glauben aus der Liebe*, [previously published earlier under the title: *Katholizismus als Gemeinschaft*], Einsiedeln 1992^3.

[18] E. Przywara, s.j., *Analogia Entis. Metaphysik. Ur-Struktur und All-Rhythmus*, Einsiedeln 1962^2.

[19] *Origenes, Geist und Feuer. Ein Aufbau aus seinen Werken*, Salzburg 1938; *Parole et mystère chez Origène*, Paris 1957.

[20] *Kosmische Liturgie. Höhe und Krise des griechischen Weltbilds bei Maximus Confessor*, Freiburg 1941; *Die Gnostischen Centurien des Maximus Confessor*, Freiburg 1941 [published in one volume as: *Kosmische Liturgie. Das Weltbild Maximus des Bekenners*, Einsiedeln 1961].

and Gregory of Nyssa[21]. These patristics studies would deeply influence Balthasar's theological style. When Pope Pius XII censored de Lubac's book *Surnaturel* in 1946, Balthasar chose de Lubac's side. Later, he would write about this event: "(...) a young David comes onto the field against the Goliath of modern rationalisation and reduction of the Christian mystery to logic".[22] In 1936, Balthasar was ordained to the priesthood. A few years later, in 1939, he was given the choice of either going to Rome to teach at the Gregorian University or to Basel to become a university chaplain. He chose the latter and passed up the opportunity of an academic career. As it would turn out, he abandoned that chance for good.

b. Catholic philosophy

Meanwhile, being an editor of the Jesuit journal *Stimmen der Zeit* in Munich, he published articles on Catholic philosophy, writing on Heidegger and the doctrine of analogy of Karl Barth, developing a philosophical metaphysics that differed radically from neothomist philosophy.[23] Christian philosophy should interpret the finite and philosophical truth in the light of Christ. Thus, grounded in this main 'vertical' task, Christian philosophy is the art of 'clarifying transpositions', which Balthasar calls 'the horizontal task' of philosophy. Instead of a rigid logical system philosophy should articulate the continuity of the Holy Spirit in the diversity of philosophical systems and languages.[24] Following his own programmatic instructions he composed a completely different concept of truth in his first major work *Wahrheit*.[25] Truth, in Balthasar's metaphysics, is not the correspondence of object and intellect but instead it is the revelation in nature, human freedom, mystery and participation, that is required by a religious attitude that balances between action and contemplation. As such, the proper metaphor for truth is 'symphony', instead of *adequatio*.[26]

---

[21] *Présence et pensée. Essai sur la philosophie religieuse de Grégoire de Nysse*, Paris 1942.

[22] *Henri de Lubac. Sein organisches Lebenswerk*, [Kriterien 38], Einsiedeln 1976, 58. Cf. Ermutigungsbrief an P. Henri de Lubac, in: E. Guerriero, *Hans Urs von Balthasar*, 409-410.

[23] Recently published essays from this period in: *Von den Aufgaben der katholischen Philosophie in der Zeit*, Einsiedeln 1998.

[24] Ibid., 30

[25] *Wahrheit*, Einsiedeln 1947. Later published as the first volume of *Theologik. Bd. 1: Wahrheit der Welt*, Einsiedeln 1981.

[26] *Die Wahrheit is symphonisch. Aspekte des christlichen Pluralismus*, Einsiedeln 1972.

3.4. Strange meetings

a. Adrienne von Speyr

Balthasar moved to Basel in 1940 where he met Adrienne von Speyr (1902-1967), a medical doctor who converted to Catholicism under his guidance in that same year. She would become an important figure for both his theology and his life.[27] After her conversion, she started writing theology, scriptural commentary and diaries, all of which she dictated to Hans because she was weakened by a severe illness. This began a lifelong partnership in theology and religious life. From an early age, she had shown a great interest in religion and has been said to have had mystical visions, which Balthasar is said to have witnessed.[28] Later, Balthasar would record these visions and seek ecclesiastical recognition of her experiences. The published works of von Speyr are almost as voluminous as those of Balthasar. He wrote an introduction to all her books and tried to bring them to the attention of other theologians. In his later works, Balthasar often quoted her, much more often than she quoted him. The final part of *Theodramatik* even contains full pages of quotations from her works. Until her death in 1967 Adrienne was part of the *Johannesgemeinschaft (Community of St. John)*, where Hans cared for her when she fell seriously ill in her final ten years. He subsequently dedicated his life to publishing her work and said that his own theological work could never be separated and interpreted without taking her work into account.[29] I fully agree with Kevin Mongrain however, that von Speyr's influence on Balthasar's work was "deforming rather than constructive".[30] Her work is important to understand Balthasar's life and work psychologically but not essential for a theological understanding of his work.

---

[27] Cf. J.S. Bonnici, *Person to person. Friendship and love in the life and theology of Hans Urs von Balthasar*, New York 1999.

[28] Several accounts of Hans's and Adrienne's partnership can be found in *Mein Werk* and in *Unser Auftrag*, Einsiedeln 1984 and in Balthasar's biography of Adrienne: *Erster Blick auf Adrienne von Speyr*, Einsiedeln 1968; Cf. Th. Krenski, *Hans Urs von Balthasar*, 123-157; J. Roten, s.m., The two halves of the moon. Marian anthropological dimensions in the common mission of Adrienne von Speyr and Hans Urs von Balthasar, in: D.L. Schindler [ed.], *Hans Urs von Balthasar*, 65-86; G. De Schrijver, Hans Urs von Balthasar's Christologie in der Theodramatik. Trinitarische Engführung als Methode, in: *Bijdragen. Tijdschrift voor filosofie en theologie* 59 (1998), 141-153.

[29] *Mein Werk*, 85-86. Research is currently taking place to determine the true author of some of the works of Balthasar (whether they are written by von Speyr) and some of the works of von Speyr (whether they are written by Balthasar).

[30] K. Mongrain, *The systematic thought of Hans Urs von Balthasar. An Irenaean retrieval*, New York 2002, 11-12.

In 1950, Balthasar decided to leave the Jesuits to lead a lay community together with Adrienne: the *Johannesgemeinschaft*.[31] Already in 1948, after years of consideration and prayer, he asked the Father General of the order to allow him to start a lay branch but this request was rejected. Balthasar's valedictory letter, however conciliatory and emotional, is very clear: obedience to God is more important than obedience to the order and he implicitly reproaches the order bitterly for its conservatism and expresses grief over personal attacks directed towards him.[32] His decision to leave the order meant that he was forbidden by canon law to teach at Catholic universities. Two years after founding the Community of St John, Balthasar founded a publishing house, the *Johannes Verlag*, especially to publish Adrienne's works, besides several series on theology and culture.[33] Furthermore, a school, already founded by Balthasar in 1944, was associated with the *Johannesgemeinschaft*. Balthasar remained the chaplain of the students of this school for the rest of his life.

b. Karl Barth

Balthasar's first great systematic-theological work was the result of his friendship of many years standing with Karl Barth, about whom he wrote a study which has become a standard work for Barth scholars.[34] In it, after presenting a chronological overview of Barth's theological work, he explains the difference between the Protestant (*analogia fidei*) and the Catholic (*analogia entis*) forms of thought (*Denkformen*):[35]

> Barth starts thinking from the viewpoint of the ultimate reality, and he considers everything else preliminary to it, potentiality of its realisation, or as Kant would say: conditions of possibility. Thinking from actuality, as if from the essence of meaning, he queries it, seeking this meaning, for that which has enabled it to be what it is. (...) scholasticism has not applied this principle[36] to

---

[31] Before he left the Jesuit order, Balthasar worked out his idea for a lay order in: *Der Laie und der Ordensstand*, Freiburg 1948; later again he wrote the rule of his own religious order in *Unser Auftrag*.

[32] The valedictory letter was published as 'Abschiedsbrief an die Gesellschaft Jesu', in: E. Guerriero, *Hans Urs von Balthasar*, 402-410.

[33] M. Lochbrunner, *Hans Urs von Balthasar als Autor, Herausgeber und Verleger. Fünf Studien zu seinen Sammlungen (1942-1967)*, Würzburg 2002.

[34] *Karl Barth. Darstellung und Deutung seiner Theologie*, Köln 1951 (Einsiedeln 1976⁴).

[35] See also chapter four.

[36] "Πρότερον γάρ εἰσι τῶν δυνάμεων αἱ ἐνέργειαι" (Aristoteles, *De anima* II 415 a 18).

[37] *Karl Barth*, 203-204.

the relation of nature and historical realisation, but has—at least methodically—followed the reverse line of reasoning: From the natures and the essences that are known as such and are at the centre of philosophical enquiry, it progresses to the destination of its activities.[37]

It is the first serious Catholic answer to the Protestant discussion about natural theology. Balthasar's amendment of Przywara's doctrine of the analogy of being (he proposes that the analogy of being should be regarded within the framework of the analogy of faith) offers a new Catholic approach to the problem of the relation between nature and grace, which still has its implications for contemporary Catholic theology.[38] Balthasar's interpretation of Barth's theology, together with Henri Bouillard's and much later Hans Küng's, has been of continuing influence on the understanding of Barth's thoughts on Catholic theology.

In the 1950s and 1960s, Balthasar worked out his own theological programme in *Die Gottesfrage des heutigen Menschen* (1956) and in *Das Ganze im Fragment* (1963). In these works, he developed a theological anthropology (an application of the philosophical doctrine of analogy in theology) and a theology of history respectively. His anthropology cannot be understood in the sense of a subjectivist practice of theology, but rather as a further determination of the essence and unicity of the God-man Jesus in His concrete historicity.[39] Balthasar regards this theological philosophy as the pivot between mythology and religion on the one hand and modern science on the other. He also wrote a concise theology of history.[40] In it he describes theology as a unique discipline compared to all others, because, on the one hand, it can never make general pronouncements, and on the other, it cannot be just a historical discipline. This

---

[38] Balthasar's later doctrine of analogy is more radical. In his book on Karl Barth, he tries to reconcile *analogia fidei* and *analogia entis*, but in the trilogy (mainly in *Theologik* II and III), both forms of analogy increasingly become each other's opposites. Despite his emphasis on the unity of nature and grace, the analogy in his theology degenerates to the only possible, but imperfect way of speaking about revelation. Cf. E. Mechels, *Analogie bei Erich Przywara und Karl Barth. Das Verhältnis von Offenbarungstheologie und Metaphysik*, Neukirchen-Vluyn 1974; J. Wissink, *De inzet van de theologie. Een onderzoek naar de motieven en de geldigheid van Karl Barths strijd tegen de natuurlijke theologie*, Amersfoort 1983, 377-388; J. Thompson, Barth and Balthasar. An ecumenical dialogue, in: B. McGregor, o.p., Th. Norris [eds], *The beauty of Christ*, 171-192; R. Chia, *Revelation and theology. The knowledge of God in Balthasar and Barth*, Bern, etc. 1999.

[39] For anthropological implications in the thought of Balthasar, see: A. Scola, *Hans Urs von Balthasar. A theological style*, [Orig. Hans Urs von Balthasar. Uno stile teologico, Milan 1991. Series: Ressourcement. Retrieval and renewal in Catholic thought], Grand Rapids 1995, 84-100.

[40] *Theologie der Geschichte*, Einsiedeln 1950 (fully revised in 1959, 1979[6]).

relation between metaphysics and history is one of the most important subjects of twentieth century Catholic fundamental theology.

3.5. Magnum opus

In the 1960s, 1970s and 1980s, Balthasar worked on a theological trilogy that would become his *magnum opus*: Theo-aesthetics (*Herrlichkeit*), Theodramatics (*Theodramatik*), and Theologic (*Theologik*). He gave the initial impetus to a theological aesthetics in his article "Offenbarung und Schönheit".[41] By the time Balthasar had started working on *Herrlichkeit*, in the 1960s, he had summarised the central ideas of his theological aesthetics again in *Glaubhaft ist nur Liebe* (1963). This should not be regarded as an extract of his theological aesthetics, however, but rather as a theology of love and encounter. Although in *Herrlichkeit* he describes the beauty of the form of divine revelation as the first and most central religious experience, in *Glaubhaft* he has already described the interaction between perception, imagination and dramatics.[42]

Balthasar continued to publish translations and works about the great mystics in the history of the church and theology throughout his life.[43] According to him, mysticism had been a forgotten or underexposed but essential pillar of theology since the Enlightenment.[44] This is why he assumed the responsibility of translating the works of all the great mystics to German.[45]

During the second Vatican Council, Balthasar was ignored as a theological advisor. This could be because he never worked at a university. For a long time, Karl Rahner tried to get Balthasar a professorship but never succeeded, which may be because he had left the Jesuits, who were

---

[41] Republished in *Verbum Caro. Schriften zur Theologie I*, 100-134.

[42] Balthasar always denied that his trilogy forms a systematic theology. Although the structure of the trilogy is very typical, almost naturally logical and very consistent in its basic principles, many contradictions can be found (e.g. the pronouncements on the order of importance of 'beauty', 'truth' and 'goodness'), as I will show in the following chapters. Cf. M. Lochbrunner, Hans Urs von Balthasars Trilogie der Liebe. Vom Dogmatikentwurf zur theologischen Summe. Zum posthumen Gedenken an Seinen 90. Geburtstag, in: *Forum katholische Theologie* 11 (1995), 161-181.

[43] For instance in *Thérèse von Lisieux*, Olten 1950; *Elisabeth von Dijon und ihre geistliche Sendung*, Köln 1952; and of course the various monographs in the trilogy (for example on St John of the Cross, Master Eckhart).

[44] This point of view has been worked out in for instance: Theologie und Heiligkeit, in: *Verbum Caro*, 195-225; Spiritualität, in: Ibid., 226-244; and in Aktion und Kontemplation, in: Ibid, 245-259.

[45] Cf. M. Lochbrunner, *Hans Urs von Balthasar als Autor, Herausgeber und Verleger*.

influential at German universities at the time. Nevertheless, the appreciation of his work started to increase in the 1960s. He received several honorary doctorates and won literary prizes and awards. In 1969 he finally received the long desired recognition of the church and was invited to become a member of the pope's International Theological Commission. In the early 1970s, although still editor of the spirituality section of *Concilium*, together with Ratzinger he established its counterpart, *Communio*, which is usually characterised as a 'conservative' theological journal.

Studies on Balthasar still seek to establish whether he really was a conservative and restorationist theologian. Those who have read his main theological works, judge him one of the most important and leading theologians of the twentieth century. Those who have read his shorter church political writings (*Streitschriften*) and his articles in *Communio*, will undoubtedly characterise him as conservative.[46] Those who consider his interest in retrieving patristic sources for contemporary theology will call him 'traditionalist' or 'premodern'. Indeed, in his writings on ecclesiastical politics Balthasar does not address the ideas progressive theologians would have appreciated (abolition of mandatory celibacy, women in the priesthood, etc.). The answer to the question whether Balthasar is a conservative theologian or not is not essential for the present research but it is important to find an answer to whether he has shaped a theology and with it a vision of faith and the church, which can be of interest for contemporary theologians and offer future perspectives for theological understanding.

In his old age Balthasar completed his trilogy, while working prolifically as a writer and editor for *Communio*. In the 1970s, he finished *Theodramatik*, a theodramatics in which he confronts Christian theology with the European theatre and integrates more than one thousand plays in it. In the 1980s the trilogy was finished with *Theologik*, of which the first part, *Wahrheit der Welt*, had already been published in 1947. In the second part, *Wahrheit Gottes*, he re-formulates his doctrine of the transcendentals and of analogy within the framework of a theology of the Trinity. At the end of his life he was to have been created cardinal deacon of S. Nicola in Carcere in the consistory of 28 June 1988, but he initially asked to be excused from receiving episcopal consecration because of advanced age. Hans Urs von Balthasar died on 26 June 1988, only two days before his elevation as a cardinal.

---

[46] M. Kehl, Hans Urs von Balthasar. Ein Porträt, in: Id., W. Löser, *In der Fülle des Glaubens. Hans Urs von Balthasar-Lesebuch*, Freiburg im Breisgau 1980, 13-60, 13-14.

4. THEOLOGICAL HERMENEUTICS AND METAPHYSICS

After giving a biographical account of Balthasar's life and works it is also necessary to introduce his theology to contemporary theologians, since his theological insights are not widely known. The reception of his work has been notably late and often filled with prejudice. However, it is almost impossible to give an adequate overview of his theology due to the quantity of his publications and the wide range of his ideas.[1] I will not attempt to give such an overview, nor will I try to mention every aspect or subject that he dealt with during his life in theology. Nevertheless, for this present research on aesthetics as a way of doing fundamental theology, it is necessary to elucidate Balthasar's view on the task of theology and in particular his understanding of the relationship between philosophy and theology (4.2). Next, I will discuss two metaphysical doctrines of his work and thought, the transcendentals (4.3) and the analogy of being (4.4). These principles are central throughout his work, and knowledge of them will be helpful in the next chapter on theological aesthetics, for the understanding of the transcendental concept of beauty in

---

[1] Some have attempted to write introductory overviews of Balthasar's work. Main introductions by one author are: E.T. Oakes, *Pattern of redemption. The theology of Hans Urs von Balthasar*, New York 1994; A. Scola, *Hans Urs von Balthasar, A theological style*, [Orig. Hans Urs von Balthasar. Uno stile teologico, Milan 1991. Series: Ressourcement. Retrieval and renewal in Catholic thought], Grand Rapids 1995; Th. Krenski, *Hans Urs von Balthasar. Das Gottesdrama*, Mainz 1995; K. Mongrain, *The systematic thought of Hans Urs von Balthasar. An Irenaean retrieval*, New York 2002. Most introductions follow the structure of Balthasar's trilogy to describe his theology, as Edward Oakes did. Others elaborate his work by linking his ideas to the people that influenced them (Erich Przywara, Henri de Lubac, Karl Barth, Adrienne von Speyr, et al.) like Thomas Krenski has done in his book. Angelo Cardinal Scola is one of few who managed to give a cross section of Balthasar's books and articles. According to Scola, Balthasar's theology can best be described as a christocentric anthropology. Kevin Mongrain reads his theology from the perspective of the Irenaean influence on his work. However, since Balthasar chose so many conversation partners from the history of thought, Mongrain's book will undoubtedly be the first of a series of introductions yet to come. Important collections of articles introducing Balthasar are: J. Riches [ed.], *The analogy of beauty. The theology of Hans Urs von Balthasar*, Edinburgh 1986; D. Schindler [ed.], *Hans Urs von Balthasar. His life and work*, San Francisco 1991 [This is partly a translation of: K. Lehmann, W. Kasper [Hrsg.], *Hans Urs von Balthasar. Gestalt und Werk*, Köln 1989. It has an article by Louis Dupré on Balthasar's theological aesthetics added.]; B. McGregor, Th. Norris [eds], *The beauty of Christ. An introduction to the theology of Hans Urs von Balthasar*, Edinburgh 1994; D. Moss, E.T. Oakes, s.j. [eds], *The Cambridge companion to Hans Urs von Balthasar*, Cambridge 2004.

particular. Finally, I will show that Balthasar's metaphysics finds its foundation in the doctrine of the Trinity (4.5). According to him, every theological statement is grounded in the incarnation, which flows out of the intratrinitarian movements. First, though, I will argue that Balthasar's theology should be placed against the background of his theological education and the cultural developments during his lifetime (4.1).

4.1. Theological context: history and method

For a critical appraisal of Balthasar's theology it is crucial to put his ideas in the perspective of the changing landscape of twentieth century theological thought. Balthasar was a reactionary thinker, at least in the literal meaning of the word. He responds strongly to the developments of his own time. In his theology he reacts especially against the excessive systematisation of the then dominant neoscholastic method. He also responds against Barth's dismissal of the analogy of being as an invention of the anti-Christ, against a demythologising and existentialist theology, and against historical-critical method.[2] It is noteworthy that he starts his theodramatics—together with his theo-aesthetics his main and most original project—with a description of the theology of his time, distinguishing nine theological trends, which are: the eventful, the historical, the orthopractical, the dialogical, the political, the prospective, the functional, the role, and finally the trend that concerns freedom and evil (TD I 23-46). It is significant that in that underlying theodramatic project, which would amount to five volumes, he purports to unify all these current trends and criticizes any theology that reduces its task to one or two of these trends.

Every trend, according to him, is a consequence of the effort to move away from a rationalist way of doing theology. The convergence of all these trends would lead to what he calls a 'theodramatic theology'. A short overview will show what Balthasar's concerns are when establishing the task of theology. Five trends concern theological method in general. The *eventful* in theology criticises both orthodox fundamentalism and historical liberalism. The *historical* element in theology demarcates Christian identity to protect it against relativism and indifference. The *orthopractical* calls for responsibility to guard against theoretical complacency. The *dialogical* character of theology is the most essential according to

---

[2] Cf. F. Kerr, Foreword: Assessing the 'Giddy Synthesis', in: L. Gardner, D. Moss, B. Quash, G. Ward [eds], *Balthasar at the end of modernity*, Edinburgh 1999, 1-14.

Balthasar because it mirrors the scriptural covenant, in which both partners affirm their relationship in freedom. The *functional* trend—Balthasar here refers to the structuralism of Lévi-Strauss, Ricoeur and Foucault—lacks drama when it tries to find a synchronicity in historical events in different ages. Structuralism thus assumes an all-embracing academic view, on which ground, according to Balthasar, it is impossible to establish a certain standpoint. However, it does provide a helpful instrument, as it not only describes social relations but also interprets humanity in the light of the performance of these relations. In the context of the church, for example, functionalism, providing an objectifying or pragmatic view on things, could expose pseudo-holiness. However, according to Balthasar, the structuralist approach can never meet the essential theological requirement of taking and clarifying one's standpoint.

From this it becomes clear that Balthasar's theological method is seeking a middle position that is neither fideist nor relativist, which integrates action and contemplation, and human freedom and obedience. Thus, the theological position that he favours should be characterised by a unifying 'and/and' rather than by the 'and/or' of either orthodoxy or liberalism. Instead of being critical and analytical, Balthasar's theological method moves from a Christian standpoint towards a Christian standpoint, without actually leaving one's position of faith. Balthasar's idea of theology is covenanted from the beginning to the end and it only abstracts from this position by describing and interpreting one's standpoint whilst performing it (H III,1 16-20).

The other four trends are concerned with the relationship of divine and human freedom. They emphasise human freedom whilst protecting divine sovereignty. Balthasar is scrupulously critical whenever he believes this balance or covenant between God and man is forgotten or ignored. *Political* theology, according to him, is the most critical theological trend. It puts the public sphere with its dynamics of power in front of the tribunal of the Christian drama, in which every utopian idea converts itself to the Christian engagement with the poor and the powerless. The *prospective* in theology is the current counterpart of the eschatological in early Christianity. However, according to him, there is a radical difference between the utopian and revolutionary perspectives of his days and the apocalyptical perspective of the early church. In the eschatological experience one touches the boundary between the unavailing finitude of life and death and the promise of eternal life, while the prospective view mainly offers a flight forward, without discarding the present state of finitude.

A theology of *role* and identity, the eighth trend in Balthasar's list, will offer a completely different answer to the question 'Who am I?' than psychology or sociology. These disciplines cannot answer the question: Who offered me the role that I have in society? In a functionalist approach it does not matter who is performing a specific role; performers are interchangeable. Balthasar argues that only a theological answer to the question of identity could integrate society, role and the individual appropriately, without subordinating one aspect to another. The topic of *freedom*, and with it the possibility of *evil*, is not a new one in modern theology. However, according to Balthasar, the view on human autonomy changed after Jacob Boehme's speculations regarding the darkness of the world as projections of the darkness in God and Schelling's determination of absolute freedom in human freedom. Therefore, the old theological answers to the questions of evil, mercy and damnation will no longer suffice in an age when the question of divine powerlessness, leading to a possible new interpretation of the abandonment at the cross, should top the theological agenda.

Balthasar is clearly a theologian of his time. He responds strongly to and mostly reacts against new theological developments. Nevertheless he is part of certain new theological developments as well. His main theological interests, developed in his own theological context, are *history* and *freedom*. He criticises the rigid and rationalistic method of neoscholasticism by emphasising the practical, the dialogical and the historical element in theology. A first consequence of this critique was his affiliation with the *Nouvelle Théologie* of Henri de Lubac and others. They applied a different hermeneutics to theology, spiritual rather than literal, historical rather than rationalistic, averse to a philosophically founded apologetic theology. Balthasar criticises the existentialist approach of Rudolf Bultmann but he is deeply influenced by Martin Heidegger's metaphysics. A second consequence of Balthasar's 'reactionary' stance was his new organisation of theological topics, resulting in a grandiose trilogy in which the ideas of freedom, hope and love are arranged in a theological symphony of aesthetics, dramatics and logic.[3] Not following the Kantian transcendental approach in theology nor the evolutionary approach of the Enlightenment, which according to him led to the same rationalism as Thomism, but influenced by the theology of

---

[3] Th. Norris, The symphonic unity of his theology. An overview, in: B. McGregor, Id. [eds], *The beauty of Christ*, 213-252.

the church fathers and Karl Barth, Balthasar proposed an ecumenical and catholic, integral and unifying principle for the task of theology.

4.2. Theological hermeneutics: incarnation as the alpha and omega of theology

a. The formal structure of theology

Balthasar wrote the following strong and dense statement about the essence of theology:

> "The Word, which is God, has become human without ceasing to be God. The Word, which is infinite, has become finite, without ceasing to be infinite. The Word, which is God, has taken on a body of flesh to be human. Because it is Word and because it has assumed the flesh as a Word, it has at the same time assumed a body of letters, writing, understanding, image, voice and proclamation. Without this, people would either not have understood that the Word has really become flesh, or that this God person, which has become flesh, truly is the Word. All problems of scripture should be approached from Christology: the letter relates to the Spirit, as the body of Christ relates to his divine nature and person" (VC 159).

This section begins Balthasar's article entitled "Was soll Theologie?" (1953). If the divine Word wants to become letter or understanding, i.e. theo*logy*, the theologian will have to find the Word through the flesh, as Paul stated, if, as the gospel of John emphasised, it has not already been heard, seen and felt. The letter is the bridge to the human mind and the human mind is the entrance to the infinity of the divine logos. Balthasar asserts that the theologian is a believer from the start and is willing to keep the entrance to the infinite divine truth open whilst acknowledging the finitude of the flesh and the letter.

Two existences therefore meet in theology according to Balthasar: that of an infinite person, the Word that has become flesh and as such gives itself as letter and content; and that of the believer, insofar as belief is the only possible adequate attitude—given by the infinite person—for man to meet that other existence (VC 160). For Balthasar, faith, as the submission to the infinite, is man's only possible a priori for understanding flesh and letter as the expression and the language of the infinite. This submission consists of the absolute will to meet God in the human, to meet the infinite content in finite understanding, which, according to Balthasar, is the definition of 'adoration'. And it consists of the will to make this infinite content the foundation of one's own existence, which he calls 'holiness', "not just in sight of the Word, but from the Word towards the Word, by virtue of the Word for the Word" (VC 161).

Faith, for Balthasar, is not just the act of faith, but also the content at which this act of faith is aimed. The emphasis on this unity of *fides qua* and *fides quae* serves to distinguish the act of faith from all other human acts. Faith is not an act like other acts, but a relation that involves man entirely and which, thanks to grace, enables him to respond to the address by God's revelation. Balthasar finds the best example of the unity of faith and knowing in the gospel of John. Although John speaks of signs, from which only believers can read the evidences of faith, these signs are not just references to a different reality, but immediate epiphanies of the divinity of Christ. The relationship of faith and knowledge gains a certain ambiguity in the gospel of John. Sometimes faith precedes knowing (Jn 8, 31-32 and 10,38), and on other occasions, this relationship is reversed and faith seems directly to be preceded by knowing (Jn 16,30 and 17,8).

Balthasar claims that the knowledge of which the bible speaks is not simply something that precedes faith. Biblical *gnosis* is not knowledge in the sense of the *praeambula fidei*. Separating this *gnosis* from the Christian act of faith and giving it its own place within the *analysis fidei* does not do justice to its original meaning. According to Balthasar, fundamental theology is not a rational exposition of faith but an analysis of the unity of faith and knowing. The formula *fides quaerens intellectum* does not exactly match the way in which the bible speaks of the relation between faith and knowing. The knowledge of faith is not merely a search or uncertain knowledge, but a form of knowledge that has already found its foundation in a form of faith, which Balthasar describes as adoration and holiness. The search for understanding nevertheless has its rightful place in faith too, insofar as faith is also striving for the evidence which can only be found in God and which can only be encountered through a discovery, a sometimes sudden happening upon of this evidence (H I 128).

Adoration and holiness are the two pillars of Balthasar's concept of Christian living and, therefore, also of that of theology. These two pillars characterise the work of the church and the office that like the priesthood, a theologian holds as well. The holiness of the church and the office is not an end in itself, however. It is a means that refers to the origin of its worldly form, which becomes redundant when the purpose is achieved. So theology itself is an office but, according to Balthasar, it is not a direct obedience to the divine Word. It is the establishment of theory, a form of contemplation that differs from adoration and holiness but is, nevertheless, aimed at these two pillars that lie at the foundation of the teachings of the church. Theology itself is also a form of teaching but it is a form of teaching that tests and corrects the teachings of the church. Like the sacraments and the teachings of the church, theology is a means to meet the infinite Word in finitude, but it has its own separate function. The one and only measure of theology is the truth that is Christ (VC 163).

Does this mean that, for Balthasar, controversy and discussion become impossible? He posits that they are possible because theology is a struggle with words, a constant weighing of postulates and positions. If anything, theology is made possible and formed by syllogisms, contradictions and deductions. However, a theological dispute is on its way to either faith or unbelief from the start. As Balthasar puts it: analogous to the words of Christ, the word of contradiction in theology is at the same time the word of atonement (VC 164). Controversies are both theology's essence and vulnerability and should form the insight that it can never find a definitive standpoint, but that it is submitted to the Word of redemption that never can be neutralised in a scientifically feasible balance. Therefore, no theological word can ever be the final word.

From this, Balthasar infers the structure of theology. He distinguishes between the general or formal and the particular or material structure of theology. The general structure of theological thought is its direction from the finite word towards the incarnated infinity. That does not mean that the finite words will be deleted in the end but they will be led beyond themselves. In the incarnation the rules of finite speech and thought became infinitely true and impossible to divide into separate rules and words. The foundation of theology therefore, is neither a historical nor a philosophical-existential premise but, for Balthasar, the incarnation, however never a-historical, cannot be reduced to the merely historical. "Not history, not development, not philosophy have the Word, but only faith itself that from the Word gives theology its form, and leads to deeper adoration and better life obedience" (VC 165).

Balthasar's concept of theology is a catholic or universal one. This means, "representing all truth, in an endless and unbound movement through death, resurrecting in heavenly truth" (VC 166). Theological knowledge would then be searching and grace-finding faith that, however characterised by controversy and finitude, is always measured by adoration and obedience. This is what Balthasar calls a 'catholic understanding', which differs from an aristotelian or platonic understanding in as far as it is not just an invitation to convert everything into a vague or even devotional infinity, but a continuous dedication of our words and thoughts to the Word of God. This is the form of scripture; how can it not be, he argues, the form of theology (VC 166).

b. *The material realm of theology*

From the general structure of theology follows the material one. The material structure of theology is determined by three differences.

Revelation and history
First, there is the difference between revelation and history.[4] According to Balthasar, all the material elements of theology should be articulations towards revelation in the way that they already have found their expression in the history of humanity and scripture. It is the task of theology, and of fundamental theology in particular, to interpret and explain the divine content of this history. Its aim, however, is not to find a definitive abstraction of history because, for Balthasar, incarnation is not an example of truth, it is truth itself (VC 166). That is why theologians cannot merely select elements from this historical story, but in their theological exposition they have to follow the essential course of historical events.

This position obviously has its consequences for reading scripture. The bible should not be read as a book, Balthasar argues, but as the expression of revelation in history. History, for Balthasar, is firstly the era of Christ and the enclosure of the whole of the history of humanity. Secondly, history is the time under the norm of Christ (TdG 23). Therefore, scripture should be read in the spirit of the church. Consequently, the aim of theological hermeneutics should not be, like other academic disciplines, a growing specialisation or differentiation. On the contrary, although differentiated in separate monographs, it is aimed at the inner unity of its infinite subject.

Balthasar complained that since theology has been fragmented in many different disciplines, all with their own methods and starting points, it is impossible to speak about *the* method or the sole subject of theology. A history of theology describes the development of doctrine, empirical theology explores religious beliefs and experiences, and philosophy of

---

[4] R. Chia, *Revelation and theology. The knowledge of God in Balthasar and Barth*, Bern, etc. 1999; L.S. Chapp, *The God who speaks. Hans Urs von Balthasar's theology of revelation*, San Francisco, etc. 1996.

religion reflects on the essence of religion. He complained about this theological fragmentation already nearly fifty years ago and regretted that there was no longer a consensus on what the theological subject was. According to him, it even became impossible to point to one contemporary source, because a choice for a particular source will reveal a theological standpoint and the preferred method. Now, of course Balthasar himself has also pointed to the many sources for theology, like scripture, tradition, the practice of daily life, contemporary issues, and so on. Although he has always been clear about the incarnation as the one and only focus and foundation of theology, and the church as its one and only context, he has never used this clarity to make a case against the world or the culture that he lived in. His complaint therefore, is rather about the consequences of theological fragmentation. He noticed that a division in theological subdisciplines could never be as prolific as a dogmatic theology that would cover all aspects of Christian faith. But, in his opinion, tradition seems to have ceased to be a source for the exegete, leaving scripture as his one and only source; faith is not a source for the dogmatician anymore but only the interpretation of faith, and so on (H I 70). This is why the determination of a single theological method became a problem for theology in general, because every specific approach of a research subject will demarcate the field of research and, inversely, every chosen subject will determine its appropriate method.[5]

Balthasar has severely criticised this diversity in theology. The most important but, to his mind, regrettable separation that took place in the history of theology is the one between philosophy and theology in the age of Descartes, when philosophy modelled its method after that of the upcoming natural sciences (H I 67-68). Ever since, philosophy uses the concepts of 'transcendence' and 'absoluteness' only as concepts of limit within the framework of a formal ontology. Balthasar deplores this rationalist turn in the history of philosophy, but it was Gotthold Ephraim Lessing, whose philosophy meant the *coup de grâce* for theology, by giving it the definition of a science of arbitrary and historical truths (H I 69). The consequence of this definition, according to him, was the degeneration of dogmatic theology into the history of dogma, and fundamental theology into a historical interpretation of church doctrine.[6] Therefore, theology

---

[5] Cf. W. Klaghofer-Treitler, *Gotteswort im Menschenwort. Inhalt und Form von Theologie nach Hans Urs von Balthasar*, Innsbruck, etc. 1992, 11.
[6] Theology as a historical discipline covers only what Augustine called *historia* and Origen called *littera*. However, according to Balthasar, in the end its real dimension should be Augustine's *intellectus* and Origen's *spiritus* (H I 71).

should have its own method, "illuminated and revered enraptured in the light of the illuminating eternal being, lightning up in the world" (H I 66).

As such, Balthasar's chosen theological method, with an emphasis on the *sensus spiritualis* and the *intellectus fidei*, determines on the one hand the object of his theology: God and His revelation; the extent of the accessibility of this object, on the other, determines this method. Theology is characterised by Balthasar as an understanding of the church in which its object itself determines and even communicates its method. Therefore, Balthasar's method raises two questions: First, how does Balthasar approach the object of theology methodically? Second, what are the implications of the specific access of the theologian to the theological object?[7] According to Balthasar, the theological object or content and theological method are one because theological method itself is part of its object. The theological standpoint is the standpoint of faith and, therefore, of adoration and holiness. To understand, interpret and explain this standpoint is founded on divine revelation in Christ (GinL 18).

How then, according to Balthasar, do theological differences occur? Why is it that the main object of theology, constituting and communicating an appropriate method, does not constitute a smooth and uniform theological content? The tradition of theology should never settle, according to Balthasar. There is no once completed theological debate, whether written down in conciliar documents or not, that is closed for future discussion. "The longer living tradition is interrupted by mere mechanically passing on of what is said, the more difficult it may become to tie in anew" (VC 168). For Balthasar, theological understanding expresses itself in a diversity directed towards the unity of revelation in history instead of being a unifying interpretation of fragmented historical events.

Revelation and mission
The second difference that theology has to deal with is the one between revelation and mission or contemporary preaching. Theology, Balthasar argues, should never submit to current needs and modern trends and he mentions the existentialist and demythologising approaches in the theology of his time as examples of this type of surrender (VC 168). Preaching therefore, should never be apologetic. Rather, it should speak from the light that the Holy Spirit shines on revelation in our present day. The theologian is a guardian, waiting for, and then proclaiming the *kairos*, not of world history but of Christian history interpreted in the light of

---

[7] Cf. W. Klaghofer-Treitler, *Gotteswort im Menschenwort*, 11-12.

revelation. Nevertheless, how can the theologian acknowledge the spirit of revelation and distinguish it from others? Primarily, says Balthasar, they can learn from the lives of the saints. Their lives are lived doctrine (VC 169). Consequently, theologians should do their work in the same light of adoration and obedience to stand in that same light of sainthood.

For Balthasar, the saints are the pillars of the church because they have understood that there is no separation between doctrine and spirituality. When they reason theologically they make no distinction between an attitude towards people within and people outside the church. Therefore, the theology of the saints, however sometimes polemical or apologetic, never happens in the portal of the church but always in the heart of it. Faith is the unity of knowledge and surrender and this unity is best represented in the lives of the saints (VC 197). Balthasar makes little distinction between a theological commentary and a sermon of someone like Origen. Although these theological genres differ in style and form, and perhaps in interest, academic or pastoral, they are explanations of the Word of God and can therefore both be called 'theology'.

Revelation and tradition
The third difference that theology has to bridge is between revelation now and the tradition of the past. In order to establish a living tradition the distance between the two needs to be spanned. Balthasar acknowledges that the guidance of the spirit in the past is not necessarily the guidance for the present, especially not when it concerns a specific situation in the past. That does not mean though, that one has to mistrust the theological statements and church formulas of the past. For Balthasar, the certainty of faith also comes, next to the plenitude of revelation and the fullness of the given spirit, from the richness of the inherited tradition. This demands a responsibility to balance between the everlasting values—he mentions the fathers, scholasticism and spirituality—and the context of every historical phenomenon. Theologians should never ignore the importance of past values. "What is needed, is neither an enthusiastic restoration of something (i.e. the fathers), nor mere historical research, but the Christian humanity that seeks the living first source of the sources" (VC 170). The representation of the living tradition comes forth from this balance between reverence for the past and the freedom to perform one's own search for values in the present.

In this section I have shown that two main interests of Balthasar's theology, *history* and *freedom*, which he emphasised against the theological background of his time, mirror themselves in his definition of the formal structure and the material realm of theology. Formally, he tries to answer the question how to reason that the incarnation has taken place historically. He interprets theological reason within the framework of faith and does not want to distinguish it radically from faith. The incarnated Word itself is the one and only foundation of theology. The ideas of history and freedom mirror themselves in the three themes that structure theology materially: history, mission and tradition. One could say that the idea of freedom is treated by Balthasar practically (mission) and theoretically (tradition). Against the background of the current theological curriculum, according to Balthasar, the idea of history should be the key issue for exegesis and dogmatic or hermeneutical theology. The idea of practical freedom should be the subject matter of theological ethics and practical theology; the idea of theoretical freedom would be an ecclesiological and historical theme. Balthasar's theology can be summarised, however inadequate and incomplete, by the following questions: How does God reveal Himself in history and how should human beings respond to that? How does this divine-human relationship structure our experiences, actions and thoughts? Despite these questions that express a positive theological standpoint, Balthasar defines theological rationality as—and he quotes Anselm—*consideratio rationabiliter comprehendit incomprehensibile esse* (GinL 100).[8]

4.3. Theological metaphysics I: the doctrine of the transcendentals

The structure of Balthasar's entire trilogy *Herrlichkeit, Theodramatik, Theologik* is determined by the three transcendental concepts of 'beauty', 'goodness' and 'truth'. This transcendental structure of Balthasar's theology is more than just a play on generic concepts. Rather, it shows that his theology is based upon a metaphysics that is deeply rooted in medieval philosophy.[9] The medieval doctrine of the transcendentals has since undergone a radical change. However, Balthasar seems to fall back on the old interpretation of the transcendental. For the present research on his theological aesthetics as a fundamental theology it is necessary to elucidate its main concept of 'the beautiful' as a transcendental one, as it is important to understand how Balthasar used and amended the

---

[8] Anselm, *Monologion* 64.
[9] Cf. J. Aertsen, *Medieval philosophy and the transcendentals. The case of Thomas Aquinas*, Leiden, etc. 1996.

metaphysical system that, together with the doctrine of analogy, is one of the two pillars of his fundamental theology.

a. Amending the philosophical doctrine of the transcendentals

The question of the foundation of thought, i.e. the search for that which an intellectual affirmation of reality cannot do without, has traditionally been called 'transcendental philosophy'. However, the term 'transcendental' is older and has been used in a completely different metaphysical context. The 'transcendental' is clearly distinguished from the 'transcendent', although these two terms have frequently been mixed up in the history of philosophy.[10] The medieval concept of the transcendental concerned the elementary structure of all of reality, of anything that is. As such, it differed from the aristotelian categories. The transcendental was seen as the transcategorical that all beings have in common. That is why the transcendentals were sometimes understood as divine predicates. The first doctrine of the transcendentals was developed by Philip the Chancellor (1160s-1236).[11] However, the concepts that would later be regarded as transcendentals can already be found in the philosophy of Pseudo-Dionysius (c. 500).[12] The term 'transcendental', in its original Latin form *transcendentia*, has been used for several concepts, but there is a consensus that 'being', 'the one', 'the true', and 'the good' are among them.[13] Others that occasionally have been mentioned are 'the beautiful', 'thing', and 'something'. The *transcendentia* were renamed *transcendentalia* by the sixteenth century philosopher Francisco Suárez (1548-1617), and have been referred to as such since.[14]

Immanuel Kant (1724-1804) radically changed the use of the concept of the transcendental. In his critical philosophy, it became a predicate for a specific type of knowledge and as such, the opposite of empirical knowledge, instead of being a concept concerning all that is. Since then, the transcendental has become the description of method. Transcendental

---

[10] "Transzendental"; "Transzendentalphilosophie", in: J. Ritter, K. Gründer [Hrsg.], *Historisches Wörterbuch der Philosophie*, Basel 1971-, 1358-1436; Cf. O. Duintjer, *De vraag naar het transcendentale. Vooral in verband met Heidegger en Kant*, Leiden 1966, 1.

[11] J. Aertsen, Medieval philosophy, 25-40; Philippi Cancellarii Parisiensis, Summa de bono, Vol. II, ed. N. Wicki, Bern 1985.

[12] Pseudo-Dionysius, *De divinus nominibus*, Migne PL 3, 4,1,95.

[13] St Thomae Aquinatis, *De veritate*, 1,1.

[14] Cf. F. Suárez, *Disputationes metaphysicae*, Salamanca 1578.

philosophy is the philosophical method that establishes the conditions for the possibility of all experience. These conditions are categorical in Kant's philosophy, in which they form the basis of every intellectual affirmation. Contrary to the medieval concept, the Kantian 'transcendental' does not concern being as such, but the a priori concepts of being and reality.[15]

By not following this Kantian turn to the transcendental categories that form the basis of every intellectual affirmation, Balthasar seems to hark back to the structure of aristotelian-thomist metaphysics, in an age in which philosophers and other theologians are actually trying to distance themselves from this kind of *philosophia perennis*. As has become clear from the two previous sections, it is not Balthasar's intention to ground his theology in an a-historical eternal metaphysical system. On the contrary, his main theological concern is to understand the historical in the light of the eternal, without actually opposing them. So, why does he structure his theology around the transcendentals as the properties of *being* itself, instead of regarding them as intellectual categories?

Balthasar argues that after Thomas Aquinas's philosophy of being, there are two ways in which the history of metaphysics continued. For Thomas, being is both the infinite and supraconceptual fullness of reality and, as it emerges from God, it attains subsistence and self-possession within finite beings. From this, the first metaphysical way was that being became the most encompassing concept of reason, with the consequence of reason having the possibility to survey and dispose of being. A being formalised in such a way could never have had the modality of beauty, Balthasar argues, because "how should the plenitude of divine mystery come forth from this emptiness?" (H III,1 374) The second way was that being was identified with God, as Meister Eckhart (1260-1328) did, according to Balthasar. Both Eckhart and Nicholas of Cusa (1401-1464) followed John Scotus Eriugena's (ca. 810-ca. 877) model of the God-world relationship in terms of complication-explication. But the identification of God and being in Eckhart's thought, and later in the philosophy of the German idealists was so exhaustive that a clear explanation of the why and the wherefore of the world became impossible (H III,1 375-377). His criticism of late medieval and modern metaphysics would lead to Balthasar's main question: Why is there a world if God is all in all?

---

[15] I. Kant, *Kritik der reinen Vernunft*, AA 16,24, B113.

He answered this fundamental question with his theological interpretation of the analogy of being, as I will show in the next section.

According to Manfred Lochbrunner, a careful examination of Balthasar's use of the medieval doctrine of the transcendentals is indispensable in Balthasar research, because the transcendental structure of his theology is not a mere non-critical copy of medieval thomist metaphysics, it signifies an amendment of the medieval doctrine of the transcendentals.[16] Thomas still distinguished five transcendentals: *ens, unum, verum, bonum, aliquid*. Balthasar limits them to just three transcendental properties of being, *verum, bonum* and *pulchrum*, introducing the last as a separate and independent concept, contrary to Thomas, who regarded beauty as a specific quality of knowledge or of the good.[17] Furthermore, Balthasar changes their order: beauty comes before goodness, and goodness before truth. Although this formal reordering matches our experience—the perception of the objective shape of revelation always precedes the confirmations that this shape is also good and true—according to him the three transcendentals should be understood in their interwovenness, presupposing one another and being inseparable (*circumincessio*).

For Balthasar, this wholesome, integrating and non-demarcating principle of the transcendental concepts of being is the fundamental structure of atonement and grace (H III,1 22). He argues that a doctrine of universal atonement can only be supported by a concept of the transcendental that concerns all being (TL II 159). An investigation into the transcendental structure and content of Balthasar's works cannot be limited to the philosophical level, therefore. It should be regarded, as will be shown now, within the theological framework of the trinitarian character of revelation. After all, according to Balthasar, every theologian is a metaphysician; but every metaphysician should also be a theologian if he does not want to belie the object of his research (TL II 159).

---

[16] M. Lochbrunner, Hans Urs von Balthasars Trilogie der Liebe, in: *Forum katholische Theologie* 11 (1995), 161-181, 174.

[17] There is an ongoing debate on whether beauty as a transcendental is a separate concept, or whether it belongs to the realm of the good. The latter position is defended by J. Aertsen, Beauty: A forgotten transcendental?, in: Id., *Medieval philosophy and the transcendentals*, 335-359, whilst the first position is advocated by G. Pöltner, *Schönheit. Eine Untersuchung zum Ursprung des Denkens bei Thomas von Aquin*, Wien, etc. 1978, esp. 135-170. Pöltner regards Thomas's concept of beauty as one that unifies all other transcendental concepts. As such, it would unexpectedly have the same function in Thomas's philosophy as it has in Kant's thought, in which beauty unifies pure and practical reason.

b. The transcendental and triune structure of the trilogy

If there is one thing that Balthasar will be remembered for as a theologian, it will be for his restructuring of systematic theology on the basis of the three transcendentals: beauty, goodness and truth. He attempted not to approach the concept of being abstractly, but according to its concrete properties. The various theological doctrines, like the doctrine of God, the doctrine of creation, the doctrine of atonement, Christology or eschatology, are not divided between Balthasar's theo-aesthetics, theodramatics and theologic. Rather, his transcendental arrangement of theology offers a triune view of the history of metaphysics and theology. As such, it shows that theological doctrine is rooted in the whole of reality, in which a creative and merciful God appears.

Balthasar provides the following justification for the order of the transcendental concepts, and with it, the structure of his trilogy: Human beings experience reality as beautiful, good and true. Being appears to them. The appearing form of being is experienced as *beauty* that enraptures them. This form does not just show itself, it also gives itself. Because being gives itself, it is experienced as *good*. In its beauty and goodness, being expresses itself, reveals itself: Being is *true* (MW 94).

Balthasar's favourite metaphor for this triune relationship with the world is that of the relationship between a mother and child. A young child will smile when he sees its mother's face. It has a first visible experience of its unity in the love with its mother. Next, it will experience trust, knowing that this unity of love is good, and therefore, according to Balthasar, it will experience that the whole of reality is good. This trust needs to be, and will be confirmed as truth in the end (GinL 49-50). The consequence of this whole process is joy (MW 92). This optimistic and maybe naïve image Balthasar often refers to in his work not only shows the order of the transcendentals but also their interwovenness and their being surrounded by the two aspects of beauty: perception and rapture.[18] However, it does not account for experiences of evil and suffering. Therefore, a theological metaphysics based on the three transcendentals might not be able to answer questions of evil. If all being is beautiful, good and true, how can ugliness, evil and falsehood be explained? Balthasar dealt with these questions by applying the doctrine of the cross and of atonement to them, as I will show later.

---

[18] The next chapter will deal with Balthasar's theological aesthetics and with the concept of the beautiful in particular.

In retrospect, Balthasar describes his own trilogy in *Epilog* as 'Dombau' (building a cathedral), dividing it into another triune structure, mirroring a classic fundamental theological scheme: 'Vorhalle' (atrium), 'Schwelle' (threshold) and 'Dom' (cathedral), which refer respectively to a Christian comparative theory of religion, a theological metaphysics and Christology. At the heart of this, the choice of the medieval doctrine of the transcendentals is accounted for (Epilog 35-66). According to Balthasar, every being in the world is real without containing a part of reality that other beings do not contain. Being real means to participate in the whole of reality in itself. Although Balthasar regards a being in the world as a fragment, it does not exist as such in isolation but instead by means of and participating in the whole of reality.[19] The *desideratum* of Balthasar's theology is seeing the totality in the fragments and being aware of the fact that only the historical, fragmented world is available to human beings, but at the same time not wanting to stick with the meaninglessness of the fragment. "Thus, we are asking for ourselves, and in doing so, we intend to be more than just a question" (GiF 13-14). To be able to realise itself, being must have had the possibility of realisation from something other than itself. This idea of causality lies at the foundation of the doctrine of the transcendentals.[20]

Eugen Biser describes Balthasar's trilogy with a somewhat more modest metaphor: 'triptych'.[21] According to Biser, the significance and the influence of Balthasar's monumental work depends upon the answer to the question of which metaphor suits his work best. If the trilogy is regarded as 'building a cathedral', it will have to maintain itself as a hermetical system, in which all diverging intuitions and new theological designs and interpretations are brought together in one overwhelmingly beautiful but closed metaphysical space, isolated from the anti-metaphysical world that surrounds it. If, on the other hand, the trilogy is seen as a triptych, it can, as Balthasar himself writes, return the various 'works of art' of the reflective and imaginative intellect to theology, to demonstrate the Christian mystery of salvation as purpose and norm at the heart of all searching for meaning and truth (TL II 178).

---

[19] Balthasar here refers to the thomist statement: "Esse significat aliquid completum et simplex, sed non subsistens", St Thomae Aquinatis, *Quaestiones disputatae de potentia*, 1,1.
[20] Cf. J. Disse, *Metaphysik der Singularität. Eine Hinführung am Leitfaden der Philosophie Hans Urs von Balthasars*, Wien 1996.
[21] E. Biser, Dombau oder Triptychon? Zum Abschluss der Trilogie Hans Urs von Balthasars, in: *Theologische Revue* 84 (1988), 177-184.

The first cluster of questions for this present research is that for the special, primary place of the transcendental concept of 'beauty' within the whole of this trilogy. Is this beauty the primary access to the objective content of our concrete experiences of reality? And how can Balthasar claim that this beauty is a property of all being? Is it not paradoxical to state that being and beauty are convertible terms? After all, is reality not experienced as both beautiful and ugly? These questions will be answered in the next chapter. The second cluster of critical questions, important for this research into the meaning of the transcendental concept of beauty in Balthasar's theology, is whether he actually succeeds in guaranteeing the confirmation of objective reality on the basis of the three transcendentals. Is this confirmation a mere formal-philosophical one, and is it able to express concrete experiences of reality in such a way that it can do justice to the historical and individual character of each separate experience? How could such a formal philosophical doctrine be foundational or even explanatory within a theological framework?

c. The theological doctrine of the transcendentals

A closer look at Balthasar's theological interpretation of the transcendental properties of being is needed. He is convinced that a theological interpretation is not a special articulation of a universal philosophical structure, but possesses its own theological content. This theological point of departure should be regarded as the foundation of philosophical thought, instead of the other way around. The aesthetic concept of glory, for example, is a divine property that God does not share with creation and which is therefore not immediately available to philosophy.[22] According to Balthasar, this theological content of 'beauty' is the foundation of the philosophical concept of 'beauty', however. To evaluate Balthasar's idea of the relation between philosophy and theology, I will expound the correspondence of the transcendental concepts and the divine properties, and the relation between the doctrine of the transcendentals and the doctrine of the Trinity in particular.

---

[22] Cf. N.D. O'Donoghue, Do we get beyond Plato? A critical appreciation of the theological aesthetics, in: B. McGregor, o.p., Th. Norris [eds], *The beauty of Christ*, 253-266, 257 n. 1.

The triangular structure of theology
How does Balthasar explain the transcendental design of his trilogy theologically? According to him, a theological aesthetics investigates the perception of the form of revelation. God appears in the world. He appears to Abraham, Moses, Isaiah and finally in Jesus Christ. Theological aesthetics therefore has to deal with the following questions: How can theophany be recognized among and distinguished from all other appearances in the world? What is characteristic of the appearance of the form of revelation in the world? How does this uniqueness relate to the various appearances of other gods? How do these theological questions distinguish themselves from philosophical and religious-historical questions? According to Balthasar, the incomparability of Christian theology with other attempts to view the glory of God in the world lies in the articulation of the life, the crucifixion and the resurrection of Christ. This is why the work of theological aesthetics should be continued in a theological dramatics. This field will have to deal with questions like "What is the relation between divine and human freedom?" and "Does the freedom of human beings actually confront them with God, or does it distance them even further from God?" Finally, Balthasar's theological logic answers the question of how God presents Himself to man. The main question here is: How can an infinite Word express itself in a finite word without losing its infinite meaning and import? (MW 94-95)

From this justification of the organisation of his systematic theology, based on the three transcendental properties, it appears that the transcendental structure is founded theologically, by the internal logic of subsequent theological questions. So far, research into Balthasar's theology has never studied this fundamental unity of the doctrine of the transcendentals and theology in detail. It may have become clear by now that the philosophical doctrine of the transcendentals in Balthasar's theology neither constitutes a universal structure of Christian faith, nor its unique content. However, the transcendental properties of being are the basic concepts of a theology that in itself could not be founded by anything but divine revelation. Therefore, it is *revelatione sola*, revelation alone that is the foundation of these basic concepts.

A trinitarian interpretation of the transcendentals
A description of Balthasar's application of the doctrine of the transcendentals to the doctrine of the Trinity will illustrate how, according to him, these basic concepts are founded on divine revelation. Trying to illuminate the relationship of divine and worldly being, and with it that

of theology and philosophical metaphysics as well, Balthasar wonders how the absolute being of God could possibly mirror itself in the world. According to him, absolute being does not give itself in any other way than in a triune way, so the question should be whether an image of the Trinity can be found in created being (TL II 159). Since the transcendental properties of being are supracategorical, they must be, Balthasar argues, predicable to both divine and worldly being. The transcendental triad of unity, truth and goodness might be easily applicable to the divine *hypostases*.

Unity signifies the countability of being, truth its knowability, and goodness its communicability. Being gets its unity insofar as it is indivisible from itself. It gets its truth insofar as it is indivisible from its form (species), and its goodness insofar as it is indivisible from its works. Constructing his own doctrine of appropriation, Balthasar applies the transcendentals to the Trinity, and calls the Father 'unity', the origin of the divine persons. Consequently, the Son is the truth and the Spirit is the good, descending from both unity and truth, the Father and the Son. Human thought reversely reconstructs this indivisible order of the transcendental properties appropriatiated to the persons in the Trinity. Truth presupposes unity, because it cannot be separated from its form in the world. Goodness presupposes truth and unity, because the form of being needs to be communicated so it can be recognised as being true. Therefore, theological metaphysics is able to relate the transcendentals to the persons in the Trinity, signifying them as origin (*Ursprung*), archetype (*Urbild*) and *telos* (*Ziel*). Theology and philosophy have the question for the archetype in common, because both theology and philosophy are seeking for the truth of being in the world (TL II 161).[23]

However, according to Balthasar, the transcendentals cannot simply be attributed to the divine essence as such. For example, 'image', being a description of all being, is at the same time the proper name for the Son. 'Freedom' is the ground of all created being, but at the same time, it is the proper name for the Spirit.[24] So, to avoid a complete identification of the transcendental concepts with the divine persons, he warns against a direct appropriation of certain properties of being to the divine persons

---

[23] Note that Balthasar chooses not to use 'the beautiful' here. Goodness however, signifies communicability in the world, which is an aspect of the beautiful as well. This gives an insight into Balthasar's theological style that, by using thomist metaphysics, presumes a certain logical rigidity, yet is at times terminologically arbitrary as well.

[24] Balthasar actually uses the Latin word '*liberalitas*', which means both 'will' and 'gift'.

in the Trinity. The divine persons are not beings in the world. Therefore, the transcendental properties do not concern them in the same way. For example, an abundance of love is a quality of the Spirit, which realises itself in creation. If it is true, Balthasar argues, that the innerworldly properties of being originate from the intratrinitarian processes, it must also be true that these properties get their fullness only when being is illuminated by its own being-spirit and the presupposition of perfect knowledge by perfect love.[25] This whole process is given by the kenotic love of the Father to the Son (TL II 162), however.[26] The transcendental properties of being are not simply grounded in divine essence, but anchored in the hypostatical process within the Trinity.

Recapitulating, it can be said that Balthasar's use of the transcendental properties of being is an amendment of the medieval doctrine of the transcendentals. He chooses not to follow the Copernican turn of Kantian epistemology in his application of the doctrine of the transcendentals to theology. Instead, he revives the medieval doctrine with some alterations, and subsequently organises his systematic theology around the transcendentals. In this organisation, 'beauty' is the first and encompassing concept, as I will show in the next chapter. This primacy of the concept of beauty is the reason why Balthasar's theological aesthetics deals with topics that usually configure a fundamental theology (H I 9). Although he is borrowing the fundamental structure of his theology from a model based on medieval metaphysics, he does not apply the properties of being directly to theology. On the contrary, Balthasar's theology of the Trinity, for example, resists any foundation of theology by philosophical metaphysics. Instead, grounded in the hypostatical process of trinitarian love, Balthasar's amended doctrine of the transcendentals offers a trinitarian image of the dynamically revealed structure of reality.

---

[25] The preceding of knowledge by love is important for Balthasar to avoid either the Hegelian mistake, where the Father begets the Son to be known as God, or the Arian mistake, where the Father begets the Son, because He has perfect knowledge of Himself (TL II 163).

[26] Here, Balthasar uses Bonaventure's *Collationes in Hexaemeron* to describe the correspondence between the Trinity and the transcendentals, adding modern interpretations of the divine hypostases by Ferdinand Ulrich (borrowing the metaphor of the unity of poverty and richness in a child) and the modern mystic Sergei Bulgakov (borrowing the image of innertrinitarian kenosis). It shows how myriad the influences on Balthasar's thought are: medieval and modern, philosophical and mystic, aristotelian and neoplatonic.

4.4. Theological metaphysics II: analogy of being

As I have shown, the doctrine of the transcendentals approaches the world from the perspective of the transcendental concepts that concern the elementary structure of all reality. However, this doctrine does not account for either the differences in the world, or the difference between God and the world. Furthermore, Balthasar's foundation of metaphysics in the trinitarian kenotic love of the Father does not explain the relationship between the intratrinitarian differences and the differences in the world. God's being in three hypostases is not a contingency, contrary to that of the created world, which could have been infinitely different (TL II 165). So why is there a world, if God is all in all? This question lies at the heart of Balthasar's theological metaphysics and his doctrine of God. In other words, as put before, how can an infinite Word express itself in a finite word without losing its infinite meaning and import? (MW 94-95)

Balthasar's doctrine of the transcendentals concerned the trinitarian foundation of all being in the world. His doctrine of analogy, the doctrine of the *analogia entis*, deals with the problem of the relationship between God and the world, which he characterises as a middle ground lying somewhere between the two extremes of identity and difference. It was, according to him, presupposed and developed in Dante's cosmos as the analogy between earth and heaven, the former age and the new age, the world of the body and the world of the spirit, nature and grace, knowledge and faith, man and God (H II 465). It has to answer questions such as why God's love is present in the world, while worldly love should not too easily be identified with divine love. In a theological aesthetics the doctrine of analogy could relate the beauty in the world to divine glory, without running the risk of identifying the two. Beauty can be a trace to the divine but its glory should be regarded as infinitely different and greater.

In the next section, (a) which is unfortunately but necessarily rather technical, I will clarify the concept of analogy and the analogy of being in particular. As stated above, Balthasar's theology must be understood against the background of the rapidly and radically changing theology of the twentieth century, which will become apparent in this section. After the general introduction, I will sketch the influence of Erich Przywara's philosophical doctrine of the *analogia entis* on Balthasar's theology (b), and Balthasar's debate on analogy with Karl Barth (c). Finally, I will analyse his own theological interpretation of the doctrine of the analogy of being (d).

a. Analogy of being and imago Dei

Analogy and analogy of being
Analogy is the essential form of discourse in Catholic fundamental theology, because the relationships between God and the world, and God and human beings, are understood analogously.[27] So, what is analogy?[28] The Greek word ἀναλογία means proportion, and in classical logic and metaphysics it referred to the comparison between two proportions. Analogy is a kind of likeness, a type of relationship characterised by a proportion of equality and inequality. As such, it is a mean between equivocity and univocity. A univocal relationship is a matter of perfect likeness, while an equivocal relationship signifies sheer diversity.

Equivocity is an accident of language. The same word can have very different meanings. For example, the word 'arms' can mean both limbs, and weapons. Conversely, two words can have exactly the same meaning. For example, the words 'heaven' and 'sky' both refer to the firmament. However, there are words that refer to things that are neither completely different, nor exactly the same. The standard example, derived from Aristotle, is the word 'health', predicated to a person, skin and food. 'Health' is used analogously in these different cases. An analogy can be applied to different phenomena in a primary and secondary sense, but it is always grounded in various kinds of attribution to its primary object, in this case to the body. This is called an *analogy of proportion*. Such an analogy is an intermediary between univocal and equivocal terms, by participating in both the extremes of univocity and equivocity.[29] Aristotle wrote that "being is used in various senses, but always with reference to one principle".[30] This is what later was going to be called the *analogy of*

---

[27] R. Latourelle, R. Fisichella [eds], *Dictionary of fundamental theology*, New York 1995, 5.
[28] G. Sieverth, *Die Analogie des Seienden*, Einsiedeln 1965, 210-234; J.F. Anderson, *The bond of being. An essay on analogy and existence*, St Louis, etc. 1949; Id., *Reflections on the analogy of being*, The Hague 1967; F. Ulrich, *Homo Abyssus. Das Wagnis der Seinsfrage*, [Mit einer Einleitung Martin Bieler], Einsiedeln 1998²; R.W. Stammberger, *On analogy. An essay historical and systematic*, Frankfurt am Main, etc. 1995; R. McInerny, *Aquinas and analogy*, Washington 1996.
[29] J.F. Anderson, *The bond of being*, 30. Doing justice to the history and systematics of the doctrine of analogy would involve a completely different book than the present one. The subject is too technical and abstract to describe it fully within the scope of this research. For the development of the doctrine of analogy, i.e. for the differences between the positions of Aristotle, Thomas Aquinas, Duns Scotus and Cajetan, as for those between the analogy of inequality, attribution and proportionality, I gladly refer to the books of McInerny and Stammberger.
[30] Aristotle, *Metaphysics*, 1003 b 5-6.

attribution. There are analogies between different kinds of relations as well, in such a way that two objects or concepts are not proportionally related to each other, but by means of an intermediary relation (A:B::C:D). This is what Thomas Aquinas called the *analogy of (attributive) proportionality*.[31]

In a theological context, the concept of analogy is especially important for the understanding of the validity of divine names. All divine names are creaturely and therefore limited. Thus, the problem of analogy in theology is how to speak in a limited way about the Unlimited. Balthasar formulates the theological problem of analogy as if from the perspective of God: How can there be a world if God is already all in all? Varying on the analogy of proportionality, he wonders how the horizontal relations in the creaturely realm are analogous to the relations in God: "The divide between being and essence in worldly being as such also mirrors the mysteries of the inner life of eternal being itself, indeed, through the window that opens itself in this non-identity, we get insights into the immense richness of divine identity" (TL I 220).

The question is whether for Balthasar the concept of analogy is just a mathematical principle that predicates a formal relationship, which functions only as a language rule that corrects distinctions and identifications of meanings that are found too easily, or whether such a formal principle could be applied ontologically as well. In other words, does the analogy between concept and being only exist in the mind, or also in reality? To answer this question, it is important to know what kind of analogy the concept of being is. Usually, the doctrine of the analogy of being defines reality as being divided horizontally into the different realities of substances and accidents, and vertically into the different realities of God and creatures. Balthasar however, applies the doctrine of the analogy of being also to the different relations in God, and regards finite being as a structural representation (*Abbild*) of the Trinity.

---

[31] Cf. G. Siewerth, *Die Analogie des Seienden*, 32-33 ; F. Ulrich, *Homo Abyssus*, 226-227. Both these authors refer to St Thomae Aquinatis, *Questionis disputate de veritate*, q 2, a 11, q 23, a 7,9. Aside from Erich Przywara, Gustav Siewerth and Ferdinand Ulrich also influenced Balthasar's doctrine of analogy. They however followed the interpretation of Cajetan (1468-1538), who made a sharp distinction between the analogy of proportionality and the analogy of proportion. Nowadays, this is regarded as a misreading of Aquinas's texts. Cf. R. McInerny, *Aquinas and analogy*. In his *De nominum analogia*, Cajetan introduced the distinction between analogy of attribution and analogy of proportionality that cannot be found in Aquinas's writings or anywhere else, McInerny argues.

Real distinction as the theological foundation of the analogy of being
Why, according to Balthasar, is the analogy of being important for theology? How could such a philosophical doctrine be applied to theological concepts? One must not forget that Balthasar was taught this doctrine by Erich Przywara, who amended it in discussion with modern philosophers like Martin Heidegger. Balthasar subsequently interpreted the doctrine of analogy in his discussion with Karl Barth, saying "nothing, in a confessional conversation, is more important than the clarification of the form of thought" (KB 201). The analogy of being and Barth's analogy of faith are such forms. Before I take a closer look at these two contexts in which Balthasar developed his own doctrine of the analogy of being, something must be said about the theological starting point of this debate.[32]

Balthasar's doctrine of analogy is grounded in a theology of creation. Regarding the analogy of being proportionally at the same time implies that the being of beings depends on something other than itself. On the one hand, while "the whole of reality exists only in finite beings, the fragment does not exist by itself; it exists only by means of the totality of being" (Epilog 38).[33] This totality, on the other hand, is not substantial and therefore cannot realise itself without having received the possibility to realise itself in fragmented beings. "This paradox refers back to a Ground that is both the inclusion of all reality and has the subsistence required by essence for its design" (Epilog 39).

For Balthasar, the human mind mirrors the divine ground of all reality when it astounds itself about the fact that the totality of reality is both given to it in finite beings and at the same time disclosed by itself in the self-consciousness realisation of being by the human mind. Therefore, human beings can be regarded as image and likeness of God because of this givenness to them of finite reality on the one hand and the self-disclosure of the human mind as non-subsisting reality on the other. They are 'like God' insofar as the essence of reality can be the object of their reflection. They are 'image of God' because their being is given to them. However, God's subsistence does not limit them but determines their humanity and therefore their freedom.

---

[32] Cf. G. De Schrijver, *Le merveilleux accord de l'homme et de dieu. Etude de l'analogie de l'être chez Hans Urs von Balthasar*, Paris 1983.
[33] "Esse significat aliquid completum et simplex, sed non subsistens", St Thomae Aquinatis, *Quaestiones disputatae de potentia*, 1,1.
[34] J. Maréchal, *Le point de depart de la metaphysique I-V*, Bruxelles 1944-1949 (1922-1927).

Balthasar's use of the doctrine of the analogy of being concerns the relationship between divine and human being. Analogy, he argues, should not only be applied to the language that is used to describe that relationship, but also concerns the reality of man, constituted by nature and grace. This pair of concepts should not be considered as opposites, but seen in their proportional relation. By applying the doctrine of analogy to theology, Balthasar found himself in the debate between neothomism and modern philosophy, and extended that debate to the confessional conversation between Catholic thinkers and Protestant theologians like Karl Barth.

b. Analogy of being: the Catholic form of thought

The Jesuits Erich Przywara and Joseph Maréchal are seen as the two Catholic philosophers who have changed the neothomist philosophy that prevailed up to their time. Their criticism was mainly targeted at the extrincistical starting point of this philosophy. This extrincism entailed that human nature had a purpose in itself but had also been given a different divine purpose, thanks to divine grace. The danger of this extrincistical position is not just that grace would be regarded as accidental to human nature, but also that the relation between nature and grace principally had to remain unaccounted for. Maurice Blondel was the first theologian who criticised this 'two-storey' idea. His theory of immanence emphasised the continuity of nature and grace, and history and revelation. As a consequence, this type of theology had to presuppose the faculty of the human spirit to reach the divine. At the same time, it should not be possible for the intellect to grasp the divine completely, or to locate the divine in the intellect or in human nature.

Joseph Maréchal's epistemological foundation of knowledge of God
Joseph Maréchal tried to solve this problem by combining aristotelian-thomist metaphysics with the starting points of Kantian epistemology.[34] The reality of abstract concepts would be founded on the non-intellectual dynamics of the mind: the dynamics from the human mind towards the infinite. Knowing therefore must be a projective act, a grasping of concepts beyond oneself, towards the infinite. The justification of the relation between nature and grace is thus based on the dynamics of the human mind. Following Maréchal, Karl Rahner developed his transcendental theology, which has been of major significance to Catholic theology in the twentieth century. The (mystical) unity of nature and grace, and with this

of God and man, is placed in the individual mind. Man as a spiritual object is forever dynamically focused in God, who is the infinite transcendent horizon of being. Although not an object (*ungegenständlich*), God is forever present in human thought.[35] The unity of God and man is completed in Jesus Christ in a unique and fundamental way. The human mind can focus on this, and thus explicitly or anonymously relate to the unity that was once completed. This theology, based on the Kantian transcendental philosophy, appeals to universal, categorical concepts of being, which as such can never confirm being in its unique historicity.[36]

Erich Przywara's ontological foundation of knowledge of God
Erich Przywara formulated the other Catholic answer to the problem of nature and grace. His critique of Maréchal entailed that the absolute transcendence of God and his irresolvable self-revelation in Jesus Christ coincide too much with the dynamics of the human mind, and can therefore be made to fit human measures all too easily. As Schillebeeckx argued:

> Therefore, the basis of the reality of our knowledge of God is neither a so-called proportional-one, actual concept, nor the subjective dynamic of the mind that creates the concept of a projection of God. Rather, it is the objective dynamic of the content of being (i.e. the so-called 'transcendentals'), which is followed by the mind in an endorsing way in an intellectually inclined or projective act.[37]

This again poses the problem of the analogy of being: Is there an objective or ontological foundation of the subjective endorsement of the divine characteristics?

Przywara's doctrine of the analogy of being is an attempt to answer this question for a new objective foundation for neothomist metaphysics. How can the relation of God and the world be accounted for within the objective unity of reality? According to Przywara, this objective reality can be characterised by the bipolarity of unity and diversity of being. In its totality, reality relates to its Creator as creation. This bipolarity is formulated

---

[35] K. Rahner, *Hörer des Wortes. Zur Grundlegung einer Religionsphilosophie*, [neu bearbeitet von J.B. Metz], München 1963², 78.
[36] Cf. H. Verweyen, *Gottes letztes Wort. Grundriss der Fundamentaltheologie*, Düsseldorf 1991, 161-162; Read also the discussion between H. Verweyen and Th. Pröpper in: *Theologische Quartalschrift* 174 (1994), 272-303; V. Holzer, C.M., *Le Dieu trinité dans l'histoire: Le concept des raisons 'esthétique' et 'transcendantale' comme accès aux logiques christologiques de Hans Urs von Balthasar et de Karl Rahner*, [Dissertatio as Doctoratum in Facultate Theologiae Pontificiae Universitas Gregorianae], Rome 1994.
[37] E. Schillebeeckx, o.p., *Openbaring en theologie*, [Theologische peilingen deel I], Bilthoven 1964, 231.

as *analogia entis*: Finite reality is analogous in its being, i.e. both identical and different to the being of God. Identical insofar as there is unity of being and essence, *Dasein* and *Sosein*. Different, however, insofar as this identity is not a complete unity, i.e. not essential.[38] Finite reality is not a necessity as such, but it gets its positive content, which is the unity of being and essence, from God. This positive content can be shifted continually in the direction of the absolute transcendence of God. Przywara refers to the position of the Fourth Lateran Council (1215): "for between Creator and creature no similitude can be noted, however great it may be, without noting a greater dissimilitude" (*quia inter creatorem et creaturam non potest tanta similitudo notari quin inter eos maior sit dissimilitudo notanda*).[39] Between the Creator and the created world all identity should be thought of in the framework of an even greater non-identity. The analogous middle that is characterised by identity and difference is forever changing because every being tends towards an even bigger identity with being. At the same time this concept of analogy points to the everlasting and insurmountable difference between God and the world: Nothing in this world can be identified with God. This is where Augustine's maxim holds true: *Deus semper maior*.

The influence of Przywara's concept of analogy on Balthasar
To both Przywara and Balthasar analogy is the fundamental mode of thought, in which the relation between God and the world should be considered. However, they emphasise different aspects. In his philosophical doctrine of analogy Przywara continually stresses the incommensurability of God and the world.[40] Balthasar, on the other hand, wants to formulate the positive value of finitude as well. According to him, the formula of the Fourth Lateran Council should not be understood as a purely negative theology. Balthasar defines any possible relation between God and the world with regard to creation as one-directional from God to man. Therefore, every human movement towards God is constituted by divine creation. All relations man can possibly have with God have an actual corresponding measure in the relation God has with man. Hence, all human relations with God only get their meaning in the revelation of God

---

[38] E. Przywara, s.j., *Analogia entis. Metaphysik. Ur-Struktur und All-Rhythmus*, Einsiedeln 1962, 124-125.
[39] DS 806; E. Przywara, *Analogia entis*, 251-254.
[40] Cf. the article 'H. U. von Balthasar, E. Przywara', in: H.J. Schulz [Hrsg.], *Tendenzen der Theologie im zwanzigsten Jarhhundert*, Stuttgart 1966, 354-359, 358.

to man (Analogie I 176). Because of the primacy of divine revelation, reality maintains its own positive content that is in no way inferior to that revelation.[41] On the contrary, revelation in beauty, goodness and truth demonstrates that it takes place in the natural environment of the world. Thus, grace perfects the created world because it actualises its potential to receive divine revelation, which will be fulfilled in redemption.

Balthasar's theological reservations towards his philosophical teacher, Przywara, were motivated by his dialogue with Karl Barth who criticised the doctrine of the analogy of being as the invention of the anti-Christ and, with it, dismissed the whole of Catholic theology. That severe criticism was directly pointed at the philosophy of Przywara which prompted Balthasar to look for ways of combining the analogy of being with Barth's alternative, the analogy of faith (*analogia fidei*). It would be safe to say that Balthasar never really moved away from the philosophical foundations of the analogy of being. However, on some rare occasions he did distance himself somewhat from his Jesuit teacher Przywara. "Przywara's centre is accordingly not the immanence of the world and man but rather the ungraspable point of encounter with the living God (...) Przywara has christened this point the analogy of being, admittedly a term that does not have much life to it but which still must be the term of choice."[42] The problem with Przywara's doctrine of analogy was its systematisation of the pathos of faith. According to Balthasar, in Przywara's scholastic treatment of the subject it became the opposite of what it should refer to, the human relationship with a living God: "As a matter of content this means the interpenetration of an unconditioned will to make everything transparent to its core, almost with a rationalistic abhorrence of all philosophies of experience that dispense with structure and substance."[43] Balthasar even blames Przywara for radicalising his own position, thereby misunderstanding Protestant theology as a theopanistic dialectic. However, Balthasar's criticisms of his philosophical teacher are very much intertwined with his account of Barth's theology and his emphasis that Przywara's concept of analogy is not necessarily *the* core Catholic concept. It is important to understand how he defended the analogy of being against Barth's criticisms, while nevertheless acknowledging his analysis.

---

[41] Cf. K. Mongrain, *The systematic thought of Hans Urs von Balthasar*, 53-57.
[42] H.U. von Balthasar in the foreword of: L. Zimmy, *Erich Przywara. Sein Schriftum, 1912-1962*, Einsiedeln 1963, 5-6.
[43] Ibid., 7-8.

c. Analogy of being within analogy of faith: in dialogue with Karl Barth

In his highly praised book on the theology of Karl Barth, acclaimed not least by Barth himself, Balthasar explores the possibility of an ecumenical dialogue based on the analysis of Catholic and Protestant forms of thought (*Denkformen*).[44] The ostensibly contradictory doctrines of analogy, analogy of being and analogy of faith, are the focus of Balthasar's exposure of Barth's theology. The thesis of his book is that these "formulas are not competing against each other—*analogia fidei* against *analogia entis*—but that two modes of understanding the sole revelation of God in Christ are measuring one another. (...) The way in which Karl Barth understands the revelation of God in creation from Christ as *analogia fidei*, contains the *analogia entis*; the way, in which the Catholic authors mentioned (Maurice Blondel, Joseph Maréchal, Erich Przywara)[45] understand the divine world plan christocentrically, only allows the *analogia entis* to gain its concreteness within the encompassing *analogia fidei* (in its broadest sense)" (KB 390). However, Balthasar does acknowledge Barth's criticism and distinguishes four of his objections against the analogy of being.

First, the concept of being is not sufficient for expressing the most decisive aspect of the relationship between God and creatures. Instead, it obscures the fact of the covenant as an event of becoming, as if it is a foundation always at our disposal rather than a moment of mystery. However, on this foundational level of being there is no similarity between God and creature. Second, the concept of being is nothing more than a concept and as such a structural scheme that improperly and irreverently goes against the sovereignty with which God decides to disclose His nature. Third, because the concept of being is a semantic and therefore relative and finite concept, any attempt to grasp the divine Absolute with it would be a grave mistake. According to Barth, it could be nothing but a projection of the creature in the divine, tending towards a creaturely self-deification. Fourth, as projection, the concept of being could become a dangerous tool for disobedience in the hands of the sinner (KB 175-176).

---

[44] Cf. W. Pannenberg, Zur Bedeutung des Analogiegedankens bei Karl Barth. Eine Auseinandersetzung mit Hans Urs von Balthasar, in: *Theologische Literaturzeitung* 78 (1953), 18-23; E. Oakes, *Pattern of redemption*, 45-71; J. Thompson, Barth and Balthasar. An ecumenical dialogue, in: B. McGregor, o.p., Th. Norris, *The beauty of Christ*, 171-192; J.B. Quash, Von Balthasar and the dialogue with Karl Barth, in: *New Blackfriars* 79 (1998), 45-55; R. Chia, *Revelation and theology*.

[45] The names of the authors are my addition.

Barth wants to avoid these dangers by making a case for the analogy of faith against the analogy of being. For him, all human knowledge of God should be considered as being preceded by the descending revelation of God in creation. However, according to him, this revelation of God in nature is not an intrinsic quality of nature itself. "God is never and nowhere an a priori of nature situated in nature (in being and in knowledge)" (KB 155). Yet he still thinks it possible to discover an analogy between God and man, but only within the act of faith, the surrendering worship of the divine power that draws human nature into the act of revelation in history. This way of receiving knowledge of the divine can only happen through Christ, in whom God has revealed Himself unequivocally (KB 176-177). Balthasar appreciates Barth's emphasis on a christocentric, historical and creational interpretation of analogy. However, precisely because of these three characteristics of human knowledge of God, he sees no radical contradiction between the analogy of faith and the analogy of being (KB 393). The analogy of faith encompasses the analogy of being, insofar as the true essence of being is revealed in Jesus Christ. According to this interpretation of being, which is also accepted by Balthasar, one can only have knowledge of God through the revelatory act in Christ.

4.5. Theology of the Trinity: katalogia trinitatis

Balthasar and others have described his *Denkform* using the word 'analogy' in combination with another concept.[46] In the second part of *Theologik* Balthasar nevertheless states that "theology, in which the logic of God finds its specific form of creaturely logic, can be nothing but trinitarian" (TL II 33). His conviction that the intratrinitarian movements are the foundation of all the other differences in the world and even the difference between God and creation (TD III 308) might be the most indigestible part of his theology for some.[47] It is obvious that, although he sustains Przywara's opting for the formula of the Fourth Lateran Council, he gives it a catalogical foundation to be able to reconcile the analogy of being with the analogy of faith. The catalogical or descending movement from God into the world through Christ is a necessary condition for every

---

[46] For example '*analogia caritatis*', '*analogia proportionis et operationis*', '*analogia adorationis et orationis*', '*analogia trinitatis*', '*analogia exinanitionis*'.
[47] Cf. A.F. Franks, Trinitarian analogia entis in Hans Urs von Balthasar, in: *The thomist* 62 (1998), 533-559, 534.

analogical statement.[48] Yet that does not solve the problem of analogy for him, because it still does not account for the possibility of an adequate expression of the incarnation of the divine triune logic in the world (TL II 155). However, there must be an analogy or image of the Trinity in the world for the revelation to be heard or seen. How else could this be the case if the world itself were not formed by the catalogical trinitarian expression in the world? Therefore, the most appropriate description of Balthasar's theological form of thought, however necessarily analogical by nature, is *katalogia trinitatis*: a condescending movement in-formed by the incarnation.[49]

a. Trinitarian presuppositions of human logic

In his third part of the trilogy, *Theologik*, Balthasar tries to find the answer to the question of how the divine truth can represent itself within the structures of created truth and (in diverse forms) come to expression there (TL I vii).[50] The faithful openness of the world to God's revelation means that it can receive the divine self-revelation in Christ. There is nothing in the world though, he argues, from which this revelation in Christ can be thought. Even in Christ, in whom God shows his similarity to humanity, He still reveals Himself as the Wholly Other. For Balthasar, Christ the mediator, unlike in the theology of Karl Rahner, is not included in every transcendental experience. On the contrary, the similarity of God and man is revealed through the free act of divine revelation.

Yet knowledge of this revelatory act is possible and includes faith: "the entirety of Jesus's being human becomes a self-utterance and self-giving of God, so unique—both in speaking (...) and in deliberate silence, in action as in passion—that from his highness (the appearing glory) and perfect servanthood (...) the truth of his whole being can be read, with a certainty that does not exclude faith, but includes it" (Epilog 70).

---

[48] Cf. W. Treitler, True foundations of authentic theology, in: D. Schindler [ed.], *Hans Urs von Balthasar*, 169-182.

[49] The word 'condescending' in English means 'patronising' or 'superior'. However, here it should be read as *con-descensio*, the descending of human beings with the incarnate Son.

[50] Cf. U.J. Plaga, *"Ich bin die Wahrheit". Die theo-logische Dimension der Christologie Hans Urs von Balthasars*, Hamburg 1997, 253-258; W. Klaghofer-Treitler, *Karfreitag. Auseinandersetzungen mit Hans Urs von Balthasars Theologik*, [Salzburger Theologische Studien; Bd. 4], Innsbruck, etc. 1997; A. Nichols, o.p., *Say it is pentecost. A guide through Balthasar's logic*, Edinburgh 2001.

According to Balthasar, the Son is the truth as the expression of the Father and is explained as such by the Spirit. As the Son is the full expression of these relations in God, the humanity in which he expresses this cannot be anything else than the image and likeness of the triune God. After all, he would not be the perfect image and likeness of God if he were not simultaneously the full image of the intratrinitarian movements. This is why Balthasar argues that there has to be an image of the Trinity in the world, in which the self-revealing *Logos* can express itself.

God revealed Himself in the world in Jesus Christ by his Spirit. In Paul's first letter to the Corinthians, it reads: "The Spirit searches all things, even the deep things of God. For who among us knows the thoughts of another, except the person's own spirit within him? Similarly, no one knows the thoughts of God, except the Spirit of God" (1 Cor 2:10-11). This is the reason why, according to Balthasar, it is possible to have certain knowledge of the Father, Son and Spirit as divine Persons, but only through the figure and nature of Jesus Christ. As it says in the gospel of John: "he is the way, and no one comes to God, the Father, except through him" (Jn 14:6). Therefore, it is only because of the economic Trinity that one can have knowledge of the immanent Trinity and are able to make statements about it. However, he maintains, ensuring that the substantial unity of God is protected, that God does not need the economy for his own self-realisation, but is eternally perfect in Himself. The triune life in three hypostases is "not a contingency, but the highest expression of the infinite fullness of the divine being" (TL II 165).

It may have become clear that, although the immanent trinity founds Balthasar's theological form of thought catalogically, his true concern is the possibility of analogical statements about the reality of God. In the second part of *Theologik*, his language shows a growing awareness of the semantics of the idea of analogy, rather than the importance of its ontological conformation of divine reality. This is best illustrated by his reference to the 'grammar' Jesus uses to explain who he is, i.e. the parable. Jesus assumes that his listeners possess a religious and moral comprehension. He addresses people, because they are created in God's image. Therefore, in some sense human beings have been prepared to understand the divine logic. Nevertheless, they cannot understand this divine logic without the clarification that has been given with Jesus's life. It not only makes the dialogue in the world but also the dialogue between God and man possible. The Spirit thus completes nature not just from above but also from below and from within. For Balthasar, Christian 'theory', therefore, is the understanding of the 'praxis' of God in the life of

Jesus Christ, which is implied in the parable. As such, the *analogia lingua* is the same as *analogia entis*, because the divine logic is, after all, completed in the life of Christ. Therefore, according to Balthasar, the structure of the human 'grammar', i.e. human nature, has its own internal condescending trinitarian structure.

b. Kenotic ontology

The key word to understand Balthasar's complex foundation of human knowledge of God is 'kenosis'.[51] Balthasar distinguishes three forms of kenosis of which the first, the intratrinitarian is primary.[52] If the incarnation is the foundation of all analogies in the world, there already has to be freedom in God and therefore a difference and a separation within the Trinity (H III,2,2 197). This difference within God, however, is at the same time absolute unity. This paradoxical unity is the primal image of the non-identity, and yet inseparability of being and essence. The cohesion between unity and difference in being is an analogical representation of that which is in God. In God there is no such thing as a static being, but rather an act, and as such a precondition of all 'becoming' in the world.[53]

Balthasar also poses the question why the absolute being of God reflects itself in the world in no other way than in the form of the Trinity. The three transcendentals 'unity', 'truth' and 'goodness' could be related to the three divine *hypostases*: 'unity' to the Father, who is the source of the persons, 'truth' to the Son, who comes from the Father as the Word, 'goodness' to the Holy Spirit that comes from both as love and a gift (H III,2,2 363). Nevertheless, some prudence is called for when

---

[51] Cf. W. Treitler, True foundations of authentic theology, 171-173; O. Davies, *A theology of compassion. Metaphysics of difference and the renewal of tradition*, London 2001, 220-221.

[52] Cf. G. De Schrijver, Hans Urs von Balthasars Christologie in der Theodramatik. Trinitarische Engführung als Methode, in: *Bijdragen. Tijdschrift voor filosofie en theologie* 59 (1998), 141-153, 142-143; G. Ward, Kenosis: Death, discourse and resurrection, in: L. Gardner, et al., *Balthasar at the end of modernity*, Edinburgh 1999, 15-68. Balthasar is not consistent in his treatment of the topic of 'kenosis'. In *Theodramatik*, Balthasar distinguishes between the intratrinitary kenoses, and three 'economic' kenoses: creation, incarnation and atonement. In *Theologik*, the latter is part of the second one. In *Theologie der drei Tage* and the final essay of *Herrlichkeit* III,1, he also distinguishes a kenosis of the human subject. See also chapter eight of this book.

[53] Cf. G. O'Hanlon, *The immutability of God in the theology of Hans Urs von Balthasar*, Cambridge 1990.

the transcendentals are appropriated to the three divine persons.[54] Resisting a transcendental theory of appropriation, Balthasar thinks that worldly categories should not simply be applied to the divine reality. Yet, the transcendentals have to be embedded in the hypostatic process. The essence of this process is love, which expresses itself in the intratrinitary kenosis, and which is the one, the true and the good in all persons of the Trinity (TL II 163).

The second kenosis is creation. As previously said, the fact that God lives in three *hypostases* has nothing to do with contingency, but is rather the expression of the fullness of divine being, while worldly being is limited by its essence. On the one hand, this means that God is absolute and sovereign and that the world is not necessary for His Being. This seems to make the chasm between God and man even more unbridgeable. On the other hand, the revelation of the Trinity does bridge this chasm in a certain manner. If there is such a thing as difference and separation in the divine identity, which is both image of the Father and primal image of all things created, if furthermore it encompasses the Spirit that is the love between the divine persons, then the fact that the creation differs from God is defined in a positive relation to God. However, according to Balthasar, this relation will become a negative one when human freedom appeals to an abstract idea of autonomy instead of owing itself to God's primal kenosis within the creational one. This kind of opposition against the free act of divine love to give human beings their freedom in the world is the very essence of sin (TD III, 306).[55]

The third kenosis Balthasar distinguishes is the incarnation. The culminating event of this last kenosis is the death of Christ on the Cross (H III,2,2 198). The final confrontation between God and man takes place when the incarnate Son gives himself away on the Cross, the decisive moment between God's love and human sin. According to Balthasar, here again all three trinitarian persons are involved. "Although kenosis thus becomes—as disclosure of the God-form—the distinguishing act of the Son's love, who allows his createdness (and with it his dependence) by the Father to flow into the expression of creaturely obedience, the whole of the Trinity nevertheless remains involved: the Father as the One Who sends the Son and forsakes him at the Cross and the Spirit as the One

---

[54] Karl Wallner interprets the Trinity as a structural principle of Balthasar's trilogy based on the three transcendentals: K.J. Wallner, OCist, Ein trinitarisches Strukturprinzip in der Trilogie Hans Urs von Balthasars?, in: *Theologie und Philosophie* 71 (1996), 532-546.

[55] Cf. W. Treitler, True foundations of authentic theology, 172.

Who only unites both in the expression of the separation" (H III,2,2 198). Note here that Balthasar speaks of a kenosis that stems from the Father, the Son and the Spirit. He awards the Spirit a directing role in the incarnation, presenting the will of the Father for the Son to follow, while the Son obeys the Father in the Spirit. This could be misleading when one thinks that Jesus is merely subordinate to the Spirit, for the Spirit is indeed also his own Spirit of love for the Father. Therefore, the Spirit is the Spirit of Jesus and yet the mediator of a will that comes to Jesus from without (PI 224).

For Balthasar, it is the incarnated Son who is determined by the Spirit, who serves as the mediator of the Father's will. Christ placed himself under the will of the Father in the primal intratrinitarian kenosis and allows the Spirit, made available by the Father in the second kenosis, to have power over him as a 'rule' of the Father's will. He does this in order to permit the Spirit resting upon him in all fullness to stream out from himself at the end of his mission in death and resurrection, which forms the third kenosis.[56] It is only in this way, through Christ, that the Spirit can do its inspirational work in the world, enabling the human mind to receive the truth of God (TL III 19-20).

In this chapter, I have introduced Balthasar's theological hermeneutics and metaphysics, and his doctrine of the Trinity. It could hardly have been an overview of his overwhelmingly rich and complex theology though, because, for example, it does not take into account his biblical or dramatic theology, nor his writings on the church and the practice of Christian life. It does, however, offer a synopsis of the foundations of his theology. The treated topics are usually part of a fundamental theology. The key concepts that I have discussed, the doctrine of the transcendentals and the doctrine of analogy, serve as a basis for the understanding of the interwovenness of form and content in Balthasar's theology.

Fundamental theology and dogmatic or doctrinal theology are intertwined in Balthasar's theology. The reciprocity of these two theological disciplines is, as might have become clear, not a formal issue for him but lies at the heart of the content of his theology. It was Balthasar's great concern to consider the possibilities and presuppositions of theological knowledge. The idea of analogy locates these possibilities in human nature and language but only because nature and language are founded by divine creation and the incarnation. His interpretation of the analogy

---

[56] Cf. E. Oakes, *Pattern of redemption*, 290.

of being, therefore, resists any theology 'from below' or 'from above', not because these movements are in some way complementary but because the incarnation enables us to make an analogous and condescending movement towards God through Christ.[57]

For this present research into aesthetics as a way of doing fundamental theology it is essential to explore Balthasar's view of the world and human nature in particular. Aesthetics is the investigation into how human beings perceive the world and the various ways they respond to it. As shown in this chapter, Balthasar characterises the world with the a real distinction between essence and existence, a reality in fragments dependent on its Creator for its realisation. Human beings are drawn into this divine self-giving process in order to respond freely to it.

For Balthasar, the task of theology is to demonstrate the possibilities of faith, not least by means of analogical statements concerning the Trinity, creation and the incarnation. These analogies are inspired and informed by the three kenotic movements I have described in this chapter. These dynamic catalogical processes clearly structure Balthasar's theology. However, they also intensify questions concerning the way human beings are touched by the divine kenoses, the possibility of receiving and perceiving divine revelation. These questions bring us closer to the content of Balthasar's theological aesthetics.

---

[57] Cf. F. LeRon Shults, *The postfoundationalist task of theology. Wolfhart Pannenberg and the new theological rationality*, [Foreword by Wolfhart Pannenberg], Grand Rapids 1999, 165-177.

5. THEOLOGICAL AESTHETICS

> It [music] is an expression of the divine. Every work of art is it as analogate: it is possible to analogically sensualise in matter properties of the divine that we grasp mentally. The truth, a thought, becomes beauty in matter. That is why beauty is just an analogical expression of truth, and both are identical insofar as they signify the divine (EdmI 42).

At the age of twenty, Balthasar wrote this in his essay, 'The development of the musical idea'. As the quotation above shows, he was interested in the relationship between the arts and the divine from the start. Some of the key ideas of his later theology are already present here, like the idea of analogy and the convertibility of beauty and truth. It is a remarkable fact that in a time of theological transition, Balthasar's ideas stayed consistent. While twentieth century Roman Catholic theology made a shift away from neothomism and its rigid attempt to create a systematic and all-encompassing *philosophia perennis*, Balthasar developed from the very beginning of his writing life a theology that was deeply rooted in the theological tradition of early Christianity. Instead of having to transform his theological method from a deadlocked neoscholasticism into a modern phenomenology like so many other theologians decades later, he established a theology that found its sources in patristics and medieval mysticism on the one hand, and in art and literature on the other. It remains to be seen, however, whether these sources also imply the application of either a pre-modern or a poetic theological method. What is clear though, is that Balthasar's interest in theology was motivated by art, especially music, and aesthetics from the start.[1] The key concepts of his theology, mentioned in the previous chapter, all serve this inspiration.[2]

In this chapter, Balthasar's theological enquiries into the relations between revelation and the history of man, as well as his amendments of the doctrines of the transcendentals and the analogy of being, will be approached from the aesthetic interest that motivated them. I will

---

[1] Cf. P. Henrici s.j., Hans Urs von Balthasar. A sketch of his life, in: D.L. Schindler [ed.], *Hans Urs von Balthasar. His life and work,* San Francisco 1991, 7-44, 33.
[2] Cf. A.M. Haas, Hans Urs von Balthasar's "Apocalypse of the German soul". At the intersection of German literature, philosophy, and theology, in: D.L. Schindler [ed.], *Hans Urs von Balthasar,* 45-58, 49.

introduce Balthasar's theological aesthetics in four parts.[3] First, by clarifying his motives for developing an aesthetics and his proposal to establish the aesthetic as a theological starting point (5.1). After that, I will present a general overview of his seven-volume work on theological aesthetics, *Herrlichkeit*, by describing its structural arrangement and its position within his *magnum opus*, the theological trilogy. He incorporated so many authors and ideas in roughly four thousand pages that it is worthwhile to map this major achievement (5.2). Then, I will explain why his theological aesthetics develops a fundamental theology at the heart of dogmatics (5.3). All this will culminate in a reconstruction of Balthasar's theological interpretations of two main aesthetic concepts that play an important role throughout his work, 'form' and 'beauty' (5.4).

5.1. Towards a theology of beauty

In 1947, Balthasar motivated his metaphysical programme in Truth (*Wahrheit*) with the desire to reconstruct a theological unity of the theoretical, the ethical and the aesthetical (TL I vii-xi).[4] The book is divided into four parts: a. Truth as nature; b. Truth as freedom; c. Truth as mystery; and d. Truth as participation. The aesthetic concepts 'image' and 'beauty' play an important role in the third part on mystery. He defines the image as the appearance of being, thereby opening the possibility for human beings to enter into dialogue with God, the creator of all things. Human perception of this configuration of being and appearance in the image offers the awareness of both the perspectivity and historicity of truth and the infinite possibility that truth is, by appearing in an infinite number of ever-changing and ever-new images (MW 21). Beauty, then,

---

[3] Other introductions are: J.A. Kay, *Theological aesthetics. The role of aesthetics in the theological method of Hans Urs von Balthasar*, Frankfurt am Main 1975; M. Lochbrunner, *Analogia caritatis. Darstellung und Deutung der Theologie Hans Urs von Balthasars*, Freiburg im Breisgau 1981, 147-200; N. O'Donaghue, A theology of beauty, in: J. Riches [ed.], *The analogy of beauty. The theology of Hans Urs von Balthasar*, Edinburgh 1986, 1-11; L. Roberts, *The theological aesthetics of Hans Urs von Balthasar*, Washington 1987; L. Dupré, The glory of the Lord. Hans Urs von Balthasar's theological aesthetic, in: D.L. Schindler [ed.], *Hans Urs von Balthasar*, 183-206; B. Leahy, Theological aesthetics, in: B. McGregor, o.p., Th. Norris, *The beauty of Christ. An introduction to the theology of Hans Urs von Balthasar*, Edinburgh 1994; F.A. Murphy, *Christ, the form of beauty. A study in theology and literature*, Edinburgh 1995, 131-194; A. Nichols, o.p., *The Word has been abroad. A guide through Balthasar's aesthetics*, Edinburgh 1998.

[4] This became the first part of *Theologik*. Balthasar 'reused' it as the metaphysical prolegomena for his trinitarian theology and pneumatology forty years later.

is "indeed nothing else but the immediate appearance of the groundlessness of Ground out of everything that is grounded. It is the transparency of the mysterious background of being through all appearances" (TL I 254).

Already in his early work Balthasar emphasises the importance of an aesthetic approach in theology. Describing the relation of truths in the world to God, he defines beauty as the primal event in which God's being appears and the image as the medium of His appearance. God, however, does not appear beyond the images in the world. The truth in the world is not a sign referring to a divine realm or a truth pointing beyond itself to another truth that is truer than itself. On the contrary, Balthasar characterises truth as mystery because it has an immanent yet ungraspable divine content. Nevertheless, he argues that the appearance of God in the world is a continuing act. Therefore, there can never be a complete identity between God and His appearance in the world. The image is a representation insofar as it is the opposite of God, but an expression insofar as God appears in it (TL I 247). For Balthasar, aesthetics is the field in which the natural world finds its true definition as appearance of the divine mystery: "But this nature is not a dead or passive determination of being, but it has the liveliness of self-grasping in the moment of the foundation of being" (TL I 248).

a. The beauty of revelation

The significance of the concept of beauty in a theology of revelation finds its explicit expression in Balthasar's article, 'Revelation and beauty' (Offenbarung und Schönheit) in 1959 (VC 100-134). The conjunction 'and' in the title is meant to be a provocative and critical starting point of a theological aesthetics. Balthasar points to Kierkegaard in his *Either-Or* (*Enten-Eller*) as being the culprit of drawing too sharp a distinction between an ethical-religious and an aesthetical dimension of human life. According to Kierkegaard, the path to true Christian life leads through the aesthetical, beyond the aesthetical. This nurtured what in Balthasar's time was the dominant ideology that revelation and beauty are two different, distinct and even contradictory events. This is understandable, he argues, because as soon as the aesthetical entered into the history of philosophy it transformed itself into myth, *erbos*, and in the end into the intellectual vision of the Hegelian absolute Spirit. The aesthetical appeared to be so inherently appealing that it dominated everything eventually. Thereby it was isolated from other cultural and religious dimensions of human life. However, to reduce aesthetics to a subdiscipline of either philosophical epistemology or a theology of the sacraments and the liturgy will not suffice (VC 100).

It was Balthasar's intention to give back aesthetics its rightful place in theology. Nevertheless, he was quite aware of the fact that the separation of ethics and aesthetics fitted the prevailing worldview. According to him, it became unthinkable for people of the twentieth century to accept a self-evident connection between the immanent perspective of science and the transcendent one of Christian revelation. A philosophy of beauty therefore calls the long gone periods of Classicism, the Renaissance and Romanticism to mind. In the philosophy of German idealism, for example, beauty was given an honoured place. However, he argues, whoever isolates beauty from the truth and the good in such a way, together these being the triadic transcendental centre of all reality, risks the danger of reducing reality to the beautiful or the aesthetic (VC 101). So how did Balthasar find a way between the Scylla of classic and romantic aesthetics, which applied beauty as an overarching concept for all reality, and the Charybdis of modern aesthetics, submitting the study of the beautiful to other philosophical disciplines like epistemology or ethics?

First and foremost, he needed to redefine the prevailing concept of beauty. For Balthasar, it appeared to have become impossible to describe beauty in union with the good and the true in an age of materialism and historicism (GdhM 94-136). Not only was a work of art according to him regarded as the expression of the human mind but thanks to museums and the study of art history, it was also to be placed solely in its context and time. Therefore, beauty became a characteristic of either the creativity or the judgment of the human subject. Balthasar blamed this development for beauty losing its transcendental meaning: it no longer signifies the divine light that shines forth from reality. Nevertheless, for it to still signify that divine light the consequence of Kierkegaard's analysis would be to require one to abstain from the joy of worldly beauty in order to be receptive to it. Balthasar noted that the people who inspired the history of aesthetics—he mentions Plato, Augustine and Bonaventure—also abandoned worldly beauty at first only to regain it afterwards in a truer sense. Therefore, he argued that one should not continue to abstain from the richness of the world-immanent constitution of beauty. The fullness of beauty in the world is a "horizontal proof for the unfathomableness of the vertically descending shock. Only then will the proof succeed, when the shock actually takes place" (VC 111).

Although Balthasar here used the word 'proof' to characterise the relation of worldly beauty with the divine, he determined the concept of beauty within the metaphysical framework of the analogy of being, acknowledging the similarity within a greater dissimilarity of immanent and transcendent beauty (H I 33). Furthermore, he understood beauty in the indivisible light that it forms with the other two transcendentals, goodness and truth. To escape the danger of either a positivism of revelation or romanticism, he suggested that a passion for beauty should always go together with a divine call to change one's life. However, the revelatory event of beauty should also be a matter of experience instead of merely a matter of responsive faith. This is the problem that especially Protestant theology sees itself confronted with, according to Balthasar. How could the disrupting event of grace come from the same source that also created the situation in which people in the world find themselves? The experience of beauty in the world and the enthusiasms it causes should neither hold fast to the event itself nor should it retreat into enthusiasm alone. For Balthasar, the beauty of revelation is the ongoing coming in the world of divine beauty, both grounding and disturbing the aesthetic events in the world itself. Thus, he argues against a Protestant positivism of revelation that emphasises the grace-event alone and against a Roman Catholic neothomist philosophy stressing a presupposed static concept of nature (VC 114).

Balthasar's theological aesthetics finds its motivation in a specific revelatory experience, although not wanting to hold at faith alone (VC 116). He argued that created beings would not be created after the image of God when its transcendental characteristics would not reveal the freedom and mystery of divine revelation. Therefore, it belongs to the world to be open to God. However, Balthasar does not characterise this openness as an *esse commune* because this would suggest that it came with the common creatureliness of all beings as a transcendental ground for the divine. Instead, the openness for the divine is an inception of salvation: "Peace in God, beatitude and glorification, the overcoming of guilt, hidden presence of paradise, everything with which the truly beautiful comforts us, without giving us more than a foretaste, an indication of the not distant, but present, totally other fulfilment" (VC 118-119).

b. Perceiving the divine form

Between 1961 and 1969, Balthasar published his theological aesthetics, *Herrlichkeit*: "a Christian theology in the light of the third transcendental, to complement the vision of the true and the good with that of the beautiful" (H I 9). It consists of three parts, divided over seven volumes, in which he develops a fundamental theology, a history of metaphysics and a biblical theology. Before I will present a short walk-through of the seven volumes in the next section, clarifying the overall structure and main themes, I want to take a closer look at Balthasar's foundations of his own project.

His aesthetic project starts with the lament of the loss of beauty in the history of theology and philosophy. For him, 'beauty' should be the first and the last word of theology. Beauty makes the double focus of theology—on truth and on goodness—comprehensible, because it is its appearance, its revelatory evidence. As such, it is not immediately tangible though, because beauty is also the splendour of the mystery of faith (H I 16). Balthasar calls 'beauty' the primal phenomenon of all experience, of all communication, and of all understanding, because it is the primary manifestation of Being. However, the beautiful is only perceived when a mystery, an inner light (*splendor*), is envisioned in the image or form, which makes that which appears believable and engaging. Balthasar characterises that mystery by the disinterested giving of a sovereign and free being, visible in an appearing body. This primal phenomenon is neither a spirit without a body, i.e. a pure experience or mere imagination, nor a body without spirit, i.e. pure matter. Rather, the primal phenomenon of beauty is experienced at a juncture where *species* and *lumen*, form and perception converge and where the perceiver is enraptured by what it sees. Balthasar interprets this configuration of experience and appearance analogously to the configuration of faith and grace. Grace belongs to the essence of the form of the revelation that can be perceived in the world because the perceiver is enraptured by grace while perceiving the form of the revelation (H I 18-19).

Balthasar's defence of the possibility of perceiving the divine form is based on the idea of the *imago Dei*. Human beings are capable of experiencing themselves as phenomena insofar as they are part of the world by means of their bodies. They perceive themselves as an appearance among other appearances. Therefore, he argues, human beings can never be understood as the primal image of being or spirit. Their appearance, both physical and spiritual, is always a response, an answering appearance. As such, they do not take the initiative to appear but they appear as if in a mirror, reacting as a responsive image. If human beings are created in God's image they are so as a mirror of God, i.e. a form that does not limit the spiritual and bodily freedom of a human being but is similar—however dissimilar—to it (H I 20).

What else would human beings have been if they had not been shaped after a primal image, Balthasar asks, echoing the metaphysical starting point of the real distinction between essence and existence. On the one hand, they cannot free themselves from being created nor from the primal image they are created in. On the other hand, this image has set them free. The created form is not an alien form but one that is so intimate that it is worthwhile to identify with it. This identification takes place through perception. The perception of beauty is a perception of a form of life which can be found in a human form. At the same time, it is the form of life that is not self-created but given, and to which it owes its freedom, corporeality and spirituality (H I 21-22).

So why does Balthasar call this a 'beautiful' form? The pleasure the perception of the form of life brings about is founded in the truth and goodness of a reality which reveals itself as infinite and inexhaustibly valuable. The appearance of this reality in a form refers beyond this form to that reality and is at the same time present in the reality of this form. The beautiful form is always the inseparability of reference and presence and, as such, this form is the basic structure of all being. The form would, however, not be a *beautiful* form if it were not the appearance of a profundity and a fullness, which nevertheless in itself remains intangible and invisible (H I 112). Through the form, the spirit of God is perceived in history as the concurrence of concealment and appearance.

5.2. Theological aesthetics I: foundations

The seven volumes consisting of more than 3500 pages of Balthasar's theological aesthetics *Herrlichkeit* are divided into three parts.[5] Although it is impossible to do justice to the richness and abundance of his work, this section will attempt to present an overview of the authors and themes he discusses. The key concepts of his theological aesthetics will be discussed in the next sections. For a better understanding of the overall structure of the project, I will start with summarizing the separate parts (with the titles of the English translation on the right):

---

[5] Originally, *Herrlichkeit* was published in five volumes. The two volumes of the second part (*Fächer der Stile*) and the first two volumes of the third part (III,1 *Im Raum der Metaphysik*, 1. *Altertum*; 2. *Neuzeit*) were published as one volume. This is the reason why the page numbering in the new edition of these two volumes continues in the second volume. The English edition starts volume 5 (*The realm of metaphysics in the modern age*) with new page numbering.

Herrlichkeit	*The Glory of the Lord*
Eine theologische Ästhetik	*A Theological Aesthetics*
H I Schau der Gestalt (664 p.)	I Seeing the Form
H II Fächer der Stile (888 p.)	Studies in theological styles
H II,1 Klerikale Stile	II Clerical styles
H II,2 Laikale Stile	III Lay styles
H III,1 Im Raum der Metaphysik (998 p.)	The realm of metaphysics
H III,1,1 Altertum	IV Antiquity
H III,1,2 Neuzeit	V The modern age
H III,2 Theologie	Theology
H III,2,1 Alter Bund (413 p.)	VI The Old Covenant
H III,2,2 Neuer Bund (540 p.)	VII The New Covenant
H III,2,3 Ökumene (not published)	Ecumenism (not published)

a. Structure: seeing the form

Part one of *Herrlichkeit*, 'Seeing the Form' (*Schau der Gestalt*), is an unfolding of the main question of theological aesthetics: How can the revelation of God's free grace be *perceived* in the world? The aim of Balthasar's investigation into the perception of God's free agency is not a theological version of a philosophical epistemology in which the Absolute is established as the ground of knowledge because of the inadequacy of knowledge towards its object. Neither is it an attempt to establish the foundations for a theological ethics, explaining how human responses like obedience or responsibility are activated. Instead, his theological aesthetics investigates the *perception* and the *rapture* of the objective form that bestows everyday life with its richness and vigour (H I 22-24). As such, it is the study of Christian contemplation, its characteristics and its conditions of possibility. Therefore, both content and method of theological aesthetics should show the diversity of the Invisible radiating in the visibility of Being in the world. This aesthetics neither is an aesthetics in the modern sense of the word, nor is it a discipline that investigates the formal qualities of imagination and perception of a work of art divorced from its content. Balthasar's *Herrlichkeit* develops a theological aesthetics that, although starting at the level of sensory perception, of light and revelation, investigates the meaning and content of the encounter with the form and beauty of divine glory.

Balthasar's theological aesthetics has the form of divine revelation as its object, but it also studies the concept of nature and man's subjective experience of nature in order to find the conditions for perceiving and understanding the form of revelation. That is why the whole of his aesthetics systematically consists of two parts. First, the doctrine of perception: This is a fundamental theology, although Balthasar is of the opinion that fundamental theology and dogmatics can only be distinguished formally, not materially. This part of the aesthetics deals with the perception of the form of revelation of God. Second, the doctrine of rapture: This is a dogmatic theology, which is aesthetics as a doctrine of the incarnation of the glory of God and man's participation in it (H I 118). The doctrine of perception compares the philosophical concept of 'beauty' to that of 'glory' in parts H I and H III,1. The doctrine of rapture discusses the form of the glory of God in part H III,2. In part H II, on theological styles, both are discussed in their interwovenness.

The title of part one, 'Seeing the form', sums up the two divisions of this book: 'Seeing' refers to the *subjective* evidence of aesthetics. In this division, Balthasar starts a first tour of the history of theology, emphasising the concept of 'faith'. 'Form' refers to the *objective* evidence of aesthetics, which in this theological context are the revelation of God in Christ, the mediation and the testimony of this form of revelation in history. His discussion of the subjective and objective evidences of theological aesthetics is preceded by a lengthy introduction, which sets out the *status quaestiones* based on the observation that Catholic and Protestant theology have eliminated aesthetics with respect to both content and method. The content explored by a theological aesthetics comes with its own specific theological method. According to Balthasar, this could never be a neoscholastic systematics. He especially blames neothomist rationality, in which he was educated, for driving aesthetics and theology apart. Instead, he attempts to find a methodical parallel for the theological harmony that emerges from mysticism and the lives of the saints (VC 195-225).

b. Key concepts: form and glory

Form
The form of revelation is the main theme of Balthasar's theological aesthetics because it is the glorious evidence of divine agency in the world. The human mind is capable of seeing in the multitude of perceptions of worldly being a unity of meaning which cannot be deduced from the various elements perceived. Balthasar calls this meaningful unity 'form'

(*Gestalt*). A form is not a sign or a reference to something else but a manifestation of that which makes it possible and inspires it. A form is a presence rather than a symbol. Jesus Christ is the ultimate, while most concrete form of revelation in Balthasar's theological aesthetics. Jesus after all does not refer to the Father but he presents the Father himself (Jn. 14,9). This means that Jesus should be called a form, not a sign or a symbol. As a form, He is not a reference to God but a theophany in the concrete history of man. Likewise, scripture, tradition and church in their roles as mediations and testimonies of divine revelation are not mere references to the Christ-event either but actual appearances and realisations of the mystery of salvation. This is why Balthasar also calls them 'objective evidences'. Thus, 'form' is the original conceptual focus of Balthasar's theological aesthetics: "Those words which attempt to convey the beautiful gravitate, first of all, toward the mystery of form (*Gestalt*) or of figure (*Gebilde*). *Formosus* (beautiful) comes from *forma* (shape) and *speciosus* (comely) from *species* (likeness). But this is to raise the question of the "great radiance from within", which transforms *species* into *speciosa*: the question of *splendor*. We are confronted simultaneously with both the figure and that which shines forth from the figure, making it into a worthy, a love-worthy thing" (H 1 18).

In philosophical aesthetics the concept of form has many different meanings, and Balthasar declares borrowing his definition of Johann Wolfgang von Goethe (1749-1832). In an interview with Peter Eicher in *Herder Korrespondenz*, he describes his choice of form as the basic concept of his theology as a choice contrary to Rahner's choice of Kantian conceptuality.[6] Now, 'form' usually relates to the aesthetical category that means either a 'shape' devoid of any meaning or an 'appearance' of a meaning or idea. The experience of a pure form is based on the composition or the harmony of an appearance, which is what Balthasar is referring to. Therefore, he does not understand form as a pure sensory experience that is still unordered. On the contrary, the experience of the appearance of meaning in the form is oriented towards the unity of content of that which appears in the form or by means of the form.[7]

Kant interprets the concept of form as the bridge between the objects of pure and practical reason. The objects of pure reason are the a priori conditions for objective, universally valid empirical judgements. The objects of practical reason are the a priori conditions for making moral

---

[6] P. Eicher, Geist und Feuer, in: *Herder Korrespondenz* 30 (1976), 76.
[7] Cf. "Gestalt", in: *Historisches Wörterbuch der Philosophie*, 540-548.

judgements. The aesthetic theory that Kant develops in the *Critique of judgement* has a distinct object too, viz. the disinterested delight in the immediately perceptible properties of an object for their own sake.[8] This disinterested pleasure is related to both moral acts, even though it concerns the beautiful rather than the good, and to theoretical knowledge, even though the object of aesthetics cannot be grasped conceptually. The aesthetic form is demarcated by the unity of reason and imagination, which distinguishes it from the theoretical demarcation of the concept, that instead is based on the distinction of reason and imagination.[9] For Kant, an aesthetic form is not the beautiful object itself, although certain elements of the object can attract us to it. The aesthetic form has no purpose in itself and should therefore be contrasted with sensation or concepts. However, perceiving the form incites knowledge and moral feelings, insofar as it prepares us to know and love something disinterestedly and esteem it far beyond or even in opposition to our own interest.

According to Goethe, a form is experienced when one is enraptured by nature, which is the expression of divine imagination. Here, 'form' is no longer a concept that can be further qualified with aesthetical judgements, such as a beautiful form, a perfect form, etc. Instead, 'form' has become an aesthetic category in itself, a quality of nature referring to the totality of divine imagination, of which creation is the outcome, right down to its smallest parts. However, Goethe does not understand it as a platonic form that is transcendent to the world but as something that is most immanent to a being in the world. A form pertains to that which lives and as such carries in it the totality of life.[10] In his later work, Goethe amends this concept of form. Form then becomes the expression of the essence of beings. Consequently, 'perceiving the form' should be understood as the experience of the essential meaning of beings. Goethe's first conception of 'form' emphasises the appearance of totality in nature. In his later conception the emphasis has shifted to the intellectual contemplation of the essence of things.

Like Goethe, Balthasar's use of the concept of form resists every type of dualism. According to him, no metaphysical truth claim can break away from its original sensory perceptions. The totality of being only

---

[8] D.W. Crawford, Kant, in: B. Gaut, D. McIver Lopes [eds], *The Routledge companion to aesthetics*, London 2001, 51-64.
[9] I. Kant, *Kritik der Urteilskraft*, [Hrsg. v. W. Weischedel, Bd. V], Darmstadt 1983⁵, 280-281 (A 5,6).
[10] E. M. Wilkinson, Goethe's conception of form, in: *Proceedings of the British Academy* 37 (1951), 186. Cf. R. Gasche, *The idea of form. Rethinking Kant's aesthetics*, Stanford 2003.

appears in separate, fragmented beings. In order to be able to perceive beings as fragments or 'contractions' of totality or absoluteness, they should be regarded as forms of being. To him, 'form' is the contemplated, independently existing totality of fragments and elements which cannot only be conceived of or understood contextually but also contains the totality of being and as such is a contracted representation or image of the Absolute (H III,1 30).[11] Given the fact that every individual being can be contemplated as form, so that even the most minimal or most contracted being can be seen as an appearance of the Absolute, it is now apparent that one can never have an exhaustive conception of any form. Balthasar quotes a passage of Goethe that shows how the perception of a form, and therefore of the totality in a fragment—no matter how minute—is an experience of glory: "When the soul becomes aware of a relation in a bud, whose harmony it would not even be able to survey and experience when in full bloom, we say this impression is exalted, and it is the most glorious impression a human soul can partake in" (H III,1 31-32).

Balthasar distinguishes the concept of form from that of image, because of the exalted experience a form can arouse. Rather than image, form is the appropriate focus of a theological aesthetics because of the possibility to apply it to theological ideas, like revelation and incarnation.[12] An image is merely the appearance of a being, but a form is the appearance of the totality of being in every individual being. Therefore, the concept of form originates in the quality of its content, which contains the totality of being, so *out of the Absolute*. To be able to perceive the content of the form the observer has to be open to that which appears, *toward the Absolute*. For example, without the intrinsic quality of the form a symphony would be invisible, and without proper perception the symphony would be inaudible (H I 493).[13] However, human perception of the Absolute can only be described as 'reception', according to Balthasar. Contrary to the concept of form in Carl Gustav Jung's (1875-1961) *Gestalt* psychology, he argues there is no finite form that can reach for the infinite. The human mind is in no way capable of finding the infinite in a finite form.

What are the consequences of the notion of form for fundamental theology? How can revelation be perceived if any attempt to find adequate

---

[11] Balthasar refers to the Cusan idea of *'contractus'*. See also chapter six, section four.
[12] Cf. L.S. Chapp, *The God Who speaks. Hans Urs von Balthasar's theology of revelation*, San Fransisco 1996, 121-136.
[13] Cf. J. Schmid, *Im Ausstrahl der Schönheit Gottes. Die Bedeutung der Analogie in "Herrlichkeit" bei Hans Urs von Balthasar*, Münsterschwarzach 1982, 88.

concepts is incommensurable with regard to revelation? Because, despite this incommensurability, Balthasar still grounds the unity of faith and knowledge on the idea of form. The form is the presence of meaningful coherence perceived by man. Together with the form, one also perceives that this form can never found itself and that therefore, it is created and borne by something else. Balthasar calls this double perception, which does not fully coincide with the form itself, the perception of divine glory. Man can behold the divine glory that is present in the forms in the world through the perception of the forms in the world. This perception is regarded by Balthasar as the basis for the unity of faith and knowledge.

Beauty and glory
The form of revelation would not be a beautiful form if it were not the appearance of a depth and a fullness, which nevertheless in itself remains intangible and invisible (H I 111). This is why for Balthasar the psychological description of the perception of beauty in theological aesthetics should always be preceded by a comprehensive ontology. In this way, he is able to interpret the concept of beauty within the framework of the transcendentals. 'Beauty', according to him, is nothing but the immediate emergence of the groundlessness (*Grundlosigkeit*) of all being. It is the appearance of the infinite in finite forms, and hence not dependent on the perception by the human subject. However, it does appear to the human subject but only to the receptive openness of graced eyes. It is a gift rather than a way of seeing things. Therefore, by 'beauty' Balthasar does not mean the aesthetical observation or appreciation of the similarity of essence and appearance, but rather the main characteristic of the divine essence appearing in a worldly form as something that is always greater and therefore never fully coincides with its appearance.[14] As such, the ground of being appears as a self-grounding immeasurability, which constitutes its disinterestedness. "Whether it appears as the classical or the romantic, as the linear or the painted, as the Apollinian or the Dionysian, it is always the helpless relinquishing of a mystery" (TL I 254-255).

According to Balthasar, the perception of the (naturally) beautiful can in no way be equated to the perception of the glory of God. Yet, a theological aesthetics will have to avail itself of philosophical concepts. However, it may have become clear by now that Balthasar's aesthetics is

---

[14] Cf. H.P. Heinz, *Der Gott des Je-mehr. Der christologische Ansatz Hans Urs von Balthasars*, Bern, etc. 1975, 15f.

ultimately theological in its source and content. Still, he closely examines beauty in the world as well, insofar as it is the theophanous realm of divine glory. He sees worldly beauty as being brought forth by the creaturely possibilities to express oneself in meaningful forms. These forms provoke a response of love and gratitude because the dignity of the whole of creation appears in them.[15] Therefore, the light of divine beauty shines forth from the beauty of worldly forms. Obviously the doctrine of analogy applies here, so that no beauty in the world can be identified with divine glory. There is, though, one concrete historical event in which divine glory is fully present: in the beauty of the Christ-form.

Balthasar, although often called 'the theologian of beauty', neither clearly defines the concept of beauty nor develops a theory of beauty. Instead of arguing for interpreting beauty as a transcendental, he merely states that the church fathers as well the mediaeval scholastics granted beauty the status of a transcendental.[16] However, in modern theology such a statement becomes problematic because one does not experience reality as a whole as beautiful, or good for that matter. If the beautiful is indeed regarded as a gift and therefore completely independent from human perception, then at least one should acknowledge that human perception often seems to be inadequate to receive this divine gift. Yet, if theology were to abandon beauty as a transcendental, it can no longer regard the world as the realm in which the divine spirit is at work so that it would lose its status as creation. "Nothing expresses more unequivocally the profound failure of these theologies than their deeply anguished, joyless and cheerless tone: torn between knowing and believing, they are no longer able to see anything, nor can they, therefore, be convincing in any visible way" (H I 167-168).

Recapitulating, Balthasar's focus on the concepts of form and glory serve a doctrine of creation and are the starting points of a doctrine of redemption. His theological aesthetics emphasises the visibility of revelation that evokes a human response to the gift of divine beauty in the world. The concept of form guarantees the perception of a meaningful unity in the appearance of being. It also safeguards the acknowledgement of divine

---

[15] Cf. Chr. Steck, s.j., *The ethical thought of Hans Urs von Balthasar*, New York 2001, 8.
[16] Balthasar is not troubled by considerations whether the beautiful was actually regarded as a transcendental or not. For example, many medieval authors did not mention beauty as a transcendental whatsoever and if they did, it was not uncommon to subordinate beauty to the good. Cf. U. Eco, *The aesthetics of Thomas Aquinas*, Cambridge Mass. 1988; F.A. Murphy, *Christ the form of beauty*, 209-214.

presence in the world. The concept of glory guarantees the ever-greater majesty of God, appearing in the beauty of His creation. It also protects theology against approaching its object in an overly rational manner. The question remains whether Balthasar sufficiently recognises human freedom in the act of perceiving the revealed form and whether he leaves room for the creation of beauty by man. In other words, are the 'evidences' of theological aesthetics, as Balthasar calls them, not the all too self-evident facts in a theological paradigm that should be described as a positivism of revelation?[17]

c. Aesthetic evidences

Balthasar's atypical use of the concepts of form and beauty demonstrates the interwovenness of objectivity and subjectivity. In philosophical epistemology these two realms are usually clearly defined and distinguished. In his theological aesthetics they seem to overlap each other and sometimes even coincide. Form is not a clearly defined object but the condition of a subjective perception of a meaningful unity. Beauty is not a subjective judgement of taste but a transcendental characteristic of all being that raptures the subject away from itself. Balthasar's aesthetics stresses the passive-receptive side of perceiving the form of divine revelation. Yet, since the first part of his aesthetics is a fundamental theology, he should account for the possibilities of the human subject not only to receive divine revelation but also to respond to it and speak about it.

Subjective evidences
Balthasar distinguishes five realms in the subjective experience of faith: world, church, liturgy, neighbour, and prayer. The logical sequence of these five moments and the way in which they relate to each other should not be regarded as a rigid theological system. This is not because it is impossible to turn faith into an open vision but because the self-revealing God remains sovereign in His appearance and is Lord of his appearance and therefore resists every theological systematisation (H I, 403). Although Balthasar's theological aesthetics itself starts with an analysis of the structure of the perception of faith, it must not be forgotten that this specific perception, which belongs to the experience of faith, is a response to the freedom of the appearing God. "The first thing to do to see objectively,

---

[17] P. Eicher, *Offenbarung. Prinzip neuzeitlicher Theologie*, München 1977, 339-343.

is to let the revealing One be (...), not to process the material of envisagements by categories of the subject, but an attitude of service to the object" (MW 63-64). This is why the objectivity of divine revelation instead of the subjectivity of human perception of revelation is the foundation of theological aesthetics. In fact, if man truly wants to perceive God in His appearance, he will have to eliminate the 'temporary'—as Balthasar calls it—subjectivity of his desires and feelings. Only then does human subjectivity respond suitably to the objectivity of divine revelation, which is itself also characterised by meekness and humiliation. Therefore, the condition for the perception of faith is being unconditionally open to the objective evidence of revelation. Within this framework of revelation and faith, the following five moments on the side of the religious perceiving subject now become possible.

First, the primary moment of the perception of faith is seeing the form of God in the *world*, i.e. Jesus Christ. Christ is seen by the eyes of faith as the centre of all images in the world. In general, no other image is seen without also seeing its relation to the images that directly surround it or without remembering the images that directly preceded it. However, from Christ the light shines on all images in such a way that the believer can simultaneously see the distance and the nearness of every image to the radiant centre that Christ is. Christ is not the focal point of the perception of faith, but the world and the people living in it are seen entirely in the light of its radiant centre: the appearance of God in Christ.[18]

If Christ is the appearance of God in the world, he is so not just for the individual or the religious elite but, according to Balthasar, for the entire world. If He is the image of all images, all images are determined by and understood through this one image. After all, there are no independent images, i.e. no images that can be understood outside the context of their relation to other images. Images are always seen within a certain environment and each of these images is capable of changing the face of this environment. Balthasar uses the example of a novel, and argues that if for example we read Goethe, we also get to know his age and a certain body of thought which has influenced Goethe and which, in turn, was influenced by him. Man always lives among images from his own historical and cultural context and is able to change this context, to form it. Those who believe in Christ do not merely get to know His historical and cultural environment but they get to know the entire creation

---

[18] Cf. M. Albus, *Die Wahrheit ist Liebe. Zur Unterscheidung des christlichen nach Hans Urs von Balthasar*, Freiburg im Breisgau 1976, 186.

and the eschatological history. To the believer the entire world he encounters is ordered by the norm of Christ's form, which is the central image of the most determining event of the world: "Beings in the world keep their right distance (from Him [Christ] and from one another) and their right closeness (to Him and to one another) through His form. For the believer, this is not a matter of faith, but a matter of perception" (H I 405). According to Balthasar, it is unimportant whether the believer possesses the sensory simultaneity of an eyewitness: "The reality of creation as a whole became the monstrance of the real presence of God" (H I 405).

Second, the individual cannot perceive the image of Christ as an image among other images. Christ reveals himself in this world in the coherence of images that form the *church*. For Balthasar, Christ himself has established the church in such a way that his light radiates from the inside to the outside. But how does the church mediate the image of Christ in such a way that the believer can actually perceive it? According to Balthasar, this is possible because of a twofold ecclesiological continuity: empirical and marian. The church's empirical continuity consists of its indissolubility as the religious community of people and its apostolic character, of which the archetypal experiences of the prophets and the apostles and the later experiences of Paul and the ecclesiastical mystics are the foundation (H I 296-309). The marian continuity consists of the motherly task of the church to teach not just the faithful the words of the faith, but also to point to the reality that is expressed in those words. The image of the church as a mother is founded in the spiritual-bodily experience of Mary: The Word springs from the image of reality and returns to it. The church should mediate the incarnate concreteness from its marian foundation. Balthasar does not want to base the mediating function of the church on the instinctive movement of the cult of Mary. Instead, he is interested in preserving the image-character of faith, viz. interpreting the continuity of Mary as Christ's bride and the church as God's People in the world. This is the counterbalance of the historical-critical method in theology which he thinks reduces the world to a composition of meaningless facts (H I 407).[19]

Third, in the space of the church the community perceives the gestures of Christ in the *liturgy*. These gestures can be perceived through the senses in the spoken word and the sacrament. Balthasar states that the Word appears in the liturgy, for where the Word of God is spoken the

---

[19] Cf. B. Leahy, *The marian principle in the church according to Hans Urs von Balthasar*, Frankfurt am Main, etc. 1996.

Word of the incarnated God is heard, which is represented in the body and blood of Christ. The sacrament also appears in the liturgy not just as a symbol but as a form in revealing concealment. The liturgy is not just a composition of symbolic acts that appeals to faith, but it also realises a historical truth. It is the sensory character of the act, which lets the believer immediately perceive the represented event here and now, according to Balthasar. "The image compels them to enter into the act by revealing to them the act, which both instituted the image and is contained in the image" (H I 408). Therefore, Balthasar declares that the church can change, add to or abolish liturgical practices as it sees fit but it can never do this with the acts that originate in the acts of Christ.

Fourth, there is one image, which according to Balthasar precedes all the other images in the world and which originates in the Son of Man like no other: the image of the *neighbour*. In his neighbour, man sees his redeemer, He who is the neighbour of all people. Throughout a human life, faith is confirmed sensually by the encounter with the neighbour. This sensual confirmation only takes place if the neighbour is seen in the light of faith, in the light that shines from Christ in the world. It is to Balthasar of lesser importance that Christ is the historical form of love. The love of the neighbour is itself (an appearance of) this form. "In a Christian perspective, love is not an act without an image, but instead, it is what creates image and bestows form absolutely" (H I 409).

Fifth and finally, the form of revelation can be perceived in *prayer and contemplation*. This realisation of the form of revelation fulfils His presence in faith. However, this sensory presence should not be sought after for its own sake, but should entirely be at the service of the love that is obedient to the reality of the love of the Lord. This obedience takes place in prayer, where God touches human fantasy and imagination. All human experience may have to be erased and all experiences may have to be transcended. Because with Christ, Balthasar says, our sensuality with all its images and thoughts has to descend into the underworld to subsequently ascend to the Father in an indescribable sensory, yet supersensory way.

By mentioning five realms of subjective perception of faith: world, church, liturgy, neighbour, and prayer, Balthasar tries to describe the human possibilities to be receptive to revelation. "To be a recipient of revelation means more and more the act of renunciation which gives God the space in which to become incarnate and to offer himself as will (...) and the Holy Spirit is still free enough to create new and unheard-of marvels for each individual believer from the material of such exemplary experiences" (H I 404). Only in this way, he believes, is there continuity, or 'integration' as he calls it, between biblical faith and the ordinary experience of faith.

Objective evidences
The subjective perception of faith is grounded in an object which can be experienced, and without which every subjective experience would become incomprehensible. If, according to Balthasar, the object of religion would be limited to 'God in Himself', the subjective experience could also be considered mere subjectively, without the need to find an objective ground for it. The result of this separation of object and subject would be either that the subjective experience only relates negatively to any objectivity whatsoever, or that subjectivity and objectivity in their independence are somehow identified without referring to any form in the world. At most, the multitude of appearances in the world would then be seen as the different modes of appearance of this one identity (H I 413). How then does Balthasar describe the objective evidences of faith as both non-reducible to the eyes of faith and yet visible in a worldly form that is more than mere matter or the appearance of a being? Balthasar distinguishes two separate, though not contradictory objective evidences: the revelation in creation and the revelation in Christ. These moments are not just the expression but also the essence of revelation. Both are mediated by scripture and the church, which includes theology as well.

In creation, all beings in the world participate in the objective revelation of God. If God has revealed himself as the Creator and if creation is necessarily a manifestation of God, it follows that this manifestation takes its form from the form of the world itself. God however, is not a being among other beings but is the Being of beings. Creation, therefore, is not an allegory or metaphor of God, Whom is perceived beyond the materiality of things. It is the divine Being, which radiates in its integrity through the medium of the Being in the world. According to Balthasar, the creature must know that it is separate in being from God. Only then can it know itself to be the most immediate object of God's love and concern; and it is precisely when its essential finitude shows it to be something quite different from God that it knows that, as a real being, it has received that most extravagant gift, participation in the real being of God (H I 414).

The presence of the divine glory in creation prefigures and anticipates the presence of God in the incarnation. However, as Balthasar frequently makes clear, this pattern must not be drawn in an overly neat fashion. It may be true that Christ is simply the visibility of divine presence which pervades all of creation. However, it would be wrong to see in this fact a license to develop an evolutionary view of the progressive nature of revelation such that the old testament, seen as the paradigmatic intensification of all creaturely longing, easily flows into the new. Much of the prefiguring of Christ in creation has the form of a radical ambiguity, which leads to paradoxical answers to vexing existential questions. One can see the fulfilment, which Christ brings, only to the extent that one antecedentally carries within oneself the felt need to find an answer to all of the aforementioned ambiguities (H I 516-519).

Although God's revelation in Christ flows from the antecedent revelation in creation and the old covenant, it is of a wholly unexpected and unpredictable nature, Balthasar says. Only the revelation of the triune God in the earthly form of Christ could fulfil all our paradoxical expectations by first shattering the illusory quality of our answers and then laying bare the heart of the question. Thus, although the historical form of Christ is the product of its historical antecedents, the true significance of this form can only be seen through the eyes of faith, which see these same historical antecedents taken up into the hypostatical union. The true significance of Christ can only be discerned through an affirmation of the theandric quality of everything that He accomplishes. What you see in Christ is the wholly unique union between the archetype (God) and the image (humanity). However, the image is of no significance to Balthasar, if not seen in its union with the archetype. The form of Christ's humanity becomes the perfect image of the form of the triune God.

Balthasar does not regard the revelation in Christ as an intensification of creation but regards creation as a preparation and a condition of the Christ-event. In Christ, heaven and earth are brought together in such a way that because of the light that radiates from Him into the world, the entire creation is now seen in this light. This is what Balthasar calls '*indirect* objectivity'. Remarkably, Balthasar situates the *direct* foundation for the objectivity of divine revelation in faith, paralleling the inversion whereby subjective experience of faith is based on the experience of objectivity. The objectivity of this revelation immediately comes to light when the historical form of Christ is seen as the appearance of the triune God. That is, if on the one hand one sees the relation between His two natures and on the other—within this first relation—his entry into the Holy Spirit, which makes Him the inner form of the church. The appearance of God as Christ is not the phenomenon of absolute identity, but of an independent Trinity. Therefore, the concrete historical form of revelation that Christ is, is not just any image of a divine nature but is its primal image and therefore not the appearance of an infinite non-form (*Un-Gestalt*) but of an infinitely determined superform (*Über-Gestalt*). The man Jesus, who is an image of God, should not be regarded independently from Christ, who is the primal image of God (H I 477-483).

In retrospect, one could ask whether Balthasar's description of the complex reciprocity of objective revelation and subjective experience answers the question how one knows that this form of God's love is not merely a projection of the mythopoetic imagination but is actually a form placed before us by God. Since God is not an infinite formlessness, but rather infinitely determined within the divine self by a triune superform, one can recognize Balthasar's emphasis on the aesthetic objectivity of revelation and its power to enrapture the beholder. The concrete historicity of the divine self-revelation should not be viewed as a concession to the pitiful material beings that God has created. Nor is the material creation as such a place which exists in opposition to God and which must be overcome in order to attain salvation in the realm of the formless Spirit. God is the author of specificity and form. Thus, Balthasar finds here the foundation to assume that there must be something analogous to form in God.

However, the concept of form should not be affirmed in an overly positivistic manner when applied to God. How does Balthasar reconcile his emphasis on the objectivity of revelation with the obvious cautions of negative theology against an exaggerated literalism in an objectivist approach to the positive aspects of revelation? According to him, even God's incomprehensibility is somehow seen and made visible in a finite form. One is metaphorically blinded, therefore, not by an absence of light but by the excess of it. The negative philosophical incomprehensibility of God is transformed and raised into the positive theological incomprehensibility of God's triune love revealed in Jesus (H I 496-505). This is the triumph of God's kenotic love over all forms of human knowledge which seek to tame God's love in either sterile rationalisms, trapping God in human concepts and systems, which Balthasar evidently avoided, or in a pious transcendentalism, holding God at a comfortable deistic distance.

5.3. Theological aesthetics II: a guide through Herrlichkeit

After Balthasar has laid the foundations of theological aesthetics in the first volume of *Herrlichkeit*, he continues with rewriting the history of theology from the aesthetic perspective. It is unfeasible to summarize all the monographs on different authors and periods in the history of myth, religion and philosophy. However, to give a general idea how comprehensive and prolific Balthasar's aesthetic project is, I will mention some of the topics and ideas he deals with in the six volumes that follow the introduction. It will become clear that Balthasar neither develops a systematic aesthetics nor a chronology of the times when the idea of beauty was mentioned in the history of theology. Instead, he circles around the formal object of theological aesthetics, accentuating the core visions of theologians but also of poets, playwrights and painters, to offer a symphonic view of the revelation of divine glory in the world (H II 20-22).

a. Studies in theological styles

The second part of Balthasars project is called 'Studies in theological styles' (*Fächer der Stile*), and takes the perception of the form of revelation clarified in part I as a starting point for a description of twelve theological expositions of this perception, like "twelve strong rays of light from a bright source of light" (H II,1 10-11). These are twelve thinkers from the history of Christianity, whom Balthasar classifies as either clerical or lay styles. Together, they do not form a history of theological aesthetics, however. On the contrary, once the differences between the authors discussed have become clear, it can only be concluded, as Balthasar ironically does, that writing a history of theological aesthetics is impossible. The field of theological aesthetics, like that of mysticism, knows no historical development, according to Balthasar (H II,1 18).

Yet, Balthasar's selection of twelve different styles has a chronological, but also a geographical and thematic basis: The first book discusses the history of theology up to about 1300, looking at five 'professional' theologians: Irenaeus from Turkey, Augustine from North Africa, Pseudo-Dionysius from Syria, Anselm from Burgundy and Bonaventure from Italy. The second book introduces seven philosophers, mystics and poets from 1300 to the present: Dante Alighieri from Italy, John of the Cross from Spain, Blaise Pascal from France, Johann Georg Hamann from Germany, Vladimir Solowjew from Russia, Gerard Manley Hopkins from England and Charles Péguy, again from France. Balthasar chooses not to discuss these twelve theological styles in the systematic form of a symposium but as twelve separate monographs. The distinction between 'clerical' and 'lay' seems confusing, since two of the lay authors were priests, and therefore not laymen in the ecclesiological sense. However, Balthasar calls them 'lay' because they wrote in their vernaculars and have the concrete personal existence as the centre of their attention.[20]

It may not surprise us that the most prolific theologian and, according to Henri de Lubac, "most cultured man of our time" had some difficulties in selecting these twelve authors from the 'Great Catholic Tradition'. Balthasar acknowledges that his choice is hardly the expression of some kind of necessity. For example, instead of Dante he could also have chosen Raymundus Lullus, Nicholas of Cusa, Desiderius Erasmus, Martin Luther or Bartolomé de Las Casas. Beside Pascal he mentions Gottfried Wilhelm von Leibniz, beside Hamann, Jacob Böhme, Francois Fénelon and Sören Kierkegaard, beside Vladimir Solowjew, Franz von Baader and Friedrich Wilhelm Joseph Schelling, and beside Gerard Manley Hopkins John Henry Newman (H II,1 13-14). Although Balthasar was not driven by some kind of necessity, the reader will discover a certain pattern in the originality of the authors he has chosen and the ones he mentions as alternatives. His preference goes clearly against the canon of the history of philosophy, especially in his choice for lay styles.

The historical and systematic connections between the twelve different positions are not discussed until in part three, where they are treated as a part of the history of western metaphysics. In part two, Balthasar follows a diachronic course, crossing horizontal, chronological lines of influence, constantly emphasising the synchronous vertical relation to God. Although the various theological positions are at times each other's opposites, Balthasar aims to present the history of theology as a harmonious composition. He sets up a dialogue between various different theological systems, without ever identifying with one of them, maintaining that no single style can do justice to the infinity of the mystery of salvation in the being of the world in a systematic way.

---

[20] Cf. A. Nichols, *The Word has been abroad*, 68. Note that the word 'lay' must have been an honoured title for Balthasar, since he left the Jesuit order to start a lay order. See also his *Der Laie und der Ordensstand*, Einsiedeln 1948; *Kleine Fibel für verunsicherte Laien*, Einsiedeln 1989³; and *Gottbereites Leben. Der Laie und der Rätestand. Nachfolge Christi in der heutigen Welt*, Einsiedeln 1993. Cf. M. Lochbrunner, *Hans Urs von Balthasar als Autor, Herausgeber und Verleger. Fünf Studien zu seinen Sammlungen (1942-1967)*, Würzburg 2002, 105 n. 22.

b. The realm of metaphysics

The third part of *Herrlichkeit* is divided into two subdivisions, which together fill four volumes. The first subdivision of this third part of the theological aesthetics is called 'The metaphysical realm' (*Im Raum der Metaphysik*) and discusses twenty-five centuries of metaphysics as a backdrop to the theological styles discussed in part two. Throughout this part of the aesthetics, Balthasar uses the term 'metaphysics' in the broadest sense of the word. To him, it encompasses Greek mythology, all of philosophy, and religion, in its diverse and highest mytho-poetical manifestations. He interprets this history of metaphysics, from Homer to Heidegger, in the light of the a priori of theological aesthetics, the revelation of the glory of God in the world.

Part III,1 is subdivided into three sections, spread over two volumes: The first section is called 'Foundations', on the relation between myth, philosophy and religion in the period from Homer to Plotinus. The second section is called 'Consequences', and deals with classical Christian thought from the church fathers to Thomas, followed by the transcendental aesthetics from the fourteenth century to German Idealism and Heidegger. The third section presents the conclusions, called 'Our inheritance and the Christian task' in possibly one of the most exalted theological essays of the twentieth century.

Looking at the number of pages awarded to individual authors or schools in the 'Foundations', Balthasar's most important influences can be traced. Here are some examples: The extensive treatment of Greek mythology (98 p.) shows that Balthasar's broad conception of the history of metaphysics starts with the mythical thought of antiquity. After all, mythology also realises the necessary relation between thought and representation, and, as such, the ultimate boundaries of philosophy are already set in Antiquity. Plato (43 p.) and Plotinus (32 p.) are the philosophers that receive most attention, as do the Greek tragedians (48 p.). The poet Virgil is also a strong presence (25 p.). However, the number of pages dedicated to one author is not always a flawless indicator. Thomas, for example, only gets 17 pages. He may not be of great importance to Balthasar's aesthetics but his ontology, which forms the framework for the entire theological aesthetics, is.[21]

Like Heidegger and Nietzsche, Balthasar has a keen interest in presocratic philosophy and mythology. He believes Greek mythology is a

---

[21] J.J. Buckley, Balthasar's use of the theology of Aquinas, in: *The thomist* 57 (1995), 517-545.

pre-figuration of the Christ-event, because nowhere in world literature can the real presence of the gods be felt as strongly as in the works of Homer. Moreover, aesthetics and ethics are truly one in the ancient world because all of life is seen in the light of the divine θεωρία. Aeschylus presents divine glory as penance and justice. The absent god of the tragedies of Sophocles reminds us of later negative theology. Euripides, however, eliminates the tragic vision from Greek thought, according to Balthasar. He believes that Euripides's plays have sadly become the model for European theatre, in which divine beauty only appears as a symbol in an inner-worldly plot (H III,1 122-123).

In Greek philosophy too, from Plato to Plotinus, the focus shifted from attention to the divine presence to the inner-worldly beauty. In Plato's philosophy the sense of measure, harmony and order conquers the sense of divine Eros. Plato himself describes the development of his philosophy as a development from epiphany to order and harmony. According to Balthasar, beauty then is only associated with the Good in order to present virtue as something that is forever controlled and in equilibrium with its surroundings. This equilibrium is associated with the symmetry of the cosmos, which leads to the notion of the sublime in philosophical aesthetics. Because of this, Balthasar argues, later western European philosophy has shifted its attention to the good and the perfect instead of to being itself. Human imagination and human agency slowly became alternatives for appearance and revelation.

The church fathers, but also Plato and Plotinus themselves, interpreted epiphany and revelation as part of a cosmological framework. Because of this, the unicity and historicity of Christ have been pushed to the background in Christian thought as well, which after all has been influenced by platonic philosophy. The platonic opposition of idea and appearance transforms into a relation of the soul to itself in Plotinus. To Plotinus, 'Beauty' is the name of the mystical unification of the soul. Unlike Plato, he no longer holds that the forms in the world are illuminated by absolute Beauty. The human soul itself becomes Light and absolute Beauty. This concept of Beauty in Plotinus's work is the common root of myth, religion and philosophy. That is why both cosmic beauty and the theological dimension of glory are subjects in Plotinus's philosophy, a dimension that was lost in the aesthetics of German Idealism (H III,1 270).

Balthasar shows his appreciation of Neoplatonism in his comment of Dionysius. The transcendental notion of beauty in the work of Dionysius combines the platonic theme of the light that illuminates all reality with the aristotelian inner-worldly properties of beauty. Balthasar also derives his own doctrine of the transcendentals from Pseudo-Dionysius. In the fourth book of the divine names Pseudo-Dionysius explicitly speaks of beauty as a transcendental property.[22] According to Pseudo-Dionysius, beauty is a property of all things, because every substance is made of light and so participates in the original light, God. Moreover, the beauty of things coincides with their goodness. Just as all things are good because they flow from the Good, they are also beautiful because God is the cause of the harmony and clarity the things possess. 'Being' here means possessing a certain order that is beautiful. Thomas adopts this analogy of the good and the beautiful yet also distinguishes between them because, contrary to the good, beauty to him implies the notion of a relation with cognitive power.

This critical line Balthasar draws in western philosophy from Plato onward does not mean he does not appreciate (neo-)platonic philosophy.[23] His interest in Greek philosophy stems from his attempts to constantly think of theology as a union of Christianity and philosophy. In the Renaissance philosophy of Cusanus, classical aesthetics reaches its apex, in his view. It combines cosmological elements from Plotinus's aesthetics with the properties of being from Pseudo-Dionysius's negative theology and the epistemological connotations of the concept of beauty in aristotelian-thomist philosophy. This unity is lost after Cusanus, and philosophy and theology stray into what Balthasar calls an anthropological reduction (GinL 19-32). However, he believes it should be possible, even today, to see Christianity "in the old almighty form of a theology which organically envelops philosophy". Cusanus was the last to fully exploit this form, but the autonomy of the sciences and philosophy has shattered the unity of theology and philosophy. This does not mean, according to Balthasar, that philosophy and theology should be equated. For him, philosophy must necessarily precede theology, because man will try to understand the form of revelation by means of reason. This is why theology will have to treat philosophy as an analogous way of speaking, indispensable for theology itself.

In the second part of 'In the metaphysical realm' Balthasar pays most attention to Goethe (65 p.), from whom, as shown in the previous section, he derives the concept of 'form'. Cusanus (40 p.), as a turning point in philosophy, Hölderlin (37 p.) and Schiller (28 p.) also seem important to him, looking at the number of pages. Heidegger merits only 17 pages, but

---

[22] *In librum beati Dionysii de Divinibus Nominibus expositio*, ed. Marietti, Rome 1950, c.4 §1.

[23] N.D. O'Donoghue, Do we get beyond Plato? A critical appreciation of the theological aesthetics, in: B. McGregor, Th. Norris [eds], *The beauty of Christ*, 253-264.

this is still more than the modern rationalism of Descartes and Leibniz, and German Idealism get. Like Thomas, Heidegger plays an important part in the works of Balthasar. To him, both thinkers have formed the fundamental ontological perspectives on the intellectual and cultural history of the west.[24]

The German idealists close this section. The beauty of a work of art is regarded as the highest form of spiritual freedom in German Idealism. Beauty becomes a human act, a mental production, and an act of free fantasy, freer than nature itself. The aesthetics of Hegel (art as the appearance of the Absolute Spirit) and Kant (aesthetics of taste) are still philosophies of the work of art, but Schelling is the last philosopher who sees the work of art as an expression of the Absolute itself.[25] Heidegger then, concludes the tradition that started with Plotinus and ran via Thomas and Eckhart. His philosophy is still rooted in German mysticism and in what Balthasar terms the metaphysics of the saints, which presents free will as abandonment (*Gelassenheit*).[26] According to Balthasar, this abandonment is man's aesthetical attitude to life because he experiences his freedom in harmony with the totality of being.

Balthasar concludes 'In the metaphysical realm' with an analysis of the Christian as the 'custodian of glory' (*Hüter der Herrlichkeit*), in which he argues that the history of metaphysics should have been a history of love. Metaphysics should start with the wonder of being, described by Balthasar by four ontological differences. A proper understanding of beauty is not possible without 'metaphysical love': "Love loves being in an a priori way, for it knows that no science will ever track down the ground of why something exists rather than nothing at all. It receives it as a free gift and replies with free gratitude" (H III,1 975).

c. Old covenant and new covenant

The second and last division of the third part of Balthasar's ambitious project is called 'Theology', and would itself have consisted of three volumes:

---

[24] M. Daigler, Heidegger and Balthasar. A lover's quarrel over beauty and divinity, in: *American Catholic philosophical quarterly* 69 (1995), 375-394.

[25] F.W.J. von Schelling, *Philosophie der Kunst*, [hrsg. u. eingel. von W. Beierwaltes], Stuttgart 1982, 388: "Consequently, I do not construct art as art, as this particular object, but I do construct the universe in the form of art."

[26] The English translators of *Herrlichkeit* have chosen to translate the word '*Gelassenheit*' with 'abandonment'. There is no English equivalent for this word but it could also be translated with the words 'submission', 'resignation' or 'yielding self interest'.

'Old covenant', 'New covenant' and 'Ecumenism'. However the last volume has never been published, although Balthasar claimed to have completed it in the form of an extensive dialogue with Luther (MW 67-68). In the last two volumes, after having clarified the concept of glory and its perception by man in part one and working through twelve styles of the aesthetic viewpoint in the history of theology in part two, he wants to approach the centre and richness of the historical diversification biblically, but not until he has also given an overview of the mythical, philosophical and poetical experience of glory in the history of mankind (H III,2,1 22). Thus, part three as a whole is an attempt to discuss the specifically Christian, first in solidarity with the history of thought and its embeddedness in a general religious metaphysics, then in isolation from all other human designs (H III,1 15).

In his treatment of the old covenant, Balthasar chooses three central concepts: glory, image and grace. 'Glory' stands at the centre of theological aesthetics because it is the essence of God's revelation. The biblical equivalence of glory is *kabod*, which means the appearance of 'weight', both in its physical and sensual meaning. Is it possible, Balthasar asks, to speak analogically from God's *kabod*? If so, then His absoluteness must at the same time mean the majesty of His power (H III,2,1 34). The concept of 'image' describes the fact that the glory of God shows itself before the Word of God is spoken at the most decisive moments in scripture. Balthasar refers to examples such as Moses at Mount Sinai, the burning bush, Isaiah's and Ezekiel's visions of their vocations, and the vision of the Son of Man at the beginning of the *Book of revelations*. However, it is also written that one cannot live after one has seen God. That is the reason why Moses sinks to his knees and Paul is thrown to the ground. All these biblical stories are examples of what will happen to every 'hearer of the Word of God': "he receives God in a rapture from himself, he hears and understands God in God and through God" (H III,2,1 14-15). In His appearing, God shows his holiness and with it the unholiness of the perceiver. This is why, according to Balthasar, a theological aesthetics could never be a peaceful contemplation of the divine. He asserts, by means of an untranslatable word play, that God's glory (*Herrlichkeit* as *Hehrlichkeit*) is at the same time His Lordship (*Herrlichkeit* as *Herrschaftlichkeit*) (H III,2,1 16). The third concept Balthasar explores in the section called 'Old covenant', is the concept of 'grace', the work of God between Himself and his image. The last and decisive question of a theological aesthetics then must be: "how it is possible that the finite and continually failing disposition of mortal being persists in the sight of the absolute and irrefutable order and how it happens that the seemly necessary, ultimate indulgence and condescension of God, to allow the human crookedness to be weighed as right, to imputate the unjust as a justness to God, coincides with *real* and true justice?" (H III,2,1 17).

This last question is elevated in the section called 'New covenant', in which the image of God becomes one with the Word of God. In a matter-of-course continuity between old and new covenant, Balthasar finally reaches the apotheosis of a biblically founded theological aesthetics. The idea of beauty is derived from the revelation in Christ that surpasses, criticises and fulfils every general or systematic conceptualisation of beauty (H III,2,2 20). In the new testament, the old-testament *kabod* becomes *doxa*: The unity of power and glory finds its ultimate form in the incarnation of the trinitarian love in Christ, as it is mirrored in the church, in its doxologies and its truth.

5.4. Aesthetics as fundamental theology

After going through Balthasar's theological aesthetics as a whole it may have become clear that he reads the history of philosophy and theology ambivalently, emphasising the 'Great Catholic Tradition' as both a work of great human achievement and as the increasing forgetfulness of glory. This oblivion leads to a philosophical aesthetics of worldly beauty and the elimination of aesthetics from theology.

a. Aesthetics as a theological criticism

In the introduction to his theological aesthetics Balthasar criticises three movements in the modern history of Christian theology, which he describes as denying a theological aesthetics its rightful place: 1. Modern philosophical aesthetics; 2. The Protestant elimination of aesthetics from theology; 3. Catholic biblical hermeneutics and its historical-critical method.[27]

Against modern aesthetics
Balthasar was deeply moved by classical music, paintings and theatre plays but he was hesitant to apply the qualities of art or aesthetic categories

---

[27] Cf. A. Nichols, o.p., *The Word has been abroad*, 8-22.

to theology. Although he acknowledges the analogy between God's creation and "the shaping forces of nature and of man as they generate and give birth" (H I 33), he goes on to warn against the misuses of the concept of analogy, i.e. subjugating divine revelation to the laws of philosophical aesthetics by applying worldly categories to the sovereignty of God. This danger occurs more frequently in aesthetics because "the beautiful brings with it a self-evidence that en-lightens without mediation" (H I 34). That will eventually lead to the application of the 'beautiful' to what happens to be an enlightening experience or a subjective judgment of what seems to be insurmountable. This could never be a theological aesthetics, which "is the attempt to do aesthetics at the level and with the methods of theology" and will "deteriorate into an aesthetic theology by betraying and selling out theological substance to the current viewpoints of an inner-worldly theory of beauty" (H I 35).[28]

It should be emphasised that by making this sharp distinction between aesthetic theology and theological aesthetics, Balthasar not only defines this field as a science of the divine form of revelation but also distinguishes it from an aestheticising form of theology (H I 74-75). His theological aesthetics is not about poetry, music or the arts, nor does it make a case for beautiful liturgy or any other form that would make the Christian life more appealing. Therefore, according to him modern philosophical aesthetics, with its analysis of inner-worldly aesthetic categories, could never be applied to theology. Instead, the touchstone of a theological aesthetics is the theodicy question.[29] It should never close its eyes to human suffering or cover it up with the veil of worldly beauty. The poetic beauty of scripture only serves the consciousness of the aesthetic dimension of the unique dramatic event in Christ. Only through this prism can it find its reflection in the cosmos and in history. (H I 40).

Against the Protestant elimination of aesthetics
According to Balthasar, Luther's defence against the replacement of the dialectic of Christ's death and resurrection by a neoplatonic scheme of an all too harmonious analogy between nature and grace eliminated aesthetics from Protestant theology (H I 42). Instead, Luther articulated the free sovereignty of the Creator whose creation cannot be deduced from any theory of Ideas. Neither the incarnation nor the mystery of the Cross could be reduced to a function of reason, "which aesthetically attempts

---
[28] Cf. B. Leahy, Theological aesthetics, 25-27; L. Dupré, The glory of the Lord, 184-185.
[29] M. Lochbrunner, *Analogia caritatis*, 164-166.

to achieve a harmony between divinity and humanity" (H I 43). Beauty then, becomes the idolatrous act of comprehending the divine through harmony. The only possible alternative is to understand the relationship between God and man within the dialectic of a self-surrendering faith. "With such a surrender the divine art can accomplish *sub contrario!* what man obstinately and vainly tries to achieve both *sub recto* and *sub contrario*" (H I 45). According to Balthasar, either Protestant interpretations of Luther's original intuition led to an irrational understanding of the mystery of God or they turned into cold and negative methodological protests. The inspiration, however, was the aesthetic "exuberant outpouring of the Gospel's nuptial love" (H I 44), which was forgotten later. A radical dialectic eventually involved the removal of aesthetics from Protestant theology.

Remarkably, Balthasar credits Karl Barth with nearly saving Protestant theology from its denial of aesthetics. Barth overcame the Kierkegaardian Either-Or and gave to God, for the first time in the history of Protestant theology, the title 'Beauty'. Balthasar thought that the concept of beauty was for Barth an indispensable aid to understand the persuasiveness of God's revelation.[30] Balthasar even enthusiastically discovers Barth's dealing with the concept of form, which he interprets as an undeniably important question for Barth while bringing to mind his "solitary treatment of the joy of faith" (H III,2,2 18). Following Anselm, Barth calls theology the most beautiful of the sciences, especially when it contemplates the perfect form of God, the Trinity and the incarnation (H I 51). Nevertheless, although he recovered a biblical concept of beauty that unmistakeably put aesthetics in the realm of theology again, he did not succeed in transforming Protestant theology, thereby leaving space for Rudolf Bultmann's existential, inner-worldly, yet imageless reading of scripture (H I 53). Again, in his criticism of the Protestant elimination of aesthetics, Balthasar emphasises the theological neglect of an objective form in

---

[30] K. Barth, *Kirchliche Dogmatik II,1*, München 1932, 732-733. "What is openness, the essence and the form of the opening in divine revelation? Here, again, we first need to consider the revelation in which God reveals Himself to Himself. Consequently we might understand how it is for us. Or are we taking things too far with this question? Should it be considered a forbidden and foolish question? Should we resign to the conclusion that God is glorious and also convincing, and thus transparent and open? Should we decline to answer the question: how, in which form He is? – decline, because it has been denied to us? (...) Or might we perhaps only be able to affirm about the 'how' of glory, God's self-glorification, that it is supported by the whole of divine omnipotence; affirm that it convinces in that it rules, conquers and controls with a simply superior power, which it creates in such a way that the Light illuminates, that something is illuminated, which, as such, receiving Light, becomes light itself?"

the world that eventually leads to a mere spiritual and therefore bodiless reception of divine revelation by faith.

Against Catholic hermeneutics and historical-critical method
Surprisingly, Balthasar reproaches Catholicism equally for banishing aesthetics from its theology. He explains this exile in terms of the historical separation of philosophy and theology. Descartes's thought experiment shows reason's independence of revelation for the first time. Since then, the exact method of the natural sciences became the dominant model for philosophy. It became impossible, Balthasar argues, for philosophy to have transcendental beauty as its subject, because it eliminated the original wonder and enthusiasm of experience as a philosophical source in order to achieve its scientific ideal. Every attempt to demonstrate the theological roots of all philosophical systems that followed this scientific development led to traditionalism, as was the case with the Catholic Tübingen School. The alternative response to the separation of theology and philosophy, according to Balthasar, was a theological rationalism in the form of hermeneutics, which merely followed the already existing philosophical idealism by considering the act of faith as the foundation of all reason, as part of the natural structure of reason (H I 69).

The consequence of these developments sketched by Balthasar, was a theological specialisation in different subjects and an unfortunate scientism. As I have mentioned in the preceding chapter, he places blame on Gotthold Ephraim Lessing for regarding theology as the science of accidental historical truths, while assuming that philosophy is the study of necessary truths of reason. Balthasar does acknowledge the historical subject of Christian theology but he is dismayed by the consequences the method of modern science and philosophy has had for theological method. He blames Catholic fundamental theology, dogmatics and exegesis equally for focusing too much on historical demonstrations, instead of giving voice to their original vision and inspiration. He laments the fact that the *fruitio* for the *sensus spiritualis* and the *intellectus fidei* are not given space in theological method anymore. He mentions Thomas Aquinas as a good example of interpreting theology as a unique type of science, "as seen by him to be founded on its participation through grace (...) in the intuitive saving knowledge of God Himself and of the Church Triumphant" (H I 71). For Balthasar, only a theological method that honours this dimension of its knowledge can do justice to the perception of the divine form that is the subject of a theological aesthetics.

b. The reciprocity of fundamental theology and dogmatic theology

To indicate the unique divine appearance in the world Balthasar quotes the preface of the birth of Christ: "Because through the mystery of the incarnate Word the new light of your brightness has shone onto the eyes of our mind; that knowing God visibly, we might be enraptured by this into the love of invisible things".[31] Although the word 'faith' does not feature in this text, it is according to Balthasar represented by two other words: *mentis nostrae oculis* and *rapiamur*. First, the 'eyes of our mind' emphasises the perceiving character of faith as a visual act. However, the most encompassing act is perception, also including hearing, which is the act of captivating that which gives itself. The 'new light', which breaks forth from the forms in the world is both a condition and the object of perception. Therefore, this light cannot be equated to any worldly aesthetical light, although there may be some form of comparison. After all, there must be something that can be seen and understood despite the mystery of God's revelation, so that man is not at the mercy of a blind belief in an absolute mystery (H I 112-113).

This expresses the second part of the preface. The rapture is not merely a passive movement from God to human beings, but it is also realised in human beings. After all, Balthasar argues, the *lux claritas* is not the same as the *amor invisibilis*. This is presupposed because man has beheld God in a human way. This rapture should therefore be understood theologically, not as a psychological answer to the witnessing encounter with worldly beauty but as a movement of man's whole being, because of the divine light of grace in the mystery of Christ, away from himself through Christ to God. *Amor* not *caritas* is the context in which faith takes place. As such, Balthasar declares that it is a more precise designation than 'faith' for the enrapturing movement that is performed by God in man. Nevertheless, it is also performed by man, although inspired by divine love (H I 114).

Balthasar here warns against interpreting the Christian *Eros* and Christian beauty platonically. After all, the soteriological moment of Christian theology indicates that God effectively realises the things he reveals. Thus, in Balthasar's interpretation a platonic imago-metaphysics and an aristotelian *causa-et-finis*-metaphysics meet in Christianity. Christian inspiration should not merely be understood in an idealistic sense. It follows

---

[31] *Quia per incarnati Verbi mysterium nova mentis nostrae oculis lux tuae claritatis infulsit: ut dum visibiliter Deum cognoscimus, per hunc in invisibilium amorem rapiamur.*

from and belongs to an existing and realistic concept of being. The splendour of Christian glory is no less than that of the worldly beautiful, but it connects the appearance and the radiance to the reality of the resurrection and the religious anticipation of this in Christian life (H I 116). Therefore, a theological aesthetics also entails the horror of the cross and the abysmal ugliness of sin and hell—all those elements a worldly aesthetics can no longer bear, Balthasar remarks.[32]

Thus, according to Balthasar, divine beauty can only be regarded in the eschatological form of the Son of Man. God's glory cannot be read from anything but God's appearance in Christ. Yet, neither can glory and appearance simply be equated, nor can glory be causally deduced from appearance, for appearance would be secondary if the latter were the case. The tension between the philosophical concept of beauty and glory thus described is the same as that between negative and positive theology. These two positions should never be separated. Likewise, fundamental theology and dogmatics should not be separated either. The theological doctrine of perception (fundamental theology) compares the philosophical concept of 'beauty' to the theological concept of 'glory', while dogmatic theology deals with (the form of -) the glory of God in itself.

This is the reason why Balthasar wants to develop his theological aesthetics in two parts: The first part can be regarded as a fundamental theology and is described by him as the doctrine of the perception of the divine form. The second part is a dogmatic theology and called the doctrine of rapture, which is about the incarnation as the concrete historical event of the glory of God and the exaltation of man taking part in this event (H I 118). As I mentioned before, Balthasar continuously emphasises the unity of dogmatics and fundamental theology. The rapture, which is the focus of dogmatics, can only take place if the human intellect in search of faith perceives what is made visible by revelation and if the human vision is cast in the right direction.

The *intellectus quaerens fidem* of fundamental theology and the *fides quaerens intellectum* of dogmatic theology are neither opposing nor mutually exclusive movements. Balthasar's fundamental theology is not a formulation of the *praeambula fidei* that are left behind as temporary securities with a leap to the object of dogmatics. The obviousness of religious experiences and perceptions, which is expounded in fundamental

---

[32] Balthasar must have overlooked the developments in art in his time. In the twentieth century, works of art were no longer necessarily connected with beauty or intended to evoke pleasure. One of the clearest examples is Picasso's *Guernica* (1937) or the paintings of Anselm Kiefer, for example his painting *Resurrexit* (1973).

theology, is in itself a rapture. The doctrine of faith as perception never reaches its own obviousness, it continually reaches for the obviousness in which it has already been founded.

Consequently, faith should not be understood as an assumption of truth based on a certain authority, which is reported in scripture. This assumption or testimony should itself be clarified as real knowledge. It should not merely be understood as the foundation or possibility of preceding knowledge (*praeambula fidei*). When Balthasar describes the act of faith he carefully avoids two extreme positions: On the one hand, the faithful human attitude towards God and his revelation cannot be understood as discontinuance of all human logic, in which only the maxim *credo quia absurdum* is true. On the other hand, human belief must not be understood within a scientifically testable structure that is composed of inner-worldly and natural categories of reason. Indeed, an analysis of the act of faith is a *contradictio in terminis* in the end, because every complete concurrence of faith and reason would take neither seriously. After all, faith is a human attitude which responds to revelation and which is as incomprehensible and mysterious to natural reason as the mystery of God in Christ itself.

According to Balthasar, the content of dogmatic theology is a double and reciprocal rapture of divine revelation and human faith. This rapture is the *admirabile commercium et conubium* between God and man in Christ as head and body. No theological perception can take place without the grace of God's appearance in Christ, who Himself already objectively belongs to the rapture and subsequently prepares the tearing away of man to God. The theologian cannot speak of these events without himself participating through faith in divine nature. Therefore, a doctrine of perception and a doctrine of rapture, fundamental theology and dogmatic theology, are reciprocal and may never be separated. The *intellectus quaerens fidem* of fundamental theology takes place in the light of divine revelation from the start, because God objectively reveals Himself in worldly forms and subjectively clarifies the human mind. Faith is an act and an *habitus*, which will be complete when human perception will be perfect. The act of faith continues to develop into a dogmatic theology as a *fides quaerens intellectum* but not as a leap away from the *praeambula fidei*. The evidence that was already gained in the enrapturing light of grace matures in faith and develops according to its own standards. In other words, that which cannot be verified in itself, can be verified indirectly in the understanding of faith, in the way in which faith reflects upon revelation and thus forms itself after the form of revelation (2Cor. 3, 18) (H I 118-119).

c. After the form of revelation

Although Balthasar emphasises the inseparability of fundamental theology and dogmatics, they can be treated separately. On the contrary, the first part of *Herrlichkeit* can be regarded as fundamental theology, while *Herrlichkeit* III,2 should be seen as dogmatic theology. But what then should be the description of volumes II en III,1? According to Balthasar himself, the exposition of the twelve theological styles in volume II is not a history of theological aesthetics but a way of illustrating something that cannot be fully expounded historically or systematically. Volume III is not a straightforward history of philosophical aesthetics either, but a history of aesthetic thought that sketches the declining interwovenness of philosophy and theology to clarify the uniqueness of theological aesthetics in comparison with mythology, theories of religion and philosophical metaphysics. In order to answer the question "What is theology?" through a confrontation with aesthetics, I would like to discuss parts of that particular volume in the following two chapters.

Volume III,1, *The realm of metaphysics*, is a comprehensive history of ideas in confrontation with the arts. As a 'custodian of glory', Balthasar discusses writers and philosophers from Homer to Heidegger, to analyse the history of ideas critically as a history of forgetfulness of glory. At the same time, he presents that same history as the 'Great Catholic Tradition', treating the Greek tragedies as prefigurations of the Christ-event, and the modern empiricists and rationalists as prodigal sons. In this gallery of philosophers and artists there are monographs on two authors which are especially pertinent to our present enquiry: Nicholas of Cusa and Friedrich Wilhelm Joseph Schelling. In the next two chapters, I analyse Balthasar's interpretation and evaluation of their philosophies of art and, in the case of Nicholas of Cusa, what could be called anachronistically 'aesthetics'.

The choice of these two authors is somewhat arbitrary, since each monograph in *Herrlichkeit* reveals a different aspect of Balthasar's own idea of what theological aesthetics should or should not be. Yet, both Cusanus and Schelling play a significant role in his account of the history of aesthetic ideas. According to Balthasar, Cusanus is the turning point in the history of metaphysics and the concurrence of ancient and modern thought. He is the first philosopher to develop a modern concept of the human subject but does this within a classic cosmological framework of interpretation. Many consider Schelling the culmination of the unity of art and philosophy and Balthasar does not disagree. He calls

Schelling the last philosopher who integrates a concept of divine glory in his thought, but criticises him for deifying both nature and the freedom of the human subject. In Balthasar's account of the history of aesthetics, by respectively introducing and glorifying the human subject, Cusanus and Schelling mark the beginning and the end of modernity. As such, reading these two monographs help to clarify his position with respect to the emergence of a scientific approach of aesthetics, the separation of philosophy and theology, and the modern primacy of the human subject.

Aside from intensifying the analysis of Balthasar's theological aesthetics, a closer look at the monographs on Cusanus and Schelling also serve to answer the questions of this present book. Balthasar's aesthetic vision of the unity of divine revelation and human faith as a theological foundation might be instructive for my attempt to understand the art of theology. And yet, some questions remain.

First, although Balthasar conquered the division of the analogy of being and the analogy of faith, he does not account sufficiently for the role of the human subject in constructing these analogies. In his theological aesthetics, the subject gains the highest freedom if it is capable of perceiving the divine light that shines in the world; but that divine light seems too self-evident in his theology. If indeed it is true that theology is formed by faith and faith is formed after revelation then what could possibly be the involvement of the human subject in the formation of theology, if faith is described by perception and rapture? What are the consequences of this kind of human involvement for the view of theology as a rational discourse about God?

Second, although Balthasar expresses his design of theology in aesthetic terms, such as 'light', 'form', 'beauty' and 'perception', he does not explain the necessity of an aesthetic approach. Would it not have been possible to describe the reciprocity of dogmatic and fundamental theology on classic doctrinal grounds? In other words: how could the art of theology be called aesthetic? Here again, the role of the human subject is important. If 'aesthetics' is not merely another description of the doctrine of revelation, an account of the new insights provided by aesthetic terms is needed. Could faith be called an aesthetic response to divine revelation? If so, what is the position of human creativity in the formation of theological ideas?

To answer these two sets of questions Balthasar's account of the thought of Cusanus and Schelling will certainly be helpful. Schelling considered art to be the expression of the Absolute and the necessary tool for understanding the project of philosophy as a whole. This might prove to be a philosophical example for this present research into aesthetics as a way of doing theology. Furthermore, as said before, it will also clarify Balthasar's distinction between a philosophy of the Absolute and a theology of divine revelation. His interpretation of Cusanus's philosophy will be useful in understanding the analogy between human and divine creation, since Cusanus was one of the first philosophers who lived and worked in the Renaissance, during which time the individual artist became an indispensable factor of modern western culture. Moreover, Cusanus was the first to rethink the subjective way of envisioning the infinite God.

6. NICHOLAS OF CUSA
THE CATALOGICAL IMAGINATION

In this chapter, I will show the importance of the philosophy of Nicholas of Cusa for Balthasar's theological aesthetics.[1] First, I will describe how Balthasar positions Cusanus's thought in the history of philosophy as the pivotal point between classic and modern metaphysics. Then, I will present an introduction to renaissance aesthetics and Balthasar's reading of Cusanus. As will become clear, Cusanus's thought holds a key position in Balthasar's account of the history of metaphysics. Finally, I will emphasise Cusanus's influence on Balthasar's theological aesthetics, philosophically and theologically, by reformulating Balthasar's interpretation of Cusanus in terms of the key concepts as defined in the preceding chapters.

6.1. The Renaissance: passage to modernity?

Before I present an analysis of Balthasar's appreciation and critique of modern metaphysics I will summarise some of the historical and philosophical commentaries on the emergence of modernity. With the rise of postmodernism, debate on the essence of modernity has intensified.[2] Part of this debate focuses on identifying the beginning of modernity. Gradually, the birth of modernity became antedated, dependent on the sociocultural stance: politics, economy, art and architecture, geographical position or science and epistemology. Originally positioned with the French Revolution and Enlightenment philosophy in the eighteenth century, the beginning of modernity has moved back through the rise of the natural sciences and the subject oriented epistemology of Descartes in the seventeenth century, until it was confronted by a period long neglected by the handbooks of the history of philosophy: the Renaissance.

The German philosopher of medieval and renaissance history Kurt Flasch has warned against delimiting a philosophical period and has

---

[1] Cf. H.U. von Balthasar, Warum wir Nikolaus Cusanus brauchen, in: *Neue Zürcher Nachrichten 60*, [Beilage Christliche Kultur 28], Nr. 29, 14 August 1964.
[2] Notably by authors like H. Blumenberg, *Die Legitimität der Neuzeit*, Frankfurt am Main 1988² (1966); and S. Toulmin, *Cosmopolis. The hidden agenda of modernity*, New York 1990.

emphasised the necessary inadequacy of any possible general outline of a specific philosophical period. The ideas of the Renaissance thinker Nicholas of Cusa are usually regarded as marking the beginning of Renaissance philosophy. Flasch however, stated that just as it is impossible to assert that Thomism is the quintessence of medieval philosophy, likewise it is impossible to assert that Cusanus is the first Renaissance philosopher.[3] It may be impossible to demonstrate a radical rift between the Middle Ages and the Renaissance or to point to a decisive moment that started modernity. However, it is possible to draw some lines, for example those that run from thirteenth century political philosophy to Machiavelli or from the twelfth and thirteenth century reception of Aristotle to the budding natural sciences in the sixteenth century. There have been authors who likewise have tried to demonstrate some of these lines in the history of philosophy during the period that has come to be known as the Renaissance. In the following sections I will first present some of the authors who interpreted the Renaissance as a period of radical change defined by characteristics fundamentally different from those of the Middle Ages. Then, I will outline the position of other authors who stress continuity between the two periods rather than discontinuity.

a. The history of philosophy discontinued

Jakob Burckhardt argues in his *Kultur der Renaissance* that the Renaissance was an intensification of the problem of the individual, through the discovery of nature and free will of human beings. A new awareness of man's own subjectivity emerges. Man recognises himself as an independent spiritual individual who can position himself opposite the cosmological structure as it was conceived in the Middle Ages. Another renowned Renaissance scholar, Peter Burke, 'exposes' this 'myth of the Renaissance', which creates a sharp caesura between the Middle Ages and the Renaissance based on the concepts of 'individualism' and 'modernity'.[4] He proposes that the Renaissance can only be described as a movement, a certain cluster of changes in western culture that took place between 1000 and 1600. The ultimate hallmark of the Renaissance would not be individuality, as Burckhardt suggested, but the attempt to revive Antiquity. The true rift with the Middle Ages only took place when

---

[3] K. Flasch, *Das Philosophische Denken im Mittelalter. Von Augustin zu Machiavelli*, Stuttgart 1987, 563-567.

[4] P. Burke, *The Renaissance*, [Studies in European history], London 1987, 7-12.

Galileo, Copernicus and Keppler dismissed classical cosmology, according to Burke.[5]

The Dutch historian Johan Huizinga also considers the Renaissance to be a period of radical transition, which should be regarded in a medieval vein rather than as the start of the modern age.[6] For him, the milestone for marking the end of the Middle Ages is that the three paths followed in one's 'longing for a more beauteous life' lead to an ever distant target and that in the Renaissance these journeys became ends in themselves. The first path leads straight out of the world, because redemption from the mortal coil is the highest medieval ideal, according to Huizinga. The second path leads to the improvement and perfection of the world itself, an aspiration hardly known to medieval man that only has its full effect in the eighteenth century. The third path leads to a more beauteous life and is the path of the clear imagination, the dream that "mitigates" the harsh reality "with the rapture of the ideal".[7] This third path is not only the subject matter of literature, but also the form and the content of social life. In the Middle Ages, this third path took shape in the ideal of chivalry. There was still a perfect harmony between art and life. During the Renaissance, however, gradually the tension between life form and reality reached vast proportions: "The light is unnatural and glaring", Huizinga says.[8] The great rift with the Middle Ages takes place after the Renaissance, when art and life truly part.

The Flemish philosopher Edgar de Bruyne demonstrates that Petrarca is the first author who does not regard man in the medieval way as a contemplative being, but as a being that possesses a free and decisive will.[9] The Renaissance, therefore, is not a struggle between (classical) paganism and Christendom, but a conflict between action and contemplation. The Renaissance emphasis on earthly life leads to a new interpretation of the concept of 'beauty', which, from this point on, is understood as 'sensuality' in the sense of a skill, an experience, and moderation. According to Renaissance man, the hunger for beauty leads to self-knowledge. Life itself subsequently leads to beauty. Therefore, Renaissance Humanism seeks to educate people in the knowledge of their being as it reveals itself

---

[5] Ibid., p. 75-76. Cf. E.H. Gombrich, *The story of art*, London 1995[15], 223-246.
[6] J. Huizinga, *Herfsttij der Middeleeuwen. Studie over levens- en gedachtenvormen der veertiende en vijftiende eeuw in Frankrijk en de Nederlanden*, Groningen 1985[18].
[7] Ibid., 30-32.
[8] Ibid., 33.
[9] E. De Bruyne, *Geschiedenis van de aesthetica. De Renaissance*, Antwerpen 1951, 9-10. Cf. A. Levi, *Renaissance and Reformation. The intellectual genesis*, New Haven 2002, 71-94.

in themselves and in their creations.[10] With the exception of Burke, who locates the beginning of modernity with the rise of the natural sciences, the abovementioned authors all consider the Renaissance as a clear break with the Middle Ages, based on the changing role of the individual.

b. The history of philosophy continued

In recent literature, the sudden emergence of the independent subject in the Renaissance is questioned and even denied by some authors. According to them, no clear line can be drawn between the Middle Ages and the Renaissance. There are changes about to take place and developments already on their way that can best be described by means of the dichotomies 'individual—cosmos', 'action—contemplation', 'reality—imagination', 'life—art', 'classical philosophy—modern philosophy' and 'Humanism—Christendom'. Thus, according to the Polish aesthetician Wladyslaw Tatarkiewicz, it is possible to distinguish two Renaissances, one best described as *renovatio hominis*, the other as *renovatio antiquitatis*.[11] The sharp contradictions that are demonstrated by means of certain dichotomies are made subtler when they are considered in the context of these two 'renovating' developments that simultaneously take place in the age of the Renaissance.

Another misconception of the Renaissance corrected by Tatarkiewicz is the idea that the philosophy of the Renaissance was mainly platonic. This overlooks the strong development of Aristotelianism, notably in aesthetics. In his renowned history of aesthetics, Tatarkiewicz differentiates between four forms of Renaissance Platonism: a) the *neopythagorite* form, which is mainly developed in Arab philosophy and the hermetic tradition. It is a breeding ground for mysteries, religious speculation, magic, astrology, alchemy, and so on.; b) the *Plotinic* form, developed from the third century onwards, later to be called 'Neoplatonism'. This is an abstract and absolute philosophy, emphasising a hierarchic and intuitive metaphysics of emanation. This form develops through Pseudo-Dionysius, Proclus and Eckhart to Cusanus; c) the *Augustine* form, which had its heyday during the Middle Ages and slowly disappears during the Renaissance. This is a Christian interpretation of Plato that forms a perfect synthesis of classical and medieval thought; d) the *scientific* form which

---

[10] E. De Bruyne, *De Renaissance*, 18.
[11] W. Tatarkiewicz, *Geschichte der Ästhetik. III: Die Ästhetik der Neuzeit. Von Petrarca bis Vico*, Basel 1987, 54.

mainly adopts Plato's aprioristic mathematical method and is only used by Cusanus in an integrative system of mathematics, epistemology and metaphysics.[12] Aristotelianism then is revived in the sixteenth century, notably in aesthetics, because of a renewed interest in Aristotle's *Poetica*.

Like Tatarkiewicz's two Renaissance 'renovations', Walter Schulz has also suggested two main trends in Renaissance philosophy which he argues have had a lasting effect on modern philosophy.[13] The first runs from Ockham to Luther and Descartes: God is no longer considered to be Being, but Will, and can therefore no longer be regarded as the foundation of harmony in the world and the order of being. The second main trend, which runs from Eckhart to Cusanus, also denies the comparability between God and the order of being. God is, on the one hand, incomprehensible and therefore not of this world that is comprehensible. On the other hand, the very comprehensibility itself of the world is incomprehensible. The truth of the world is a certainty that is conscious of its own shortcomings. As such, God is the incomprehensible foundation of the comprehensibility of the world and this is why God can be called '*intelligere*', to comprehend in an incomprehensible way. The concept of God is defined by subjective characteristics in the modern sense of that word.[14]

Even when the differences between the Middle Ages and modernity are not considered to be radical, the shifts that take place in the Renaissance are still interpreted based on the changing role of the human subject, with the consequence of an altered concept of God. At the end of the Middle Ages the relations in the metaphysical triangle God-man-world are no longer seen as following in that order, as was the case in classical thought. In modern philosophy each aspect of metaphysics can be a starting point for understanding the totality of things. The three exponents of medieval reality are no longer regarded in their hierarchical relations. From now on, every interdependency of any set of aspects determines the thought process. This development has greatly influenced the ambivalence of Christian theology. On the one hand, theology is anthropocentric: scholastic rationality had already expounded the transformation of the reality of salvation of the biblical God in history to the complete world order of nature, history and man. On the other hand, theology is theocentric: one tries to surpass the rationality of scholasticism by strongly emphasising the transcendence, the sovereignty and the mysteriousness of God. According to Hans Blumenberg, who opened the debate on the essence

---

[12] W. Tatarkiewicz, *Geschichte der Ästhetik*, 61-62.
[13] W. Schulz, *Der Gott der neuzeitlichen Metaphysik*, Pfullingen 1982[7], 11-30.
[14] Ibid., 12.

of modernity, anthropocentrism tries to bring together the metaphysical triangle theology-anthropology-cosmology in one system, while theocentrism separates the various lines of thought and perspectives.[15] Blumenberg asserts that the preservation of the theocentric position from the Middle Ages to the modern age is due to the lack of systematic consistency and heterogeneity of anthropocentrism.

More recently, Louis Dupré has argued for the importance of a new and careful hermeneutical reading of early modernity.[16] This new reading is mainly based on the statement that modernity should be seen as a development of fourteenth-century nominalism and fifteenth- and sixteenth century humanism, especially on the philosophy of Nicholas of Cusa and Giordano Bruno, rather than seventeenth-century rationalism or the philosophy of the Enlightenment. According to Dupré, the Enlightenment reads modernity in terms of "too hardened a set of once flexible modern categories, too narrow, even dogmatic, a way of understanding the meanings by both its proponents and its critics."[17]

Strongly influenced by Balthasar, Dupré proposes an alternative hermeneutical concept for the individual by emphasising the concept of form as central to western thought.[18] The classic concept of form provided for the idea of the link between reality in the world and the realm of the divine. In nominalist theology, this intermediary function of the form was discarded and the link with the divine became increasingly external[19]. Thereafter, in humanist and Renaissance philosophy the function of the concept of form developed to denote the essence of expression. Nominalism also anticipated the coming scientific revolution by using words and forms as independent symbols of expression. However, according to Dupré, in early humanism, the creative subject is still embedded in a cosmological structure in which the transcendent God is omnipresent and as such constitutive for human creation[20].

The philosophy of subjectivity is indeed still distant future in the Renaissance. The concept of the subject is, as it was in the Middle Ages,

---

[15] H. Blumenberg, *Die Legitimität der Neuzeit*, 558-559.

[16] L. Dupré, *Passage to modernity. An essay in the hermeneutics of nature and culture*, New Haven, etc. 1993.

[17] D. Tracy, Fragments of synthesis? The hopeful paradox of Dupré's modernity, in: P.J. Casarella, G.P. Schner, s.j., *Christian spirituality and the culture of modernity. The thought of Louis Dupré*, Grand Rapids, etc. 1998, 9-26, 12-13.

[18] Cf. L. Dupré, The glory of the Lord. Hans Urs von Balthasar's theological aesthetic, in: D.L. Schindler [ed.], *Hans Urs von Balthasar. His life and work*, San Francisco 1991, 183-206.

[19] L. Dupré, *Passage to modernity*, 40.

[20] Ibid., 41.

applied to a being that shows itself to us, while the 'object' is a being of representation. According to Schulz, it is only since Kant and the German Idealists that the subject has become the act that performs itself. Hegel, finally, stated that the truth should not be expressed as substance, but as subject. In Cusanus's age this concept of the subject does not exist.[21] However, it can be said that, from Eckhart on, actual being is no longer determined as an available being (*vorhanden*), but as spirit.[22] That spirit is considered to be able to transform reality. In the Renaissance, however, it is not clear yet whether that transformation is dominated by the human subject or equally by God, nature and the subject. The modern project, then, consists in establishing a balance between these three factors of meaning-and-value-giving function, and may still not be finished. The Renaissance humanist philosophy of art and poetry, though, started to consider the increasing active relation of the human subject with the divine and cosmic realm.[23]

6.2. The history of metaphysics: before and after Cusanus

In the twentieth century, the ideas of Nicholas of Cusa were revived by philosophers like Ernst Cassirer and Hans Blumenberg.[24] Very few theologians however, have paid serious attention to the ideas of Cusanus. The scholar of Cusanus, Rudolf Haubst, has written treatises on some theological topics in Cusanus's work.[25] His findings, however, did not attract much attention from theologians.[26] Karl Jaspers's introduction to the ideas of Cusanus has been much more significant in that respect.[27] For the main part theologians have been dependent on philosophical approaches to the Renaissance thinker. However, despite the central role he plays in

---

[21] Cf. W. Schulz, *Der Gott der neuzeitlichen Metaphysik*, 12-13.
[22] Cf. W. Göbel, *Okzidentale Zeit. Die Subjektgeltung des Menschen im Praktischen nach der Entfaltungslogik unserer Geschichte*, Freiburg 1996.
[23] Cf. L. Dupré, *Passage to modernity*, 249-253.
[24] E. Cassirer, *Das Erkenntnisproblem in der Philosophie und Wissenschaft der neueren Zeit*, [Erster Band], Darmstadt 1994³ (1906), 21-61; H. Blumenberg, *Die Legitimität der Neuzeit*, 558-638.
[25] His essays are collected in: R. Haubst, *Streifzüge in die cusanische Theologie*, München 1991.
[26] With some notable exceptions: A. Kaiser, *Möglichkeiten und Grenzen einer Christologie 'von unten' bei Piet Schoonenberg und dessen Weiterführung mit Blick auf Nikolaus von Kues*, Münster 1992; M. Thurner, *Gott als das offenbare Geheimnis nach Nikolaus von Kues*, Berlin 2001.
[27] K. Jaspers, *Nikolaus Cusanus*, München 1987 (1964).

Balthasar's theological aesthetics he has failed to influence either philosophers or theologians, with the notable exception of Louis Dupré.

Balthasar's treatise on Cusanus is an attempt to determine his philosophy as a re-assimilation and completion of classical philosophy. In this sense, Balthasar advocates the continuity between Antiquity and modernity. At the same time, he considers Cusanus's thought to be a radical renewal of classical thought, by which Cusanus, according to Balthasar, set the tone for modern philosophy. Therefore, his systematic analysis of Cusanus's metaphysics must be understood within the framework of his own account of the history of philosophical developments before and after Cusanus.

When Balthasar was working on the first volumes of *Herrlichkeit* he wrote a small book dedicated to "a mysticism of love".[28] In it, he describes the love of God as the light of the world. Because of the theme of light, but also because of themes like 'perception of love' and 'love as revelation', he calls *Glaubhaft* an outline of his main work on aesthetics. In this short introduction to his aesthetics Balthasar describes the classical and modern periods as the age of the cosmological reduction and anthropological reduction respectively, asserting that God's everlasting love cannot be thought of from either perspective alone.[29] God's love can only be thought of as the coherence of eternity and individuality. Balthasar argues that philosophy should never have traded its cosmological starting points for the merely anthropological. According to him, it should have sought to find a union of the classical and the modern, a union that would lead to the heart of western thought. As will be shown further in this chapter, he thought that Nicholas of Cusa was one of few thinkers in the history of Christian thought who managed to find a form of thought that expressed that very union.

a. Metaphysical developments before Cusanus

One of the main achievements of Cusanus's philosophy, according to Balthasar, is the reincorporation of the original forms of thought as they

---

[28] H.U. von Balthasar, *Glaubhaft is nur Liebe*, Einsiedeln 1963 (GinL).

[29] Balthasar does not strictly distinguish between a cosmological and an anthropological *period* but he generally classifies the period before the Renaissance as 'cosmological' and the period after the Renaissance 'anthropological'. However, authors such as Boehme, Hegel and Schelling are classed by him as part of the cosmological reduction as well (GinL 8-32).

were articulated in Greek philosophy. The days of scholasticism are over, and Balthasar remained highly critical of the rationalistic method of this period throughout his work. Cusanus and Balthasar would agree that there could be no such thing as a scientific theology, for true theology cannot be captured in books or arguments. There can be no scientific doctrine of God next to a mystical doctrine of God. Instead, Balthasar distinguishes two types of theological metaphysics in the history of mythology, philosophy and religion toward the end of the Middle Ages: the metaphysics of the saints and the metaphysics of the fools. Both types signify a return to the metaphysical questions of the classical world, in which the ontological problem of unity and diversity is developed (H III,1 371-551). Nevertheless, this position is no mere restoration of classical thought. Rather it is an attempt to reflect upon the religious and mythical foundation of the Christian unity of late medieval culture. According to Balthasar, they should be seen as a follow-up of Neoplatonism, a philosophical movement he has both criticised and adopted in his theology.[30]

Let us examine these two types of metaphysics that Balthasar distinguishes. First, the metaphysics of the saints, which is also termed the 'metaphysics of holy reason'. This type of metaphysics can be found especially in the thought of Eckhart, Tauler and Ruusbroec, and has as its main characteristic *indifferentia* or disinterestedness. It is mainly developed by the mystics in the period between Thomas and the Renaissance and is reminiscent of several themes in Greek tragedy. The core idea of this type of metaphysics is that being human means 'suffering'. This, according to Balthasar, should be understood as the true characteristic of finitude and therefore as both a physical but, above all, spiritual feature. The person who suffers can do nothing but to resign herself to her being and fate. The theme of 'resignation' has often been forgotten in Christian philosophy, according to Balthasar, because Christian thought is a continuation of classical philosophy, which failed to digest the themes of

---

[30] "The touching Protestant seriousness, which likes to cover itself with disparaging remarks about the "aesthetic" lack of seriousness in the Catholic realm, and is surely right where biblical observation slips into "neoplatonic" aesthetic contemplation, will nevertheless have to be reminded constantly of the glory of God, which is revealed fully and objectively." Balthasar adds a note to the word 'slips': "I had to be aware that I would be dismissed as neoplatonic, even before I had finished speaking." (HIII,1 17-18). Balthasar is responding to a book review by H.E. Bahr—himself an author on theological aesthetics—who calls *Herrlichkeit* a return to the period before Thomas (Balthasar adds an exclamation mark when he quotes this line) and at the same time a renewed neoplatonic-Christian mysticism. Balthasar himself takes part in causing this confusion, by including appreciatively, among others, many platonists in the origins of western thought and consequently, of the Christian theology of revelation (H III,1 958-964).

the Greek tragedies. This is why Christendom does not use the idea of tragic resignation but the 'way of Christ' for interpreting and undergoing suffering. However, undergoing suffering has always been interpreted in a metaphysical sense as well, as a deliverance of the finite beings into an infinite Being, as exaltation from being-image to being-without-image, as being accepted into the world of the eternal light. Following Thomas, the theme of resignation gained a different, more active meaning, the intellectual openness of the *intellectus possibilis*, which is followed by the *intellectus agens*. According to Balthasar, Eckhart interpreted this intellectual openness of humans to God as an intellectual form of 'freedom', but not as the freedom of the will. In contrast, modernity views the freedom of man as separate from the freedom of God (H III,1 407-491, esp. 407-410). This position would entail the end of the metaphysics of the saints, which advocates the selfless vision of the divine glory and therefore interprets its own freedom within the framework of divine freedom.

Second, he distinguishes the metaphysics of foolish reason, which Balthasar characterises by *Geworfenheit*, thrownness. This metaphysics can be found in the works of François Villon, Cervantes, Shakespeare and Dostoievsky and the paintings of Rouault. Although most of these writers and painters lived and worked long after Cusanus, Balthasar discusses them in his analysis of the beginning of modernity in contrast with the metaphysics of the saints with which it forms a metaphysical counterpart to thomist metaphysics. If the world of the classic tragedies can be characterised by melancholy, the world of the fool certainly cannot be characterised in the same way. Saints experience a chasm between finitude and infinity or use contemplation to ascend into the intangible infinite light. In literature and the plastic arts, the difference between God and human beings often finds its only expression in a simple man, the fool or the clown. Quite often, these fools accompany saints and heroes. Furthermore, saints and heroes show a great resemblance to the fools, in the forms of a contemplation that sometimes leads to madness, a temporary experience of hell, or in the often abnormal gestures and rituals that have to be performed to bridge the chasm with eternity (H III,1 492-551, esp. 492-496).

b. Metaphysical developments after Cusanus

The passivity of both types of metaphysics reaches its completion in the life and work of Ignatius of Loyola, according to Balthasar. Ignatius considered the passivity and the spontaneity of the human intellect to be united in their relationship with God. Those that deny the activity and the spontaneity of the human mind in the light of divine revelation, or even dismiss it as mere foolery, will quickly identify the analogy of Creator and creature with the contradiction of the sinful and apostate human and the delivering and atoning God. Both the metaphysics of the saints and the metaphysics of the fools have been guilty of searching for divine glory in the world in the form of something unmediated and supernatural. Later, the two types of metaphysics are joined by a third, the metaphysics of the reformers, characterised by being 'unmediated', which according to Balthasar also institutionalises the chasm between God and human beings too rapidly. A further similarity is its foundation in pre-scholastic philosophy:

Balthasar proposes that the modern age, from fifteenth century humanism, sixteenth century Renaissance, seventeenth century Baroque, and eighteenth century Enlightenment to nineteenth century German Idealism, has three main themes which are addressed in these three different metaphysical variants, again finding their origin in classical thought but eventually leading to a loss of divine glory. First, there is a continuing mediation of classical thought in the works of Origen, Augustine, Boethius, Eriugena, Dante and Bruno. This neoplatonic line in the history of philosophy has always related best to Christian thought, Balthasar argues, because it regards the world as revelation and thereby questions the division between the world and the cosmos. Christ then, being the divine or cosmic revelation, would be the definitive Christian answer to the questions about the relation between world and cosmos. However, the modern age does not return to this 'naive classical relation to the divine', as he calls it, and therefore a new doctrine of God needed to be developed.

That brings Balthasar to the second theme of modernity, which is a new speculative doctrine of God. This new type of theology, already prepared by Plotinus and subsequently reinterpreted in a Christian way by Augustine, assumes a direct experience between the finite and the infinite self. Not until Eckhart does this experience gain its full meaning of diffidence and veneration by means of the direct vision of God, interpreted as the mystagogical way. Balthasar argues that Eckhart could not have foreseen that the combination of these themes—cosmos/world and the inward witnessing of God—would eventually lead to the loss of divine glory.

A third theme that for Balthasar defines the essence of modernity is the idea of evolution, especially in the philosophy of Ludwig Feuerbach and

Karl Marx (H III,1 594). According to Balthasar, the evolutionary concept of the world is developed within the space of the relation of the finite and the infinite self, as a result of which the sovereignty of God and His glory are diminished. What is left, Balthasar laments, is nothing but the idea of the absolute identity of the self and the human search for it.

Balthasar's account of the modern history of metaphysics seems rather critical. Every theme and development in modernity he describes has led to a loss of divine glory (*Herrlichkeitsvergessenheit*). Nevertheless, these developments have their origin in classical thought and therefore cannot be interpreted as modern inventions. Balthasar's criticism of philosophical metaphysics does not advocate a return to premodern times. According to him, the history of metaphysics is not a history of radical caesuras but of continuity (with the possible exception of nominalism), as a history of catholicity. In his *magnum opus*, *Herrlichkeit*, his criticisms are especially directed towards the application of philosophical concepts to theological aesthetics. In the modern age, philosophy and theology have become separate disciplines. A theological aesthetics, based on what he calls philosophical and, therefore, 'innerworldly' concepts will necessarily confuse natural or artificial beauty with divine glory. According to Balthasar, Nicholas of Cusa was the last philosopher who was able to maintain the concurrence of a cosmological and anthropological worldview in a form of thought best described by *coincidentia oppositorum*, one of Cusanus's own favoured concepts.[31] In Cusanus's theory of art and imagination there is no radical opposition between the divine Creator and the artist. Nevertheless, he establishes a modern change of roles in the interplay of the human and the divine.

6.3. Cusanus and Renaissance aesthetics

a. Aesthetics from the Middle Ages to modernity

To position Cusanus's aesthetics, a presentation of Renaissance aesthetics in general will be helpful. The arts experienced a golden age during the Renaissance. According to the renowned historian of aesthetics Monroe Beardsley, however, no philosopher made an important contribution

---

[31] Cf. the opposite opinion in P. Sloterdijk, *Sphären II. Globen*, Frankfurt am Main 1999, 429ff.

to aesthetics.[32] While this seems a gross underestimation of the emergence of new genres of texts trying to justify the arts, dealing with individual artists (e.g. Giorgo Vasari[33]) or the theory of the work of art, on perspective, proportion, colour, etc. (e.g. Leon Battista Alberti[34]) or poetry (Philip Sidney[35]), Beardsley is right to assert that no new theories of art were developed in this period. In these texts, the work of art is measured by its technical qualities rather than by its quality of beauty or their original representation of reality. Moreover, neoplatonic philosophy does not have a renewing effect on aesthetics. Yet, the reintroduction of classical philosophy (*renovatio antiquitatis*) in the Renaissance is not the only new development. Although philosophy still has its classical form, its themes have changed: The human mind is no longer seen as part of a much larger cosmological structure but cosmos and mind have become two separate and relatively independent units (*renovatio hominis*).

In the Middle Ages 'beauty' is regarded as a general quality of being: *ens et pulchrum convertuntur*. The whole of the natural world is beautiful since God has created it. This means that 'beauty' is closely connected with 'goodness', which, like 'beauty', is regarded as a quality of being and therefore as a form of perfection. Apart from the beauty that is experienced in the world, there is a supernatural and superhuman beauty. Natural beauty is conceived of as a reflection of this supernatural beauty. Nature has been created by God and its beauty, therefore, must be more absolute than that of the work of art, which has been made by man.[36] These metaphysical starting points in the medieval theory of beauty originate in the philosophy of Pseudo-Dionysius and are still employed in neoscholastic philosophy.[37]

The ideas and concepts of the Greek artists form the basis for the theory of the work of art. These are developed further in medieval theories

---

[32] M.C. Beardsley, *Aesthetics from classical Greece to the present. A short history*, Tuscaloosa, etc. 1991[8], 117.
[33] Giorgo Vasari, *Le vite de' più eccelenti pittori, scultori e architettori* (1550/1568).
[34] Leon Battista Alberti, *Della pittura* (1435); Id., *Della statua* (1435); Id., *De re aedificatoria* (1452).
[35] Sir Philip Sidney, *A defence of poetry*, Oxford 1966 (1595).
[36] U. Eco, *Art and beauty in the Middle Ages*, New Haven 1988.
[37] J. Aertsen, Die Transzendentalienlehre bei Thomas von Aquin in ihren Hintergründen und philosophischen Motiven, in: *Thomas von Aquin. Werk und Wirkung im Licht neuerer Forschungen*, [Miscellanea Mediaevalia. Veröffentlichungen des Thomas-Instituts der Universität zu Köln. Band 19. Hrsg. v. A. Zimmerman], Berlin, etc. 1988, 82-102; Id., Beauty in the Middle Ages: a forgotten transcendental?, [Cardinal Mercier lecture at the Catholic University of Louvain on 22 February 1990], in: *Medieval philosophy and theology* 1 (1991), 68-97; Id., *Medieval philosophy and the transcendentals. The case of Thomas Aquinas*, Leiden, etc. 1996.

of music, poetry and architecture. Art is a form of knowledge that can be described by general concepts and rules. The visual arts are part of the mechanical skills (which are taught in the workshop), poetry and music belong to the free arts (part of the *quadrivium* of the *artes liberales*, taught at the cathedral schools). Medieval aesthetics does not make a clear distinction between art and craft, but the arts are said to have a didactical and moral value because they express a desire for the truth.[38]

There are aspects of medieval aesthetics that have their reverberations in the modern age. Contrary to the classical definition, Thomas Aquinas limits his definition of 'beauty', *pulchra sunt quae visa placent*, to two elements: vision and gratification of judgement. This means that the beauty of the object is no longer completely dependent on the object itself but also on the subject. Modern aesthetics radicalises this point of view but the tension between the object and the subject will remain central. Thomas also unites two contrary qualities of beauty from classical thought: *commensuratio* and *claritas*.[39] Art and beauty are regarded as composite appearances of form and content. Various interpretations of beauty now become possible: formal, exemplary, symbolic, etc. This also means that the idea of art as *imitatio* fades into the background and that the concept of *imaginatio* will receive more emphasis, although it is still not common to distinguish between art and craft.[40]

It is only in the modern age that the familiar distinction is made between the arts, crafts and the sciences respectively. Beauty is seen as a subjective judgement, as something that can be experienced and assessed in various appearances.[41] Art begins to express itself in different styles as well. This puts the idea of man as a creator of forms in the foreground. The human creator does not merely have to satisfy a number of rules in his work of art but can also express his or her own individuality, talent, inspiration and genius, thereby appealing to human feeling and the inner self. Because of this, the work of art becomes an increasingly isolated event that has its own specific truth, which is not identical to the scientific or revealed truth.

---

[38] For this passage, I have used the handbook by W. Tatarkiewicz, *Geschichte der Ästhetik*, 28-30.
[39] Cf. H I 18, where Balthasar explains the unity of splendour (*Glanz*) and form (*Gestalt*).
[40] W. Tatarkiewicz, *Geschichte der Ästhetik*, 30-31.
[41] Cf. M. Mothersill, "Beauty", in: D. Cooper [ed.], *A companion to aesthetics*, [Blackwell companions to philosophy, Vol. 3], 44-51.

In the transition to the modern age, whilst some of the medieval qualities of beauty disappear, others, mostly aesthetical qualities that were also used in classical philosophy, get a new emphasis. The idea of a supernatural and absolute beauty disappears, as does the idea of cosmic beauty. In a mainly platonic framework of interpretation, the negative appreciation of art, already present in the works of Plato, does not return. However, the Renaissance sees the return of the aristotelian idea of art as a representation of nature, and the concepts of 'form', 'inspiration' and 'creativity'.

Renaissance aesthetics cannot be described as simply a return of Neoplatonism or rebirth of classical thought. The Renaissance sees the advent of new ideas next to the reintroduction of many classical ideas. It can be established that the individual has gained an independent role in theories of art, however. As an inspired being, man is able to create something new himself. The variety of images and styles is also appreciated. The work of art has its own content, which does not necessarily have to correspond to reality. It creates its own artistic reality. From now on, the work of art is slowly given its very own and independent position as a cultural form that has its rightful place in society next to politics, science and technology.

b. A reconstruction of Cusanus's aesthetics

Coming from the North of Europe, Cusanus did not implement all the new aesthetic ideas of the mainly Italian Renaissance in his own philosophy. Instead, his ideas on the human subject have partly influenced these developments. Originally from Kues in Germany, Cusanus spent some time at Deventer, in the Netherlands, with the Brethren of the Common Life, in his early years. Later in life, he spent a considerable amount of time in Italy as a church diplomat, where he must have become acquainted with the Italian Renaissance. Nevertheless, Nicholas preferred the 'medieval' gothic music and paintings from the Low Countries, such as the music of Johannes Ockegem (1410-1497) and the work of the painter Rogier van der Weyden (1399/1400—1464) and Hans Memlinc (1430?-1494). Although Cusanus never developed an explicit theory of art and aesthetics, he plays a key role in Balthasar's theological aesthetics. Other handbooks of the history of aesthetics do not mention him, though. This is why I will reconstruct his aesthetics before I evaluate the importance of his thought for Balthasar.[42]

Some histories of aesthetics refer to Cusanus merely to mark the beginning of Renaissance philosophy. His contemporary, Marsilio Ficino, seems to be much more important for the history of philosophical aesthetics. Cusanus himself did not devote a single work exclusively to art or the concept of beauty.[43] Nevertheless, the works of a philosopher like Cusanus, who is deeply influenced by Neoplatonism, contain many passages that deal with form, light, harmony or proportion. The Flemish philosopher, Edgar De Bruyne, argues that Cusanus's treatment of beauty and art lacks originality. According to De Bruyne, Cusanus's ideas are only interesting when viewed in the framework of his entire philosophical system.[44] Tatarkiewicz calls Cusanus's aesthetics a return to Platonism, although he emphasises that Cusanus lends little weight to the platonic-idealistic starting points of his aesthetics. Instead, he seems to be more interested in the activity of the human mind.[45]

According to Cusanus, the function of art is to arrange and assemble substances (*congregat omnia*) to give multiplicity and diversity, unity

---

[42] I have used the following Latin-German edition of the works of Cusanus: *Nikolaus von Kues. Philosophisch Theologische Schriften (*from here on *PTS),* [3 Bde., lat.-dt.Studien- und Jubiläumausgabe, hg. und eingef. v. L. Gabriel. übersetzt und kommentiert von D. und W. Dupré], Freiburg 1964-67; For Cusanus's biography, see E. Meuthen, *Nikolaus von Kues. Skizze einer Biographie,* Münster 1964. Other works on Cusanus: R. Haubst, *Das Bild des Einen und Dreieinen Gottes in der Welt nach Nikolaus von Kues,* Trier 1952; Id., *Die Christologie des Nikolaus von Kues,* Freiburg 1956; K.H. Volkmann-Schluck, *Nicolaus Cusanus. Die Philosophie im übergang vom Mittelalter zur Neuzeit,* Frankfurt am Main 1957; K. Jaspers, *Nikolaus Cusanus*; M. Alvarez-Gomez, *Die verborgene Gegenwart des Unendlichen bei Nikolaus von Kues,* München 1968; G. Schneider, Gott—Das Nichtandere. Untersuchungen zum metaphysischen Grunde bei Nikolaus von Kues, in: R. Haubst [Hrsg.], *Mitteilungen und Forschungsbeiträge der Cusanus-Gesellschaft 8,* Mainz 1970, 246-254; K. Flasch, *Die Metaphysik des Einen bei Nikolaus von Kues. Problemgeschichtliche Stellung und systematische Bedeutung,* [Studien zur Problemgeschichte der antiken und mittelalterlichen Philosophie VII], Leiden 1973; W. Beierwaltes, *Identität und Differenz. Zum Prinzip cusanischen Denkens,* Opladen 1977; Th. van Velthoven, *Gottesschau und menschliche Kreativität. Studien zur Erkenntnislehre des Nikolaus von Kues,* Leiden 1977; P.M. Watts, *Nicholas of Cusa. A fifteenth century vision of man,* Leiden 1982; I. Bocken, *Waarheid en interpretatie. Perspectieven op het conjecturele denken van Nicolaus Cusanus 1401-1464,* Maastricht 2002; Id., *De kunst van het verzamelen. Historische inleiding tot de conjecturele hermeneutiek van Nicolaas Cusanus,* Budel 2004.
[43] G. Santinello, *Il pensiero di Nicola Cusano nella sua propetiva estetica,* Padova 1958.
[44] E. De Bruyne, *De Renaissance,* Antwerpen 1951, 227-229.
[45] W. Tatarkiewicz, *Geschichte der Ästhetik,* 81-86.

and form (*unitas in pluritate*).⁴⁶ He calls this method of working a creative act. After all, the artist can create a work that does not exist in nature, for example, when he creates a casket or a spoon from a tree that was created by nature.⁴⁷ The world in which people live has therefore been created by both God and humans. For Cusanus, there is nothing in this world, which is exclusively natural or artificial. He usually compares the work of an artist with that of the artisan. The work of the painter, however, still has its example in nature, but the artisan's work finds its example in the human mind since, for example, the spoon cannot be found in natural reality. In Cusanus's days, of course, the visual arts produced mainly images and representations of natural reality. His choice of the artisan is not unique in the history of aesthetics.⁴⁸ However, his interpretation of the artisan's work, capable of creating something new that expresses the creative power of the human mind, is original.⁴⁹ In this respect, Cusanus's aesthetics differs from the medieval conception of art as pure productivity and technical skill, although he does not have a modern theory of art as a separate discipline yet.

The creative process of the artist does not start with the creation of a work of art but with a vision, the mind's image. 'Vision' here is not the mere sensory act but a mental act. As such, vision is the beginning of all art, according to Cusanus. Creation is just a result of this vision. This point of view makes Cusanus appropriate to mark the beginning of modern philosophy. Art is not just the work of hands but also the work of the human mind. Because vision precedes art, Cusanus can be said to have instigated a Copernican turn *avant la lettre*. Although, in the philosophy of Cusanus, human knowledge is aimed at objects, the mind is the measure of all things in art. The work of art completely conforms to the human mind.

The human mind is not capable of creating the absolute proportion, which is the highest norm for a work of art in platonic philosophy. According to Cusanus, the mind is only capable of forming conjectures: assumptions or assessments. The proportions of a work of art are grounded in comparisons performed by the mind and are therefore always relative. The form one creates out of substance is only likeness and image (*similitudo et imago*). This idea, which resounds the idea of analogy, is valuable to Balthasar in the works of Cusanus.

---

[46] Cusanus also uses both concepts in his philosophy of religion, especially in his philosophy of religious freedom in *De pace fidei, PTS III*, 707-796.
[47] *Idiota de mente, PTS III*, 490ff.
[48] Similar interpretations of the artisan as an artist can already be found in the works of Aristotle. Cf. W. Tatarkiewicz, *Geschichte der Ästhetik. III*, 82-84.
[49] Cf. H. Blumenberg, *Die Legitimität der Neuzeit*, 558-638.

6.4. Human vision as analogy: a philosophical appraisal

> His [Cusanus] design for a philosophy between Spirit and God can, but does not have to be evaluated as transcendental in the modern sense of the word. From a classical point of view (as a philosophy of being), as well as from the modern point of view (as a philosophy of the Spirit and of Freedom), Nicholas's effort is unfalteringly devoted to the completion of the analogia entis. (H III,1 568-569)

According to Balthasar, Cusanus is the starting point for a philosophy of mind based on classic thought. The analogy of being, which according to him is formally prepared by Plotinus, is completed by Cusanus introducing the creativity of the human mind. In the following sections I will reconstruct Balthasar's appreciation of Cusanus's thought in Balthasar's own theological terminology.

a. Cusanus and the analogy of being

The analogy of being is the expression of the first philosophical act, Balthasar states. For the purpose of this argument, he uses Cusanus's language: seeing the *complicatio* in the *explicatio*. "God is all in all, because He is irretrievably all above all" (H III,1 556). A human being always has a one-sided vision of the One extracted in all and, at the same time, he sees that the One can never be fully extracted. In this sense, one sees the invisible in the visible. There can be a world next to a God who is already everything, if and only if God is thought of as being above everything. This simultaneity can only be grasped in an imperfect way, in the form of a longing.

Balthasar interprets Cusanus's epistemological starting points within his own structural analysis of the metaphysical developments at the beginning of modernity. According to him, Cusanus adds a metaphysics of the *desiderium* to a metaphysics of *Gelassenheit* and a metaphysics of *Geworfenheit*. As a philosopher, he calls himself *idiota*. Balthasar's own concept of the metaphysics of fools resounds here. For Cusanus, philosophy is the deepening and exploration of the understanding that we know nothing. The more we realise this, the more we start longing.[50] The desire for God is fed by the understanding that He is the Invisible, and the more we realise this, the more we comprehend God in an incomprehensible way (*docta ignorantia*).

---

[50] *De quaerendo Deum III, PTS II*, 596ff.

This epistemological doctrine of God, based on the concept of desire, is also at the heart of Cusanus's theory of divine and human creativity. Balthasar distinguishes between four moments in what he calls Cusanus's philosophical and theological aesthetics and presents it as a unity of a material, and a formal aesthetics. First, the moment of creation: the world has been created for God's glory, for its announcement and for knowledge. Second, the role of the creative creature: the created and creating human spirit should praise, as it is the reflection of the Praiseworthy. Being the reflection of the Praiseworthy, praising comes naturally to it. Third, divine sovereignty: the divine freedom decides for how long the mystery remains a mystery to human beings and when the inner-divine glory is revealed to be beheld. Four, catalogy and analogy: the catalogical vision of earth from heaven sees order, harmony, and beauty. The analogous vision of heaven from earth sees the divine love through grace, and God decides when and how man can answer this divine love (H III,1 564-565).

Cusanus is the last pre-reformation philosopher who reflects upon the paradoxes of the *analogia entis*, says Balthasar. His concept of the *coincidentia oppositorum* does not mean the coexistence or combination of *contradictions* but rather the coincidence of *opposites*. Incarnation, for example, is the coincidence of God and man; the church is the coincidence of historicity and universality; faith is the coincidence of seeing the invisible and visualising this vision, and so forth. Balthasar understands the Cusan idea of coincidence as an *intellectus fidei*. For both Balthasar and Cusanus, the *intellectus* is always combined with an Anselmian *fides*: considered to be a search for understanding faith, within faith towards faith (H III,1 559).

Though Balthasar praises Cusanus's application of the analogy of being, he has a series of critical questions about the remainder of Cusanus's philosophy. Does Cusanus neglect the infinite difference between God and humanity? Does his explanation of the analogy of being mean a dissolving of the reception of divine glory into a totalitarian, cosmological scheme? If so, how could this do justice to the concrete historical events of the cross and resurrection? Balthasar argues that despite these dangers, Cusanus succeeds in bringing cosmos and gospel together in a way unique to the modern age. This is why Cusanus, according to Balthasar, is not just the pivotal point between the old and the new age. His philosophy also confronts all the former images of God with the modern idea of the human mind. Cusanus's God is at the same time the One

(Plotinus), the Shining One (Homer), the Dark One (Sophocles), the Longing (Virgil) and the biblical God. For Plotinus, Proclus and Eriugena, the world itself is the appearance of the non-appearing God (H III,1 559-560). Furthermore, Balthasar argues that Eckhart has interpreted God's non-appearance as His absolute freedom, while Cusanus has intertwined the theme of divine freedom with the themes of divine glory and love.

b. Glory and analogy

The appearance of the divine glory in the world is developed on two levels by Cusanus. First, on a trinitarian level: The relation between the divine Love and the human mind appears in the glory between Father and Son. 'Glory' in this case is the mutual giving and receiving of love. Second, on an innerworldly level: The God-world relation in Christ is present in the mystery of the Spirit in the Church. Trinitarian glory appears in the church because of the Spirit's work in the human mind. Thus, both the analogy between the trinitarian relations and the innerworldly relation of God and man can already be found in the philosophical works of Cusanus. I will now present how Balthasar reads Cusanus's philosophy through the lens of his own doctrine of analogy.

Cusanus describes the infinite forming principle of all forms in the world as the Primal Image, which appears in the human mind as the truth of every image, as measure (harmony, proportion, number) and foundation. This Primal Image is an infinite living Person—for it appears to the human mind as a spirit, not just as a worldly being that thinks and speaks.[51] The sensory world could be represented as a book or a text that can be read and that contains the words God has spoken to the world through his Son. His Word is heard in every sound. Each creature should be understood as an intention, a resolve to be understood as divine self-communication. People, who see themselves as a creature and the world as creation, understand themselves and the world they live in as divine self-communication. Because of this Cusan image, Balthasar finds a double aesthetical dimension in the works of Cusanus. First, a material or horizontal aesthetics that is characterised by *consonantia*: All sounds in the world are only heard in imitation of one or the other, belonging together as in a melody in which every note has its place, a simultaneous

---

[51] Cf. *Idiota de mente V, PTS II*, 512-520.

preceding and proceeding. The world could not be understood as world if the different tones within the melody, the different words, were not heard in a sentence or in a meaningful context.[52] Secondly, a formal or vertical aesthetics that is characterised by *claritas* and *resplendentia*: The things in the world could not be seen if there were no light to illuminate them. Things receive clarity from the reflection of something, which is not a thing itself, but a light which can only be seen indirectly through its action upon objects in the world.

Balthasar claims that Cusanus attributes a transcendental beauty to a person simultaneously in the form of a *having* (in a spiritual way) and in the form of *being* (as being-spirit). This reflects the cohesion between the horizontal and the vertical aesthetics. According to Cusanus, the human mind *has* the ability to behold the world as the appearance of the non-appearing God (and with it beholding God Himself). As spirit, a person *is* a created image of the divine primal beauty. Seeing oneself as the image of God, a person understands his or her seeing of God in the world as an image of how God sees people and everything else in the world. Consequently, this intellectual vision is the image of God. People see the world and themselves as an image. With this, they see the Creator of the image. The insight follows that only the act of seeing itself, makes a person into an image. Seeing God is seeing the divine glory in worldly beauty, which also includes people.

Knowledge of worldly beauty is no guarantee of knowledge of the divine glory. On the contrary, glory can only be seen if the divine light itself breaks through in the world. Only then can one realise that although glory cannot be defined conceptually, it can be comprehended in an incomprehensible way. This comprehension only exists in the coincidence of the descent of identity into non-identity and the ascent of non-identity into identity. For Cusanus, analogy is *evocat idem nonidem in idem*.[53] In other words, the light of faith alone, and not one's own conceptual capabilities, enables one to become *speculator majestatis*, but the human mind realises this because it already has faith when it does so.

---

[52] Here, the doctrine of the *docta ignorantia* resounds: All knowledge is only knowledge because of a preceding knowledge. All new knowledge can only come into existence because of the application of a measure, formed by what we already know.
[53] W. Schulze, *Zahl, Proportion, Analogie. Eine Untersuchung zur Metaphysik und Wissenschaftshaltung des Nikolaus von Kues*, [Buchreihe der Cusanusgesellschaft, Bd. VII, Hrsg. von R. Haubst, E. Meuthen und J Stallmach], Münster 1978, 232-242.

c. Analogy as negative theology

How does the horizontal aesthetics in the world, expressing itself in proportion and number (*analogia proportionalitatis*), relate to the vertical aesthetics that expresses itself in terms of light (*analogia attributionis*)? Between God and the created world, one finds the created spirit that, just like the Creator, can also be the light and principle of all things. According to Cusanus, the spirit expresses the relation between God and the world. The inadequacy of that expression corresponds to the inadequate comprehension of the infinite spirit. Even the inadequacy of mental expression constitutes a similarity to the difference between the finite and the infinite spirit. This is a similarity in the face of an ever greater dissimilarity. Like the infinite spirit, the human mind has the infinite possibility of contemplating, determining and naming things in the world. This infinite possibility is actualised in a finite way, however. Insofar as the world is beheld by the human mind it becomes intelligible that it is seen by the infinite Spirit and that this seeing of the Spirit constitutes the human freedom of imagination.[54]

This is the paradox that expresses the analogy of being, according to Balthasar: God is everything and yet the world exists, although not in any way altering the fact that God is everything. God is all in all, yet He does not coincide with the world, He does not mix with it, even though He is completely immanent to it, because He is all in all the unfolded (*extractus*) particularities, in a forever folded (*contractus*) way (H III,1 571). Some Cusanus scholars deny the importance of the analogy of being in his philosophy. Their main argument is that Cusanus himself never used the term 'analogy'. He did however use the word *proportio*, e.g. *finiti ad infinitum proportio non est*. In this last statement, Cusanus seems to deny the analogy of the infinite and the finite. Others argue that Cusanus's metaphysics is a metaphysics of unity instead of difference, in which there is no room for analogy. Moreover, all inner-worldly characteristics ascribed to God should be regarded in a metaphorical sense only.[55]

---

[54] "Apparuisti mihi Domine aliquando ut invisibilis ab omni creatura, quia es Deus absconditus infinitus. Infinitas autem est incomprehensibilis omni modo comprehendi. Apparuisti deinde mihi, ut ab omnibus visibilis, quia in tantum res est, in quantum tu eam vides. Et ipsa non esset actu nisi te videret. Visio enim praestat esse, quia est essentia tua. Sic Deus meus es invisibilis pariter et visibilis. Invisibilis es uti tu es, visibilis es uti creatura est, quae in tantum est, in quantum te videt." *De visione Dei XII, PTS III*, 142.

[55] J. Hirschberger, Das Prinzip der Inkommensurabilität bei Nikolaus von Kues, in: R. Haubst [Hrsg.], *Mitteilungen und Forschungsbeiträge der Cusanusgesellschaf, Bd. 11*, Mainz 1975, 39-54; R. Haubst, Nikolaus von Kues und die analogia entis, in: Id.,

Despite these different interpretations of Cusanus's metaphysics, Balthasar reads his doctrine of the Non-Other analogously. The beings in the world relate to other things as being different. However, God can never be such an opposite, for He is never just a particular being, according to Cusanus. On the contrary, he is not different, the Non-Other, because beings are no more than what they are, and because human beings keep noticing the other in the world, which presupposes the Non-Other. How else would it be possible to conceive of the other? Both moments of non-otherness, of the things in the world itself (identity) and of the possibility of thinking of things in such a way (the idea of *Non-Aliud*), reflect two moments in Cusanus's aesthetics. The identity of the world is the *consonantia* of the material or horizontal aesthetics. The idea of *Non-Aliud* is the *claritas* and *resplendentia* of the formal or vertical aesthetics, which can be read from things as the appearance of the Non-Appearing.

Eventually, *coincidentia oppositorum* must be understood as convergence (non-otherness). This convergence or analogy is expressed by Cusanus as reduplication: *omne ens non entiter, essentia essentiarum*, etc. This is how he avoids taking a pantheistic stance. The analogy of being does not just apply to all beings in the world, it also applies to all (metaphysical) knowledge: Only in the idea of God can things become exact.

6.5. Seeing the present God: a theological critique

The problems Cusanus exposed in his philosophical epistemology are theologically resolved in *De visione Dei,* and *De Possest*, according to Balthasar. Nevertheless, he laments that these theological texts retain a philosophical style, strongly influenced by Plotinus and Proclus. Plotinus for example regarded the contingency of finitude as the worldly counterpart of absolute freedom. Aesthetically, finitude is then understood as the unselfish radiation of the Good. According to Balthasar, Cusanus interpreted this unselfish act appropriately and without any hesitation in the light of the Person and the Love of God as Creator and revelation. The consequence, however, was that he had to carefully tailor his philosophical elaboration of the analogy of being to fit Christian doctrine, especially the doctrine of God. This section presents Balthasar's reading

---

E. Meuthen, J. Stallmach [Hrsg.], *Streifzüge in die cusanische Theologie*, [Buchreihe der Cusanusgesellschaft, Sonderbeitrag zur Theologie des Cusanus], Münster 1991, 232-242.

of the aforementioned texts, emphasising the scheme of catalogical analogy that characterises his own theology.

a. Analogy as positive theology

Cusanus interprets God's incomprehensibility within the framework of the even greater incomprehensibility of divine love.[56] God's love reveals itself to human beings because God wants it, even though it is not necessary. Subsequently, human beings are free to comply with this divine free will. Balthasar argues that this conquers the position of negative theology in classical thought.[57] In Christian theology, God's negative incomprehensibility is transformed into a positive incomprehensibility. The analogy of love shows that the human relation to God does not entail mere determinism but also an act of free will of human beings. This relation to God, which Augustine once described as *"Videntem videre"*, is explained by Cusanus in *De visione Dei* (1453) through the celebrated example of a portrait that seems to look back at the beholder.[58] Here, an insight into God's love is provided by means of the metaphor of vision, of seeing and being-seen.

In *De visione Dei* Cusanus attempts to introduce the monks of Tegernsee to mystical theology. He tries to explain the inaccessible light of God, which transcends any sensory, rational and intellectual comprehension, in nevertheless intelligible terms. He does this by means of the self-portrait of Rogier van der Weyden, which had been painted in such a way that the portrayed appears to look at everything and everyone.[59] The gaze of the portrait moves to both a certain position and to all other positions simultaneously. It seems to move without moving itself, as though it sees everything at the same time. Cusanus calls this, 'the image of God'.

---

[56] Cf. *Idiota de sapientia I, PTS III*, 432: "Et haec est gaudiosissima comprehensio amantis, quando incomprehensibilem amabilitatem amati comprehendit. Nequaquam enim tantum gauderet se amare secundum aliquod comprehensibile amatum, sicut quando sibi constat amat amabilitatem esse penitus immensurabilem, infinibilem, interminabilem ac incomprehensibilem. Haec est gaudiosissima incomprehensibilitatis comprehensibilitas."

[57] For the opposite position, see Th.P. Tighe, A neglected feature of neoplatonic metaphysics, in: P.J. Casarella, G.P. Schner, s.j., *Christian spirituality and the culture of modernity. The thought of Louis Dupré*, Grand Rapids, etc. 1998, 27-49.

[58] Cf. *PTS III*, 93-219. Especially in the *praefatio* and chapters I to III.

[59] In his text, Cusanus refers to a large panel on which Rogier Van der Weyden had painted himself among a large group of people. He is the only one looking at the beholder. This panel used to hang in the city hall of Brussels but it no longer survives. A goblin copy of the panel can be found in the Bern museum. Cusanus presumably sent the brothers of Tegernsee a similar portrait.

Cusanus does not describe this analogy of the portrait merely to educate the monks by simplifying something that is otherwise too difficult to understand. Nor does the description of the portrait serve to point out that people are trapped in images because they can only think in images. Instead, Cusanus articulates a fascination with the image. It is the image itself which is so complex and incomprehensible that it invites exploration. The incomprehensibility of the image is evoked by the fact that it appears to contain a infinite amount of possible perspectives and meanings. Every act of beholding and understanding is the vision of that out of which one creates an image to constitute reality. God's reality is actualised here not as one of the many meanings enclosed in the image but as the condition for all possible meanings. This insight in the image simultaneously comes objectively and subjectively. 'Constituting reality' in this case means marking out a certain configuration of identity and difference within the whole of possible meanings of the image.

God, whom Cusanus describes with the gazing portrait, is not primarily a reality that is inaccessible and therefore has to be represented. In this example, he is presented as the limit of the image. We do not see God in the image but, because we see the image, we see God. Seeing God by means of the portrait is seeing infinite possibilities, precisely by taking seriously first one's own position and subsequently that of the other, and finally confronting the many possible positions with each other. Although man knows that the infinity of the number of points of view cannot be known by him, he keeps longing for the one point of view from which he can oversee all points of view. Cusanus's description of the portrait of Rogier Van der Weyden shows that man will never take this point of view himself, but will always have been and always will be looked at from this point of view. Being-seen from the point of view of all points of view is part of the seeing every beholder does. Seeing and being-seen are one in the image of God.

Rather surprisingly, Balthasar describes the idea illustrated with the example of the gaze as 'biblical', although he argues that Cusanus has thought through it in an all too Plotinian way, i.e. in the abstract form of the reduplications: God is the face of all faces, the vision of all visions, and so on. Even so, the idea remains biblical still because the vision of God is not just determined as all-encompassing but also as love and compassion (H III,1 577). Balthasar states that here, Cusanus transforms the analogy of being into an analogy of freedom and love. The relation to God is borne by the free and simultaneous choice of both God and humans.

"It is obvious (...) that God's pure givenness will only be received when man too has freely and personally chosen God, in a choice that is both God's and his own" (H III,1,2 578)."

A person's vision of God is contained in God's vision of the person. Every human vision sees the divine truth in a human way. In that sense, one does not see anything but one's own truth. Yet, in another sense, this is also the divine truth insofar as there can be nothing but truth in the divine truth. Otherness and difference belong to the image and to human vision. With regard to God Himself, human vision can be nothing but the vision of God.[60] One knows, however, that this seeing of God is nothing else than seeing one's own truth. Because of this, a person knows that what is comprehended by seeing is only comprehended because the person is seen. Therefore, it is a way of comprehending the incomprehensible. Balthasar considers Cusanus's completion of the relation to God in the person seen by God as introducing the Pauline idea (H III,1 578): Human beings regard themselves as being an image and they know that as such they are not the truth, but are created by God, Who is Truth itself.[61] The truth of being human is nothing more and nothing less than the truth of being an image of Truth itself. Although Cusanus places this biblical idea into the Plotinian scheme quite stubbornly, according to Balthasar, he nevertheless reveals its Christian and, therefore, positive theological qualities.

b. Created in the image of the possibility-to-be

In *De Possest* (1460), Cusanus emphasises that God's Being and his infinite potential Being coincide. According to Balthasar, the difference with Thomas's *distinctio realis* is that the possibility of the human-made image of God is clarified by means of an identification of God as *actus purus* and the idea of otherness. Since worldly being does not coincide with possible being, there must be a position where being and possibility coincide. This is God's position. Therefore, the creation of an image of God is an act that, although it is founded on the act of creation of the Creator, is infinitely different from it. However, despite this emphasis on infinite

---

[60] Cf. *De visione Dei VI, PTS III*, 112: "Omnis igitur facies, quae in tuam potest intueri faciem nihil videt aliud aut diversum a se, quia videt veritatem suam. Veritas autem exemplaris non potest esse alia aut diversa, sed illa accidunt imagini, ex eo, quia non est ipsum exemplar."

[61] Cf. Gal. 4,9; 1Cor. 8,3; 2Cor 5,11; Phil. 3,12.

difference, Cusanus also departs from the tradition of negative theology, according to Balthasar, because the creation appears as the positive intention of the Creator. This appearance is founded on seeing the infinite possibilities of the human mind.[62]

Otherness can only be thought of because of the distinction between possibility and impossibility, which can be made based on the image in which being and potential being coincide. The wherefore of things in themselves can never be constituted by creatures. The essence of the otherness of something is always formulated in the sense of being non-other than what it is. A creature can never answer why something is nothing but that which it is. If this were possible, the creature would become creator. Balthasar identifies this as the point in Cusanus's philosophy where the real problems arise. He acknowledges, however, that Cusanus wants to maintain a classical metaphysical position with the analogy of being as its central idea, without ignoring the biblical-Christian body of thought.

Balthasar shows that the problem of the Creator-creature points back to the idea of Thomas, who regarded creation both as *emanatio* and as *receptio*. 'Emanation' is the classical aspect of the analogy of being, looking at creation as the emanation of the fullness of being of God. 'Reception' is the Christian aspect of the analogy of being, insofar as people's free act of receiving corresponds to the free Potential Being of God. The potential only reveals itself in being insofar as the ability to see this revelation corresponds to the infinite being, without this infinite being being totally enclosed in the ability to see infinite possibilities. In the idea of emanation, God is dependent upon Himself. The idea of reception responds to God's infinite Love without which there could be no love (H III,1 580).

Cusanus's concept of *possest* is more than the simplicity of being, according to Balthasar.[63] It is the concept of being infinitely predominated by itself and therefore the openness of the totality of being, wherein God even without Himself can be Himself. In this respect, Cusanus differs from Plato and Plotinus, who raised the idea of the Good above that of Being, into being able to understand why Being should be understood as manifestation. Furthermore, Cusanus differs from Eckhart, who thinks God is Being because He is Spirit and Freedom. He even assimilates and adapts the Anselmian *id quo maius cogitari*. The vision of the human

---

[62] Cf. the postmodern reception of this idea in R. Kearney, *The God who may be. A hermeneutics of religion*, Bloomington 2001, 103-105.

[63] *Possest* is best translated by 'the possibility-to-be', or even better: 'the freedom-to-be'.

mind gets its final positive confirmation *vis-à-vis* God's incomprehensibility: not just founded on the intangibility of His infinite greatness but also on the glory of His Love and Majesty.[64]

Balthasar concludes that Cusanus's position differs not only from negative theology, but also from positive theology.[65] If Cusanus regards human desire to behold the divine glory as an intellectual transcendental possibility, there is a greater intimacy of the human desire and divine self-revelation in his works than in those of the fathers. Cusanus uses the classical scheme of the dynamics of divine Eros, because the dynamics of human reason cannot be recovered in the world. In Cusanus's works, however, this idea never approaches the attitude of indifference and resignation that characterises the metaphysics of the saints. The desire is maintained despite the realisation of imperfection. However, human desire is only possible thanks to divine grace, which is God's personal self-revelation in the world. This, Balthasar remarks, is where classical thought effortlessly changes into Christian doctrine. The distinction between philosophy and theology made in scholastic thought is rejected in favour of a classical metaphysics of totality. However, Balthasar realises that this threatens a form of mystical rationalism and so argues that Christology should be reintroduced in its Origenian form: Christ will have to be regarded as the presence of the absolute Intellect in the creaturely intellect. Thus, faith is enlightened from within to achieve a better understanding of the mystery of God, "as Sun of all spirits" (H III,1 583).

---

[64] "Collige igitur haec, ut videas omnia ad hoc ordinata, ut mens ad posse ipsum quod videt a remotis, currere possit et incomprehensibile meliori quo potest modo comprehendat, quia posse ipsum est solum potens, cum apparuerit in gloria maiestatis satiare mentis desiderium." *De apice theoriae, PTS II*, 372.

[65] Cf. *De Deo abscondito, PTS I*, 299-309. This dialogue between a Christian and a heretic is about the absence of God but does not emphasise a negative theology: "Christian: I know that everything I know is not God, and that everything I imagine is not like Him, but that He is beyond everything. Heretic: So, nothing is God. C: He is not nothing because this nothing has a name: nothing. H: If He is not nothing, than He must be something. C: Neither is He something. After all, something is not everything. God, on the other hand, is not rather something than that He is everything. H: It is amazing what you are claiming about the God you worship: That He is neither nothing, nor something. It is incomprehensible. C: Well, God is beyond nothing and beyond something. After all, nothing obeys Him to become something. And therein consists His omnipotence, by which He is beyond everything that is or is not, so that everything that is or is not, obeys Him. He is nothing of everything that is below Him; He is nothing of everything that He in His omnipotence precedes. Therefore, it cannot be claimed that He is rather this than that. After all, everything originates from Him." *PTS I*, 303.

6.6. Balthasar's primacy of catalogical vision

a. Seeing non-otherness in otherness

I have presented Balthasar's discussion of Cusanus's thought in two parts, philosophically and theologically. According to Balthasar, Cusanus succeeded in developing a modern approach to philosophy that nevertheless assimilated elements of classical philosophy. Central to Balthasar's aesthetical approach of Cusanus is the relation between God and humanity. He argues that this relation is best expressed in the analogy of being. For him, Cusanus has found the exact character of analogy: a similarity in the face of an even greater dissimilarity.

What is most characteristic of the idea of analogy in the works of Cusanus is the fact that it is borne by the freedom of both God and humanity. Therefore, human freedom should not be characterised by resignation (*Gelassenheit*) or by being thrown (*Geworfenheit*) alone, but also by longing. In Cusanus's philosophy the longing for God is expressed in the human intellect, which is capable of comprehending who God is in an incomprehensible way. God is comprehended as the coincidence of opposites, as an identity, without being able to lift the differences of thought itself. Balthasar, acknowledging the importance of Cusanus in the history of western thought, also warns against the danger of his philosophy, which too hastily emphasises the identity of human and divine freedom, ignoring the fact that human freedom should be regarded as being subject to the norm of difference and imperfection.

Nevertheless, Balthasar is of the opinion that Cusanus has succeeded in gauging the value of identity and difference in the relation between God and humanity because of his use of the aesthetical category of vision. Cusanus succeeds in doing so because he does not interpret the appearance of God in the world as merely an innerworldly event. That said, he does read it from the innerworldly appearances and forms. A horizontal aesthetics is thus founded on a vertical aesthetics. Cusanus characterises human freedom by its unlimited possibilities but this limitlessness is also a human inability. For one can never carry out all of these possibilities let alone see them at once or consider them in a single thought. Seeing God is longing for God. This constitutes the difference between God and humanity and the paradox of the analogy of being: One can only see otherness in the world and only sees this otherness as otherness because one knows that God sees the otherness as nothing but that which it is. The vision of God should therefore be understood as a seeing of non-otherness in the otherness.

The theme of the relation between human and divine freedom is continued in Cusanus's theological aesthetics. According to Balthasar, Cusanus goes beyond the ideas of the difference between God and humanity, and the inadequacy of the human intellect to know God familiar from Plotinus or the negative theology of Pseudo-Dionysius. He also approaches it in a biblical way. The selflessness with which God sees the world and through which one can see the divine glory in the world, can only be understood within the framework of the love of God, which is even more incomprehensible than His selflessness. Cusanus sees human freedom as a gift out of love. Thus, he conquers negative theology. Human beings are capable of a positive confirmation of the love of God despite the inadequacy of their vision of God. According to Balthasar, Cusanus's philosophy is completed in the idea of potential being. It regards human freedom as both emanation and reception. A creature has been given an infinite number of possible ways of answering the love of God. According to Balthasar, this positive statement fulfils the idea of a biblical interpretation of the analogy of being in a modern philosophical framework.

The intelligibility of the world finds its foundation in its infinite possibility. The vision of God is a precondition for seeing the world. However, according to Balthasar, at this point Cusanus shifted the whole perspective of theology. Neoplatonic philosophy usually proceeds from affirmations to negations analogously, in an ascending movement. In contrast, Cusanus proceeds from the incomprehensible God to an expression in the world in a catalogical descending movement (TL II 195). This catalogical perspective is assumed in every analogical movement and yet it is infinitely unapproachable. In other words, although faith is the condition of meaning and understanding, this insight cannot be explained except by understanding itself (TL II 191).

Only within this complex structure of the interwovenness of the catalogical and analogical movement is it understandable that the Father can be seen in the Son (John 14,9). The human nature of Jesus Christ subsists in his divine personhood so that nature itself is encompassed in this unity of divinity and humanity.[66] This unity finds its climax in the cross, where the coincidence of opposites, the coincidence of catalogy and analogy, is fulfilled by Christ, because He descends in utmost humility, without losing His divinity (TL II 194).

b. The catalogical imagination

To recapitulate, Balthasar's main questions in his reading of Cusanus are: What is the importance of the analogy between the human vision of God and God's vision of human beings for theological aesthetics? Can the unifying divine vision (the catalogical movement) and the diversifying human imagination (the analogical movement) provide a solution for the problem of analogy? Confronted with the ideas of Cusanus, Balthasar raises again the fundamental question of his theology: How can there be a world apart from God, when God is all in all?

To contemplate the theme of analogy in Balthasar's aesthetics and its consequences for theological imagination as a whole, let us glance once more at Cusanus's example of the portrait. First, Cusanus demonstrates that people have images of reality which, they realise, are not reality itself but only images of it. Seeing and being seen, although separate in human images, are associated. From this follows the insight that it is of no use to consider reality as something completely different from that which is represented in it. It is for the sake of this unrepresentable reality that this image is formed. Conversely, the reality that cannot be represented can only be conceptualised thanks to the image; it cannot be thought of independently of the image. Finally, it can be concluded that the creation of images is a constitutive element of being human. This human constitutive act is a limited, yet transcendental method of relating to reality as a whole, and in particular to God. The creation of an image actualises but one of the many possible configurations of identity and difference. In this way, one also appears to oneself as an image and therefore as a limit. It is this observation that makes one susceptible to the reality in images and the possibilities that appear in them.

Limit and difference are the constructive elements of every act of imagination and, therefore, of faith and theology as well. They serve not to point to whatever lies outside the limits of the image. Nor do they serve to illustrate that humans are trapped in their own images from which they will never be able to reach reality. To a certain extent, image and reality are inextricably intertwined. Reality is the limit of the image during the

[66] Cf. *De visione Dei XIX*, *PTS III*, "To me, a humble person, You reveal, my God, such a hidden mystery, that I can understand that humans can't understand You, Father, unless through and in your Son, Who is comprehensible and intermediary. And now I understand that to comprehend You is to become one with You. Humans can become one with You, through your Son, Who is the medium of unification."

creation of the image because image and reality never fully coincide. The creation of an image is the actualisation of one of the many possibilities of imagined reality. Indeed, this is how it presents that reality. However, this reality can only be thought of within the image that actualises it. Therefore, the image is both limit and possibility of the susceptibility to that reality.

For human beings, seeing precedes the statement of being, because the practice of seeing is a coincidence of seeing and being seen. With every perception, human beings form the image they have of reality and therefore of themselves. It is the hallmark of the human situation that if one chooses it, one can go on forever questioning the limits of the image in which one lives. According to Cusanus, this fundamental infinity is God's freedom, which is at the same time the limit of human imagination and the human image. Freedom is the limit of imagination because it is constituted by it. God *is* freedom and man *has* freedom. This freedom is the creativity of human imagination, the ability to endlessly confront one image with another and, by doing so, to create a new image of oneself and the surrounding reality.

To actualise this human freedom, humans beings have to be forever different from the reality that confronts them in images and the images they create of reality. This is why being is never fully constituted by the act of seeing. The fact that human beings are forever different from the images they behold is the tension with which they have to live. This tension is the context of human longing for a potential which seems to be forever inaccessible. This inaccessibility should not, however, be characterised by failure and inability but by infinite possibility. This infinite possibility is not some distant ideal that is beyond the limits of this life. It is a reality that human beings are constantly confronted with and which they constantly emanate.

Human beings are not simply passive and resigned towards this confronting reality. They meet it repeatedly and actualise it by means of the image. The image is the presence of the ever-newly created reality. As such, human imagination is not regulated by the ever-failing longing for the one or the whole. Instead, it is regulated by the desire to look in the same direction as the image. But ultimately this direction diverges into many perspectives of the one reality that holds all these perspectives together. In doing so, it also draws all these visions to itself.

7. FRIEDRICH WILHELM JOSEPH SCHELLING
THE ABSOLUTE IN ART

In the previous chapter, I stressed the importance of two characteristics of Nicholas of Cusa's philosophy for Balthasar's theological aesthetics. First, Cusanus's biblical interpretation of classical philosophy and his modern definition of the human subject distinguishes him as a key thinker in the history of western metaphysics. Second, Cusanus's catalogical foundation of the human imagination mirrors Balthasar's own design of theological aesthetics. He approves of the perfect balance in Cusanus's thought between the negativity of the analogical dissimilarity between Creator and creature and the positivity of the given possibility of participating in the catalogical imagination. Thus, reading Cusanus through the eyes of Balthasar clarified and confirmed Balthasar's doctrine of analogy. Furthermore, the choice of a philosopher in a time of cultural transition is a good example of how he reformulates the history of metaphysics aesthetically.

From the start it has been my intention to answer the question "What is theology?" by confronting the subject matter of theology with aesthetics. Balthasar has been the main guide until now. Before I leave him as a guide, I still expect the answers to the following questions. First, why is an aesthetic approach to theology necessary? Second, how are aesthetic perceptions and expressions applicable to theology? To find answers to these questions, I will look to Balthasar's treatment of the philosophy of Friedrich Wilhelm Joseph Schelling. Balthasar says that "more so than any other modern philosophy, the philosophy of Schelling, as a balance between the Infinite and the finite, is an aesthetic one" (H III,1 898). Moreover, Schelling's philosophical project to create a 'new mythology' has great similarities with Balthasar's own aesthetical project. In his own words: "This *kairos* of an 'aesthetic theology' in Schelling is decisive for our theme, because it appears (more originally even than in Hegel) as the recapitulation of that which was developed in our first volume (Seeing the Form), and also as the idealistic representation of the primary matter of the present volume" (H III,1 899). But beside these similarities recognised by Balthasar himself, there are some straightforward reasons for choosing Schelling as a thinker who could answer my questions. He called art the organ of philosophy and considered it capable of expressing the Absolute.

In the following, I begin by sketching Balthasar's account of the developments in the history of modern philosophy from Cusanus onwards (7.1). I will then introduce Schelling's aesthetics by giving an overview of the culture and philosophy of his time, the ideas of Romanticism and German Idealist philosophy in particular (7.2). Next, I will take a closer look at Balthasar's reading of Schelling's aesthetics (7.3) and confront his appreciation and criticism with his own theological program (7.4). Finally, I will conclude with an analysis of Balthasar's characterisation of modern aesthetics being 'promethean' (7.5).

7.1. The advancement of modernity

a. Three modern developments

The return to Antiquity was a way out of late medieval formalism, according to Balthasar. He approves of Cusanus's reintroduction of classical philosophy during the Renaissance. Cusanus's Christian interpretation of platonic philosophy could have had positive consequences in the further development of modern thought, Balthasar argues, if it had not been interpreted as a religious-cosmic archetype of modern philosophy, which Christianity had merely utilised to its full intellectual potential. He believes however, that classical philosophy ultimately could not offer sufficient possibilities for understanding the unique character of Christian revelation (H III,1 788).

Balthasar makes the provocative assertion that Eckhart was the first thinker to offer a viable alternative to classical philosophy.[1] Eckhart, and not Descartes, was the first to point at the human mind as the essence of all non-spiritual being, and to explain this spiritual constitution of all being from the personal relation between the finite and the infinite spirit as it is revealed in the scriptural covenant. As I have mentioned in the previous chapter, this early modern philosophy has evolved into what Balthasar calls 'the metaphysics of the saints', characterised by *indifferentia* and a mystical, non-philosophical foundation.

Balthasar believes, however, that the metaphysics of the saints degenerated into a philosophically reduced idealism. As shown, Cusanus adopted a philosophy in the spirit of Eckhart and from it developed his idea of 'analogy'—in the classical philosophical sense—of the archetypal

---

[1] Cf. C. O'Regan, Balthasar and Eckhart. Theological principles and catholicity, in: *The thomist* 60 (1996), 203-239.

image of the Creator and the image of the creative human mind, which Cusanus refers to as *secundus deus*, a second god. After Eckhart and Cusanus, philosophers like Giordano Bruno (1548-1600) and Anthony Ashley Cooper, Earl of Shaftesbury (1671-1713), turned the human mind into "the one who from the inner apprehension and experience of the divine, creative, universal nature and from the fullness of his ethical personality becomes himself a creator—and now we hear the Plotinian word—of inward form" (H III,1 641-642). The result was a type of aesthetics that positioned the creative artist in the foreground as a creator in his own right: a modern Prometheus who, once more, threatens to steal the fire of the gods.

According to Balthasar, this new perspective on human creativity was certainly an advancement in the history of philosophy but, at the same time, it also led to a corrosion of classical metaphysics. Some nominalist philosophers had completely reversed the hierarchy of the cosmos, nature and the human mind. The cosmos had been reduced to a material entity that can be calculated and used by man.[2] The consequence was that certain strands of modern philosophy no longer position the mediation between the infinite and the finite in the cosmos or in nature but in the human mind. It has thus become the biggest threat to Christianity, even though it is the fruit of Christianity at the same time, (H III,1 789). Warning against the dangers of this displacement of the cosmos and the human mind, Balthasar describes three consequential aspects of the history of modern philosophy.

First, Descartes unified philosophy and the natural sciences. He did this by regarding the outside world as matter (*res extensa*) on the one hand, and by moving the focal point of metaphysics to the *ego cogito* on the other. Since then, both the finite and the infinite spirit can be deduced from the *ego cogito*. According to Balthasar, the Christian position in philosophy may have been safeguarded in this way but it also clears the way for modern science. From that point on, the human mind would have to bridge the chasm between the inner world and the outside world, either by regarding matter as a mode of the spirit, as Leibniz did, or as deception and mere appearance, as Berkeley did.[3]

---

[2] To stress this point, Balthasar refers critically to Francis Bacon's *Of the proficiency and the advancement of learning divine and human*, London 1973 (1605). Cf. L. Dupré, *Passage to modernity. An essay in the hermeneutics of nature and culture*, New Haven, etc. 1993, 128.

[3] Cf. Ph. Clayton, *The problem of God in modern thought*, Grand Rapids 2000, esp. 224 and 256-262.

Second, as the natural sciences gain greater independence, metaphysics gains strength. The success of science and technology can be regarded as the success of man as co-creator. Balthasar is concerned, however, that the difference between the creation of God and that of man may be obscured. If the starting point of philosophy is reduced to the *ego cogito*, and if this is subsequently regarded as the absolute identity of all reality— be it in the form of Descartes's formal philosophical starting point of the *ego cogito*, or Fichte's *Ich*, or Schelling's point of identity, or Hegel's Absolute Spirit—, how can divine glory be the subject matter of metaphysics? After all, if the supposed subjective starting point of modern philosophy is taken seriously, there can only be a glory of the human mind, or as Balthasar puts it, a *Selbstherrlichkeit* (H III,1 790).

This is why Balthasar believes Eckhart's and Cusanus's alternatives should be given serious consideration as a third way in modern philosophy. To view the creative artist as *secundus deus* should not only be regarded as a *causa secunda* but, as being involved from the start in the *Causa Prima*, which has formed man materially and spiritually. Without wanting to return to a neoplatonic worldview, in which the relationship of the infinite and finite is explained by the concept of manifestation, Balthasar suggests that it is necessary to reinterpret the concept of participation in modernity. His main metaphysical problem: How can there be a world if God is all in all? is a question about how things in the world can be individuated. A classic cosmological reduction can only account for the way the world is related to its primary source.[4] However, the modern anthropological reduction, he argues, can only conceive of the difference between God and man in terms of the difference between a formal fulfilment of the absoluteness of the human mind and all its intrinsic, realised potential. Henceforth, reality can only be regarded as the evolution of nature to the human mind.[5] However, idealistically it can only be interpreted as the human mind anticipating its own infinite potential, which is the foundation of its intrinsic totality. Balthasar is of the opinion that a modern philosophy of mind should be aware of this circular idea.

In modernity, cosmos and nature are understood as objects of philosophy. The development from matter to spirit sketched by Balthasar reveals the mismatch between Christianity and the tendencies in modern philosophy, which presuppose that the thinking subject precedes the

---

[4] Cf. Ibid., 477.
[5] Cf. L. Dupré, *Passage to modernity*, 252.

objectivity of nature, thereby forgetting that the mind itself is subject to cosmological processes as well. In Balthasar's words: "Nature, which somehow comprehends the finite spirit, is not intelligible without the prior projection of an (absolute) spirit, but the source of that projection is now the human spirit at the same time, which thus also grasps its own process of becoming within the universe (in the evolutionary sciences) and thus possesses the latter definitively as its own material beneath itself" (H III,1 791).

b. Second god or modern Prometheus?

The abovementioned three developments in modern philosophy that follow one another consequentially originally start with a new form of thought that originated in the ideas of Eckhart and Cusanus. The idea of man—the creative artist in particular—as *secundus deus*, was the expression of a new concept of human freedom. It emphasised the sovereignty of the human subject and yet confirmed the biblical idea of human freedom, in covenant with God. Balthasar is of the opinion that Christianity reaches its maturity in modernity because it applies a new metaphysics of subjective creativity to the biblical narrative of divine creation. Divine creation in Genesis is not merely a cosmological idea that should be philosophically interpreted with the *exitus-reditus*-model of neoplatonic philosophy but is also the establishment of the human-divine covenant and, therefore, the confirmation of human freedom at the same time (GinL 10). Peter Eicher accurately calls Balthasar's theology an apology of divine grace and revelation.[6] However, it could also be called a Christian plea for human freedom of desire, which is analogous to the freedom of belief. The reception of the grace of God finds its form in the figure of desire, not least in the philosophical form of desire. Balthasar repeats Spinoza's idea of the *amor intellectualis Dei* to describe the task of philosophy but warns against the Spinozean form of self-love.

It is clear that Balthasar appreciates certain developments in modern metaphysics. But he is certainly not uncritical of them. Both the rise of the natural sciences and the emergence of philosophical idealism eventually led to the identification of the creative imagination and divine revelation. This development did not start in modernity, however. He does

---

[6] Cf. P. Eicher, *Offenbarung. Prinzip neuzeitlicher Theologie,* München 1977, 339-343.

not blame Descartes or say, Francis Bacon for the *Gottvergessenheit* (forgetfullness of God) of modernity but he uses the complete first part of *Herrlichkeit III* to describe a process from Homer onwards that signifies the difference between Christian theology and philosophical metaphysics, which intensified in modernity in a particular way. Just as the cosmological reduction of neoplatonic philosophy could not explain biblical revelation fully, the anthropological reduction of modernity failed to account for the analogy of being. The modern turn towards the subject resulted not only in the denial of the ever-greater dissimilarity between God and man, but even to the declaration of the death of God (GinL 26).

For that reason, Balthasar repeatedly compares these developments with the myth of Prometheus, who stole the fire of the gods in order to give it to the "creatures of a day", to mankind (H III,1 641).[7] The gods fought back, not wanting to be burned out or to become redundant after man would have gained all the hidden knowledge necessary to rule the earth self-determinately. So they chained Prometheus to the rocks on the shore to show their supremacy and his dependency. In the history of western culture, Prometheus became the teacher of man, educating him in both science and virtue. To be able to do so he had to possess at least a spark of divine wisdom. Consequently, Prometheus was considered the demiurge, which places that divine spark within man. This interpretation of the Prometheus myth is utilised by the Romantic tradition, especially by the early Romantics of the *Sturm und Drang* (Storm and Stress) movement. Think of the subtitle of Mary Shelley's *Frankenstein, or the modern Prometheus*. Other Romantic poets such as Johann Wolfgang von Goethe (1749-1832), Lord Byron (1788-1824), John Keats (1795-1817) and, not least, Percy Bysshe Shelly (1792-1822) in *Prometheus unbound*, all saw Prometheus as the symbol of the tormented but independent artist.[8] Balthasar's references to the Prometheus myth therefore are highly appropriate in relation to German Idealism and the Romantic movement. There is a thin line however between his appreciation of the idea of the creative artist as a second god and his criticism of the promethean genius in Romantic literature. He expresses this ambivalence towards the aesthetics of German Idealism in his monograph on Schelling, as I will show in the following sections.

---

[7] Cf. D. Verene, *Philosophy and the return to self-knowledge*, New Haven 1997, 1-38.
[8] Ibid., 13.

7.2. Schelling and the aesthetics of German idealism

At a very young age, Schelling became the key figure of both Romanticism and German Idealism. He was not only strongly influenced by the early Romantics, and would later in his life become the leading philosopher of late Romanticism, but he also declared art to be the organ of philosophy. Before I turn to Balthasar's analysis and critique of Schelling's philosophy of art, I will introduce Schelling and the philosophical context in which his ideas emerged. But first, I will give a historic overview of German Idealism and the Romantic movement before examining the different stages in Schelling's philosophy and his aesthetics in particular.

a. German Idealism

The age of revolution
It is impossible to understand the philosophy of Schelling without knowing something of the period he lived in and of his philosophical conversation partners.[9] The period was characterised by radical political and cultural changes: the Enlightenment and the Kantian revolution in philosophy, the French Revolution, the beginning of the industrial revolution and the rise of Romantic art and literature. Ideas of art and politics were strongly interwoven. In his *Über die ästhetische Erziehung des Menschen* (On the aesthetical education of man) Friedrich Schiller (1759-1805) argues that the promethean idea of man must be made comprehensible to the public, as the embodiment of a republican citizenry.[10] The four philosophers who mark the period of German Idealism (Kant, who provided the conceptual framework for it, and Fichte, Schelling and Hegel) were strongly influenced by these cultural changes. Fichte for example explicitly identified his philosophy with the French Revolution. Fichte, Schelling and Hegel responded to Kant and each other's philosophies, and most of them knew one another personally as well. It would be insufficient, however, to restrict the philosophical description of this period to these four figures. Two of them, Hegel and Schelling, actually lived

---

[9] Cf. T. Pinkard, *German philosophy 1760-1860. The legacy of Idealism*, Cambridge 2002; D. Simpson [ed.], *German aesthetic and literary criticism. Kant, Fichte, Schelling, Schopenhauer, Hegel*, Cambridge 1984; N. Schneider, *Geschichte der Ästhetik von der Aufklärung bis zur Postmoderne. Eine paradigmatische Einführung*, Stuttgart 1996.
[10] F. Schiller, *Über die ästhetische Erziehung des Menschen in einer Reihe von Briefen*, in: Id., *Über Kunst und Wirklichkeit*, Leipzig 1975, 261-374.

together with the poet Hölderlin when they studied in Tübingen. But the cultural capital of this age was Jena.[11] It was there that Fichte, Schelling and Hegel successively taught philosophy but it was also the city where the Romantics, like Goethe, Schiller, Hölderlin, Novalis and Friedrich Schlegel, lived and worked.[12]

Because of the cultural diversity and philosophical complexity of this era, any short introduction to German Idealism as a whole will most likely misrepresent it. There are some remarks to make about the term 'idealism' however, and some rough distinctions to sketch between the main philosophers and between Idealism and Romanticism. The Idealism of this period differs from the idealism of philosophers like George Berkeley (1685-1753). Although the objectivity of reality is conditioned by the subjective judgment in Kant's transcendental idealism, the subject does not have to constitute the existence of the object, as is the case in Berkeley's philosophy.[13] Therefore, the term 'idea' in 'idealism' does not indicate that which is not real or does not exist at all. Fichte and Schelling contemplated the unity of object and subject, thereby constructing 'the ideal': the understanding of an optimal form of the objective world that surrounds us. Idealism in this sense means the philosophy that considers the possibilities of the subject to think beyond the separation and limitation that mark individual existence. This type of Idealism fitted the Romantic movement, which was concerned with the representation of the unrepresentable Absolute and the cosmic influence on the individual.[14] Romanticism, however, was by no means intended as an irrational movement. On the contrary, it looked for representations of universal meaning that according to the Romantic poets and painters could not be expressed formally as the neo-classicists claimed.

The story of German Idealism is usually told as a chronology that goes from Kant to Hegel. Indeed, it starts with Kant's *Critiques* and his definitions of the Enlightenment and the university. In the days of the French Revolution his works were not only read as academic treatises but also as harbingers of a new world order.[15] In Jena the first lectures on Kant were in given 1785. Fichte was one of the first main figures in philosophy

---

[11] Cf. Th. O'Meara, *Romantic Idealism and Roman Catholicism. Schelling and the theologians*, Notre Dame 1982, 19-36.
[12] Cf. K. Ameriks, Introduction. Interpreting German Idealism, in: Id. [ed.], *The Cambridge companion to German Idealism*, Cambridge 2000, 1-17.
[13] A. Bowie, *Aesthetics and subjectivity. From Kant to Nietzsche*, Manchester, etc. 1990, 41-42.
[14] Cf. W. Vaughan, *Romanticism and art*, London 1994².
[15] T. Pinkard, *German philosophy 1760-1860*, 84.

to question the Kantian system, by radicalising the turn towards the subject. According to Fichte, the presupposition of a *Ding an sich* is false and nature as a whole should be regarded as a product of the human subject. However, to interpret this subjective production a phenomenological constitution of the world by a kind of Husserlian transcendental Ego *avant la lettre*, would be incorrect. For Fichte, philosophy is the exploration of the structure of self-consciousness in order to reveal the irreducibility of the Ego to objectivity. Fichte's Ego constitutes the ground that precedes the division of subject and object. Schelling consequently continues this project in his philosophy of the identity of object and subject but the attention shifts from the Ego to nature and eventually to the Absolute thinking itself. Schelling is usually positioned between Fichte and Hegel, preparing the move from subjective to absolute idealism. Fichte emphasised the subject and Schelling nature, while Hegel brought subject and object together in the synthesis of the Absolute Spirit. However, Schelling lived twenty years after Hegel's death and this is where the standard chronology misrepresents historical fact. Schelling lived to comment on Hegel's philosophical system of the Absolute Spirit. Hegel's concept of the end of art and, indeed, of the end of philosophy as a whole, might mark the end of an era but not the decline of German Idealism.[16] To reduce Schelling's thought to a philosophy of nature, however, would be a misrepresentation because an emphasis on nature only characterises a very short period in his philosophy.

The aesthetics of Romanticism and Idealism
Many concerns of the idealist philosophers are still on the agenda of contemporary philosophy and of aesthetics in particular. It should not be surprising that German Idealism as a philosophical movement developed in the wake of Baumgarten's identification of aesthetics as a separate philosophical discipline and of Kant's *Critique of judgment* (1790), which was designed as the capstone of the whole system of his transcendental philosophy, has art and aesthetics at its core.[17] Furthermore, the rise of the Romantic art movement had a strong influence on philosophy, especially on the style of philosophical writing. Under this influence, the idea of philosophy itself changed and became increasingly defined by its similarities with art and poetry. The result was a mixture

---

[16] Schelling's later philosophy however, is called 'the end of idealism' by many scholars. Cf. Th. Buchheim, *Eins von Allem. Die Selbstbescheidung des Idealismus in Schellings Spätphilosophie*, Hamburg 1992; D. Snow, *Schelling and the end of idealism*, New York 1996.

[17] See also chapter two of this book.

of a critical orientation of philosophy, seeking the limitations of knowledge and philosophical claims, and an anti-systematic and very often literary style of philosophical expression.[18] The claims were universal. In the age of Enlightenment, when the exact scientists established their own method as the paradigm of human rationality, Romanticism and German Idealism tried to establish art and poetry as the foundation of all academic disciplines. In this anti-systematic spirit, the Idealist philosophers tried to develop a universal philosophical system that paradoxically acknowledges the limitations of every analytical systematisation.

While Baumgarten focused on perception and Kant on the judgment of taste, the Romantics considered art as the medium of cognition. The eighteenth century philosopher Johann Georg Hamann (1730-1788) was the first to criticise Enlightenment rationality in his *Aesthetica in nuce* (1762), asserting that poetical language, not mathematics or physics, is the medium of cognition. Hamann's insight highly influenced the *Sturm und Drang* movement and later the Romantics. To see art and poetry as the appropriate media of cognition was explicitly opposed to the Kantian dichotomies between noumena and phenomena, and nature and freedom. Although Kant called the 'transcendental synthesis of apperception' the apogee of philosophy, it did not bridge the chasm between noumena and phenomena but only brought together the manifold of perceptions.[19] According to Fichte, the Ego is the ground of the unity of subject and object. The Romantics however considered art to be the expression of this foundational unity and shifted the attention from the Ego and its *Sturm und Drang*-variant of the poet-genius, to art itself.

Although the Romantics and the Idealists were acquainted with and mutually influenced one another, the movements can be distinguished. Romanticism was also an art movement and therefore concerned with the emergence of a new artistic style that differed from classical formalism. The opposition against a formal and mimetic artistic style followed from the reception of the Kantian notion of the sublime, which indicated the inability to represent the infinite and became the essence of the Romantic spirit. At the same time the experience of the sublime by means of strong feelings of the tragedy of finitude invokes the expression of the infinite. But because of the unrepresentability of the infinite, Romantic art was necessarily considered to be an expression of a longing, at most an attempt to understand the unrepresentability of the Absolute.[20]

---

[18] K. Ameriks, Introduction. Interpreting German Idealism, 10-11.
[19] I. Kant, *Kritik der Urteilskraft*, B 136.
[20] A. Bowie, *Aesthetics and subjectivity*, 43.

Notwithstanding the similarities between Romanticism and Idealism, Fichte, Schelling and Hegel tried to bridge between the subject and the Absolute. With Schelling, however, Romanticism and Idealism parted ways to some extent. Instead of regarding the expression of longing in art as the way to understand the unrepresentability of the Absolute, Schelling posited art over against philosophy. For him, The Absolute could never be an object of knowledge because that would bring back the division between subject and object.[21]

b. *Friedrich Wilhelm Joseph von Schelling*

Life and works
Friedrich Wilhelm Joseph von Schelling (1775-1854) was born in Leonberg.[22] He was much younger than his fellow students, due to his early entrance at the university of Tübingen at the age of fifteen. There, at the so-called *Tübinger Stift*, he lived with Hegel and Hölderlin and studied theology and the philosophies of Kant and Fichte. Advised not to write a dissertation on Fichte, he wrote one on the concept of myth in the first chapters of Genesis. At the age of twenty-two, after he had already published *Philosophische Briefe über Dogmatismus und Kritizismus* (Philosophical letters on dogmatism and criticism, 1795), *Die Möglichkeit einer Form der Philosophie überhaupt* (On the possibility of a form for philosophy) and *Vom Ich als Princip der Philosophie* (On the I as a principle of philosophy), all inspired by the philosophy of Fichte[23], he became a professor of philosophy at Jena. He became acquainted with the Jena Romantics, especially the Schlegel brothers and the poet Novalis. He also met Caroline Schlegel, who was August Schlegel's wife at the time and whom he would marry in 1803 after her divorce.

In 1800, Schelling published his *System des tranzendentalen Idealismus* (System of transcendental idealism) that is widely regarded the most important work of his early period. In it he further developed a philosophy of

---

[21] K. Hammermeister, *The German aesthetic tradition*, Cambridge 2002, 67.
[22] Cf. J. Kirchhoff, *Friedrich Wilhelm Joseph von Schelling*, Reinbek 1982.
[23] For the works of Schelling, I used the edition of K.F.A. Schelling: F.W.J. Schelling, *Sämmtliche Werke*, [herausgegeben von K.F.A. Schelling, I. Abtheilung Bde. 1-10; II. Abtheilung Bde. 1-4], Stuttgart and Augsburg 1856-1861. Selections of this edition are published in: F.W.J. Schelling, *Ausgewählte Werke Bde. 1-6*, [Unveränd. reprograf. Nachdr. d. aus d. hs. Nachlass hrsg. Ausg. von 1856 bis 1861], Darmstadt 1980-1990; and: F.W.J. Schelling, *Ausgewählte Schriften Bde. 1-6*, Frankfurt am Main 1985. I will refer to the pages of the K.F.A. Schelling edition. For specific collections of lectures, I will refer to recent editions.

nature, by establishing the grounds of unity of all forms of life and expression of organic and dynamic principles. He started a new project in 1801 that became known as the philosophy of identity. In 1803 he left the university of Jena to hold several academic positions in Bavaria.

Schelling's philosophy is usually divided into several, sometimes overlapping periods: 1. Disciple and critic of Fichte (1794-1797); 2. Philosophy of nature (1797-1800); 3. Transcendental Idealism (1800); 4. Philosophy of identity (1801-1804); 5. Philosophy of art (1802-1803); 6. Philosophy of freedom (1804 or 1806-1815); 7. Philosophy of mythology and revelation (1827-1854).[24] Such a scheme, however, pays too much attention to Schelling's first decade of writing and the supposed discontinuities between the different 'systems' he developed, and neglects the diachronic themes in his work, for there are many continuities in his oeuvre. For these reasons the renowned Schelling scholar Xavier Tilliette has argued, as Schelling himself suggested, that his work should instead be viewed as moving through just two phases: one positive and one negative.[25] This has become the common view of Schelling's work.[26]

After Caroline's death in 1809, Schelling did not publish any major works and worked for nearly twenty years on *Die Weltalter* (The ages of the world), a manuscript that he would later abandon. In 1841, Schelling staged the most famous comeback in the history of academia, and became the successor to Hegel at the university of Berlin. At the end of his life he mainly worked in the field of philosophy of religion, writing *Philosophie der Offenbarung* (Philosophy of revelation) and *Philosophie der Mythologie* (Philosophy of mythology), both published posthumously. His lectures on the philosophy of revelation and mythology did not get a good reception. Schelling died in 1854 in Bad Ragaz, on a journey through Switzerland.

Schelling's works on art and aesthetics
Among the German idealists, Schelling can be regarded as the philosopher of art.[27] In his *System des tranzendentalen Idealismus* (System of

---

[24] R.F. Brown, *The later philosophy of Schelling. The influence of Boehme on the works of 1809-1815*, Lewisburg 1877, 16.
[25] Cf. X. Tilliette, *Schelling, une philosophie en devenir. I. Le système vivant, 1794-1821; II. La dernière philosophie, 1821-1854*, Paris 1970.
[26] Cf. W.E. Ehrhardt, F.W.J. Schelling. Die Wirklichkeit der Freiheit, in: J. Speck [Hrsg.], *Grundprobleme der großen Philosophen. Philosophie der Neuzeit II*, Göttingen 1988³, 109-144, 116; Id., Nur ein Schelling, in: *Studi Urbinati di storia, filosofia e letteratura*, [Anno LI, Nuova serie B], 1-2 (1977), 111-122.
[27] For introductions to Schelling's aesthetics, see: H. Paetzold, *Ästhetik des deutschen Idealismus. Zur Idee ästhetischer Rationalität bei Baumgarten, Kant, Schelling, Hegel*

transcendental idealism, 1800), however, the concept of art plays a key role. It is considered not merely as one of the objects of philosophy but as the integral part of it. This encompassing idea of art was a central topic in Schelling's early period. In the first and last letters of the *Philosophische Briefe über Dogmatismus und Kritizismus* he deals with the problem of freedom in Greek tragedy and the work of art in general.[28] In *Das älteste Systemprogramm des deutschen Idealismus* (The oldest systematic program of German idealism, probably written in 1796), the manifesto of the German Idealists most likely written by Schelling, it is declared that beauty is the idea that unites all other ideas and that therefore the philosopher must have the same skills as the poet.[29] Although there is still dispute about the authorship of this manuscript, it is partly because of the central position of poetry and art that *Das älteste Systemprogramm*, although written in Hegel's handwriting, is clearly most influenced by Schelling's ideas and less so by Hölderlin's, Hegel's or someone else's.

After Schelling developed the idea of art as the capstone of philosophy in *System des tranzendentalen Idealismus* in 1800, his philosophy of art changes. Although art remained an important topic in his thought, it became increasingly subjugated to conceptual knowledge. This development is clearly present in his dialogue *Bruno* (1802) and his lecture series *Philosophie der Kunst* (Philosophy of art, 1802-1803 and 1804-1805), all written in the same period.[30] Art is also the subject matter of the second and fourteenth lectures of the *Vorlesungen über die Methode des akademischen Studiums* (Lectures on the method of academic studies,

---

und Schopenhauer, Wiesbaden 1983, 119-173; J. Schmidt, *Die Geschichte des Genie-Gedankens in der Deutschen Literatur, Philosophie und Politik. Band 1. Von der Audklärung bis zum Idealismus*, Darmstadt 1988², 390-403; A. Bowie, *Aesthetics and subjectivity*, 80-114; W. Schulz, Einleitung, in: H.D. Brandt, P. Müller [Hrsg.], *F.W.J. Schelling, System des transzendentalen Idealismus*, Hamburg 1992, IX-XLIV; N. Schneider, *Geschichte der Ästhetik von der Aufklärung bis zur Postmoderne*, 66-73; J. de Mul, Inleiding, in: Id., *Schelling, Filosofie van de kunst*, Meppel 1996, 7-47; K. Hammermeister, *The German aesthetic tradition*, 62-86.

[28] F.W.J. Schelling, *Briefe über Dogmatismus und Kritizismus*, [herausgeg. und eingeleitet von Otto Braun], Leipzig 1914.

[29] F.W.J. Schelling, Das älteste Systemprogramm des deutschen Idealismus, in: P. Sloterdijk [Hrsg.], *Schelling*, [Ausgewählt und vorgestellt von Michaela Boenke], München 1995, 95-97; Cf. F. Rosenzweig, *Das älteste Systemprogramm des deutschen Idealsinus. Ein handschrifter Fund*, Heidelberg 1917; Cf. X. Tilliette, Schelling als Verfasser des Systemprogramms?, in: M. Frank, G. Kruz [Hrsg.], *Materialien zu Schellings philosophischen Anfangen*, Frankfurt am Main 1975, 193-211.

[30] F.W.J. Schelling, *Bruno oder über das göttliche und natürliche Prinzip der Dinge. Ein Gespräch*, Berlin 1802. Recently published in: Id, *Ausgewählte Werke. Philosophie der Kunst*, [Unveränd. reprograf. Nachdr. d. aus d. hs. Nachlass hrsg. Ausg. von 1859], Darmstadt 1990.

1803). In these lectures, he considers philosophy to be the construction of the universe in a work of art. The idea of philosophy and the idea of art are still closely related in this period of Schelling's philosophy. However, in *Über das Verhältniss der bildende Künste zu der Natur* (On the relation of the visual arts to nature, 1807) art becomes one of the objects of philosophy.[31] In this lecture he describes the primacy of art to nature. Although the artist imitates nature, people are taught by the arts to judge nature aesthetically. As such, the work of art is a transcendental condition for the human perception of nature.

After this period Schelling did not write about art again except to mention individual works of art, using them as illustrations in his late philosophy on revelation and mythology. This does not mean that Schelling's interest in the arts faded away completely. For the later Schelling, the idea of mythology which he already mentioned in *Das älteste Systemprogramm*, is still an aesthetic idea because it needs to be expressed by means of the poetic imagination.

Unfortunately, it is beyond the scope of this book to present an exhaustive analysis of the different stages in Schelling's philosophy of art or to demonstrate the continuities and discontinuities between his early objective philosophy of nature and identity and his later philosophy of revelation and mythology. Since Balthasar was not concerned by the differences and contradictions in Schelling's thought that preoccupy contemporary secondary literature, I concentrate on the main topics in Schelling's philosophy of art that serve the main questions of this book and are discussed by Balthasar as well.

Schelling's philosophy of art
In the *System des transzendentalen Idealismus* Schelling considers a work of art to be the synthesis of nature and spirit. It is his attempt to solve the Kantian dualism of nature and freedom. According to Schelling, only the Absolute precedes both object and subject and should therefore be considered the unity of the two. As such, the Absolute cannot be an object of knowledge, since that would perpetuate the subject-object divide, but it can be the 'object' of art. Art is the expression of the Absolute because it is the identity of human consciousness and unconscious nature. It is therefore not only the result of human acts or an expression of the will, but also the result of human intuition. The Schlegel brothers had already defined Romantic art as the symbolic representation of infinity. They

---

[31] F.W.J. Schelling, *Ausgewählte Werke. Schriften von 1806-1813*, [Unveränd. reprograf. Nachdr. d. aus d. hs. Nachlass hrsg. Ausg. von 1860 u. 1861], Darmstadt 1990.

considered the poetic moment in art religiously and the experience of beauty was thought of as a religious experience. The poet as the inspired genius who is able to express the way infinity comes into finitude, became the 'priest' of the Romantic movement. Schelling's philosophy of art is called a 'Romantic programme', because he worked out these Romantic ideas philosophically.[32]

Schelling describes the artistic process as being both conscious and unconscious. The identity of the intellectual apprehension of reality and the aesthetical apprehension cannot be created by consciousness alone. Knowledge is an ongoing process of objectifying the products of intellectual apprehension. This objectification in art is always accompanied by intuition. There is a danger of terminological confusion here. 'Intuition' is a word that can be used to mean a direct *intellectual* apprehension of some truth but it can also be used, as Schelling does, to indicate an *intellective* apprehension of a perceptual *gestalt*, with the consequence of an organized perceptual configuration which is unmediated by concepts. Hence, the aesthetical apprehension is the objectified intellectual apprehension that cannot be created by consciousness alone.[33]

The artist thus creates intuitively a form of the Absolute. It is, according to Schelling, impossible to determine whether the Absolute is present in the artist or only in the work of art as the product of the artistic process. Nevertheless, the Absolute in art can never be interpreted as a product of human imagination alone but is also the presence of the Absolute. This presence can only be experienced through a form, which is the reason why the work of art and not the artist is at the heart of Schelling's aesthetics.[34] To describe the work of art, he distinguishes two moments: the poetic and the artistic. The poetic is that through which an object has life and reality in itself. It is the sublime experience that reality is created and actually there, in a moment of grace. The artistic moment is the creation of finitude in the infinite. It is art in the sense of *technè*, that is, skill and practice. Schelling combines the artistic moment with the realm of the beautiful.[35]

Art is thus the capstone of Schelling's system of transcendental idealism because he considers it the condition for the project of understanding

---

[32] H. Paetzold, *Ästhetik des deutschen Idealismus*, 127. Cf. W. Vaughan, *Romanticism and art*, 9-13.
[33] F.W.J. Schelling, *Sämmtliche Werke*, I/7, 148-149.
[34] Ibid., I/3, 619-625. Cf. O. Marquard, *Aesthetica und Anaesthetica. Philosophische Überlegungen*, München 2003 (1989), 103-106.
[35] F.W.J. Schelling, *Sämmtliche Werke*, I/5, 461.

the whole process of knowledge.[36] Schelling puts it as follows in a well-known quotation from the conclusion of *System des transzendentalen Idealismus*:

> When the aesthetical apprehension is nothing but the objectified transcendental, it stands to reason that art simultaneously is the only true and the eternal *organon*, and a document of philosophy, which again and again testifies of that which philosophy cannot represent externally, viz. the unconscious in acts and production, and its original identity with the conscious. That is why art is the ultimate to philosophers, because it opens the holy of holies to them, as it were.[37]

Unlike any previous philosopher, Schelling attributes a central role to art. After the Kantian turn to the subject, Schelling's philosophy can be regarded the turn to art. The work of art becomes the first principle of philosophy because it is the form of the Absolute: the unity of the intellectual and the intuitive apprehension. Art can be considered the most complete act that grounds philosophy. The similarity between philosophical ideas and art is the fundamental contradiction they express between finitude and infinity, which is characteristic of all forms of objectivity. The difference however is the possibility of art to show this contradiction in a synthesis. Thus, art demonstrates the core of the philosophical process because it shows that human imagination is capable of bringing together contradictions.[38]

Following the publication of *System des transzendentalen Idealismus* in 1800, Schelling lectured on the concept of art for some years until 1804, after which it became less central his philosophical work. Although he continued to lecture on the topic the following years, art loses its honoured position in his philosophy. Art and philosophy became one another's equals but the later Schelling was even hesitant towards the role of art in philosophy. In his lecture, *Über die Verhältniss der bildende Künste zu der Natur*, art is said to mimic nature and thus lose its primacy. Ultimately in Schelling's philosophy of religion, art and religion become contradictory *magisteria*, with art condemned as "worldly and pagan in its nature".[39]

---

[36] Cf. W. Kasper, *Das Absolute in der Geschichte. Philosophie und Theologie der Geschichte in der Spätphilosophie Schellings*, Mainz 1965, 53; Ph. Clayton, *The problem of God in modern thought*, 475-481.
[37] F.W.J. Schelling, *Sämmtliche Werke*, I/3, 627-628.
[38] H. Paetzold, *Ästhetik des deutschen Idealismus*, 125-126.
[39] Quoted in K. Hammermeister, *The German aesthetic tradition*, 66.

7.3. Absolute beauty: a philosophical appraisal

Balthasar neglects the differences and nuances in Schelling's aesthetics in favour of the continuities in Schelling's thought. Although he expresses his sympathy for Schelling's project, he is also highly critical of both the absolute identity between nature and spirit and the concept of mythology. In the following sections it will become clear that through his criticisms, Balthasar makes plain his own doctrine of the analogy of being and establishes the starting point of his theological aesthetics: the glory of God. I will also demonstrate that, according to Balthasar, Schelling is a key figure to understand the idea of human freedom in modernity.[40]

a. The Ego and the sublime

Fichte and the evolution of modernity
Balthasar's account of the philosophy of Schelling follows his rejection of Fichte's philosophy of the Ego. This is not because he considers Fichte's philosophy as merely an extreme form of subjectivism, lacking any sense of transcendence. On the contrary, Balthasar emphasises that his philosophy, like that of Cusanus, bears witness to both a classical and a Christian piety. The ethical is Fichte's fundamental inspiration and it has to be understood as the prime measure for religion, given that he acknowledges that the love of the good is sought after for its own sake. However, Balthasar speculates, if the Ego is considered the foundation of absolute knowledge, which in turn is based on the elusiveness of being, and God is consequently conceived of as Spirit, then would the idea of God not stay as elusive as being itself? In other words, does Fichte's philosophy leave us with nothing but a radically and insuperable negative view of God and the self?[41] When one wants to confirm the beauty of things, but one discovers that all beautiful things are grounded in a neutral and ungraspable Being, philosophy "becomes a gazing into the abyss" (H III,1 889-890).[42]

---

[40] Cf. G. De Schrijver, Die analogia entis in der Theologie Hans Urs von Balthasars. Eine genetisch-historische Studie, in: *Bijdragen. Tijdschrift voor filosofie en theologie* 38 (1977), 249-281, 257-262.

[41] Cf. H. Verweyen, *Gottes letztes Wort. Grundriss der Fundamentaltheologie*, Düsseldorf 1991, 306-311.

[42] In the philosophy of Fichte, Balthasar sees a foreshadowing of the pessimistic philosophy of Schopenhauer.

The result of Fichte's philosophy is a pantheistic worldview, which is quite contrary to Balthasar's own proposal for a third way in modern philosophy: the metaphysics of the saints.[43] "Who in Fichte's world", Balthasar asks, "can call out in such a way that the finite person can know himself to be determined by this call and to be able to take hold of it in total obedience?" (H III,1 885). Here he uses the vocabulary and imagery of the metaphysics of the saints. This type of metaphysics is his alternative for the cosmological and the anthropological reductions. The ideas of 'vocation', 'obedience' and 'mission' that are essential for the life of the saints ask for a third way in modernity that he describes in *Glaubhaft ist nur Liebe* as 'the third way of love' and which is principally developed to safeguard the givenness of human freedom (GinL 33-39). In a cosmological view, God becomes a mysterious ground that "strives in eternal movement into this ground and, for the sake of this movement, releases the concrete world from itself" (H III,1 885). In the anthropological view, of which Fichte's philosophy is a clear example, the self evolves from the universe, and this in turn presupposes the principle of the self. Balthasar argues that both the modern ideas of evolution and its often neglected response, the idea of revolution, which is the ever greater self-giving of the world in God, did not necessarily have to lead to the deistic concept of the Enlightenment. The philosophy of Schelling offers a modern alternative.

The sublime nothingness of absolute freedom
As shown above, Balthasar finds it necessary to repeat his standpoint in the history of metaphysics before he begins his analysis of Schelling's philosophy. For Balthasar, Schelling's philosophy offers a form of thought that is very similar to his proposal of the third way. Nevertheless, because he adopted Fichte's irrational basis of all knowledge and "changed the perspective of philosophy from a prophetic to a sibylline one" (H III,1 890), pantheism and subjectivism are ever present dangers in his thought as well.[44]

Fichte, Hegel and the later Schelling share a commitment to design a philosophy of identity which has dominated philosophy until this day. On this point, Balthasar's judgment about that influence of German Idealism is very severe and he states that the Idealist's life-view that emerges

---

[43] Cf. chapter six, section two.
[44] The Sibylline Books are three books from ancient Rome that contain oracles, supposedly from the Sibyl of Cumae. It is a collection of Jewish and Christian apocalyptic texts from the period of the second century BC to ca. 600.

from a point of identity cannot lead to anything else but to sublime nothingness. This destructive influence of the German Idealists on the history of philosophy makes Balthasar speculate as to why it was so important to determine this point of identity, and why in particular for Schelling, to whom he feels philosophically related.

Schelling's motivation for developing a philosophy of identity, which establishes the point at which the subject postulates itself but at the same time realises that it is not open to objectification, is grounded in a belief that the essence of human beings consists solely in their absolute freedom. Instead of things or objects of the mind, they are determined in such a way that they can never be thought of as pure objects. Nevertheless, being and consciousness coincide in such a way that the self can only be thought of as indistinguishable from its own being. This circular idea, according to Balthasar, is the pitfall of Schelling's thought because it leaves space for a concept of nature, which stands completely under the norm of the spirit.

b. *The Absolute in art*

Nature and spirit

Balthasar divides Schelling's thought into a *philosophy of nature* and a *philosophy of the spirit*. In the philosophy of nature, the spirit emerges in nature because of an increasing awareness of nature and the objectification or realization of nature by the human mind. In the philosophy of the spirit, the spirit incarnates morally and culturally in reality and thereby raises itself up above nature. Balthasar argues that the difference between subject (spirit) and object (nature) is thus postulated in Schelling's philosophy of the absolute identity, but eventually removed again by the spiritual act. The unity of subject and object is realized by the human mind through the objectification of nature. The latter entails that the infinity that emerges in this spiritual act—as an identity-founding spirituality—appears in a form that can itself be understood as an expression of infinity. Balthasar identifies this form in Schelling's philosophy as a form of beauty (H III,1 898).

The human mind can thus form a unity between the finite and the infinite and, as said before, for Schelling this can only be achieved through a work of art. A work of art thus becomes the condition for the appearance of infinity, which is the identity of subject and object, in finitude. That is why Balthasar calls Schelling's philosophy 'aesthetic' throughout. He hesitates to call it a philosophy of glory, however, because he believed a philosophy of identity could never account for a concept of glory. After all, any attempt to identify the glory of God with something else or to interpret it as an identity of which nature and spirit are parts, is doomed to failure since glory is incomparable to any beautiful form (H III,1 898).

Balthasar considers Schelling's philosophy of art a reconciliation of the classical philosophy of his days with the ideas of the poets Schiller and Hölderlin. This is a rather daring interpretation, considering that Romanticism was mainly opposed to classical formalism. Schelling considers, however, that the romantic idea of organic nature, which envelops the spirit, should be in harmony with the classical idea of nature, above which the spirit raises itself to give nature its reality. Furthermore, the philosophy of nature and the philosophy of spirit should both result in a point of identity of the conscious and the unconscious. Balthasar is right to see a similarity here between classic philosophy and Romanticism because both philosophical forms developed the ideas of the genius and the sublime. Occasionally, and this is his main concern, these ideas have taken on divine characteristics or have even been identified with God in the history of philosophy.

Beauty, the sublime and the glory of God
Balthasar blames a romantic misinterpretation of the Kantian concept of the sublime for the identification of the genius with God.[45] He thinks that the idea of the sublime in the philosophy of Kant was already nothing more than a relic of the objective glory of God (H III,1 898).[46] In the aesthetic writings of Schiller, Kant's clear distinction between the sublime and the beautiful is eroded. The sublime is interpreted anthropologically and finally subsumed under a total and all-encompassing beauty. The result is an identification of beauty and sublimity in Schelling's philosophy.[47] It is the necessary consequence of Schelling's philosophy of identity, according to Balthasar, that there can no longer be a difference between sublimity and beauty. Absolute beauty is always sublime and the sublime is always beautiful. The dichotomy of Kantian philosophy is resolved, as was Schelling's original intention. Hegel subsequently reduces the sublime to mere transience and announces the end of art. Thus, says Balthasar, Schelling has prepared the way for Hegel's radical and nihilistic position.

---

[45] Cf. chapter two, section two.
[46] Cf. C. Crockett, *A theology of the sublime*, London 2001, 23-36.
[47] Cf. The twenty-second letter in: F. Schiller, *Über die ästhetische Erziehung des Menschen in einer Reihe von Briefen*, 337-341.

In Schelling's work, however, the beautiful also makes its final appearance as a transcendental property of all being, and this is why Balthasar's account of Schelling is also highly apologetic, despite the concerns he expresses throughout *Im Raum der Metaphysik* and not only in his account of Schelling's philosophy. The latter interprets the totality of being in itself as a divine work of art. Art may be the *organon* of philosophy but the totality of being itself is said to be beautiful and, as such, it is the only true work of art. The beautiful is therefore a characteristic of the totality of being, in Schelling's thought, rather than of the individual work of art.

Balthasar believes that Schelling's aesthetics reconstructs the infinite universe in the form of the work of art and subsequently determines the philosophy of art as the study of infinity in the shape of art. Individual works of art can therefore only be understood in the light of eternity and nature itself will only be experienced as a work of art if it is first objectified by man. Every perception of a beautiful form, regardless of whether it is nature itself or a work of art, is considered the perception of the totality of being in a form. Balthasar recognises in Schelling's philosophy a mutual interpenetration (*circumincessio*) of the transcendentals 'truth' and 'beauty'. As in Balthasar's own metaphysical view, 'beauty' has a systematic primacy over the truth and the goodness of being.[48] The beautiful work of art is for Schelling the key to a better understanding of the religious because as the Absolute appears in the world in a work of art, so the world is perceived as divine revelation.

7.4. Being and God: a theological critique

According to Balthasar, Schelling is the last thinker in the history of philosophy to interpret 'beauty' as a transcendental concept of being in the medieval sense. Therefore, several classical ideas of absoluteness return in Schelling's philosophy of identity: unity, freedom, the embodiment of reality, substance, omnipotence and immortality. Schelling connects these ideas of absoluteness with God, or even identifies them with Him in their pure form. According to Schelling, philosophy should concentrate on thinking the Absolute and thus, he resists the position *si comprehendis non est Deus*. Consequently a philosopher does justice to the wonder that is the starting point of his thought if he simultaneously continues to search for the wonderful and mysterious aspects of Being and the Absolute.

---

[48] See also chapter four, section three.

Schelling's determination of the task of philosophy reminds Balthasar of Cusanus's philosophy of the *desiderium*. For Schelling too, philosophy is *comprehendere incomprehensibile* (Anselm) or *docta ignorantia* (Cusanus). The later Schelling of *Philosophie der Offenbarung* and *Philosophie der Mythologie* proposes that philosophy should ultimately find a point of rest that, once found, cancels out all the searching that preceded it. This point of rest is the Absolute or the point of 'indifference', which forms an end to all thinking because God is greater than anything that can be thought. Balthasar wonders how this 'positive philosophy' could be possible if the absolute identity that should be regarded as being beyond thought has its starting point in the thinking subject. How could a philosophy of identity go beyond this point? And how could the thinking subject ever be questioned after that (H III,1 891)?

a. Freedom between the Absolute and the Ego

In order to answer these questions Balthasar discusses two works of the early Schelling: *Philosophische Briefe über Dogmatismus und Kritizismus* (1795) and *Philosophische Untersuchungen über das Wesen der menschlichen Freiheit* (Philosophical investigations of the essence of human freedom, 1809). In the philosophical letters Schelling analyses Spinoza's radical philosophical attitude, in which the subject as *amor intellectualis Dei* coincides with an absolute Object and, as such, exceeds all its own limitations to dissolve into the Absolute. Schelling himself considers this Spinoza's self-deception. After all, the subject cannot annihilate itself for the simple reason that to be able to annihilate itself it would have to survive its own annihilation, which is impossible. The subject cannot regard itself as being annihilated in an absolute object, for it would still be regarding itself as a subject. To be aware of this, it would have to exist and be annihilated at the same time. Schelling believes absolute surrender must therefore also be a form of the highest and most free form of self-determination. In Schelling's early philosophy, identity is always a coincidence of object and subject, of being and consciousness. He understands this identity as the coincidence of two radical attitudes in which the Ego has the final word. After all, the Ego is the identity of being and consciousness, of subject and object. Moreover, it would be the greatest freedom of the Ego to find itself in the highest state of resignation after the most intense effort. Therefore, Schelling's philosophical position mirrors Balthasar's own theology. In *Glaubhaft ist nur Liebe* for example, he speaks of love as absolute self-sacrifice and love which is its own reward (GinL 72). In his trinitarian theology, developed much later in *Theologik* in the 1980's, he explored the concept of the divine persons as selfless selves (TL II 38).

As has been shown, Balthasar severely criticises Schelling's philosophy of identity. The univocal concept of being (Balthasar refers to Avicenna, Scotus, Suarez) may be abolished here by transcendental thought, but the transcendental unity of subject and object is a univocity, which as in classical metaphysics, is characterised by *Seinsvergessenheid* (forgetfulness of being). After all, classical metaphysics constructed an abstract concept of being beyond the difference between God and beings. According to Balthasar, the same line of thought of classical metaphysics can be found in Schelling in the form of idealism. In Schelling's early philosophy God eventually is placed under the norm of the identity of the I. The absoluteness, therefore, is an imaginable absoluteness that places God in the range of thought of the Ego. Thus, Schelling has opened the way to an idealistic atheism, according to Balthasar (H III,1 893).

Balthasar calls Schelling's philosophy forgetful of Being (*Seinsvergessen*) because it cannot clearly distinguish between the ideal and the real. The coincidence of the ideal and the real is not a point that lies beyond the Kantian distinction between concept and conception[49], nor, for example, beyond Husserl's distinction between *noesis* and *noema*[50]. Ultimately in Schelling's philosophy, the ideal is the universal even while the beginning of all reality is a contraction of the universal that forms the beginning of all particularity. God only becomes real because he contracts from the general, or being, to a distinct being. This contraction of

---

[49] Kant analyses reason as the ability to construct concepts, sensual perception as the ability to behold. In the *Kritik der reinen Vernunft*, reason is analysed in the transcendental logic and sensual perception in the transcendental aesthetics. Beholding precedes the concepts but the concepts just as much precede the beholding. The conditions for beholding are space and time, the Kantian categories that are the condions for the construction of concepts. "None of these characteristics is preferable over the others. Without sensual perception we would have no object and without reason we would not be able to think it. Thoughts without content are empty, intuitions without concepts are blind.." (*Kritik der reinen Vernunft*, B75)

[50] In the *Logische Untersuchungen* (Logical investigations), Husserl defines the '*noema*' as the thing itself, as it manifests itself to us through a given act of perception, and the '*noesis*' as the phenomenological consciousness (in Husserls later works: the transcendental ego) of the perceived object. In any given perception, the thing only appears in a certain aspect, viz. that of being-thought, but as such, the thing appears in its totality. Cf. E. Husserl, *Logische Untersuchungen. Erster Band: Prolegomena zur reinen Logik*, [Text der 1. und der 2. Auflage. *Husserliana. Gesammelte Werke*, Vol. 18], Dordrecht 1975, 227-257.

God from the general to the particular, however, is analogous to the condescension (*Herablassung*) of a real being to its ground (*Seyn*). This second moment of the contraction of being to its ground is a condition for the created world to have part in divine being, without actually becoming identical with God himself. From this it follows that God is the non-real in identity for, after all, the real exists in the difference between the general and the particular.

Schelling presupposes that God needs creation to become real. Despite this dependence of God on creation, His descent into the world remains an act of absolute freedom, because He decides whether to descend into this world or not. This coincidence of freedom and dependence is according to Balthasar, the cause of Schelling's *seinsvergessene* philosophy, in which the ideal and the real can only be real within a universal concept of the ideal. Only within this all-encompassing ideal appears the individuation of reality as a constructed unity of the ideal and the real. Such a concept of reality, Balthasar argues, is intrinsically contradictory because it lacks an essential and independent dimension of being (H III,1 893-894).

b. Identity and analogy

Cusanus revisited
At this point Balthasar returns to Cusanus's philosophy to compare it with that of Schelling. Cusanus's central problem was the question: How can God be everything while there is another world outside God? or to put it differently: How can God be all in all without formally being the being of things? Schelling describes the same problem thus: God is not a separate, independent being because then it would be impossible for him to be *Non-Aliud*. This is what Schelling calls the danger of 'dogmatism'. But God is not a general substance either, intrinsic to all things, as pantheism claims. Schelling posits that God is both. God is the essence of all creatures but he needs to exist too and, as such, he needs to be grounded in something. For this reason the essence of all beings should not be regarded as generality but as individuality and, therefore, as grounded. God's individuality is the foundation of the universal. This individuality is a condition for the universal in Schelling's philosophy.

But, Balthasar asks, how can an individual God meet the conditions to be everything (*Non-Aliud*) at the same time? Cusanus calls God *Non-Aliud* only insofar as he is *Possest*, the One insofar as He is the Only, the

General insofar as He is the Almighty. Subsequently, the power over all that is possible belongs to the identity of subjectivity and objectivity, of ability and being. Balthasar proposes that God must be entirely modelled after either that of man or the universe, if Schelling conceives of God and the world from the perspective of the I-identity of human reason. This is indeed Schelling's solution: if God's individuality is a condition for his universality, one must regard God as entirely human. Furthermore, if one presumes that His life has the greatest analogy to the human, it means that in Him there is eternal becoming as well as external being and that he has everything in common with man save dependence.

A tritheistic God
According to Balthasar, Schelling's introduction of the greatest analogy of the humanity of God neglects the definition of the analogy of being as a similarity within an even greater dissimilarity. For Schelling, however, it is the only way to avoid the separation of the world into an unnatural God and a godless nature. Balthasar argues that Schelling can only maintain the analogous unity of God and world through a duplication or even triplication of God: first, God is the all encompassing, yet still contracted identity; next, God will have to exist and therefore be individual; and finally, nature itself is an unfolding of divine nature. However, Balthasar believes the individuality of God can never be encompassed by yet another absolute divine identity. The unity of divine individuality and universality can never be conceived of within the scheme of absolute identity because this would necessarily entail the sort of dualism that Schelling wanted to avoid. Balthasar argues that divine individuality cannot be encompassed by divine universality because something that encompasses God must necessarily be something other than God, yet just as all encompassing, and this can only be nothingness.

Thus, Balthasar thinks that Schelling attributes the same origin to both God and man: the human mind. God emerges as a spirit from the pre-divine darkness which, as such, is also the pre-creaturely ground. This ground is matter, as yet unformed, the unconscious part of God. Thus, the ideal must necessarily form a superstructure on top of the real. According to Balthasar, Schelling's philosophy leads thus to the same materialism he tried to fight. Unformed matter unconsciously precedes any form of the ideal. This matter is the foundation of all thought and thus, according to Schelling, of all being, the tragic consequence of the "beingless concept-thinking of univocity" (H III,1 896). The basic attitude of the philosopher in Schelling's thought is the heroic stand against the sibylline gaze into the abyss. With Schelling, Balthasar refers to Dante's hell but adds that Dante described the journey through hell as a Christian sinner and not a philosopher.

To explain the failure of German Idealism, Balthasar points to its attempt to simplify the thomist *actus essendi*, which is the doctrine in which being is considered an act, limited by an essence with primary matter, a substantial form and accidents. The act of being is neither God, nor the neutral concept beyond God and the world, nor the possibility of matter. It is rather the mystery of God giving Himself. Only from being and by referring to being, it is possible to speak of being. Schelling, however, replaced the concept of being with a conceptual identity. This has degenerated into the concept of an Absolute without which philosophy is impossible.

c. Mythology and revelation

Balthasar is highly critical of Schelling's philosophy of identity. The concept of the Absolute, which finds its best expression in art, could never be compared to the theological concept of glory. Art is the foundation of philosophy but, according to Balthasar, it cannot be the foundation of theology if it is interpreted as the expression of the absolute identity of nature and spirit. Yet he recognises a theological theme in Schelling's thought. Schelling's aesthetics is a philosophy of the appearance (*Erscheinung*) of the infinite in a finite form. In this sense it is similar to mythology or, to use Schelling's term, pre-Christian religion.[51] Because of this, Balthasar sees opportunities to define Schelling's aesthetics in terms of 'revelation' and 'Christian religion' (H III,1 899).[52]

Mythology
Balthasar believes that the distinction Schelling makes in his *aesthetic theology* between mythology and Christian revelation is a recapitulation of his own design for a theological aesthetics in *Schau der Gestalt* and the idealistic variant of the theme elaborated in volume III,1 of *Herrlichkeit*, viz. the relation between theological aesthetics and philosophical metaphysics (H III,1, 899). This is a remarkable statement considering the fact that only one and half pages earlier Balthasar claims that

---
[51] F.W.J. Schelling, *Sämmtliche Werke*, I/5, 430.
[52] Ibid.

Schelling's philosophy is *not* a philosophy of glory.[53] Yet the reversal of the terms 'theology' and 'aesthetics' is telling.[54] He defined aesthetic theology as the study of worldly beauty, while divine glory is the subject matter of theological aesthetics. The identity of appearance (nature) and imagination (spirit) is postulated by the human mind in Schelling's philosophy. In Balthasar's theology however, divine creation makes the covenant between God and man possible. For Schelling, art is the expression of identity; for Balthasar, art should express analogy. Only the idea of analogy can do justice to the human-divine relationship that is expressed in art and beauty. Considering these fundamental differences, why does Balthasar recognise his own project in Schelling's philosophy?

According to Balthasar, the differences and the similarities between theological aesthetics and aesthetical theology can be articulated in terms of Schelling's 'philosophy of mythology'. For the interpretation of it, Balthasar does not just draw from the collection of lectures by that title but also and mainly from the *Philosophie der Kunst*, in particular the introduction, and from an early essay *Über Mythen, historische Sagen und Philosopheme der ältesten Welt* (On myths, historical sagas and philosophemes of the ancient world, 1793). Already in this early essay, religion is treated in its original form of *mythical* beauty. Religion has to be mythology first, before it is possible to be understood and transfigured into *revealed* beauty. Before God became man, he had to appear in human consciousness in a temporary form, which is mythology. Schelling calls the mythical beauty a pre-figuration of Christian art, and Balthasar agrees that indeed "Christ is the end of mythology, before it becomes transfigured within the infinite (Spirit) form of revelatory beauty in which God first becomes man, authentically suffers in his finiteness, only to return by resurrection to the eternal world of ideas where he assimilates the real

---

[53] This type of ambivalent evaluation of other people's work, in which Balthasar emphasises the similarities with his own philosophy and the whole of the Christian theological tradition, is typical of his work and of *Herrlichkeit* in particular. I have mentioned it before and it is important here to repeat my warning for anyone planning to read parts of *Herrlichkeit*: It refers to most other people's work with great sympathy. The reader has to be aware, however, of the fact that he does that repeatedly. This means that it is virtually impossible to determine Balthasar's theology based on the influence of some theologians and philosophers from the history of Christianity. After all, to explain his own theological standpoint he identifies with the whole of tradition (H III,1 16-20). This is why Balthasar's theology is usually referred to as 'universalist' and 'catholic'. In a sense, Balthasar's concept of 'tradition' is a history of dissimilarities with an even greater similarity. Cf. C. O'Regan, Balthasar and Eckhart. Theological principles and catholicity, in: *The thomist* 60 (1996), 203-239.

[54] Cf. chapter five, section four.

man into this new reality" (H III,1 900). Balthasar reads in Schelling the idea of the end of the ancient world of the gods in Christ since, after all, those gods were nothing but possible deities and forces of the one, true God. Only in Christ is the possibility of God in the world realised and historical, in a word: revealed.

Revelation
To this extent, Balthasar endorses the relation Schelling outlined between mythology and revelation, particularly in *Philosophie der Kunst*, but he opposes the explanation, which he consistently denounces as Enlightenment philosophy, in which myth was considered a primitive form of religious imagination. Balthasar, however, does not make a distinction between a primitive mythological phase and a mature Christian one. Instead, he distinguishes between mythology and revelation. Mythology is esoteric insofar as the gods stay outside the symbolic and sacramental expressions, while revelation adds an esoteric side to these expressions, which is the reconciliation that God makes possible by entering into the world. While Balthasar calls revelation the definitive event of Christianity, Schelling says that mysticism lies at the heart of Christianity.[55]

In Schelling's philosophy, ancient mythology turns historically into a philosophy of art and not into a theology of revelation. Human imagination has become a condition for witnessing infinity in finitude. The foundation of the idea of this human necessity should be Christ himself, who is the divine representation of the final identity of God and man. This is why Balthasar calls the relation between God and man in Schelling's thought a philosophical one because it is a difference that can only be conceived of based on the indifferent foundation that is the mind. Thus, says Balthasar, Schelling created space for the philosopher-artist, the divine human being who can realise this indifferent foundation, to take Christ's place. The idea that the difference between God and man forms a foundation that is itself infinite and divine must necessarily lead to a duplication of God. Any difference can thus be conceived of from the spiritual indifference. Balthasar's final judgment of Schelling is that he reduces all mysteries of faith to philosophy, which is ultimately the identity of reason with art as its *organon*. Thus, the foundation for Hegel's philosophy of the Absolute Spirit, which Balthasar believes the culmination of *Selbstherrlichkeit*, is laid here (H III,1 901-904).

Balthasar proposes that any Christian theology should first distinguish between the Christian doctrine of atonement and a philosophy of mediation

---

[55] F.W.J. Schelling, *Sämmtliche Werke*, I/5, 443.

before it produces a metaphysical synthesis of philosophy and theology. The subsuming of theology to philosophy in the idea of mythology, according to Schelling, is only possible because he believes that there had never been an elevation of theology over philosophy, which should, according to Balthasar, be a characteristic of any form of Christian thought.[56] In Schelling's aesthetics this means that the grace and freedom of the divine revelation is always thought of within the necessary process of deification and incarnation, which simultaneously means the incarnation of God but also the deification of man. Consequently, the human freedom to capture infinity in a work of art can mean little more than 'voluntariness', according to Balthasar. This is so because the free act of human creation is no longer preceded by divine revelation, after which human creation is modelled. In Schelling's aesthetics, man can only show himself his own spiritual foundation. Consequently, the idea of beauty is not signifying a relation of the freedom of both God and man, but rather the freedom of the human subject to realise its own foundation (TD I, 532-542).

7.5. Prometheus rebound

> I sought the fount of fire in hollow reed
> Hid privily, a measureless resource
> For man, and mighty teacher of all arts.
> This is the crime that I must expiate
> Hung here in chains, nailed 'neath the open sky.[57]

Balthasar characterises the developments in modernity repeatedly by calling them "promethean flaws". The mythological figure Prometheus is a significant theme throughout his theological work. In 1947 he published the first volume of the extended version of his dissertation and gave it the title *Prometheus*.[58] A few years ago the *Johannes Verlag* decided to publish all three volumes of that dissertation despite Balthasar's hesitations to republish it.[59] That decision however, was important, because it demonstrates

---

[56] Cf. J. Milbank, *The Word made strange. Theology, language, culture*, Oxford 1997, 36-52.
[57] From: Aeschylus, *Prometheus bound*, [Ed. by Mark Griffith], Cambridge 1983.
[58] *Prometheus. Studien zur Geschichte des deutschen Idealismus*, Heidelberg 1947, 7f: "This "meaning" says nothing against the true "objectivity" of the image, nothing against its absolute validity, as long as there are people."
[59] "Even though the work has not fully matured—most chapters should be written again —, some of it might still be valid" (UA 32).

how Balthasar's work developed from the study of literary themes to theological ones. This gradual shift is not merely a matter of method and style but mainly a matter of content that needs a specific theological argumentation. To evaluate Balthasar's reading of Schelling in the context of modern metaphysical developments, I will now focus on the Prometheus theme in his work. I will show how the story of Prometheus both mirrors his disapproval of modernity and illustrates the motives for his critical search for a theological foundation of the history of mythology, religion and philosophy.[60]

In *Apokalypse der deutschen Seele* Balthasar anthologises poets, writers and philosophers of then recent German history from Lessing to Rilke. He treats their work systematically from a Christian theological perspective: death and eschatology. *Herrlichkeit* deals with the perception of the glory of God and, in volume III,1, Balthasar describes how philosophy, and metaphysics in particular, has treated this subject, although at best insufficiently, in the course of history. The method of *Apokalypse der deutschen Seele* consists of the attempt to survey philosophy, theology and the arts as one. Balthasar believes it is typical of all three disciplines that they do not use direct language but instead they speak in terms of meaning (*meinen*). In his opinion, however, this does not detract from the objectivity of the image they employ. Likewise, the method of *Herrlichkeit* is entirely theological but it is in theology that the profound connection between image and reality is ultimate, not least because of the suspense of the absent presence of God. But theology speaks of a message to the world here and now, and should, therefore, be much more concrete and imaginative (*bildhafter*) (UA 7).

Balthasar's method in *Prometheus* is 'inter-textual', in the double sense of the word. First, Balthasar chooses the treatment of the eschatological theme of death in a wide range of authors and texts. Second, he refuses to neatly categorise the various texts into separate disciplines—philosophy, history, poetry, and literature—and he does not consider them within their own genre, by means of their own methods of study.[61] Therefore,

---

[60] Cf. H. Blumenberg, *Arbeit am Mythos*, Frankfurt am Main 1979.
[61] Cf. E.T. Oakes, s.j., *Pattern of redemption. The theology of Hans Urs von Balthasar*, New York 1994, 74f. Oakes, who originally studied German literature and culture, dedicates a chapter to the influence of German Idealism on Balthasar's theology in his excellent introduction to the theology of Balthasar ("Goethe, Nietzsche and the encounter with German Idealism", 72-101). In this chapter, he only deals with Kant, Goethe, Hegel and Nietzsche though, but not with Schelling, or for example Hölderlin, who also play a significant role in Balthasar's early work.

one may conclude that his theological method bears similarities to mythology rather than to literature or science. From his early writings onwards, Balthasar searched for new ways of doing theology and discovered ancient resemblances in mythology and the arts.

In his dissertation, Balthasar tries to establish the three main mythical characteristics that according to him lie at the heart of German literature: 1. Prometheus; 2. Dionysus; and 3. *Götterdämmerung* (twilight of the gods). He posits that all these three characteristics deny the analogy between God and the world. Although the theological implications of Balthasar's dissertation are obvious, instead of being a theology of literature, it is a systematic consideration of mythological history in German literature. He argues that the central role of mythology and the accompanying negation of the analogous relation of God and the world will lead to either the deification of the world or to nihilism. His conclusion is that (the history of) German literature suffers from a *reductio ad crucem*:

> The expansion of being between 'life' and 'spirit', between 'Prometheus' and the 'goddess Soul', between existential and ideal world, between earth and heaven, this extension of being, which gives it its final attitude and its full truth, this extension is a crucifixion. The 'contradiction' of idealistic dialectics, like the 'contradiction' between nature and spirit, is mythical and concrete like the meeting of the arms of the cross (...) This is where 'Prometheus bound' and 'Dionysus crucified' find there explanation too (AddS III 434-435).

Balthasar considers the bound Prometheus to be a pre-figuration of Christ on the cross. The myth of Prometheus, however, needs according to him to be related to scripture to reveal the ultimate meaning of Prometheus's suffering (TD I 116). The catholic dialectic of nature and grace is a condition for understanding human freedom. After all, God has given man his freedom and, with it, a certain natural knowledge of his origin. This type of knowledge may be presupposed in mythology but it is also obscured and taken away repeatedly. Because of God's gift of freedom to human beings, there is a dramatic suspense between them and God, in which both parties are involved and both parties act. This dramatic suspense is completed in Christ's expiatory death. There is, however, no such redemptive completion in the myth of Prometheus, Balthasar argues. Prometheus does not sacrifice himself but offers the fire of the gods to human beings, which he then has to pay for with his own freedom. Jesus Christ brings about reconciliation between God and man with his own life. Modern idealism could never account for this consequence. Schelling's idea of freedom cannot be redemptive, because it finds its foundation in the human mind, instead of in divine revelation.

Balthasar calls idealist philosophy a recapitulation of the myth of Prometheus, because the relation between God and man is obscured anew, albeit in a different way than in Hellenic times. Man is no longer at the mercy of the capricious gods, but instead has grown so great in his own freedom, that he has forgotten that this freedom was received from God. Balthasar considers the modern subject as bound like Prometheus in a world that will meet its nemesis in the twilight of the gods. It was this same forgetfulness or hubristic denial of dependence that made the gods of the old myth chain Prometheus to the rocks.[62]

Balthasar points to Anthony Ashley Cooper, better known as the third Earl of Shaftesbury, as the first philosopher of the modern age to rediscover Prometheus as the symbol for creative man (H III,1 637-641). In *A letter concerning enthusiasm* (1708) he trades the experience of prayer with that of philosophical enthusiasm, and God with philosophical genius. The idea of promethean man may remind us of the idea of man as *secundus deus* but Balthasar believes that man eventually degenerates into a true titan as a consequence of Shaftesbury's philosophy. Whereas, at first, the artist is still "a second maker, a just Prometheus under Jove", the "under Jove" is completely lost to the artists of *Sturm und Drang* and the romantic movement. When Goethe finally distances himself from the Prometheus principle the damage has already been done in the history of philosophy: the principle continues to make itself felt in Fichte's philosophy of the *Ich*, Schelling's philosophy of freedom and Hegel's philosophy of the Spirit (H III,1 643).

According to Balthasar, the return of Prometheus to philosophy is a much more serious mistake than the one that was made at the time of Plato. Plato's concept of the δαιμόνιον is the philosophical counterpart of the relation between Ulysses and Athena, which is an analogous relation[63] and therefore dissimilar to the idea of absolute identity, as it is worked out in German Idealism. Idealist philosophy presents man as a titan: a being that does not need the fire of the gods, and a being that can shine its own

---

[62] For an alternative position, cf. D. Verene, *Philosophy and the return to self-knowledge*, 1-38. Verene considers the Prometheus-theme an opportunity for modern philosophy to recapitulate the well-known Greek maxim: "Know thyself".

[63] Cf. H III,1, 55-56. In Homer's Odyssee, the goddess Athena cares for the life of Ulysses, who can only accept this in gratitude. Balthasar presents the relation between God and man in Homer as a "relation between the god, who is flash and light in himself, and man, who becomes apparent to itself and all others in its autonomous value, its exaltedness and dignity when elevated into the merciful light of God: light from darkness, life from death" (H III,1 51).

light on the world. Balthasar argues that this will have apocalyptic consequences for the German soul. Even the myth of Prometheus does not suppose the identity between God and man, but describes a power struggle between the titans and the gods that will ultimately degenerate into an apocalyptical battle between the gods and the primal forces, which is just what Prometheus sought to protect man from (H III,1 108).

C.

THEOLOGICAL AESTHETICS AS FUNDAMENTAL THEOLOGY

8. THE ART OF THEOLOGY

Hans Urs von Balthasar's work is wide-ranging and voluminous. Indeed, the sheer volume of his writings together with his consistent and systematic criticisms of modern metaphysics and the theology of his time make it an arduous task to give an adequate assessment of his theology. Without intending to construct a closed system of thought, he developed an encompassing vision forcing one to either join from the outset or analyse and assess by the standards of contemporary theology, which he dismissed for its scientific specialisation and forgetfulness of revelation. In an attempt to avoid becoming either an epigone of Balthasar's theology or a blind critic who inscrutably repeats what has already been discharged, I will suggest ways to supplement his vision.

In previous chapters I have introduced Balthasar's theological aesthetics and his idiosyncratic synopsis of the history of metaphysics, exemplified by the ideas of Cusanus and Schelling. I will now present a critical evaluation of his theo-aesthetic vision and suggest ways of supplementing it in order to meet the tasks of contemporary fundamental theology. To reconstruct Balthasar's description of theology as 'perceiving glory', I will examine his closing essay on the aesthetics of glory in *Herrlichkeit* III,1, reading it alongside his criticism of modernity (8.1). Next, to develop a theological aesthetics that addresses the problem of how to communicate faith, I propose to supplement Balthasar's ideas with an interpretation of human creativity as actively seeking forms of faith, particularly in theological imagination and construction (8.2). Finally, I will present the consequences of this proposed supplement for doctrinal theology and return to the original question of this book: What is theology (8.3)? I will show that aesthetics has proven to be an adequate theological approach to reason about God and to communicate faith.

8.1. Perceiving glory

Is it possible to maintain a theo-aesthetic concept of glory after modernity? At the end of his overview of the history of metaphysics and aesthetics, Balthasar's conclusions are pessimistic: "Being no longer possesses any radiance, and beauty, banished from the transcendental dimension, is confined to a purely worldly reality where only tensions and contradictions, encompassed only by univocity, remain to overcome" (H III,1 928).[1] In a gloomy forward-looking vision of postmodernity, he laments that aesthetics will only be capable of seeing fragments and aspects that cannot become a whole. Yet, he acknowledges that a fragmentary perspective on the truth also yields genuine glimpses of the comprehensive whole because in its descent divine revelation can "make use of the worldly and the fragmentary in order to become manifest at that level and indeed to achieve self-expression" (H III,1 930).[2] Balthasar therefore sets himself the task of expressing the positive content of a theological aesthetics, different from, yet in dialogue with the modern conception of aesthetics as science.

a. The legacy of modernity: appearance, production, charis

In the closing section of Balthasar's historical review of the relation between metaphysics and aesthetics he hesitantly extracts three aspects from modern aesthetics which he subsequently applies to the organisation of the biblical volumes of *Herrlichkeit* III,2: 'appearance', 'production' and *'charis'*. 'Appearance' (ἐπιφάνεια) is undoubtedly the permanent aesthetic characteristic of the beautiful throughout the history of western thought.[3] This, which eventually and, according to Balthasar, regrettably led to a misconceived unity of the divine and human spirit in German Idealism, once started as the vision of "worldly beauty to be the appearance of the One who does not appear, and who shows His transcendence in the unifying order of the manifold" (H III,1 930). Schelling's identification of nature and the Absolute in a work of art confronted modern aesthetics with the paradoxical ability of the beautiful or that which appears in a beautiful form to express its own opposite in ugly forms. It raises the obvious question as to why a form is called 'beautiful'.

Thus, in the history of philosophy the idea of appearance of the beautiful gave birth to a philosophy of form. Two paths can be followed to

---

[1] Cf. L. Dupré, *Passage to modernity. An essay in the hermeneutics of nature and culture*, New Haven 1993, 248.
[2] Cf. R. Williams, Afterword. Making differences, in: L. Gardner, et al., *Balthasar at the end of modernity*, Edinburgh 1999, 173-179, 175.
[3] Cf. G. Steiner, *Real presences. Is there anything in what we say?*, London 1989, 226: "Be it in a specifically religious, for us Judaeo-Christian sense, or in the more general platonic-mythological guise, the aesthetic is the making formal of epiphany. There is a shining through."

interpret this relationship between beauty and form. Either, as is the case in both rationalism and idealism, beauty is derived from experiences and phenomena as a value independent of their being; this results in a type of aesthetics that can never reach beyond a philosophy of experience, since the relation between value and experience is simply and irreducibly conceived of as given. Or, as is the case in atomic, Pythagorean or Leibnizian approaches, the freedom of appearances is captured within the structure of appearance, resulting in a type of aesthetics that can only deal with harmony or other static relationships. Both developments, Balthasar argues, cannot be of any use to a theological aesthetics that has as its starting point the free epiphany of Absolute Being, which needs to be confirmed in both its freedom and its being.

The second aspect of philosophical aesthetics, useful in understanding the free appearance of divine beauty in the world, is 'production' (ποίησισ). The artist is capable of conceiving and confirming the appearance of divine beauty by producing a work of art in a way that goes beyond the rational and discursive faculties because it mirrors the givenness of beauty in a form in a similar intuitive and unified fashion. From Cusanus to Schelling this aspect is explicitly explored by modern philosophers. Their enquiries concerned the ability to respond constructively to the epiphany of the beautiful in worldly forms. Thus, the classic ideas of Plato's μανία and Plotinus's ἔνδον εἶδοσ (inward form) were pursued in the modern idea of *secundus deus* and the intuitive mind of the romantic genius (H III,1 934-935). However, instead of as an intensification of intuition by means of the generation of forms, Balthasar characterises the developments in modernity as a forgetfulness of analogy. In particular, Schelling's romantic idea of art as the expression of the Absolute does not leave any space for the analogy that was articulated in the idea of Cusanus's 'catalogical imagination' of the divine Creative Spirit into the creative spirit of man. To distinguish sharply between artistic (passive) and sexual (active) production, Balthasar suggests an adjustment of the idea of artistic production with the concept of 'empathy' or openness: "that prerequisite of powers, dispositions and expectations of the subject, whereby it draws the object into its own sphere, clasping and permeating it with its sentient organs which bestow both light and warmth in order thus to enjoy it as its own possession" (H III,1 938).

However, for the subject to reach the attitude of self-giving to Being in its entirety, instead of only letting the categorical beauty of the object appear to a subjectively structured aesthetic judgment of taste, an openness towards the transcendental is needed. Only after this transcendental turning point can the epiphany be called theophanous. The human response to this theophany is what Balthasar calls 'metaphysical *eros*', which is the foundation of the lover's freedom to purify natural love into a spiritual one to make it universal and, indeed, more than a figment of the imagination. "It is only this background of the metaphysical *eros* which prevents the particular *eros* from misapprehending itself as a bitter illusion and a scurrilous trick of nature, on which the individual who has been informed and made a fool of avenges himself through his a priori frigidity and insolence" (H III, 1 939).

The third and final aspect of the beautiful that Balthasar derives from modern aesthetics is giftedness (χαρισ), which he defines as loveliness, dignity, brilliance, favour, grace and gratitude all in one.[4] Being all these qualities at the same time, it is the most vague and most enigmatic of aesthetic concepts but crucial for understanding the whole of being in a fragment in which the beautiful appears. '*Charis*' is the light from within, and as such, after the encounter with the beautiful and the artistic erotic response to it, it leaves man with nothing but the "remembrance of the mystery of Being itself" or the "helpless melancholy of *eros*", as Balthasar poetically puts it (H III,I 940).

According to Balthasar, it is possible to integrate modern aesthetics in theology by means of these three aspects. He adds some comments to these aspects, mainly stressing the gift-character of appearance, creativity and grace, to do justice to what it means to perceive the glory of God. The beholder of glory strives towards it as *eros* and proceeds from it as intuition. In ancient times people were more piously open to that intuition, even when it overwhelmed them as an all-encompassing beauty, while in modernity they titanically started to enforce their own idea of beauty upon the universe. Balthasar does not necessarily reject the latter attitude, but he insists that neither of these responses must ignore that, in the first instance, the beauty of Being as a whole causes wonder. Theological reflection should always do justice to this original moment, which is its inspiration and aim. The next section summarises and evaluates one of the most visionary and sublimely written theological essays of the twentieth century, in which Balthasar defines the ground and tasks of theological aesthetics.

---

[4] In the context of modern aesthetics I suggest that χαρισ be translated as 'talent' or 'giftedness'. Balthasar, however, leaves it untranslated.

b. Analogical foundation: love beyond expression

To illustrate the original experience of beauty, Balthasar refers to the words from the gospel of Matthew: "Unless you change and become like little children, you will never enter the kingdom of heaven (Matthew 18:3). As the *id quo majus cogitari non potest* of faith, he considers this a tautology and the expression of an initial yet ultimate experience that existence is both glorious and a matter of course. The original experience of the incomprehensible light of grace, described by Balthasar from the metaphorical perspective of a child not yet constrained by duties, privation, guilt or death, shows existence as the invitation to take part as an object of love (H III,1 963). The awareness that love, experienced in this way, is distinct from the love of God only follows in a second instance. It is theology's task to articulate this distinction by finding its way back to the original experience that to be is to be loved, only to understand that no attempt of the human spirit to reconstruct it will find the same necessity and wonder as generated by its prototype.

What is Balthasar's solution to the problem in theological aesthetics, which on the one hand should reflect the original and wondrous experience of the light of grace, while on the other should and will be aware of the fact that it will never be able to actively reconstruct that experience based on the experience of worldly beauty? To explain this problem, unmistakably under the influence of Heidegger's philosophy of being that was prevalent at the time, Balthasar makes use of ontological discourse to describe a fourfold distinction:[5] After the first experience of being thrown into existence (1), a being becomes actual through participation in the act of Being (2). From this, it follows that it is only possible for the fullness of Being to attain its actuality in its dependence of existent beings (3).[6] Consequently, through the understanding of the beauty in and of the world, one will gain the awareness that Being cannot be made responsible for bringing essences into existence from itself, just as the human spirit cannot construct the real world, since it is part of that world. With reference to Kant, Balthasar declares that not only "concepts without intuition are empty" but the abundance of Being also remains empty. Therefore, even if the totality of Being were to be reconstructed, it would still find itself confronted with the unsurpassable abundance of glory (4) that only has a 'reflection' in the beautiful (H III,1 945-947).

---

[5] Cf. M. Heidegger, *Einführung in die Metaphysik*, Tübingen 1987^5, 101, 121.
[6] Cf. F. Ulrich, *Homo abyssus. Das Wagnis der Seinsfrage*, Einsiedeln 1998^2, 46-60.

To describe this reflection of glory in worldly beauty, and having explained that the overpowering wonder at the very fact of being itself cannot be derived from "gazing at Being", Balthasar rejects the term 'expression'. The idea of expression presupposes a plan and a decision to express oneself, which are categories of the human spirit, but should not be applied to the abundance of Being, which instead he characterises by 'indifference', the antonym of planning and decision-making. Especially at this point he is highly critical of Cusanus and Schelling, who were both influenced by the modern idea of 'evolution', put forward in the Cusan idea of the Absolute Spirit which explicates itself in the world, or in Schelling's idea of art as a way of the Absolute in search of Itself. These interpretations account for neither the Absolute's perfection that presupposes an intelligence and a freedom, which are completely different from the constraints of nature, nor the reason why the Absolute expresses itself in a natural order of forms and not in another unnatural randomness. "Within the world, 'expression' remains a category of the 'beautiful' whose radiance and charm easily brings the word 'glorious' (*herrlich*) to our lips but which can only inauthentically lay claim to the sense of 'lordship' (*herrschaftlich*) and 'majesty' (*hehr*) within it" (H III,1 951-952). Balthasar suggests that to understand the freedom of non-subsisting beings, it must be grounded in an ultimate and subsisting freedom of absolute Being, which is God, whose works cannot be described in terms of expression or any other concept that involves causality or necessity.

So, to characterise the incomprehensibility and freedom of Being in its glory and sovereignty, one must look beyond the real distinction of Being and beings, which comes immediately into view when one sees the beauty of the world. Instead, Balthasar thinks a turning point in modern metaphysics is necessary, one that is best to be described as a theological turn. Theology's speculative perception of glory directs the human gaze from freedom to grace and from the actuality of being to salvation. It is the only possible perspective to break out of the circular polarity of Being and beings, in which each being is infinitely dependent on one another, and which might as well not be. Borrowing Cusanus's concept of *Possest*, Balthasar states that only the absolute freedom of God can break this circle by being a power whose potency is all potential, which proceeds in the world as the abundance of gift and love.[7] Another Cusan concept grounds all metaphysical understanding of the world in the freedom of God. God appears in the world as "the Wholly Other only as the

---

[7] See also chapter six for the description of Cusanus's example of the 'portrait' of God, in which the gaze of the portrayed makes all other perceptions possible.

Non-Aliud, the Not-Other: as He who covers all finite entities with the one mantle of His indivisible Being in so far as they are able to participate in His reality at an infinite remove—as 'entities', which are not Him, but which owe their possibility to His power, and their wealth (to grasp Him as the One who is actual and to shelter in Him) to His creative freedom" (H III,1 956).

Here, Balthasar's theological interpretation of the analogy of being is expressed in full. The difference between God and Being must not be explained in a pantheistic or theopanistic manner by some kind of correspondence between two things that gradually differ, but as the presence of the free divine act in the world (TD II 118-119). God does not reveal Himself in the transcendental openness of Being, but instead He is present freely in Being as a whole. This idea of analogy has far-reaching implications for a theological aesthetics. The beauty of God can be recognised in nature as well as in works of art but it can only be recognised as such by revelation and not by that which pleases the senses or what seems to be without interest.

Balthasar thus presents a theologically grounded metaphysics as the positive methodological starting point of his theological aesthetics. Its subject matter is not primarily the beauty in the world, nor the beauty of the whole world, but the glory of God. Finite beauty can only be regarded as the likeness and image of the Infinite glory, if the finite subject allows itself a removal from itself. Balthasar makes use of the idea of kenosis to describe the perceptive recognition in the 'darkness of Being', as he describes it metaphorically, of both the limits of Being in which it participates and the God who, infinitely different from Being itself, reveals Himself as the abundance of potential that proceeds from Him as gift and love.

c. Catalogical foundation: trinitarian kenosis

The starting point of Balthasar's theological aesthetics is the light of grace revealing itself in the primal ontological difference that emerges in the experience of being thrown into existence, which proceeds from the love of God. As such, this procession determines the historical events between God and man, and must not be interpreted, as Hegel did, as the necessity to go outside the inner dialectic of the absolute Spirit to find the dynamism revealed in scripture. Nor should it be equated with the event of the destiny of Being, as Heidegger did. Instead, the limitation of Being opened the possibility of conceiving the Absolute and sovereign freedom of God in a kenotic moment of rapture, which is founded on a prior movement of the divine kenosis. It is therefore impossible to characterise Balthasar's work as a "fundamental ontological reduction".[8]

To understand Balthasar's task for theology to bring revelation in relation with history, mission and tradition and following his intention to rethink the problem of analogy (How can there be a world, if God is already all in all?), it is important here to speak about intratrinitarian love. God does not change when he reveals His love in the world, but chooses freely to appear and to create human beings in his image.[9] In Balthasar's theology the metaphysical concept of God is fulfilled and secured in the revelation of trinitarian love. So, although prior to the historical events of creation and salvation and therefore necessarily incomprehensible, Balthasar tries to comprehend analogically the intratrinitarian kenoses in order to understand the aesthetic rapture as a consequence of the perception of grace.[10]

He describes the fact that the innerworldly rapture by the light of grace points to the intratrinitarian kenotic movements within God as follows: "The exteriorisation of God (in the incarnation) has its ontic condition of possibility in the eternal exteriorisation of God, which is His tripersonal self-gift. With that departure point, the created person too, should no longer be described as subsisting in itself, but more profoundly (if he is created after God's image and likeness) as a "returning (*reflexio completa*) from exteriority to oneself" and an "emergence from oneself as an interiority that gives itself in self-expression" (TddT 33). It is important to note here that Balthasar not only establishes the primal divine kenosis as the ground of the subsequent kenoses in creation, incarnation and atonement, but also as the ground of rapture of the human subject. This rapture, which follows the outpouring of divine love, directs towards the promise eventually to be taken up in the immanent Trinity because, within the intratrinitarian movements, God's self-giving coincides with God's infinite self-possession. But again, this self-possession can only

---

[8] L. Roberts, A critique of the aesthetic theology of Hans Urs von Balthasar, in: *The American Benedictine review* 16 (1965), 486-504, 503; cf. Id., *The theological aesthetics of Hans Urs von Balthasar*, Washington 1987, 53-54.

[9] Cf. G. O'Hanlon, *The immutability of God in the theology of Hans Urs von Balthasar*, Cambridge 1990, 21ff.

[10] Cf. G. De Schrijver, Hans Urs von Balthasars Christologie in der Theodramatik. Trinitarische Engführung als Methode, in: *Bijdragen. Tijdschrift voor filosofie en theologie* 59 (1998), 141-153, 142-143.

be understood analogically in terms of kenotic self-abandonment which truly reveals the meaning of God's love in the world: the absolute freedom to establish a relation defined by an infinite distance and, precisely because of this distance, an infinite intimacy and presence. The distance within the Trinity should be interpreted as the distance of infinite love and self-giving which grounds the existence of Being and calls the Christian to restore all things in Christ.

d. Theology: revelation and form

In his critique of modern metaphysics Balthasar shows a discord with the separation of theology and philosophy, and of faith and reason. For him, the rise of the human subject in modernity is not as much the entry of a competitor of the divine as it is a forgetfulness or eclipse of glory. While Cusanus's concept of the *secundus deus,* or even the promethean theme in Schelling's philosophy, can be understood within the framework of the analogy of being, the results of modern metaphysics endanger the very ground of theology: the Word of God that reveals both the foundation for the fact that Being proclaims grace and the origin of the permission to be (*Seindürfen*) (H III,1 963). Thus, the problem of modernity, according to Balthasar, is not primarily the titanic struggle between divine and human freedom but the focus on the nihilistic realm of Being in which this struggle is fought. The legacy of modernity is a gloryless metaphysics and the end of theology.[11]

How then will theology survive this crisis?[12] Balthasar's own organisation of the tasks of theology—revelation and history, revelation and mission, revelation and tradition—structures the answer to that question.[13] To address the first task of understanding revelation in history, he defines the Christian contribution to metaphysics in a twofold manner. First, the Christian theologian who searches for the understanding of faith must admit that the ground of Being cannot be found within this world, which is exactly the place where the philosopher and the scientist mistakenly assume to find it. Second, the Christian theologian is the 'custodian of

---

[11] C. O'Regan, Balthasar and Eckhart. Theological principles and catholicity, in: *The thomist* 60 (1966), 203-239, 207 n. 6.

[12] G. Pattison, *The end of theology—And the task of thinking about God*, London 1998, especially 19-29.

[13] Note that Balthasar's three tasks (history, mission, tradition) differ from the ones I presented in chapter one (diversity, particularity, freedom).

glory', the guardian of the metaphysical wonderment which is the point of origin for theology, but also for philosophy and science, although these latter disciplines fall into the danger of turning the light of grace into a cosmological admiration of existence as a whole. This admiration, however, Balthasar argues, is not love, because "Love loves Being in an a priori way. (...) It receives it as a free gift and replies with free gratitude. Here that light weaves, which is the source of all authentic images and cyphers together with the 'sacred words of origin' and thus of all art which remains close to the origin" (H III,1 975).

Balthasar's criticisms towards modern science and philosophy apply to a certain branch of aesthetic theology as well. He severely rejects an understanding of God as the creator of the world based on its beauty, branding this view 'tasteless'. Viewed in the light of suffering or used as a theory to justify eternal damnation, Balthasar finds such an aesthetic theology wholly intolerable. Not the fullness of Being but its poverty is the ultimate test for theology because, he argues, the light of grace usually shines in darkness, which is the preferred place of revelation and hardly of aesthetic contemplation.[14]

Thus, he addresses the second task of theology: to explain the relation between revelation and mission. Balthasar's theology of beauty can be called a theology of engagement. His theological aesthetics, with its emphasis on the analogy of being, rejects a disinterested aesthetic contemplation that leads to a glorification of worldly beauty, and shows a great involvement with the world and freedom of man. Therefore, and for some critics perhaps unexpectedly, one might say that his analysis of modernity resists any interpretation of his theology being a distasteful aestheticised elevation of the Christian faith. He describes his ideas of Christian life and Christian attitude as the mission to love one's neighbour, which he says can only be understood as the kenotic work of a selfless self that follows the rapture by the glory of God.[15] As such, he defines the practice of Christian mission in terms of worship and obedience. This

---

[14] Balthasar's aesthetics is not a theology of art. Had he discussed works of art, he would have had to acknowledge that metaphors like 'poverty' and the biblical image of 'darkness, where the light comes in' do not necessarily contradict the aesthetic contemplation. By the time he finished *Herrlichkeit* III (1969), Picasso's *Guernica* and Edvard Munch's *Scream*, for example, had already had an enormous impact on western European culture. These paintings are just two examples of a radical change in artistic expression in the twentieth century, asking for a change in responsive contemplation and demonstrating a new and critical position of art in society.

[15] Cf. O. Davies, *A theology of compassion. Metaphysics of difference and the renewal of tradition*, London 2001, 32.

description finds its theoretical background in his design of the metaphysics of the saints that is characterised by the self's disinterestedness, embodied in the lives of saints. Here, it becomes clear that Balthasar's theological aesthetics is embedded in the practice of the church. At the same time, however, theology is also a church practice. The consequence of the idea of mission for theology is a 'kneeling attitude', a spiritual understanding that is not concerned with the self but with the self's servitude towards that which is beyond comprehension, through the free and responsible act of giving one's life to others (VC 220).

By pointing towards revelation as a gift, to the Christian response to revelation as worship and obedience, and thus to faith as being a mainly receptive act, Balthasar fails to fully address the third task of theology, which is the relation between revelation and tradition. In his dispute with nominalist and scholastic schools of thought, and with modern scientific and subjectivist approaches, and by reintroducing the mystic elements in theology through aesthetics, he interprets the whole enterprise of theological aesthetics by means of perception and being enraptured. The result is a passive, contemplative view on faith and theology. "Faith is always obedience, even when it is seeking insight and understanding: it is never permission for us to give vent to our hunger for novelty in vain speculation. And many questions that human curiosity tends to ask of revelation are rejected by revelation, and exposed as false and irrelevant" (KB 39).

Furthermore, his view on aesthetics ignores the idea of creativity but focuses completely on inspiration. Instead of opposing action and contemplation, he places actions such as worship and obedience in the midst of contemplation (VC 257). He might have done this to save theology from degenerating into moralism but the consequence is a type of theology that describes the beginning and the end of salvation history in terms of grace, while failing to address what happens in between.

Balthasar defines theological aesthetics as perceiving the glory of God. It is a discipline that is embedded in the active practice of the church and grounded in the self-disclosure of the glory of the triune God, which he considers to be perceivable in the historical form of tradition. The implications of this definition for his idea of theology in general are far-reaching. His concern is wonder instead of scientific exploration, and intuition instead of systematic thought. Wonder and intuition are human faculties illuminated by and drawn to, but not actively directed at divine revelation. Balthasar's image of the believer is that of the beholder and not that of the artist. Consequently, since theology has to conform itself to its subject matter, it follows that the theologian must not be compared to the creative artist.

This inevitably has its consequences for Balthasar's view of tradition. Instead of taking the diversity of tradition into account, he concentrates on the historicity of tradition and its receptivity to divine grace. The consequence is an aesthetic interpretation of scripture, Christ and tradition as forms, without taking seriously either the multitude within these subsequent forms or the plurality of receptions. The idea of form as a plurality in unity is interpreted by Balthasar from the perspective of the perceiver who, enraptured by the light of grace, should see unity rather than plurality. Although an experience of faith should not merely be communal, no Christian believer can have an isolated perception of glory either. All faith perceptions must be understood within the framework of tradition, as tradition is constituted by a variety of perceptions. This variety composes the historical dynamics of tradition. That process of tradition is fed by an ongoing internal debate that cannot be settled due to the differences in perceptions of revealed forms. Furthermore, Christians and Christian communities are participants in a broader culture that influences their perceptions.

Balthasar's theological standpoint of the faithful perceiver seeing the form explains neither tradition's historical and cultural dynamics, nor its internal diversity. Instead, he interprets tradition as the result of the one true vision that is enlightened by divine revelation. Theology then, participating in that vision within tradition, is defined as the verbal and intellectual articulation of that vision. As a consequence, Balthasar takes the continuity between the ground of faith and the ground of theology for granted, thereby risking confusion of the two. Theology however, instead of being a self-description of faith alone, should be the internal and external communication of the perceived forms of faith and their content. Only thus it can account for the specific position of a community of faith within a changing cultural context in order to understand or stress not only the particularity of that community but hopefully also its inner dynamics.

8.2. Fides quaerens imagines: faith seeking forms

It is now time to return to the questions about the nature of theology raised in chapter one. Balthasar's theological aesthetics has provided several insights into the central question: "What is theology?" His main concern was to reinscribe the sense of beauty in theology but at the same time he indicated the danger of confusing the beauty of divine glory with one's own taste judgment, the beauty of nature or the beauty of works of art. Art and beauty are neither expressions of the Absolute, nor ways to reach or experience God. Therefore, neither a comparison of faith and art, nor an illustration of the content of faith by means of art, are sufficient to address the nature of theology. The lesson to learn from this is that theology should not surrender to the prevailing idea that all art is religious and all beauty divine, or that all artists are religious.[16] Thus, making use of works of art to demonstrate the truth claims of faith violates the iconoclastic rule that one should not see the divine in beauty and art. A straightforward *demonstratio aesthetica* is not a viable way to do fundamental theology.

Balthasar correctly dismisses another justification for applying aesthetics to fundamental theology: the observation that both the primary speech of religion and the language of theology itself are figurative and poetic.[17] The exploration of this observation leads to linguistic studies of the genres and styles of holy texts, or to structuralist approaches to myths and symbols. Art in these cases would have to be considered as the expression of that which cannot be addressed scientifically and the analysis of figurative language or the symbolic imagination serves to explain the mediation between a concept and the divine reality that cannot be conceived directly. However important such an approach may be, the purpose of aesthetics is not to admit a theological weakness based on the presumed impossibility of approaching the subject matter of theology rationally; nor should it serve to conceal the scientific limitations of theology by restricting theological explorations to the conceptual clarification of religious language. Theological aesthetics should strive to think beyond these implications of linguistic or symbolic approaches of the 'grammar' of faith.[18]

Although an artistic or linguistic awareness has been eliminated as a possible justification for theological aesthetics, it is still possible to use art in theology or to do theology through the arts. Theological aesthetics at least enables an expansion of the theological field of operation beyond

---

[16] F.B. Brown, *Good taste, bad taste, and Christian taste. Aesthetics in religious life*, Oxford 2000, 122.

[17] P. Avis, *God and the creative imagination. Metaphor, symbol and myth in religion and theology*, London 1999, 68.

[18] Cf. H. Frei, *Types of Christian theology*, New Haven 1993, 20-21; D.Z. Phillips, *Religion and the hermeneutics of contemplation*, Cambridge 2001.

ethics and logic. Thus, it approaches faith with a set of concepts that differs from the customary epistemological, ethical or doctrinal concepts. The present research serves to defend the thesis that, besides a broadening of possible theological concepts, aesthetics makes one aware of different sources and changes the very nature of theological method. This change is needed to meet a task of contemporary fundamental theology: to freely explore the possibilities of communicating faith theologically in the church and the culture to which it belongs. To do this, the definition of theology should not be constituted by the internal logic of faith alone, nor by the search for similarities with other academic disciplines or artistic forms of expressions. Instead, theology should be understood as seeking forms to describe and reasonably explain what is perceived and witnessed in faith to a variety of audiences.

Speaking to academic, cultural and ecclesiastical—both lay and clerical—audiences, Balthasar succeeded in exploring and expressing the essence of faith in aesthetic terms. Despite the successes of his approach he failed, however, to address the problem of faith in a secularised culture and the variety of theological responses to a changing position of the church in the world after the Second Vatican Council. In his aesthetics he defines faith as 'seeing the form' but that definition does not suffice to describe the interconnectedness of the various communications of faith within the dynamics of history: with God, church and culture. 'Seeing the form' expresses a revelatory positivism which understands the perception of God through the analogical forms of scripture and tradition alone. Although Balthasar's aesthetics deals with the historicity of these forms, his analysis remains esoteric and susceptible to accusations of fideism.[19] He maintains that faith is only available within a particular pattern of experience and refuses to submit it to any external assessment.[20] As he would put it: it cannot be judged by worldly standards.

To deal with the problem of fundamental theology, the problem of doing justice to the various forms of communications that are involved in faith, I propose that theological aesthetics, besides *seeing* the form, is also *seeking* the form by means of the reasonable exploration of a diversity of religious forms that mark the pattern of the particularity of faith. Theological aesthetics as fundamental theology then would be faith seeking

---

[19] Cf. J. Disse, *Metaphysik der Singularität. Eine Hinführung am Leitfaden der Philosophie Hans Urs von Balthasars*, Wien 1996, 229-236.
[20] N. Lash, Ideology, metaphor, and analogy, in: S. Hauerwas, L.G. Jones [eds], *Why narrative? Readings in narrative theology*, Grand Rapids 1989, 134.

images: *fides quaerens imagines*. It is a search for meaning that is mediated by a diversity of perceptions and responses. Defined this way, it is the methodological analogue of, or at least an important moment in fundamental theology that seeks to understand faith: *fides quaerens intellectum*.

The search for understanding and the search for images are complementary and inseparable. Theological aesthetics therefore does not signify the impossibility of or the decline in theological reasoning. Nor is it a desperate apologetic attempt to find a broadly supported or fashionable description of theological content. The main importance of theological aesthetics lies in its twofold contribution to Christian theological reasoning: to complement Christian self-description and to improve the communication with various audiences. Thus, it meets the first two tasks of contemporary fundamental theology: to understand Christian particularity in its expressive forms and to explore the possibilities of forms of communication in conversation with a diversity of others. In what follows, I will describe the aesthetic aspects that constitute the search for these forms.

a. Perception: sense and sensibilities

In chapter two I claimed that the type of theological aesthetics that takes the work of art as its starting point represents an impoverished view of the systematic perspectives aesthetics might open for theology. Nevertheless, works of art can be main sources of theological inspiration instead of merely theological illustrations. The artist's imagination evokes the beholder's response and in so doing breaks through existing ideas and calls up new theological insights. However, my preference for a theological aesthetics which takes a broad concept of theological imagination and the religious interpretation of the concept of beauty as its centre not only addresses the spiritual senses but also bodily, sensory perception. Aesthetics is grounded in the awareness that the senses and corporality are inextricably connected to human perception. Indeed, from its origins in the works of its founder, Alexander Baumgarten, aesthetics has always also sought to describe perception from a physical and not just a spiritual or intellectual point of view. To this, Kant added that the perception of beauty cannot be explained teleologically but is disinterested.

What is the importance of the notion of a bodily and disinterested perception to theology? Perception is an essential aspect of faith. This does not mean that there is something like a pure experience that can be interpreted religiously. 'Perception' does not refer to a purely sensory experience although, in principle, it is possible—be it with some considerable effort—to isolate the aspect of the senses from other types of experiences and our interpretations.[21] Faith does not begin with a certain perception that can be backtracked theologically to one single moment of sensual experience. It does however come with a strong sense of belonging, the recognition of impressions and an atmosphere which is shared and mediated by the religious community. This recognition involves smells, gestures, a sense of space, the nearness of others, but also the sound and the joy or the gravity of spoken words. There are other examples of what could be regarded as perception of faith. For example, faith is motivated by the perception of what is true and good. This can be encountered in the face or the actions of fellow human beings or in nature.[22] All these recognitions and encounters form the variety of aesthetic experiences that constitute the perception of faith, as they are sensory or can be characterised as immediate, gratuitous or disinterested.

Perception of faith differs from other types of perception insofar as it emerges in a specific context and is accompanied by a religious interpretation. Sensory experiences are part of faith experiences, but no faith experience can be regarded detached from religious interpretation and understanding. Conversely, religious interpretation and understanding are not available detached from any experienced clues in the surrounding objective reality. Theological interpretation is needed to understand scripture, tradition, culture and the original perception of faith which lies at the heart of all theological sources. This, the perception of faith itself, becomes a source of theology, which incidentally does not mean that a theological interpretation of sensory perception will necessarily lead to a theology that finds its first or only starting point in experience. Instead, the search for an understanding of faith should take the perceptions of individuals and communities of faith as seriously, as it does scripture and tradition. Furthermore, faith perception is something that is shared by the theologian, who should, therefore, if only as a means of self-criticism, consult and evaluate the perceptions of others. In addition, our visual and virtual culture, which increasingly appeals to our senses and at the same time questions their limits and possibilities, also requires a theology of sensory perception.

[21] Cf. B. Maund, *Perception*, Chesham 2003.
[22] Cf. D. Ford, *Self and salvation. Being transformed*, Cambridge 1999.

The classic theological interpretation of the senses explains them as the necessity of a home to the human soul. According to this idea, the whole of creation finds its purpose in the incarnation and the body with its senses are merely instruments of grace. This position fails to do justice to the suffering and the imperfections of the body. After all, what does it mean that "the eyes of the blind be opened and the ears of the deaf unstopped" (Isaiah 35,5)? A classic theological understanding of the senses not only underlines that the material, physical world has been made possible by an immaterial God but also shows that God has created the senses and the body to allow man to physically experience and enjoy creation.[23]

There is a growing sensibility for the senses in theology. In recent years the ideas of physicality and perception have been the domain of feminist theologians. Their reintroduction of the body into theology has undoubtedly been of great importance for a renewed interest in aesthetics.[24] Also, the Barthian T.J. Gorringe has recently written a 'dogmatics in outline', based on sensory perception.[25] Philip Blond, a member of John Milbank's theological movement 'Radical Orthodoxy', has made the idea of perception the central focus of a new brand of philosophical theology.[26] According to Blond, 'perception' is a theological concept *par excellence* which will necessarily remain incomprehensible in philosophy. It is an openness to the givenness of existence which, according to him, only acquires a certain order and meaning within a Christian vision. Without this specific vision of faith, the given would appear as a bare reality that cannot even be called 'world'. However, Blond too strictly separates perception and Christian interpretation. If perception is only interpreted as an openness to a given world that consequently can only be understood within a Christian vision, then the implication for that vision is that it must be blind itself, since it only in second instance determines the original perception instead of evoking specific perceptions from the start.

---

[23] Cf. F.B. Brown, *Good taste, bad taste, and Christian taste*.
[24] Cf. J. Bekkenkamp, M. de Haardt [eds], *Begin with the body. Corporeality, religion, and gender*, Louvain 1998.
[25] T.J. Gorringe, *The education of desire. Towards a theology of the senses*, London 2001.
[26] Ph. Blond, Introduction. Theology before philosophy, in: Id. [ed.], *Post-secular philosophy. Between philosophy and theology*, London 1998, 1-66; Id., Theology and perception, in: *Modern theology* 14 (1998), 523-534; Id., The primacy of theology and the question of perception, in: P. Heelas, D. Martin [eds], *Religion, modernity and postmodernity*, Oxford 1998, 285-313; Id., Perception. From modern painting to the vision in Christ, in: J. Milbank [ed.], *Radical orthodoxy. A new theology*, London 1999, 220-242.

Against Blond, I would argue for the reciprocity of perception and imaginative interpretation. Christian visions are developed by free people with open ears and eyes (Matthew 13:16). Right from the beginning, the perception of faith has a context and an interpretational framework to which every individual observer must relate.[27] This relation comes with a receptiveness that is not, as yet, unintentional, but is grounded in the experience of the gratuitousness of being. This aesthetic, perceptive aspect is a necessary and grounding moment in the search for an understanding of fundamental theology. The perception of faith points to the fact that faith is experienced and is therefore alive and vivid, regardless of how difficult it may sometimes be to express this experience in words. This vividness is an aspect of human freedom, which starts with individual perception and searches for credible forms by means of the religious imagination. Like perception, imagination is a gift but one that can be exercised as an active and unifying power.

b. Imagination: playing the field

Although the philosophical concept of 'imagination' has a long history—it was a key concept in medieval and modern epistemology—it has not attracted serious theological attention until relatively recently when it became central to the theologies of David Tracy, Gordon Kaufman and currently, David Brown.[28] Thomas Aquinas considered the imagination to be the bridge between sensory and intellectual knowledge: all knowledge starts in the senses, although true knowledge is not sensory. The sensory image is interchangeable but the concept is not. The intellect participates in the universal truth and needs imagination to express its meaning. Despite its own creative force, imagination guarantees the receptive or mimetic character of thought because it is an expressive result of participation in

---

[27] The idea of 'perception without imagination' does not mean that, because all perception occurs in an existing interpretational framework, conversion is impossible. On the contrary, imagination enables it to relate to existing interpretations in a new way. Imagination therefore will play an important role for a new generation that is not brought up within a self-evident Christian context, to freely relate to the Christian narrative.

[28] For the genesis of the concept of 'imagination', cf. R. Kearney, *The wake of imagination. Toward a postmodern culture*, London 1988; G. Green, *Imagining God. Theology and the religious imagination*, San Francisco 1989; Id., *Theology, hermeneutics and imagination. The crisis of interpretation at the end of modernity*, Cambridge 2000; R. Viladesau, *Theological aesthetics. God in imagination, beauty and art*, Oxford 1999, 39-72; A. Grøn, Imagination and subjectivity, in: *Ars disputandi* 2 (2002), 27-36.

reality.²⁹ In his *Kritik der reinen Vernunft*, Kant also locates the imagination between the senses and reason.³⁰ Imagination forms a synthesis between the material representations of the senses and the categorical concepts of reason. Thus, it structures experience and renders it comprehensible. However, in his *Kritik der Urteilskraft*, Kant distinguishes another type of imagination: intuitive or creative imagination (*Einbildungskraft*).³¹ The relation between this form of imagination and reason is not necessary but it is the product of human freedom.

Human imagination always has to find a balance between receptivity and construction. It is, as John Milbank puts it, "the medium in which the judgment of the higher soul swims".³² Thus, it is more than sheer receptivity because it is accompanied by creative or artistic effort. It also differs from the ideas of pure construction, insofar as it always more or less refers to perceived aspects of reality. Theological aesthetics then, should describe and value the human imagination for its ability to endure the tension between receptivity and construction. Theological imagination may point out the place of revelation in the world but it is unable to determine the source or the content of revelation.³³ The key to the imagination of faith cannot therefore be found in a philosophical or psychological analysis of mental processes. The imagination of faith is not only the expression of an experience but is always embedded in a tradition of (imaginative) interpretation. This is why Garrett Green introduced the concept of 'paradigmatic imagination', in which the paradigm is the material content of imagination.³⁴ Only the objective content of Christian imagination can lay claim to the truth, which in turn can only be represented by imagination. According to Green, the human connection with divine revelation is formally the imagination and materially the image of God. This raises the question as to whether a theology of imagination can only relate formally to the materiality of the image of God. After all, the material given of man as the likeness of God is a product of the imagination too. That is why man cannot construct an image based on a clearly defined religious perception which does not subsequently influence this image. The imagination of faith is forever part of a tradition of images

---

[29] St Thomae Aquinatis, *Quaestiones disputatae de veritate*, q. 1, art. 11.
[30] I. Kant, *Kritik der reinen Vernunft*, A 104-105.
[31] Id., *Kritik der Urteilskraft*, B 86-87.
[32] J. Milbank, Beauty and the soul, in: Id., G. Ward, E. Wyschogrod [eds], *Theological perspectives on God and beauty*, Harrisburg 2003, 1-34, 22.
[33] Cf. G. Green, The mirror, the lamp, and the lens. On the limits of imagination, in: *Ars disputandi* 2 (2002), 75-86.
[34] Cf. G. Green, *Imagining God*, 61-80.

that convey religious content. In turn, this tradition influences our religious perceptions. Still, human imagination does not have to be trapped in this dialectic. It may lead to changes in religious perception and religious content.

Gordon Kaufman and David Tracy have put imagination at the centre of contemporary fundamental theology.[35] According to them, an ambiguous world leaves theologians with only one option, which is to clarify the mystery of God by means of accepted concepts of faith and shared interpretations of texts. Imagination is involved in the language used to express the meanings of those texts.[36] Tracy thinks the creative imagination in texts is mainly at work in the genre and style of these texts.[37] In Kaufman's theology too, 'imagination' is the key concept of theological method. He believes that theology—like the natural sciences and literature, politics and the arts—is an expression of human imagination.

Both theologians regard imagination as the ability to actualise and integrate theology. According to Tracy, imagination is centrally involved in the translation of existing faith concepts to new contexts, in which the theologian encounters other situations and conversation partners. Kaufman thinks that imagination can demonstrate the communality of faith with other cultural expressions and calls on theologians to consult other sciences and literature. However, neither Tracy nor Kaufman use the concept of 'imagination' to answer questions of theological self-description, such as to what extent Christian imagination distinguishes itself from other forms of religious imagination, or in what way Christian imagination contributes to a relation of the faithful to their own religious traditions. Fundamental theology's search for understanding should not ignore its self-descriptive task. Imagination is not just a means of entering the dialogue with other religions or academic disciplines but also the pre-eminent medium for theological self-description.

If Kant was right when he claimed that the creative imagination is entirely based on human freedom, what does this mean for theological self-understanding? Christian religious imagination may be able to rid itself of its biblical and traditional seedbed temporarily but certainly not permanently. As shown, even religious perception does not start with a pure sensory experience but rather is determined by its traditional environment.

---

[35] D. Tracy, *The analogical imagination. Christian theology and the culture of pluralism*, Londen 1981; G. Kaufman, *An essay on theological method*, Atlanta 1995³.
[36] D. Tracy, *The analogical imagination*, 54
[37] Ibid., 128-129. Cf. K.-J. Kuschel, *Im Spiegel der Dichter. Mensch, Gott und Jesus in der Literatur des 20. Jahrhunderts*, Düsseldorf 2000.

Does this mean that religious imagination is never a form of creative imagination and always held to a given religious content? Put differently: to what extent do revelation and tradition limit the possibilities of theological aesthetics when it finds new constructions based on religious perception and religious imagination?

c. Construction: building a theory

The idea that, strictly speaking, only God has a concept of God is no doubt an important theological axiom for both 'liberal' and 'orthodox' theologians.[38] Any image of God or concept of God is indeed nothing more than human construction. This observation offers endless possibilities for further examination of the concept of God and for trying new models and metaphors but that does not mean that anything is possible. After all, the dynamics of the history of the changing image of God is embedded in a tradition of debate, habit and a variety of contexts. However, theologians search both inside and outside their own traditions for a better understanding of their own faith. It means that these traditions are subject to change without ever ceasing to be tradition. Theologians are responsible for analysing images of God, criticising them and reconstructing them.[39] They can even put tradition aside to make room for new perceptions. However, they cannot avoid having to present the fruits of their labour, their religious constructions, to the forum of tradition.

Theological aesthetics describes the free play of human imagination, realising that religious imagination itself cannot escape the relation between tradition and construction. On the one hand, tradition is construction right from its beginning. On the other hand, it can only be tradition by limiting construction. This makes religious tradition as a living reality both limit and condition to the creation of new religious content.[40] That is why theological construction as an activity is usually situated between dogmatic and fundamental theology. Theological construction would then mediate between the historicity of dogma and the universal

---

[38] Cf. K. Barth, *Kirchliche Dogmatik I,1*, München 1932, 97; Id., *Fides quaerens intellectum. Anselms Beweis der Existenz Gottes im Zusammenhang seines theologischen Programms*, [*Gesamtausgabe II. Akademische Werke*, Hrsg. von E. Jüngel, I. Dalferth], Zürich 1981.

[39] Cf. G. Kaufman, *The theological imagination. Constructing the concept of God*, Philadelphia 1981, 265-267.

[40] Cf. G.P. Schner, s.j., Metaphors for theology, in: Id., J. Webster, [eds], *Theology after liberalism. A reader*, Oxford 2000, 3-51, 12-24.

conditions of the *humanum*,[41] or it is regarded as constituting the link between historical and practical theology.[42] However, religious construction does not so much mediate between different theological approaches as it emphasises the fact that faith and theology always use language and images that are the product of human creativity. That is why construction plays an important role in all subdisciplines of theology.[43]

The idea of human creativity as an inevitable part of faith and theology seems to contradict the receptive character of Christian—pneumatological, soteriological, eschatological—thought. A theological aesthetics that regards imagination in a radically constructive sense would risk forgetting that theology does not just find its foundations in faith as the creative self-understanding of the individual or the religious community but also in a religious certainty that in the history of Christian theology has been described as trust and as a gift from God. The reticence in using 'construction' as the key concept in theology is understandable, founded as it is in the apprehension of violating divine sovereignty or disobeying church authority. Yet, regarding theology as the mere explanation and dogmatic specification of biblical imagination will not enable to take into account current religious perceptions.[44]

Theology is a creative and constructive enterprise. Fundamental theology consequently, is an ongoing critical self-reflection through traditional and newly constructed theological concepts. Instead of violating divine sovereignty by positing human creativity in opposition to divine creativity and regarding it as a dichotomy of divine and human freedom, religious construction will ultimately demonstrate the infinite difference between divine creativity and human creativity. Unlike man, God does not have to keep searching for or constructing new images, while only by means of human construction can it be discovered that God is unconstructable. Edward Schillebeeckx called this the non-projective moment of reality in our images of God.[45] Human creativity enabled Kaufman to come up with a name for God: 'serendipitous creativity'. God is the creativity that arbitrarily—not necessarily but coincidentally—produces the

---

[41] F.J. van Beeck, *God encountered. A contemporary Catholic systematic theology, I: Understanding the Christian faith*, San Francisco 1989, 43.

[42] P.C. Hodgson, *Winds of the Spirit. A constructive Christian theology*, London 1994, 35-36.

[43] Cf. P.L. Berger, Th. Luckmann, *The social construction of reality. A treatise in the sociology of knowledge*, New York 1967, 68.

[44] Cf. D. Brown, *Discipleship and imagination. Christian tradition and truth*, Oxford 2000, 354-359.

[45] E. Schillebeeckx, *Mensen als verhaal van God*, Baarn 1989, 94.

valuable and the beautiful.[46] The receptivity of faith is guaranteed in such a constructive doctrine of God, or to put it more accurately, the receptivity caused by divine revelation is mediated by religious imagination and its expressive products demonstrate this receptiveness. The question remains however, whether these constructions are able to express more than just the human openness to divine revelation, so that they indeed can be tools for a constructive doctrine of God.

With the concept of 'religious construction', theological aesthetics emphasises the finite character of each image, which is not merely an epistemological but also an eschatological limitation. Human creativity searches for images, experiments with and examines the possibilities of (as yet) non-existent connections. This enables man to create beautiful things and offer a different view on reality. In a Christian context, any representation of a possible divine reality is created in the awareness of its own finitude. Of course, nobody is able to single-handedly or even communally create the kingdom of God by means of religious construction. However, this very fact can only be demonstrated by human imagination and creativity, be it in the way Hans Küng described, when works of art represent the current crisis of meaning, or in the form proposed by Eberhard Jüngel, in which beauty breaks all natural and moral restraints of this earthly life. This way, art and beauty can anticipate the kingdom of God, and thus contribute to the prospect of redemption.

Religious construction shows that human beings are not bound to an objectifiable world. This is ultimately the redemptive character of the subject matter of theological aesthetics. Religious construction shows that the eschatological 'not yet' lead to impossibility but also to one of the most exalted and 'glorious' human possibilities. In the realisation, understood in its double meaning of openness and finitude, of every religious image as an expression of human freedom in the light of eternity, it tries to glimpse the glory of divine beauty.

Theological aesthetics supplements the customary ethical and metaphysical ways of reasoning in theology. I have proposed that aesthetics should be a central part of every fundamental theology and, to elucidate this, I introduced three aesthetic acts that mark key moments in faith and theology: perception, imagination and construction. These acts may be distinguished formally but they are inextricably interwoven in the act of

---

[46] Cf. G. Kaufman, On thinking of God as Serendipitous Creativity, in: *Journal of the American Academy of Religion* 69 (2001), 409-424; Id., *In face of mystery. A constructive theology*, Harvard 1993.

faith. I did not intend to dictate a strict order in which religious content comes about. Religious perception, for example, is fed by current religious content. However, the three aesthetic acts do not describe a closed hermeneutical circle either. On the contrary, the free play of human faculties desires to keep exploring new images with respect to transcendence and infinity, and in so doing, it keeps religious tradition alive. In a Christian context, this means that, in the light of God who is forever greater and a kingdom that is yet to come, any creative attempt to represent God or his kingdom will reveal its own finitude and thus make way for a more intimate and yet still incomprehensible revelation. This is the sometimes glorious, sometimes god-forsaken field of play of the *fides quaerens imagines*, faith seeking images.

8.3. Understanding the sublime

To avoid a revelatory positivism, I have proposed to supplement the first part of Balthasar's theological aesthetics, the doctrine of perception, with a 'doctrine of imagination' and a 'doctrine of construction'. The question remains, however, whether the aesthetic acts of perception, imagination and construction can become points of revelation. If the answer to this question is negative or indeed, if this question cannot be answered at all, then the whole enterprise of fundamental theology, to communicate the grounds of faith and theology both self-descriptively and dialogically, will prove impossible. In this final section, I will counter this nonfoundationalist claim, not only to avoid a positivism of revelation but also to argue against the reduction of theological reasoning to the self-descriptive project of the church.

Introducing aesthetics as a way of doing fundamental theology is not to deny that theology has a self-descriptive task. However, theology must do more than seek forms of faith by means of philosophical, in this case aesthetic ideas. For that reason, Balthasar made a distinction between aesthetic theology and theological aesthetics. Theological aesthetics is not the result of the method of correlation but is inherent to faith and theology. Aesthetics is not borrowed territory but belongs intrinsically to the field of theology. This must be made explicit in doctrinal aesthetics.

Therefore, I will start this final section with a doctrinal presentation of how the aesthetic acts of perception, imagination and construction are intertwined with the act of faith. Grounded in the divine act of revelation, they form the foundation of theology, in particular of Christian doctrine.

Next, I will show that the aesthetic acts must not displace divine revelation. That iconoclastic rule does not reduce them to sheer receptivity, though. To reflect the kenotic spirit in the world, apart from expressing receptivity to revelation, they should also anticipate redemption. Finally, I suggest that the consequence of this aesthetic approach is the definition of theology as a discipline, which specifity is to reason kenotically.

a. Doctrinal aesthetics

Until now, I have discussed aesthetics as fundamental theology. The unintended implication of that treatment could be that aesthetics only has a function as a 'theology of theology'. In this section, I will show that aesthetics itself is a discipline that is intrinsically theological. Indeed, I have presented it as the discipline that offers possibilities of understanding Christian faith theologically. In explaining how faith is experienced and expressed, it is important to make this theological character of aesthetics explicit. That 'demonstration' is directed towards a variety of audiences, not least the audience of the church, for the need for Christian self-description emerges in that context. However, in the western secularised culture, that self-description can no longer be understood as merely a doctrinal extension of the creed. On the contrary, being part of a changing culture, the ecclesiastical need for self-description increases under the influence of a growing awareness of both the differences with other worldviews and one's own secularisation. The western understanding of the particularity of faith by means of doctrine therefore, is aligned with the diversity of developments in the broader cultural environment.

Yet that does not mean an end to the particular emphases of doctrinal theology. On the contrary, an aesthetic reformulation of doctrinal theology may help to intensify the awareness that Christian faith emerges amidst a secular culture and is deeply influenced by it. For this reason, I would like to sketch a number of starting points for a future theological programme: doctrinal aesthetics.

Theological aesthetics should address the trinitarian patterns of faith. Trinitarian theology teaches how God is to be perceived, as it enables one to see the gift of reciprocity of revelation in a way that analogically corresponds to God's intratrinitarian being.[47] A trinitarian view resists

---

[47] I agree with John Webster, who believes that the Trinity is theology's *conditio sine qua non*: "The holy God is not merely some subject-matter entertained by the all-surveying

the idea of God as sheer creativity but offers possibilities of participating creatively in the kenotic and saving life of the divine.[48] Indeed, if the loving harmony of the intratrinitarian relationships is projected onto a salvific plan for humanity, then it is necessary to explore the perception of trinitarian patterns in the light of human sin and suffering.[49] A christological focus that only mirrors the historically manifested form of Christ, mimetically envisioned in (liturgical) memories of the past, will not suffice.[50] Instead, theological aesthetics should search for new ways of perceiving God today. A trinitarian starting point will centre the attention on communion in divine life rather than on obedience to divine law and thus on the freedom to seek and create forms that make that communion perceptible and show possibilities of how to participate in it.

The focal point of this communion is the work of the Holy Spirit, who makes redemption present in the form of an always-already but not-yet reality, and evokes a free response.[51] This would be the subject matter of pneumatological aesthetics, claiming that the Spirit communicates the glory of God to the world in the createdness of natural beauty and in the creaturely freedom of artistic beauty.[52] The themes of pneumatological aesthetics are inspiration and intuition, the possibilities of an ongoing revelation, and the freedom to respond to these events with the Spirit, who enables one to realise the aesthetic acts of imagination and construction as a response to divine revelation. This theological idea is as old as Irenaeus, who, playing on John 14:7, stated that without the Spirit it is impossible to see the Son, and without the Son, no one can reach the Father.[53]

The degree of christocentrism of a particular theology determines whether christological aesthetics will regard Christ's descending form as the sole analogue between God and the world, as for example Irenaeus

---

theological mind; he is the majestic one, the one whose communicative presence makes theology possible", in: J. Webster, *Holiness*, London 2003, 12.

[48] R. Williams, *On Christian theology*, Oxford 2000, 178-179.

[49] Cf. C.M. LaCugna's efforts to join together God's *theologia* and *oikonomia* in her *God for us. The Trinity and Christian life*, London 1991.

[50] As is suggested by J. Milbank, Beauty and the soul, 8.

[51] Cf. O. O'Donovan, Freedom and reality, in: J. Webster, G.P. Schner, s.j. [eds], *Theology after liberalism*, 132-151, 133.

[52] Patrick Sherry is the first theologian who developed a pneumatological aesthetics, and indeed the first to write a doctrinal aesthetics with his *Spirit and Beauty. An introduction to theological aesthetics*, London 2002².

[53] Irenaeus, *Adversus Haereses*, V, 36, 2. Cf. the gospel of John: "No one comes to the Father except through me. He who knows me, knows the Father, and he who sees me sees the Father" (John 14:6-7,9).

and Karl Barth did.[54] Balthasar, although his theology is christocentric in some respects, did not and thus he created the possibility for developing christological aesthetics by also taking the ascending forms of the receptive imagination into account. To know Christ aesthetically then, means to see and hear Him through the faces and words of fellow human beings and through the sensitive grasp of their physical features and gestures.[55] That means that christological aesthetics will also deal with human sin and suffering and thus, with the ugliness of the cross. I agree with both Barth and Balthasar that theological aesthetics cannot ignore the horror of the cross in seeking a 'glorious' Christ as one who is not crucified. It would go too far to call the crucifixion a beautiful experience but it can be considered a beautiful act of the divine, in as much as it is the expression of divine love and the divine identification with human suffering. Consequently, christological aesthetics will differ radically from philosophical aesthetics because it envisages God's beauty embracing joy, the fear of suffering, life, death and the life beyond. It directs attention away from a worldly beauty that ignores ugliness, towards the divine beauty that feeds a fallen humanity with redeemed sensibilities through Christ.

Trinitarian, pneumatological and christological aesthetics all point to a soteriological understanding of the beautiful and thus, to the inextricable relationship of theological aesthetics and ethics. Soteriological aesthetics could emphasise contemplation in action and argue against a theological idea of art for art's sake.[56] The issue at stake in theological aesthetics is not a matter of sensual pleasure and is not concerned with the decoration of liturgy or churches. Theological aesthetics does not interpret religious contemplation as an event apart from the world but instead as a way of enabling responsible action in the world. For the South African theologian John de Gruchy for example, aesthetics has to do with the way in which

[54] Note however, that Barth never developed a christological aesthetics, and the part of his *Church Dogmatics* that could be called 'aesthetics' concerns the attributes of God. See also chapter two, section three.
[55] Cf. F.A. Murphy, *Christ, the form of beauty. A study in theology and literature*, Edinburgh 1995, 131-194.
[56] Again, Patrick Sherry was the first to write a 'soteriology of the arts': *Images of redemption. Arts, literature and salvation*, London 2003. However, contrary to his pneumatological aesthetics, this work develops a theology through the arts, rather than developing a soteriological aesthetics. He shows how painters and writers have created images of redemption in the history of art. Cf. N. Wolterstorff, *Art in action. Towards a Christian aesthetic*, Grand Rapids 1980. Wolterstorff writes about the religious and political implications of works of art, rather than exploring the possibilities of a soteriological approach in theology based on works of art. 'Aesthetics' in his theology means: how to contribute artistically to the Christian life. The 'aesthetic' signifies an attitude, rather than a perception.

art in the church stimulates Christian involvement in society.[57] Thus, theological aesthetics can demonstrate that the life of faith not only takes place through doctrine or holiness, truth or goodness, but also through the cultivation of perception and a sense of taste for what is genuinely beautiful in a world of competing images and ugliness.

Doctrinal aesthetics can only perform this task if it participates in both religious life and its cultural environment, by constructing images and forms that anticipate redemption and the life to come. Eschatological aesthetics might prove a highly imaginative and constructive subdiscipline. It is no coincidence that the Book of Revelations, Michelangelo's *Last Judgment* and Dante's *Divina Commedia* are impressive examples of human imagination, which express a complexity of human hopes and fears combined with theological ideas of damnation and glorification. The sublime idea of redemption can only be anticipated imaginatively, however straightforward and noncorrelational doctrinal reasoning may be.[58] Eschatological aesthetics will have to reflect the possibility for the divine to disrupt every straightforward repetition or presumed doctrinal continuity of the Word of God in history.

Theological aesthetics will show, even more so than theological ethics and epistemology, that all theology is necessarily eschatological in a double sense: First, theological statements are finite human constructs, grounded in the intuitive perception of divine revelation and imaginative anticipations of God's purposes for creation. Second, the diversification of theological statements is a given freedom in which divine freedom has revealed itself. Balthasar was right to articulate that theology is necessarily a diversification, when he defined theology as reasoning about God: "Because it is Word and because it has assumed the flesh as a Word, it has at the same time assumed a body of letters, writing, understanding, image, voice and proclamation" (VC 159).

b. Sublime redemption

Based on the perception of the incarnate givenness of all creaturely forms of understanding, images, writing and so forth, every aspect of human

---

[57] Cf. J.W. de Gruchy, *Christianity, art and transformation. Theological aesthetics in the struggle for justice*, Cambridge 2001, 254.
[58] J. Webster, *Holiness*, 21.

creativity can be understood as an opportunity for God to mediate revelation. This does not mean that human creativity is a 'definitive' transcendental ground that opens up a possible condition for God to reveal Himself, but it confirms the idea that God enters the human condition of contingency and mortality kenotically in the appearing forms of the world and in the flesh, and thus evokes the perceptions of that event. If subsequently, redemption is considered the destiny of all flesh and thus of faith and theology as well, how then can fallible ideas be recognised? Equally, on what grounds could they be rejected? In the coming light of redemption these questions become important because, instead of theoretically confirming sheer creatureliness and with it, the practices of sin and suffering, the theological vision of redemption is meant to describe the extrication of human beings from the situation they find themselves in. To fight the ghost of Ludwig Feuerbach, the following question needs to be answered: How can theories of perception, imagination and construction become articulations of revelation, instead of merely mimetic confirmations of creation? Put differently: what is the theological relationship between the beautiful and the sublime?

Human imagination and construction cannot be interpreted as constitutive methods for receiving divine revelation: Christian believers do not become receptive to divine revelation by the creative power of human imagination. Nor is the event of revelation a human construction. Were this the case, and if revelation grounded itself in human acts, it would be impossible to account for the fact that God indeed reveals Himself in human images and constructions. However, if revelation were to be understood as a pure gift and human creativity as pure construction, it would be equally impossible to explain the relationship between divine revelation and human creativity. Theological aesthetics should therefore characterise the aesthetic faculties of perception, imagination and construction as modes of receptivity, and revelation as the gift of creative reciprocity. Consequently, if the idea of revelation is not only limited to the law of creation but also covers the event of redemption, then the gift of reciprocity offers the possibility to be accomplished in these aesthetic acts.[59] Theological aesthetics explains man's ability to receive and respond to divine revelation in the hope that this response will be taken up by God. Thus, anticipating the given possibility of a divine-human relationship, it hopes for a divine response that once will restore that relation in the sublime event that is the redeeming return to God.

---

[59] Cf. C. Gunton, *Intellect and action*, Edinburgh 2000, viii.

The accomplishment of the given reciprocity should be performed with the awareness that nothing can redeem itself and with the hope that there is nothing that cannot be redeemed. Theological aesthetics defines the always-already but not-yet reality of creation and redemption by means of the double event of rapture. First, rapture is the primal wonder of being-there, which evokes both the gratitude for participating in the possibility-to-be (*possest*) and the confirmation that possibility exists. In other words: it is the amazing experience that human becoming is grounded in God's becoming in history. This is the meaning of the prologue to the gospel of John when it is said that the Life of God was the light of men (John 1:4). Second, rapture is seeing the glory of God in the ineffable and overwhelming moments of fascination and fear. This evokes a longing to be redeemed, which is a longing to return to the original relation in God.

Both these moments of rapture describe faith as the ecstatic movement away from the self to the infinite love of the divine.[60] The sublime event of creation reveals that God's being is in becoming, which grounds human becoming. The sublime event of redemption reveals that human becoming will be taken up in God's becoming. Human beings have been given the freedom to respond to these events with gratitude and anticipation. Thus, rapture is reflected in the catalogical givenness to create the eschatological vision of human beings returning to God. That return itself is analogously envisioned as the catalogical act of God's becoming. This is the true meaning of catalogical analogy.[61]

The analogical free-play of human imagination and construction should not isolate itself from or even displace the catalogical and sublime movements of creation and redemption that cause the twofold rapture described above. On the contrary, worldly beauty and the sublime are inseparable because the double event of rapture calls the freedom of man into being and establishes him as a created co-creator participating in the work of redemption. Here one finds the continuity of the beautiful and the sublime. The sublime is divine becoming in the world as an ongoing gift of freedom to human beings to anticipate the elevating return to the divine. The 'beautiful' has the double meaning of experiencing that gift and of responding to it through imagination and construction.

---

[60] 1Thess 4:16-18: "For the Lord himself will descend from heaven with a cry of command, with the archangel's call, and with the sound of the trumpet of God. And the dead in Christ will rise first; then we who are alive, who are left, shall be caught up together with them in the clouds to meet the Lord in the air; and so we shall always be with the Lord. Therefore comfort one another with these words."

[61] See also chapter six, section six.

This is why the philosophical separation of the beautiful and the sublime, as found in the modern aesthetic projects of Kant and Nietzsche, fails to appeal to theological aesthetics. In Kantian aesthetics, the subject is not a co-creator but instead limited to the contemplation of beauty in creation and the creative enterprise of human freedom. The disinterested contemplation of beauty, despite Kant's efforts in *The critique of judgment* to invest it with a communal quality, is a solipsistic event; and human creativity is not a given in Kantian philosophy but a pure subjective exploration of the imagination. The sublime then is a formless limitation of the beautiful, confining it to the finite realm and serving the ends of a moral sublime.[62] Nietzsche does the exact opposite by purging the sublime of any subjective perception and viewing it from the perspective of the artist.[63] Instead of considering the sublime as a formless and ungraspable event, as Kant does, Nietzsche speaks of the sublime as the ideal quality of artistic forms and styles. According to him, the sublime does not need to be perceived but occurs when a work of art gives birth to itself. The Nietzschean sublime therefore is the unilateral artistic expression of the will to power.

Neither the Kantian nor the Nietzschean sublime can be applied to a theological aesthetics that seeks to emphasise human-divine reciprocity. By positing the sublime either in the subjective experience or in the work of art, the dynamics between the objectivity of the gift and the subjectivity of being enraptured is lost, and with it any possible analogy of beauty.[64] Instead, the sublime should be defined as the work of the Spirit, which is the event of divine becoming in the world. It is the aesthetic description of the transfiguration of Christ, prefigured in the aesthetic acts of perception, imagination and construction. These 'prefigurations' should reflect the splendour of the kenotic act that has brought them into being.

It may have become clear that aesthetics is presented here as a theological approach in understanding the work of creation and redemption. The

---

[62] D.W. Crawford, Kant, in: B. Gaut, D. McIver Lopes [eds], *The Routledge companion to aesthetics*, London 2001, 51-64, 58-60. Cf. J. Milbank, Beauty and the soul, 4-7; For the contrary position: C. Crockett, *A theology of the sublime*, London 2001, 23-36. See also chapter two, section two.

[63] Cf. G. Agamben, *The man without content*, Stanford 1999, 1-7.

[64] C. Crockett, *A theology of the sublime*, 28-32. Crockett's standpoint is philosophical and he correctly criticises John Milbank for interpreting the givenness of divine glory too positively. His own proposal however, to interpret the sublime as stretching and disrupting the beauty of worldly forms, will not be sufficient to meet the task of theological aesthetics to understand the positive relationship between human and divine creativity.

use of aesthetic terminology does not serve to constitute the philosophical *praeambula fidei* of theology, nor the discovery of beauty as a transcendental ground of faith, nor the articulation of the idea of the sublime to understand the transcendence of God. The concepts of the beautiful and the sublime however, can be considered the axes of theology if they are understood in their interwovenness, mirroring the work of the kenotic Spirit and anticipating the return to the divine.[65]

c. Kenotic reasoning

> Where shall the word be found, where will the word
> Resound? Not here, there is not enough silence
> Not on the sea or on the islands, not
> On the mainland, in the desert or the rain land,
> For those who walk in darkness
> Both in the day time and in the night time
> The right time and the right place are not here
> No place of grace for those who avoid the face
> No time to rejoice for those who walk among noise and deny the voice
>
> From: T.S. Eliot, *Ash-Wednesday*.[66]

If I had heeded the words of T.S. Eliot, I might not have written the preceding chapters. If indeed, divine revelation can only be heard in the silence because it breaks that silence, then theological speech might possibly signify a denial of the voice and an expression of the Word

---

[65] Cf. Balthasar's evaluation of the poetry of St John of the Cross: "Then there is the recalling of the hallowed words and images of the Bible, which are theologically interwoven and caught up to the heights of interior inspiration. Finally, there is the whole range of expressive material formed by natural images and the beloved and long-cherished symbols familiar from literature. Who can confirm this and neatly separate the various levels? Who can divide the spheres of supernatural and natural inspiration? Why should the direct inspiration of the Holy Spirit not at the same time awaken all of the powers of artistic enthusiasm and creative inventiveness where such powers exist? And who would want to maintain that such elevation of man's creative ability to the service, both passive and active, of the divine Word is impossible or inadmissible from a Christian point of view or incompatible with supreme holiness? On the contrary, this poetry claims to be a direct expression and incontrovertible testimony to such engraced holiness, a reflection of its splendour. The expression as such, of course, is not 'necessary', because the holiness could occur without poetry, but the two originate from the same sphere of loving freedom in the soul's relationship with God; both are the overwhelming splendour of grace, an 'inundation with glory'" (H II 483-484).
[66] T.S. Eliot, Ash-Wednesday V, in: Id., *Collected poems 1909-1962*, London 1963, 102.

"unheard, unspoken".[67] Yet, in the words of the prologue to the Gospel of John "everything is made by the Word, and without the Word nothing of what was made was made. Life was in the Word, and life was the light of humanity". These two texts utter the sound of theological speech. Theology rejoices in the light of life, when it hears the voice that breaks the silence and subsequently reiterates and rearticulates it creatively in the face of others.

What is theology? After all that has been written, this main question must seem too general and too indefinite. The short answer to it: theology is reasoning about God and communicating faith, raised all kinds of new questions: How to reason about an invisible God? What is revelation? What is religious experience? How to do theology in a both secularised and multireligious culture? To whom is theology addressed? Taking the viewpoint and terminology of aesthetics in order to answer these questions again has raised new and more specific questions: Is all art religious? Is faith an artistic construction? What is religious perception? What is the relationship of the beautiful and the sublime with God? What is the role of imagination in theology? The choice of Hans Urs von Balthasar as a theological guide once more produced a specific set of enquiries which concerned his interpretation of the history of theology, of the modern period in particular, and his own contribution to that history. Yet, despite the variety of questions and enquiries and the scope of problems they addressed, the main question about the nature of theology has been answered along the way: the focus on aesthetics has shown that theology reasons and communicates about the kenotic act it participates in. It performs this kenotic participation in two movements:

First, theology communicates faith with others. Reflecting the divine Spirit that empties itself in the world by becoming something other and yet remaining the same, theology performs its task by surrendering to a broad cultural audience of others, believers and non-believers alike, without ceasing to be self-descriptive. It reads scripture and interprets tradition in and for the culture to which it belongs. However, a straightforward continuity between scripture and tradition cannot be assumed. At some point, it might even occur that tradition needs to be displaced by perception. If theology

---

[67] From that same poem: "If the lost word is lost, if the spent word is spent / If the unheard, unspoken / Word is unspoken, unheard". Cf. O. Davies, Soundings. Towards a theological poetics of silence, in: Id., D. Turner [ed.], *Silence and the Word. Negative theology and incarnation*, Cambridge 2002, 201-222.

mirrors the kenotic Spirit, then it must to all intents and purposes be anti-apologetic. It ought not to point exclusively to one's own standpoint but should instead be willing to 'empty itself' to address the questions and concerns of contemporary culture. The kenotic motivation for this subordination to culture constitutes theology's self-descriptive task as being co-creative, rather than merely responsive or explanatory.[68] Although the material of theology consists partly of its own tradition, it must at some point look away from it in search of what it means to reflect the given possibility of becoming truly human. In doing so, it attempts to awake the perceptive sensibilities that are necessary for the renewal of tradition.

This is a significant amendment to the definition of theology as merely 'the study of tradition', although that definition is not incorrect. Tradition however, is more than just the historical context of biblical interpretation or the socio-political motivation behind theological studies. Tradition is also the given freedom to imaginatively explore one's own perceptions of revelation. Nevertheless, theology's dealings with tradition surround it with suspicion, especially since, to contemporary observers, traditional religious doctrines may appear to be either obscure or even to serve only to bolster church authority. Indeed, the history of Christian theology has shown that traditional doctrines are susceptible to manipulation and abuse, but this is precisely one of the reasons why theology must study them both critically and imaginatively. In any case, aside from evoking valid questions about obscurity and authority, the content of tradition deserves to be encountered freely with academic curiosity and integrity for the very fact that it is culturally present.

Although the presence of religious traditions may be less urgent for others, theologians should be given the academic freedom to explore new perspectives or even possibilities of decentring their own tradition, which

---

[68] Constituted by the analogy of divine kenosis, theology will not fall into the danger of 'false humility' that John Milbank has warned against: "The pathos of modern theology is false humility. For theology, this must be a fatal disease, for once theology surrenders its claim to be a metadiscourse, it cannot any longer articulate the word of the creator God, but is bound to turn into the oracular voice of some finite idol, such as historical scholarship, humanist psychology, or transcendental philosophy. If theology no longer seeks to position, qualify or criticize other discourses, then it is inevitable that these discourses will position theology: for the necessity of an ultimate organizing logic cannot be wished away. A theology 'positioned' by secular reason suffers two characteristic forms of confinement. Either it idolatrously connects knowledge of God with some particular immanent field of knowledge — 'ultimate cosmological causes, or 'ultimate' psychological and subjective needs. Or else it is confined to intimations of a sublimity beyond representation, so functioning to confirm negatively the questionable idea of an autonomous secular realm, completely transparent to rational understanding."
J. Milbank, *Theology and social theory. Beyond secular reason*, Oxford 1990, 1.

in itself is and always has been a matter of diversity. Moreover, although theologians should positively acknowledge that they are the pupils of that myriad tradition, they should also allow themselves to put the governing streams of tradition aside and make room for new perceptions of givenness and hope, and thus for the possibility of ongoing revelation. This is exactly what Balthasar has done and his greatest legacy is the effect of an original rereading of that which remained hidden for a long time. Although regarded by many as a restorationist, and despite his unitive vision of form, he took a pluralist and anti-monolithic stance towards tradition. In search of the 'symphony of truth' and interpreting tradition as a catholic unity of differences by treating it as the sum of theological deposits without excluding any of these, Balthasar presented certain traditional developments in a new key.[69] As a consequence, he provided the insight that tradition is not the authority but the inviting availability of the history of ideas and beliefs, because it has generated forms in which all may partake freely and responsibly.

This characterisation of tradition as 'invitation' resists the need for the deconstruction of tradition as a whole but it does offer the possibility of decentring certain dominant streams within tradition.[70] Theology therefore, must mediate and inspire an open communication, with room for the articulations of new perceptions and yet unexplored images of faith. Thus, theology performs the communication of faith with others in a kenotic fashion, analogical to the experience of divine communication: away from itself and inviting a variety of possible responses.

Second, theology imaginatively anticipates the life in the Kingdom to come, through the sublimity of the redemptive ascension in Christ. This anticipation entails that every proposed construction of faith should express the awareness of the fallibility and indefiniteness of human perception and imagination. Fallibility qualifies all theological statements, thereby safeguarding the dynamics of a living tradition of free and equal human beings. In fact, it also shows that the communication with others, described above in the first kenotic movement of theology, anticipates the mediation of God's giving of freedom and thus in a sense of becoming "Christ to others".[71]

---

[69] Cf. C. O'Regan, Balthasar and Eckhart, 238-239.
[70] Cf. K.J. Vanhoozer, Scripture and tradition, in: Id. [ed.], *The Cambridge companion to postmodern theology*, Cambridge 2003, 149-169.
[71] This is a quotation of Luther by Richard Bauckham from his *God and the crisis of freedom. Biblical and contemporary perspectives*, Louisville 2002, 209.

The indefiniteness of perception and imagination constitutes the human longing for God. That longing is expressed in other words than the Word it is assumed to proceed from. More often than not, these words do not find their way back to their origin. This is why longing for the divine is envisioned in terms of human impossibilities and often grounded in feelings of guilt and the experiences of human sin and suffering. Theological aesthetics does not serve to confront these experiences with their counterparts by imagining the divine kingdom as an ideal. Instead, theological reasoning must take up the responsibility to present the Christian narrative as the affirmation of human life in its furthest consequences, without ignoring its impossibilities. Christ is the image in which these consequences are conceived to the full and Christian theological reason is ultimately subordinate to that image, which transforms darkness into light and thus gives human beings the freedom to long for the life in a world that is wholly other.

Because of this double 'surrender', to culture and Christ, I suggest defining theology as 'kenotic reasoning'.[72] The art of theology is to reason kenotically. It finds its foundation in the divine *Logos* that progressively appears in the givenness of being. Consequently, it is imaginatively anticipated in the hope for sublime redemption. Both givenness and hope thus constitute theological reason and provide the tools to read scripture and interpret tradition for a variety of audiences and a diversity of beliefs. Only within this spirit of givenness and hope, by means of perception and imagination, can theology engage in the *logos* of either modernity or postmodernity and share in the discourse of other disciplines and the particular articulations of meaning in the life of others.

At the same time, theology can only address its tasks kenotically by engaging in the communication with others. This engagement constitutes the life of faith and does not merely lead to the theological description of the content of faith but also encourages possible ways of transforming both culture and tradition to share in the spirit of givenness and hope. And yet, it paradoxically envisions the desire that its hope is met with something

---

[72] Cf. R.H. Niebuhr, *Christ and culture*, New York 1951. In this book, Niebuhr distinguishes five basic ways that Christians deal with culture: Christ against culture, Christ above culture, Christ and culture, Christ transforming culture, and Christ as culture. To define theology as 'kenotic reasoning' means that I, like Niebuhr, choose the fourth option, that interprets culture as something that will be the restoration of creation to its original, God-given purpose. See also: R.W. Jenson, Christ as culture. Christ as polity, in: *International journal for systematic theology* 5 (2003), 323-329.

utterly inexpressible and unhoped for. In other words, that its poetic constructions are embraced by the kenotic rapture of life in the Word of God.

That embrace, however inexpressible, is made visible by a flame in the last words of Charles Ryder, the central figure of Evelyn Waugh's postwar novel *Brideshead Revisited*. In beautiful prose that balances between prayer and (auto)-biography, Waugh expressed, through Ryder, the indefiniteness of tradition and the hope that shines through it despite its ugliness.

> The builders did not know the uses to which their work would descend; they made a new house with the stones of the old castle; year by year, generation after generation, they enriched and extended it; year by year the great harvest of timber in the park grew to ripeness;
> (...)
> Something quite remote from anything the builders intended, has come out of their work, and out of the fierce little human tragedy in which I played; something none of us thought about at the time; a small red flame—a beaten-copper lamp of deplorable design relit before the beaten-copper doors of a tabernacle; the flame which the old knights saw from their tombs, which they saw put out; that flame burns again for other soldiers, far from home, farther, in heart, than Acre or Jerusalem. It could not have been lit but for the builders and the tragedians, and there I found it this morning, burning anew among the old stones.[73]

---

[73] E. Waugh, *Brideshead revisited*, Middlesex 1986 (1945), 330-331.

BIBLIOGRAPHY

1. Hans Urs von Balthasar

Hans Urs von Balthasar. Bibliographie 1925-1990, [Bearbeitet von Cornelia Capol], Einsiedeln 1990.

1.1. Primary sources

Analogie und Dialektik. Zur Klärung der theologischen Prinzipienlehre Karl Barths, in: *Divus Thomas* 22 (1944), 171-216.
Analogie und Natur. Zur Klärung der theologischen Prinzipienlehre Karl Barths, in: *Divus Thomas* 23 (1945), 3-56.
Apokalypse der deutschen Seele. Studien zu einer Lehre von letzten Haltungen: Bd. 1: *Der deutsche Idealismus;* Bd. 2: *Im Zeichen Nietsches;* Bd. 3: *Die Vergöttlichung des Todes*, Einsiedeln 1998² (1937-1939).
Von den Aufgaben der Katholischen Philosophie in der Zeit, Einsiedeln, etc. 1998².
Cordula oder der Ernstfall, [Kriterien 2], Einsiedeln 1987⁴.
Credo, Meditationen zum Apostolischen Glaubensbekenntnis, [Kriterien 95], Einsiedeln, etc. 1996.
Die Entwicklung der musikalishen Idee. Versuch einer Synthese der Musik, Einsiedeln, etc. 1998².
Epilog, Einsiedeln 1987.
Die Gottesfrage des heutigen Menschen, Wien, etc. 1956.
Das Ganze im Fragment. Aspekte der Geschichtstheologie, Einsiedeln 1990².
Geschichte des eschatologischen Problems in der modernen deutschen Literatur, Einsiedeln, etc. 1998².
Glaubhaft is nur Liebe, Einsiedeln 1985⁵.
Herrlichkeit. Eine theologische Ästhetik I. Schau der Gestalt, Einsiedeln 1961.
Herrlichkeit. Eine theologische Ästhetik II. Fächer der Stile, [2 Bände: *1. Klerikale Stile, 2. Laikale Stile*], Einsiedeln 1962.
Herrlichkeit. Eine theologische Ästhetik III,1. Im Raum der Metaphysik, [2 Bände: *1 Altertum, 2 Neuzeit*], Einsiedeln 1965.
Herrlichkeit. Eine theologische Ästhetik III,2. Theologie, 1 Alter Bund, Einsiedeln 1966.
Herrlichkeit. Eine theologische Ästhetik III,2. Theologie, 2 Neuer Bund, Einsiedeln 1969.
Das Herz der Welt, Einsiedeln, etc. 2002.
Homo creatus est, [Skizzen zur Theologie V], Einsiedeln 1986.
Katholisch, [Kriterien 36], Einsiedeln 1993³.
Karl Barth. Darstellung und Deutung seiner Theologie, Einsiedeln 1976⁴.

Mein Werk—Durchblicke, Einsiedeln 1990.
Pneuma und Institution, [Skizzen zur Theologie IV], Einsiedeln 1974.
Prüfet Alles, das Gute behaltet. Ein Gespräch mit Angelo Scola, [Neue Kriterien 3], Einsiedeln, etc. 2001².
Spiritus Creator, [Skizzen zur Theologie III], Einsiedeln 1967.
Sponsa Verbi, [Skizzen zur Theologie II], Einsiedeln 1971.
Theodramatik I. Prolegomena, Einsiedeln 1973.
Theodramatik II. Die Personen des Spiels: II,1 Der Mensch in Gott, Einsiedeln 1976.
Theodramatik II. Die Personen des Spiels: II,2 Die Personen in Christus, Einsiedeln 1978.
Theodramatik III. Die Handlung, Einsiedeln 1980.
Theodramatik IV. Das Endspiel, Einsiedeln 1983.
Theologie der Geschichte. Neue Fassung, [Christ Heute, 8. Heft], Einsiedeln 1979⁶.
Theologie der drei Tage, Einsiedeln 1990.
Theologik I. Wahrheit der Welt, Einsiedeln 1985.
Theologik II. Wahrheit Gottes, Einsiedeln 1985.
Theologik III. Der Geist der Wahrheit, Einsiedeln 1987.
Unser Auftrag. Bericht und Entwurf. Einführung in die von Adrienne von Speyr gegründete Johannesgemeinschaft, Einsiedeln 1984.
Verbum Caro, [Skizzen zur Theologie I], Einsiedeln 1990³.
Die Wahrheit ist symphonisch. Aspekte des christlichen Pluralismus, [Kriterien 29], Einsiedeln 1972.
Warum wir Nikolaus Cusanus brauchen, in: *Neue Zürcher Nachrichten* 60 (1964), [Beilage Christliche Kultur 28, Nr. 29, 14 August], 1-2.
Das Weizenkorn. Aphorismen, Einsiedeln 1989³.
Zur Ortsbestimmung christlicher Mystik, in: Beierwaltes, W., BALTHASAR, H.U. VON, HAAS, A.M., *Grundfragen der Mystik*, [Kriterien 33], Einsiedeln, etc. 2002².
Zu seinem Werk, [Orig. *Mein Werk—Durchblicke*. Neu hinzugefügt wurde: ALBUS, M., Geist und Feuer. Ein Gespräch mit Hans Urs von Balthasar, in: *Herder Korrespondenz* 30 (1976), 72-82.] Einsiedeln, etc. 2000².

1.2. Secondary sources

ALBUS, M., *Die Wahrheit ist Liebe. Zur Unterscheidung des Christlichen bei Hans Urs von Balthasar*, Freiburg im Breisgau 1976.
ALBUS, M., Geist und Feuer. Ein Gespräch mit Hans Urs von Balthasar, in: *Herder Korrespondenz* 30 (1976), 72-82.
BECKER, W.M., *The historical Jesus in the face of his death. His comprehension of its salvafic meaning in the writings of Edward Schillebeeckx and Hans Urs von Balthasar*, Rome 1994.
BISER, E., Hans Urs von Balthasar, in: SCHULTZ, H.J. [HRSG.], *Tendenzen der Theologie im 20. Jahrhundert*, Stuttgart 1966, 524-529.
BISER, E., Dombau oder Triptychon? Zum Abschluß der Trilogie Hans Urs von Balthasars, in: *Theologische Revue* 84 (1988), 179-184.

BONNICI, J.S., *Person to person. Friendship and love in the life and theology of Hans Urs von Balthasar*, New York 1999.
BUCKLEY, J.J., Balthasar's use of the theology of Aquinas, in: *The thomist* 57 (1995), 517-545.
CHAPP, L.S., *The God who speaks. Hans Urs von Balthasar's theology of revelation*, San Francisco, etc. 1996.
CHIA, R., Theological aesthetics or aesthetic theology? Some reflections on the theology of Hans Urs von Balthasar, in: *Scottish journal of theology* 49 (1996), 75-95.
CHIA, R., *Revelation and theology. The knowledge of God in Balthasar and Barth*, Bern, etc. 1999.
COBB, J., A question for Hans Urs von Balthasar, in: *Communio* 5 (1978), 53-59.
DADOSKY, J.D., The dialectic of religious identity: Lonergan and Balthasar, in: *Theological studies* 60 (1999), 31-52.
DAIGLER, M.A., Heidegger and Balthasar. A lover's quarrel over beauty and divinity, in: *American catholic philosophical quarterly* 69 (1995), 375-394.
DALZELL, TH.G., Lack of social drama in Balthasar's theological dramatics, in: *Theological studies* 60 (1999), 457-475.
DALZELL, TH.G., The enrichment of God in Balthasar's trinitarian eschatology, in: *Irish theological quarterly* 66 (2001), 3-18.
DAVIES, O., Von Balthasar and the problem of being, in: *New Blackfriars* 79 (1998), 11-17.
DE SCHRIJVER, G., Die Analogia Entis in der Theologie Hans Urs von Balthasars. Eine genetisch-historische Studie, in: *Bijdragen. Tijdschrift voor filosofie en theologie* 38 (1977), 241-281.
DE SCHRIJVER, G., *Le merveilleux accord de l'homme et de dieu. Etude de l'analogie de l'être chez Hans Urs von Balthasar*, Paris 1983.
DE SCHRIJVER, G., Hans Urs von Balthasars Christologie in der Theodramatik. Trinitarische Engführung als Methode, in: *Bijdragen. Tijdschrift voor filosofie en theologie* 59 (1998), 141-153.
DISSE, J., *Metaphysik der Singularität. Eine Hinführung am Leitfaden der Philosophie Hans Urs von Balthasars*, [Philosophische Theologie; Bd. 7], Wien 1996.
DORAN, R.M., S.J., Lonergan and Balthasar: Methodological considerations, in: *Theological studies* 58 (1997), 61-84.
DUPRÉ, L.K., Hans Urs von Balthasar's theology of aesthetic form, in: *Theological studies* 49 (1988), 299-318.
EICHER, P., Geist und Feuer, in: *Herder Korrespondenz* 30 (1976), 76.
ENDEAN, PH., S.J., Von Balthasar, Rahner, and the Commisar, in: *New Blackfriars* 79 (1998), 33-37.
ESCOBAR, P., *Zeit und Sein bei Hans Urs von Balthasar*, [Dissertation], Paris 1973.
FESSIO, J., *The origin of the church in Christ's kenosis. The ontological structure of the church in the ecclesiology of Hans Urs von Balthasar*, [Dissertation], Regensburg 1974.
FIELDS, S., S.J., Balthasar and Rahner on the spiritual senses, in: *Theological studies* 57 (1996), 224-241.

FOLEY, G., The catholic critics of Karl Barth. In outline and analysis, in: *Scottish journal of theology* 14 (1961), 136-155.
FRANKS, A.F., Trinitarian *analogia entis* in Hans Urs von Balthasar, in: *The thomist* 62 (1998), 533-559.
GADIENT, L., *Wahrheit als Anruf der Freiheit. Hans Urs von Balthasars theodramatischer Erkenntnisbegriff in vergleichender Auseinandersetzung mit der transzendentalphilosophischen Erkenntniskritik Reinhard Lauths*, [Münchener theologische Studien. II. Systematische Abteilung—55. Band], St. Ottilien 1999.
GARDNER, L., MOSS, D., QUASH, B., WARD, G., *Balthasar at the end of modernity*, [Foreword by F. Kerr and Afterword by R. Williams], Edinburgh 1999.
GREINER, M., *Drama der Freiheiten. Eine Denkformanalyse zu Hans Urs von Balthasars trinitarischer Soteriologie*, Münster 2000.
GUERRIERO, E., *Hans Urs von Balthasar. Eine Biographie*, Einsiedeln 1993.
GUTWENGER, E., BALTHASAR, H.U. VON, Der Begriff der Natur in der theologie. eine Diskussion zwischen Hans Urs von Balthasar, Zürich, und Engelbert Gutwenger, s.j., Innsbruck, in: *Zeitschrift für katholische Theologie* 75 (1953), 452-464.
GUTWENGER, E., Natur und Übernatur. Gedanken zu Balthasars Werk über die bartsche Theologie, in: *Zeitschrift für katholische Theologie* 75 (1953), 82-97.
HAAS, A., *Vermittlung als Auftrag. Vorträge am Symposion zum 90. Geburtstag von Hans Urs von Balthasar*, [27.—29. September 1995 in Fribourg (Schweiz)], Einsiedeln, etc. 1995.
HAAS, A. [HRSG.], *Wer ist die Kirche? Symposion zum 10. Todesjahr von Hans Urs von Balthasar*, Einsiedeln 1999.
HARRISON, V.S., Homo orans: Von Balthasar's christocentric philosophical anthropology, in: *Heythrop journal* 15 (1999), 280-300.
HARRISON, V.S., *The apologetic value of human holiness. Von Balthasar's christocentric philosophical anthropology*, Dordrecht, etc. 2000.
HARRISON, V.S., Theology as revelation and apologia, in: *Theology* 104 (2001), 284-255.
HARTMANN, M., *Ästhetik als ein Grundbegriff fundamenteler Theologie. Eine Untersuchung zu Hans Urs von Balthasar*, [Dissertationen theologische Reihe, Bd. 5], St. Otillien 1985.
HEINZ, H., *Der Gott des Je-mehr. Der christologische Ansatz Hans Urs von Balthasars*, Bern, etc. 1975.
HOLZER, V. C.M., *Le Dieu trinité dans l'histoire: le conflit der raisons 'esthétique' et 'transcendentale' comme accès aux logiques christologiques de Hans Urs von Balthasar et de Karl Rahner*, [Dissertatio as Doctoratum in Facultate Theologiae Pontificiae Universitas Gregorianae], Rome 1994.
IDE, P., *Être et mystère. La philosophie de Hans Urs von Balthasar*, [Série Présences 13], Bruxelles 1995.
KAY, J.A., Aesthetics and a posteriori evidence in Balthasar's theological method, in: *Communio* 2 (1975), 289-299.
KAY, J.A., *Theological aesthetics. The role of aesthetics in the theological method of Hans Urs von Balthasar*, Frankfurt am Main 1975.

KEEFE, D.J., A methodological critique of von Balthasar's theological aesthetics, in: *Communio* 5 (1978), 23-43.

KEHL, M., *Die Kirche als Institution. Zur theologischen Begründung des insitutionellen Charakters der Kirche in der neueren deutschsprachigen katholischen Ekklesiologie*, [Frankfurt Theologischen Studien 22], Frankfurt am Main 1976.

KEHL, M., Hans Urs von Balthasar. Ein Porträt, in: ID., LÖSER, W. [HRSG.], *In der Fülle des Glaubens. Hans Urs von Balthasar-Lesebuch*, Freiburg im Breisgau 1980.

KERR, F., O.P., Adrienne von Speyr and Hans Urs von Balthasar, in: *New Blackfriars* 79 (1998), 26-32.

KIM, S., *Christliche Denkform: Theozentrik oder Anthropozentrik? Die Frage nach dem Subjekt der Geschichte bei Hans Urs von Balthasar und Johann Baptist Metz*, Freiburg im Breisgau 1999.

KLAGHOFER-TREITLER, W., *Gotteswort im Menschenwort. Inhalt und Form von Theologie nach Hans Urs von Balthasar*, Innsbruck, etc. 1992.

KLAGHOFER-TREITLER, W., *Karfreitag. Auseinandersetzung mit Hans Urs von Balthasar's Theologik*, [Salzburger Theologische Studien; Bd. 4], Innsbruck, etc. 1997.

KÖRNER, B., Fundamentaltheologie bei Hans Urs von Balthasar, in: *Zeitschrift für katholische Theologie* 109 (1987).

KRENSKI, TH., *Hans Urs von Balthasar. Das Gottesdrama*, [Theologische Profile], Mainz 1995.

KRENSKI, TH., *Passio Caritatis. Trinitarische Passiologie im Werk Hans Urs von Balthasars*, Einsiedeln 1990.

LAMADRID, L., Anonymous or analogous Christians? Rahner and von Balthasar on naming the non-christian, in: *Modern theology* 11 (1995), 363-384.

LAUBACH, J., Hans Urs von Balthasar, [Orig. Theologen unserer Zeit, München 1960, 1966], in: REINISCH, L. [ED.], *Theologians of our time*, Notre Dame 1964.

LEAHY, B., *The Marian principle in the church according to Hans Urs von Balthasar*, Frankfurt am Main, etc. 1993.

LEHMANN, K., KASPER, W., [HRSG.], *Hans Urs von Balthasar. Gestalt und Werk*, Köln 1989.

LOCHBRUNNER, M., *Analogia Caritatis. Darstellung und Deutung der Theologie Hans Urs von Balthasars*, Freiburg im Breisgau 1981.

LOCHBRUNNER, M., Hans Urs von Balthasars Trilogie der Liebe. Vom Dogmatikentwurf zur theologischen Summe. Zum posthumen Gedenken an Seinen 90. Geburtstag, in: *Forum katholische Theologie* 11 (1995), 161-181.

LOCHBRUNNER, M., Unterwegs zu einer Balthasar-Biographie? Marginalien zu Elio Guerrieros Monographie "Hans Urs von Balthasar", in: *Communio* 25 (1996), 75-90.

LOCHBRUNNER, M., Guardini und Balthasar. Auf der Spurensuche einer geistigen Wohlverwandtschaft, in: *Forum katholische Theologie* 12 (1996), 229-246.

LOCHBRUNNER, M., *Hans Urs von Balthasar als Autor, Herausgeber und Verleger. Fünf Studien zu seinen Sammlungen (1942-1967)*, Würzburg 2002.

LÖSER, W., Das Sein—ausgelegt als Liebe, in: *Communio* 4 (1975), 410-424.

LÖSER, W., *Im Geiste des Origenes. Hans Urs von Balthasar als Interpret der Theologie der Kirchenväter*, Frankfurt am Main 1976.
LOUGHLIN, G., Sexing the trinity, in: *New Blackfriars* 79 (1998), 18-25.
LUBAC, H., Ein Zeuge Christi in der Kirche. Hans Urs von Balthasar, in: *Communio* 4 (1975), 390-409.
MARION, J.L., Verklärte Gegenwart (Himmelfahrt Christi). Über Hans Urs von Balthasar, in: *Communio* 12 (1983), 223-231.
MCGREGOR, B., O.P., NORRIS, TH. [EDS], *The beauty of Christ. An introduction in the theology of Hans Urs von Balthasar*, Edinburgh 1994.
MILLER, M., The sacramental theology of Hans Urs von Balthasar, in: *Worship* 64 (1990), 48-66.
MONGRAIN, K., *The systematic thought of Hans Urs von Balthasar. An Irenaean retrieval*, New York 2002.
MOSS, D., OAKES, E.T., S.J., *The Cambridge companion to Hans Urs von Balthasar*, Cambridge 2004.
MUERS, R., A question of two answers: Difference and determination in Barth and von Balthasar, in: *Heythrop journal* 15 (1999), 265-279.
MURPHY, F.A., *Christ, the form of beauty. A study in theology and literature*, Edinburgh 1995.
MURPHY, F.A., Inclusion and exclusion in the ethos of von Balthasar's Theodrama, in: *New Blackfriars* 79 (1998), 56-64.
NADUVILLEKUT, J., *Christus der Heilsweg. Soteria als Theodrama im werk Hans Urs von Balthasars*, St. Ottilien 1987.
NICHOLS, A., O.P., An introduction to Balthasar, in: *New Blackfriars* 79 (1998), 2-10.
NICHOLS, A., O.P., *The word has been abroad. A guide through Balthasar's aesthetics*, [Introduction to Hans Urs von Balthasar], Edinburgh 1998.
NICHOLS, A., O.P., Von Balthasar's aims in his theological aesthetics, in: *Heythrop journal* 15 (1999), 409-423.
NICHOLS, A., O.P., *No bloodless myth. A guide through Balthasar's dramatics*, [Introduction to Hans Urs von Balthasar], Edinburgh 2000.
NICHOLS, A., O.P., *Say it is Pentecost. A guide through Balthasar's logic*, [Introduction to Hans Urs von Balthasar], Edinburgh 2001.
O'DONNELL, J., S.J., *Hans Urs von Balthasar*, [Outstanding Christian thinkers], London 1991.
O'HANLON, G., S.J., *The immutibility of God in the theology of Hans Urs von Balthasar*, Cambridge 1990.
O'HANLON, G., S.J., The Jesuits and modern theology—Rahner, Von Balthasar and Liberation theology, in: *The Irish theological quarterly* (1992), 25-45.
O'MEARA, TH., O.P., Of art and theology. Hans Urs von Balthasar's systems, in: *Theological studies* 42 (1981), 272-276.
O'REGAN, C., Newman and von Balthasar. The christological contexting of the numinous, in: *Église et théologie* 26 (1995), 165-202.
O'REGAN, C., Balthasar and Eckhart: Theological principles and catholicity, in: *The thomist* 60 (1996), 203-239.
O'REGAN, C., Von Balthasar and thick retrieval: Post-Chalcedonian symphonic theology, in: *Gregorianum* 77 (1996), 227-260.

O'REGAN, C., Balthasar: Between Tübingen and postmodernity, in: *Modern theology* 14 (1998), 325-354.
OAKES, E.T., S.J., *Pattern of redemption. The theology of Hans Urs von Balthasar*, New York 1994.
OLSEN, G.W., Hans Urs von Balthasar and the rehabilitation of St. Anselm's doctrine of the atonement, in: *Scottish journal of theology* 34 (1981), 49-61.
PANNENBERG, W., Zur Bedeutung des Analogiegedankens bei Karl Barth. Eine Auseinandersetzung mit Hans Urs von Balthasar, in: *Theologische Literaturzeitung* 78 (1953), 18-23.
PLAGA, U.J., *"Ich bin die Wahrheit". Die theo-logische Dimension der Christologie Hans Urs von Balthasars*, Hamburg 1997.
PROTERRA, M., Hans Urs von Balthasar. Theologian, in: *Communio* 2 (1975), 270-288.
QUASH, J.B., 'Between the brutely given, and the brutally, banally free': Von Balthasar's theology of drama in dialogue with Hegel, in: *Modern theology* 13 (1997), 293-318.
QUASH, J.B., Von Balthasar and the dialogue with Karl Barth, in: *New Blackfriars* 79 (1998), 45-55.
RAGUZ, I., *Sinn für das Gott-Menschliche. Transzendental-theologisches Gespräch zwischen den Ästhetiken von Immanuel Kant und Hans Urs von Balthasar*, Würzburg 2003.
RAHNER, K., Hans Urs von Balthasar, in: *Civitas* 20 (1965), 601-604.
REEDY, G., The christology of Hans Urs von Balthasar, in: *Thought* 45 (1970), 407-420.
REIFENBERG, P., HOOFF, A. VAN [HRSG.], *Gott für die Welt. Henri de Lubac, Gustav Siewerth und Hans Urs von Balthasar in ihren Grundanliegen*, Mainz 2001.
RICHES, J., The theology of Hans Urs von Balthasar, in: *Theology* 75 (1972), 562-570, 647-655.
RICHES, J. [ED.], *The analogy of beauty. The theology of Hans Urs von Balthasar*, Edinburgh 1986.
RICHES, J., Von Balthasar as biblical theologian and exegete, in: *New Blackfriars* 79 (1998), 38-44.
ROBERTS, L., A critique of the aesthetic theology of Hans Urs von Balthasar, in: *The American Benedictine review* 16 (1965), 486-504.
ROBERTS, L., The collision of Rahner and Balthasar, in: *Continuum* 5 (1968), 753-757.
ROBERTS, L., *The theological aesthetics of Hans Urs von Balthasar*, Washington 1987.
SACHS, J., Die Theologie der Zukunft. Hans Urs von Balthasar, in: *Zeitschrift für deutsche Theologie* 34 (1977), 234-256.
SAWARD, J., *The mysteries of March. Hans Urs von Balthasar on the incarnation and Easter*, London, etc. 1990.
SCHEUER, M., *Die Evangelischen Räte. Structurprinzip systematischer Theologie bei H.U. von Balthasar, K. Rahner, J.B. Metz und in der Theologie der Befreiung*, [Studien zur systematischen und spirituellen Theologie 1. Herausg. von G. Greshake, M Kehl, W. Löser], Würzburg 1990.

SCHINDLER, D.L. [ED.], *Hans Urs von Balthasar. His life and work*, San Francisco 1991.
SCHMID, J., *Im Ausstrahl der Schönheit Gottes. Die Bedeutung der Analogie in "Herrlichkeit" bei Hans Urs von Balthasar*, Münsterschwarzwach 1982.
SCHULZ, M., *Hans Urs von Balthasar begegnen*, Augsburg 2002.
SCHUMACHER, M.M., The concept of representation in the theology of Hans Urs von Balthasar, in: *Theological studies* 60 (1999), 53-71.
SCHWAGER, R., Der Sohn Gottes und die Weltsünde. Zur Erlösungslehre von Hans Urs von Balthasar, in: *Zeitschrift für katholische Theologie* 108 (1986), 5-44.
SCOLA, A., *Hans Urs von Balthasar. A theological style*, [Orig. Hans Urs von Balthasar. Uno stile teologico, Milan 1991. Series: Ressourcement. Retrieval and renewal in catholic thought], Grand Rapids 1995.
SEIFERT, J., Person und Individuum. Über Hans Urs von Balthasars Philosophie der Person und die philosophischen Implikationen seiner Dreifältigkeitstheologie, in: *Forum katholische Theologie* 13 (1997), 81-105.
SPLETT, J., Wahrheit in Herrlichkeit. Auf Balthasar hören, in: *Theologie und Philosophie* 69 (1994), 411-421.
STECK, CHR., S.J., *The ethical thought of Hans Urs von Balthasar*, New York 2001.
VORGRIMMLER, H., Hans Urs von Balthasar, in: VAN DER GUCHT, J.W. [HRSG.], *Bilanz der Theologie im 20. Jahrhundert. Bahnbrechende Theologen*, Freiburg im Breisgau 1970, 122-142.
WALLNER, K.J. OCIST., Ein trinitarisches Strukturprinzip in der Trilogie Hans Urs von Balthasars?, in: *Theologie und Philosophie* 71 (1996), 532-546.
WERBICK, J., Gottes Dreieinigkeit denken? Hans Urs von Balthasars Rede von der göttlichen Selbstentäusserung als Mitte des Glaubens und Zentrum der Theologie, in: *Theologische Quartalschrift* 176 (1996), 225-240.
WOOD, R.E., Philosophy, aesthetics, and theology: A review of Hans Urs von Balthasar's The Glory of the Lord, in: *American catholic philosophical quarterly* 67 (1993), 355-382.

2. Aesthetics

2.1. Philosophical aesthetics

AERTSEN, J.A., Beauty in the Middle Ages: a forgotten transcendental?, [Cardinal Mercier lecture at the Catholic University of Louvain on 22 February 1990], in: *Medieval philosophy and theology* 1 (1991), 68-97.
AGAMBEN, G., *The man without content*, Stanford 1999.
ALLISON, H.E., *Kant's theory of taste, A reading of the 'Critique of aesthetic judgment'*, Cambridge 2001.
BAUMEISTER, TH., *De filosofie en de kunsten. Van Plato tot Beuys*, Best 1999.
BAUMGARTEN, A.G., *Aesthetica*, Hildesheim 1961 (1750-1758).
BEARDSLEY, M.C., *Aesthetics. From classical Greece to the present. A short history*, Tuscaloosa, etc. 1991[8].

BERGER, H., *Ik noem het: God. Reflecties bij Luc Ferry, L'homme-Dieu ou le sens de la vie*, Tilburg 1998.
BOWIE, A., *Aesthetics and subjectivity: from Kant to Nietzsche*, Manchester, etc. 1990.
BRAEMBUSSCHE, A.A. VAN DEN, *Denken over kunst: een kennismaking met de kunstfilosofie*, Bussum 1994.
BREDIN, H., SANTORO-BRIENZA, L., *Philosophies of art and beauty. Introducing aesthetics*, Edinburgh 2000.
CASSIRER, E., *Die Grundprobleme der Ästhetik*, [Aus: Die Philosophie der Aufklärung], Berlin 1989.
DE BRUYNE, E., *Het aesthetisch beleven*, Antwerpen, etc. 1942.
DE BRUYNE, E., *Études d'esthetique médiévale*, Brugge 1946.
DE BRUYNE, E., *Philosophie van de Kunst. Phaenomenologie van het Kunstwerk*, Antwerpen, etc. 1948³.
DE BRUYNE, E., *Geschiedenis van de Aesthetica. De Renaissance*, Antwerpen, etc. 1951.
DE BRUYNE, E., *Geschiedenis van de Aesthetica. De Griekse oudheid*, Antwerpen, etc. 1952.
DE BRUYNE, E., *Geschiedenis van de Aesthetica. De christelijke oudheid*, Antwerpen, etc. 1954.
ECO, U., *Art and beauty in the Middle Ages*, New Haven 1988.
ECO, U., *The aesthetics of Thomas Aquinas*, Cambridge 1988.
EVERETT GILBERT, K., KUHN, H., *A history of esthetics*, Bloomington 1953.
GADAMER, H.G., *Die Aktualität des Schönen. Kunst als Spiel, Symbol und Fest*, Stuttgart 1993.
GAUT, B., MCIVER LOPES, D. [EDS], *The Routledge companion to aesthetics*, London 2001.
GERWEN, R. VAN, *Kennis in schoonheid. Een inleiding tot de moderne esthetica*, Meppel, etc. 1992.
GOMBRICH, E.H., *The story of art*, London 1995¹⁵.
GRØN, A., Imagination and subjectivity, in: *Ars disputandi* 2 (2002) 27-36.
HAMMERMEISTER, K., *The German aesthetic tradition*, Cambridge 2002.
HEIDEGGER, M., *Der Ursprung des Kunstwerkes*, [Mit einer Einführung von H.G. Gadamer], Stuttgart 1992.
HOSPERS, J., *Introductory readings in aesthetics*, New York 1969.
KANT, I., *Kritik der Urteilskraft und Schriften zur Naturphilosophie*, [Hrsg. von W. Weischedel], Darmstadt 1983⁵.
KEARNEY, R., *Poetics of imagining. Modern to postmodern*, Edinburgh 1998².
KEARNEY, R., *The wake of imagination. Toward a postmodern culture*, London 1988.
LOTZ, J.B., *Ästhetik aus der ontologischen Differenz. Das Anwesen des Unsichtbaren im Sichtbaren*, München 1984.
MARQUARD, O., *Aesthetica und Anaesthetica. Philosophische Überlegungen*, München 2003 (1989).
MAUND, B., *Perception*, Chesham 2003.
MERLEAU-PONTY, M., *L'oeil et l'esprit*, Paris 1964.
MOTHERSHILL, M., *Beauty restored*, Oxford 1984.

PAETZOLD, H., *Ästhetik des deutschen Idealismus. Zur Idee ästhetischer Rationalität bei Baumgarten, Kant, Schelling, Hegel und Schopenhauer*, Wiesbaden 1983.
PETERS, J.M., *Het beeld. Bouwstenen voor een algemene iconologie*, Antwerpen, etc. 1996.
PÖLTNER, G., *Schönheit. Eine Untersuchung zum Ursprung des Denkens bei Thomas von Aquin*, Wien, etc. 1978.
SCHILLER, F., *Über Kunst und Wirklichkeit. Schriften und Briefe zur Ästhetik*, Leipzig 1975.
SCHNEIDER, N., *Geschichte der Ästhetik von der Aufklärung bis zur Postmoderne. Eine paradigmatische Einführung*, Stuttgart 1996.
SIMPSON, D. [ED.], *German aesthetic and literary criticism. Kant, Fichte, Schelling, Schopenhauer, Hegel*, [Intr. by D. Simpson], Cambridge 1984.
SÖHNGEN, G., *Theologie der Musik*, Kassel 1967.
STEINER, G., *Grammars of creation*, [Originating in the Gifford Lectures for 1990], London 2001.
STEINER, G., *Real presences. Is there anything in what we say?*, London 1989.
TATARKIEWICZ, W., *Geschichte der Ästhetik*, Basel 1987.
VAUGHAN, W., *Romanticism and art*, London 1994².
WEBER, W.M., *Het wezen van de schoonheid. Een dwarsdoorsnede door de westerse filosofie*, Kampen 2003.

2.2. Theological aesthetics

AVIS, P., *God and the creative imagination. Metaphor, symbol and myth in religion and theology*, London 1999.
AYRES, L., Representation, theology and faith, in: *Modern theology* 11 (1995), 23-46.
BAHR, H.E., *Theologische Untersuchungen der Kunst. Poiesis*, München, etc. 1965.
BAYER, O., *Gott als Autor. Zu einer poietologischen Theologie*, Tübingen 1999.
BEGBIE, J., *Voicing creation's praise: towards a theology of the arts*, Edinburgh 1991.
BEGBIE, J. [ED.], *Beholding the glory. Incarnation through the arts*, London 2000.
BEGBIE, J. [ED.], *Sounding the depths. Theology through the arts*, London 2002.
BELTING, H., *Bild und Kult. Eine Geschichte des Bildes vor dem Zeitalter der Kunst*, München 1991².
BENTLEY HART, D., *The beauty of the infinite. The aesthetics of Christian truth*, Grand Rapids 2003.
BIESINGER, A., Gegen der Verlust der Augen. Gott in Farben sehen, in: *Theologische Quartalschrift* 175 (1995), 337-346.
BLOND, PH, The primacy of theology and the question of perception, in: HEELAS, P., MARTIN, D. [EDS], *Religion, modernity and postmodernity*, Oxford 1998, 285-313.
BLOND, PH., Theology and perception, in: *Modern theology* 14 (1998) 523-534.
BOHREN, R., *Dass Gott schön werde*, München 1975.

BROWN, D., *Tradition and imagination. Revelation & change*, Oxford 1999.
BROWN, D., *Discipleship and imagination. Christian tradition & truth*, Oxford 2000.
BROWN, F.B., *Religious aesthetics. A theological study of making and meaning*, Princeton 1993².
BROWN, F.B., Theological table-talk. The startling testimony of George Steiner, in: *Theology today* 54 (1997), 419-423.
BROWN, F.B., *Good taste, bad taste, and Christian taste. Aesthetics in religious life*, Oxford 2000.
COULSUN, J., *Religion and imagination. In aid of a grammar of assent*, Oxford 1981.
CROCKETT, C., *A theology of the sublime*, [With a foreword by Charles Winquist], London 2001.
DELATTRE, R.A., *Beauty and sensibility in the thought of Jonathan Edwards*, New Haven 1968.
DELRUE, M., Kunst en liturgie als epifanie, in: QUAGHEBEUR, R., VERBIEST, D. [RED.], *Epifanie. Actuele kunst en religie*, Antwerpen 2000.
DILLENBERGER, J., *A theology of artistic sensibilities. The visual arts and the church*, New York 1986.
DIXON, J.W., *Art and the theological imagination*, New York 1978.
DYRNESS, W.A., *Visual faith. Art, theology and worship in dialogue*, Grand Rapids 2001.
ECKHOLT, M., *Poetik der Kultur. Bausteine einer interkulturellen dogmatischen Methodenlehre*, Freiburg im Breisgau 2002.
ENGEL, U., *Umgrenzte Leere. Zur Praxis einer politisch-theologischen Ästhetik im Anschluss an Peter Weiss' Romantrilogie "Die Ästhetik des Widerstands"*, Münster 1997.
ERP, S.A.J. VAN, Fides quaerens intellectum. Esthetica als fundamentele theologie, geloof op zoek naar beelden, in: *Tijdschrift voor theologie* 43 (2003), 15-39.
ERP, S.A.J. VAN, Eindige schoonheid. Schepping tussen hybris en hoop, in: KALSKY, M., LEIJNSE, B., OOSTERVEEN, L. (RED.), *Het heil op de hielen. Over de belofte van het vervulde leven*, Zoetermeer 2003.
FARLEY, E., *Faith and beauty. A theological aesthetic*, Aldershot 2001.
FOREST, J., *Praying with icons*, New York 1997.
FRASER, H., *Beauty and belief. Aesthetics and religion in Victorian literature*, Cambridge 1986.
FULLER, P., *Theoria. Art, and the absence of grace*, London 1988.
FÜRST, W., *Pastoralästhetik. Die Kunst der Wahrnehmung und Gestaltung in Glaube und Kirche*, Freiburg im Breisgau 2002.
GANOCZY, A., *Der schöpferische Gott und die Schöpfung Gottes*, Mainz 1976.
GARCÍA-RIVERA, A., *The community of the beautiful. A theological aesthetics*, Collegeville 1999.
GARCÍA-RIVERA, A., *A wounded innocence. Sketches for a theology of art*, Collegeville 2003.
GORRINGE, T.J., *The education of desire. Towards a theology of the senses*, [The 2000 Diocese of British Columbia John Albert Hall Lectures at the Centre for Studies in Religion and Society in the University of Victoria], London 2001.

GREEN, G., *Imagining God. Theology and the religious imagination*, San Francisco 1989.
GREEN, G., *Theology, hermeneutics, and imagination. The crisis of interpretation at the end of modernity*, Cambridge 2000.
GREEN, G., The mirror, the lamp, and the lens. On the limits of imagination, in: *Ars disputandi* 2 (2002), 75-86.
GRUCHY, J. DE, *Christianity, art and transformation. Theological aesthetics in the struggle for justice*, Cambridge 2001.
GUARDINI, R., *Über das Wesen des Kunstwerkes*, Tübingen 1965^9.
HALDER, A., WELSCH, W., Kunst und Religion, in: BÖCKLE, F., U.A. [HRSG.], *Christlicher Glaube in moderner Gesellschaft, Bd. 2*, Freiburg im Breisgau 1981, 43-70.
HARRIES, R., *Art and the beauty of God. A Christian underdstanding*, London 1993.
HEINEN, W., *Bild—Wort—Symbol in der Theologie*, Würzburg 1969.
HEUMANN, J., MÜLLER, W.E. [HRSG.], *Auf der Suche nach Wirklichkeit. Von der (Un-)Möglichkeit einer theologischen Interpretation der Kunst*, [Religion in der Öffentlichkeit; Bd. 1], Frankfurt am Main 1996.
HOEPS, R., *Bildsinn und religiöse Erfahrung: Hermeneutische Grundlagen für einen Weg der Theologie zum Verständnis gegenstandsloser Malerei*, [Disputationes Theologicae; Bd. 16], Frankfurt am Main 1984.
HOEPS, R., *Das Gefühl des Erhabenen und die Herrlichkeit Gottes. Studien zur Beziehung von philosophischer und theologischer Ästhetik*, Würzburg 1989.
HOWES, G., Theology and the arts: Visual arts, in: FORD, D. [ED.], *The modern theologians: an introduction to Christian theology in the twentieth century*, Oxford 1997², 669-685.
JANTZEN, G., Beauty for ashes. Notes on the displacement of beauty, in: *Literature & theology* 16 (2002) 4, 427-449.
JÜNGEL, E., Auch das Schöne muss sterben—Schönheit im Lichte der Wahrheit. Theologische Bemerkungen zum ästhetischen Verhältnis, in: *Zeitschrift für Theologie und Kirche* 81 (1984), 106-127.
KARFIKOVÁ, L., Die Rettung des Flüchtigen. Die Schönheit in der Theologie Hugos von St. Viktor, in: *Forum katholische Theologie* 13 (1997), 271-282.
KÖLBL, A., LARCHER, G., RAUCHENBERGER, J. [HRSG.], *ENTGEGEN. ReligionGedächtnisKörper in Gegenwartskunst*, [Ausstellung anlässlich der II. Europäischen Ökumenischen Versammlung in Graz, 23. Mai – 6. Juli 1997], Ostfildern-Ruit 1997.
KÜNG, H., *Kunst und Sinnfrage*, Zürich, etc. 1980.
KUSCHEL, K.J., Theologen und ihre Dichter. Analysen zur Funktion der Literatur bei Rudolf Bultmann und Hans Urs von Balthasar, in: *Theologische Quartalschrift* 172 (1992), 98-116.
KUSCHEL, K.J., *Im Spiegel der Dichter. Mensch, Gott und Jesus in der Literatur des 20. Jahrhunderts*, Düsseldorf 2000.
LAARHOVEN, J. VAN, *De beeldtaal van de christelijke kunst. Geschiedenis van de iconografie*, Nijmegen 1992.
LANGENHORST, G. [HRSG.], *Auf dem Weg zu einer theologischen Ästhetik*, Münster 1998.
LARCHER, G. [HRSG.], *Gott-Bild. Gebrochen durch die Moderne*, [Für K.M. Woschitz], Graz, etc. 1997.

LARCHER, G., Bildende Kunst und Kirche. Fundamentaltheologisches zu ihrem Verhältnis heute, [Für Hermann Josef Pottmeyer], in: GEERLINGS, W., SECKLER, M. [HRSG.], *Kirche sein: nachkonziliare Theologie im Dienst der Kirchenreform*, Freiburg im Breisgau, etc. 1994, 431-442.

LARCHER, G., Fundamentaltheologie und Kunst im Kontext der Mediengesellschaft. Neue Herausforderungen für eine alte Beziehung, in: VALENTIN J., WENDEL, S. [HRSG.], *Unbedingtes Verstehen?! Fundamentaltheologie zwischen Erstphilosophie und Hermeneutik*, Regensburg 2001, 161-176.

LEEUW, G. VAN DER, *Wegen en grenzen, Een studie over de verhouding van religie en kunst*, Amsterdam 1955³ (1932). [English translation: Sacred and profane beauty: The holy in art, New York 1963.]

LESCH, W. [HRSG.], *Theologie und ästhetische Erfahrung. Beiträge zur Begegnung von Religion und Kunst*, Darmstadt 1994.

LEUENBERGER, R., Theologische Reflexionen über die Kunst, in: *Zeitschrift für Theologie und Kirche* 81 (1984), 127-137.

LOMBAERTS, H., MAAS, J., WISSINK, J. [EDS], *Beeld & gelijkenis. Inwijding, kunst en religie*, Zoetermeer 2001.

LORETZ, O., *Die Gottesebenbildlichkeit des Menschen*, München 1967.

MAAS, F.A., *Schoonheid vraagt om goed gezelschap. Katholieke cultuur tussen esthetiek en ethiek*, Vught 1997.

MAAS, F.A., Beauty and religion. Being touched by a sense of openness and underlying unity of all things, in: DERKSE, W., ET AL. [RED.], *In Quest of humanity in a globalising world. Dutch contributions to the jubilee of universities in Rome 2000*, Leende 2000, 275-292

MACKEY, J.P. [ED.], *Religious imagination*, Edinburgh 1986.

MARITAIN, J., *Art et scholastique*, Paris 1920.

MARTIN, JR., J.A., *Beauty and holiness. The dialogue between aesthetics and religion*, Princeton 1990.

MARTLAND, T.R., *Religion as art. An interpretation*, Albany 1981.

MCINTYRE, J., *Faith, theology and imagination*, Edinburgh 1987.

MERTENS, H.-E., Ook schoonheid is een naam voor God. Kunst als bron van theologie. Een pleidooi, in: *Collationes. Vlaams tijdschrift voor theologie en pastoraal* 26 (1996), 227-249.

MERTENS, H.-E., *Schoonheid is uw naam. Essay over esthetische en religieuze ervaring*, Leuven, etc. 1997.

MERTIN, A., WENDT, K. [HRSG.], *Magazin für Theologie und Ästhetik* (http://www.theomag.de/).

MILBANK, J., WARD, G., WYSCHOGROD, E. [EDS], *Theological perspectives on God and beauty*, Harrisburg 2003.

MÜLLER, W.E., HEUMANN, J. [HRSG.], *Kunst-Positionen. Kunst als Thema gegenwärtiger evangelischer und katholischer Theologie*, Stuttgart, etc. 1998.

MÜLLER, W.E., *Kunst als Darstellung des Unbedingten. Theologische Reflexionen zur Ästhetik*, Frankfurt am Main, etc. 1976.

NAVONE, J., S.J., *Enjoying God's beauty*, Collegeville, Minnesota 1999.

NAVONE, J., *Toward a theology of beauty*, Collegeville, Minnesota 1996.

NEBEL, G., *Das Ereignis des Schönen*, Stuttgart 1953.

NOLTE, J., Unterscheidung der Bilder. Vorläufige Erkundungen zu einer christlich bestimmten Ästhetik, in: *Theologische Quartalschrift* 175 (1995), 294-305.

NORDHOFEN, E., *Der Engel der Bestreitung. Über das Verhältnis von Kunst und negativer Theologie*, Würzburg 1993.
O'CONNELL, R., S.J., *Art and the Christian intelligence in St. Augustine*, Cambridge 1978.
OBERTI, E., Ästhetik, in: *Sacramentum Mundi. Theologisches Lexikon für die Praxis I*, Freiburg im Breisgau, etc. , 351-356.
PATTISON, G., *Art, modernity and faith. Towards a theology of art*, London 1998².
PELIKAN, J., *Fools for Christ. Essays on the true, the good and the beautiful (Impressions of Kierkegaard, Paul, Dostoevsky, Luther, Nietzsche, Bach)*, Philadelphia 1955.
PELIKAN, J., *Imago Dei. The Byzantine Apologia for Icons* [A.W.Mellon Lectures in the Fine Arts, 1987], Princeton 1990.
PLOEGER, A.K., *Dare we observe? The importance of art works for consciousness of diakonia in (post-)modern church*, Leuven 2002.
RAHNER, K., Priester und Dichter, in: *Schriften zur Theologie. Band III: Zur Theologie des geistlichen Lebens*, Einsiedeln, etc. 1956, 349-375.
RAHNER, K., Theology and the arts, in: *Thought* 57 (1982), 24.
SAWARD, J., *The beauty of holiness and the holiness of beauty. Art, sanctity and the truth of catholicism*, San Francisco 1997.
SCHILLEBEECKX, E., O.P., Cultuur, godsdienst en geweld: Theologie als onderdeel van een cultuur, in: *Tijdschrift voor theologie* 36 (1996), 387-404.
SCHMIDT, P., *In de handen van mensen. 2000 jaar Christus in kunst en cultuur*, Kampen 2000.
SCHMIDT, TH., *A scandalous beauty. The artistry of God and the way of the cross*, Grand Rapids 2002.
SHANKS, A., *'What is truth?' Towards a theological poetics*, London 2001.
SHERRY, P., *Images of redemption. Arts, literature and salvation*, London 2003.
SHERRY, P., *Spirit and beauty. An introduction to theological aesthetics*, London 2002² (1992).
STOCK, A., *Keine Kunst. Aspekte der Bildtheologie*, Paderborn, etc. 1996.
STOCK, A., *Poetische Dogmatik. Christologie: 1. Namen; 2. Schrift und Gesicht; 3. Leib und Leben; 4. Bilder*, Paderborn, etc. 1995-2001.
STOCK, A., *Zwischen Tempel und Museum. Theologische Kunstkritik; Positionen der Moderne*, Paderborn, etc. 1991.
TAYLOR, M.C., *Disfiguring. Art, architecture, religion*, Chicago 1992.
TILLICH, P., *On art and architecture*, New York 1987.
TILLICH, P., *Theology of culture*, New York 1959.
VILADESAU, R., *Theological aesthetics. God in imagination, beauty and art*, Oxford 1999.
VILADESAU, R., *Theology and the arts. Encountering God through music, art and rhetoric*, New York, etc. 2000.
WILDER, A.N., *Theopoetic*, Philadelphia 1976.
WISSINK, J., *Te mooi om onwaar te zijn. Theologische vragen naar het schone*, Vught 1993.
WOHLMUTH, J., Überlegungen zu einer theologischen Ästhetik der Sakramente, in: BAIER, W. [HRSG.], *Weisheit Gottes—Weisheit der Welt. Festschrift für Joseph Kardinal Ratzinger zum 60. Geburtstag*, St. Otilien 1987, 1109-1128.

WOLTERSTORFF, N., *Art in action. Towards a Christian aesthetic*, Grand Rapids 1980.
ZEINDLER, M., *Gott und das Schöne: Studien zur Theologie der Schönheit*, [Forschungen zur systematischen und ökumenischen Theologie; Bd. 68], Göttingen 1993.

3. Fundamental theology—Philosophical theology—Methodology

ANDERSON, J.F., *The bond of being. An essay on analogy and existence*, St. Louis, etc. 1949.
AVIS, P. [ED.], *Modern theology. The dream of reason*, Basingstoke 1986.
BEECK, F.J. VAN, S.J., *God encountered. A contemporary catholic systematic theology*, Collegeville 1989-.
BLONDEL, M., *Lettre sur les exigences de la pensée contemporaine en matière d'apologétique et sur la méthode de la philosophie dans l'étude du problème religieux*, Paris 1956 (1896).
BRAATEN, C.E., Scripture, church and dogma. An essay on theological method, in: *Interpretation* 50 (1996), 142-155.
DALFERTH, I.U., *Kombinatorische Theologie. Probleme theologischer Rationalität*, [Quaestiones Disputatae 130], Freiburg im Breisgau, etc. 1991.
DALFERTH, I.U., *Gott. Philosophisch-theologische Denkversuche*, Tübingen 1992.
DE PETTER, D.M., Impliciete intuïtie, in: *Tijdschrift voor philosophie* 1 (1939), 84-105.
DÖRING, H., KREINER, A., SCHMIDT-LEUKEL, P., *Den Glauben denken. Neue Wege der Fundamentaltheologie*, [Quaestiones disputatae; Bd. 147], Freiburg im Breisgau, etc. 1993.
DREY, J.S. VON, *Die Apologetik als wissenschaftliche Nachweisung der Göttlichkeit des Christentums in seiner Erscheinung*, Mainz 1844-1847.
DULLES, A., S.J., *Models of revelation*, Dublin 1992³.
DULLES, A., S.J., *The craft of theology. From symbol to system*, New York 2000².
DUPRÉ, L.K., *Religious mystery and rational reflection. Excursions in the phenomenology and philosophy of religion*, Grand Rapids 1998.
EBELING, G., Erwägungen zu einer evangelischen Fundamentaltheologie, in: *Zeitschrift für Theologie und Kirche* 67 (1970), 479-524.
EHRLICH, J.N., *Leitfaden für Vorlesungen über die allgemeine Einleitung in die theologische Wissenschaft und die Theorie der Religion und Offenbarung als I. Theil der Fundamental-Theologie*, Prag 1859.
EHRLICH, J.N., *Leitfaden für Vorlesungen über die Offenbarung Gottes als Thatsache der Geschichte. II. Theil der Fundamental-Theologie*, Prag 1862.
FORD, D.F., Hans Frei and the future of theology, in: *Modern theology* 8 (1992), 203-214.
FORD, D.F., *Theology. A very short introduction*, Oxford 1999.
FREI, H.W., *Types of Christian theology*, New Haven 1992.
FRIES, H., *Fundamentaltheologie*, Graz, etc. 1985².
GRENZ, S.J., FRANKE, J.R., *Beyond foundationalism. Shaping theology in a postmodern context*, Louisville 2001.

HAILER, M., *Theologie als Weisheit. Sapientiale Konzeptionen in der Fundamentaltheologie des 20. Jahrhunderts*, [Neukichener theologische Dissertationen und Habilitationen; Bd. 17], Neukirchener 1997.
HAUERWAS, S., MURPHY, N., NATION M. [EDS], *Theology without foundations. Religious practice and the future of theological truth*, Nashville 1994.
HELM, P., *Faith with reason*, Oxford 2000.
HODGSON, P.C., *Winds of the spirit. A constructive Christian theology*, London 1994.
HOFF, G.M., *Aporetische Theologie. Skizze eines Stils fundamenteler Theolologie*, Paderborn, etc. 1997.
JENSON, R.W., Christ as culture. Christ as polity, in: *International journal for systematic theology* 5 (2003) 323-329.
JOEST, W., *Fundamentaltheologie. theologische Grundlagen- und Methodenprobleme*, Stuttgart 1974.
KAMITSUKA, D.G., *Theology and contemporary culture. Liberation, postliberal and revisionary perspectives*, Cambridge 1999.
KAUFMAN, G., *The theological imagination. Constructing the concept of God*, Philadelphia 1981.
KAUFMAN, G., *In face of mystery. A constructive theology*, Cambridge 1993.
KAUFMAN, G., *An essay on theological method*, Atlanta 1995³.
KAUFMAN, G., *God, mystery, diversity. Christian theology in a pluralistic world*, Minneapolis 1996.
KAUFMAN, G., On thinking of God as Serendipitous Creativity, in: *Journal of the American Academy of Religion* 69 (2001) 409-424.
KEARNEY, R., *The God who may be. A hermeneutics of religion*, Bloomington 2001.
KESSLER, M., PANNENBERG, W., POTTMEYER, H.J. [HRSG.], *Fides quaerens intellectum. Beiträge zur Fundamentaltheologie*, Tübingen 1992.
KNAUER, P., *Der Glaube kommt vom Hören. Ökumenische Fundamentaltheologie*, Freiburg im Breisgau 1991⁶.
LARCHER, G., MÜLLER, K., PRÖPPER, TH. [HRSG.], *Hoffnung, die Gründe nennt. Zu Hansjürgen Verweyens Projekt einer erstphilosophischen Glaubensverantwortung*, Regensburg 1996.
LATOURELLE, R., O'COLLINS, G. [HRSG.], *Probleme und Aspekte der Fundamentaltheologie*, [Hrsg. d. dt. Ausg., Endred. d. Übers., Bearb. d. Apparats Johannes Bernard], Innsbruck, etc. 1985.
LATOURELLE, R., FISICHELLA, R. [EDS], *Dictionary of fundamental theology*, [Orig. Dizionario di teologia fondamentale], New York 1994.
LERON SHULTS, F., *The postfoundationalist task of theology. Wolfhart Pannenberg and the new theological rationality*, [Foreword by Wolfhart Pannenberg], Grand Rapids 1999.
LERON SHULTS, F., *Reforming theological anthropology. After the philosophical turn to relativity*, Grand Rapids 2003.
LINDBECK, G., *The nature of doctrine. Religion and theology in a postliberal age*, Philadelphia 1984.
LONERGAN, B., *Method in theology*, Toronto 1996.
MACKEY, J.P., *The critique of theological reason*, Cambridge 2000.
MACKEY, J.P., The preacher, the theologian, and the Trinity, in: *Theology today* 54 (1997), 347-366.

MARÉCHAL, J., *Le point de depart de la metaphysique I-V*, Bruxelles 1944-1949 (1922-1927).
MARKS, D.C. [ED.], *Shaping a theological mind. Theological context and methodology*, Aldershot 2002.
MECHELS, E., *Analogie bei Erich Przywara un Karl Barth. Das Verhältnis von Offenbarungstheologie und Metaphysik*, Neukirchen-Vluyn 1974.
MIGLIORE, D.L., *Faith seeking understanding. An introduction to Christian theology*, Grand Rapids 1991.
MILBANK, J. [ED.], *Radical orthodoxy. A new theology*, London 1999.
MÜLLER, K. [HRSG.], *Fundamentaltheologie. Fluchtlinien und gegenwärtige Herausforderungen*, [In konzeptioneller Zusammenarbeit mit Gerhard Larcher], Regensburg 1998.
MÜLLER, K., *Gott erkennen. Das Abenteuer der Gottesbeweise*, Regensburg 2001.
MÜLLER, K., *Gottes Dasein denken. Eine philosophische Gotteslehre für heute*, Regensburg 2001
MURPHY, N.C., *Beyond liberalism and fundamentalism. How modern and postmodern philosophy set the theological agenda*, Valley Forge 1996.
NEUNER, P., WAGNER, H. [HRSG.], *In Verantwortung für den Glauben. Beiträge zur Fundamentaltheologie und Ökumenik*, [Für Heinrich Fries], Freiburg im Breisgau, etc. 1992.
NIEBUHR, R.H., *Christ and culture*, New York 1951.
O'COLLINS, G., S.J., *Fundamental theology*, New York, etc. 1981.
O'COLLINS, G., S.J., *Retrieving fundamental theology. The three styles of contemporary theology*, London 1993.
OTT, H., *Apologetik des Glaubens. Grundprobleme einer dialogischen Fundamentaltheologie*, Darmstadt 1994.
PANNENBERG, W., *Wissenschaftstheorie und Theologie*, Frankfurt am Main 1987.
PATTISON, G., *The end of theology – And the task of thinking about God*, London 1998.
PHILLIPS, D.Z., *Faith and philosophical enquiry*, London 1970.
PHILLIPS, D.Z., *Religion and the hermeneutics of contemplation*, Cambridge 2001.
PLACHER, W., *Unapologetic theology. A Christian voice in a pluralistic conversation*, Louisville 1989.
PRÖPPER, TH., Erstphilosophischer Begriff oder Aufweis letztgültigen Sinnes? Anfragen an Hansjürgen Verweyens "Grundriss der Fundamentaltheologie", in: *Theologische Quartalschrift* 174 (1994) 4, 272-287.
PRÖPPER, TH., *Evangelium und freie Vernunft. Konturen einer theologischen Hermeneutik*, Freiburg im Breisgau 2001.
RAHNER, K., *Hörer des Wortes. Zur Grundlegung einer Religionsphilosophie*, [Neu bearbeitet von J.B. Metz], München 1963².
RAHNER, K., Theologie und Anthropologie, in: *Schriften zur Theologie VIII*, Einsiedeln 1967, 43-65.
RAHNER, K., *Grundkurs des Glaubens. Einführung in den Begriff des Christentums*, Freiburg im Breisgau, etc. 1976.
SCHILLEBEECKX, E., O.P., *Openbaring en theologie*, [Theologische peilingen deel I], Bilthoven 1964.
SCHREURS, N., J.S. Drey en F. Schleiermacher aan het begin van de fundamentele theologie. Oorsprongen en ontwikkelingen, in: *Bijdragen. Tijdschrift voor*

filosofie en theologie 43 (1982), 251-288.
SCHÜSSLER FIORENZA, F., *Foundational theology. Jesus and the church*, New York 1986.
SCHÜSSLER FIORENZA, F., GALVIN, J.P., *Systematic theology. Roman Catholic perspectives Vol. I*, Minneapolis 1991.
THIEL, J., *Nonfoundationalism*, Minneapolis 1994.
TRACY, D., *On naming the present. God, hermeneutics and the church*, Maryknoll 1994.
TRACY, D., *The analogical imagination. Christian theology and the culture of pluralism*, London 1981.
VERWEYEN, H., *Ontologische Voraussetzungen des Glaubensaktes. Zur transzendentalen Frage nach der Möglichkeit von Offenbarung*, Düsseldorf 1969.
VERWEYEN, H., *Gottes letztes Wort. Grundriss der Fundamentaltheologie*, Düsseldorf 1991².
VERWEYEN, H., Glaubensverantwortung heute Zu den "Anfragen" von Thomas Pröpper, in: *Theologische Quartalschrift* 174 (1994) 4, 288-303.
VERWEYEN, H., *Botschaft eines Toten? Den Glauben rational verantworten*, Regensburg 1997.
WAGNER, H., *Einführung in die Fundamentaltheologie*, Darmstadt 1996².
WALDENFELS, H., *Kontextuelle Fundamentaltheologie*, Paderborn, etc. 1988².
WALDENFELS, H., *Einführung in die Theologie der Offenbarung*, Darmstadt 1996.
WEBSTER, J., SCHNER, G.P. [EDS], *Theology after liberalism. A reader*, Oxford 2000.
WEBSTER, J., *Theological theology*, [An inaugural lecture delivered before the University of Oxford on 27 October 1997], Oxford 1998.
WENTZEL VAN HUYSSTEEN, J., Book review of J. Thiel, Nonfoundationalism, in: *Theology today* 52 (1996) 4, 521-524, 522
WENTZEL VAN HUYSSTEEN, J., *Essays in postfoundationalist theology*, Grand Rapids 1997.
WERBICK, J., *Den Glauben verantworten. Eine Fundamentaltheologie*, Freiburg im Breisgau 2000.
WILES, M., *What is theology?*, Oxford 1976.
WISSINK, J., *De inzet van de theologie. Een onderzoek naar de motieven en de geldigheid van Karl Barths strijd tegen de natuurlijke theologie*, Amersfoort 1983.
WOLDE, E. VAN, The limits of linearity. Linear and non-linear causal thinking in biblical exegesis, philosophy and theology, in: *Bijdragen. Tijdschrift voor filosofie en theologie* 62 (2001), 371-392.
YANDELL, K.E., *Philosophy of religion. A contemporary introduction*, London 1999.

4. Other

AERTSEN, J.A., Die Transzendentalienlehre bei Thomas von Aquin in ihren Hintergründen und philosophischen Motiven, in: *Thomas von Aquin. Werk und Wirkung im Licht neuerer Forschungen*, [Miscellanea Mediaevalia.

Veröffentlichungen des Thomas-Instituts der Universität zu Köln. Band 19. Hrsg. A. Zimmerman], Berlin, etc. 1988, 82-102.

AERTSEN, J.A., *Medieval philosophy and the transcendentals. The case of Thomas Aquinas*, Leiden, etc. 1996.

ALVAREZ-GOMEZ, M., *Die verborgene Gegenwart des Unendlichen bei Nikolaus von Kues*, München 1968.

ANDERSON, J.F., *Reflections on the analogy of being*, The Hague 1967.

BARTH, K., *Kirchliche Dogmatik, I,1. Prolegomena*, München 1932.

BARTH, K., *Fides quaerens intellectum. Anselms Beweis der Existenz Gottes im Zusammenhang seines theologischen Programms*, [*Gesamtausgabe. II. Akademische Werke*, Hrsg. von E. Jüngel und I. Dalferth], Zürich 1981.

BAUCKHAM, R., *God and the crisis of freedom. Biblical and contemporary perspectives*, Louisville 2002.

BEEK, A. VAN, *Ontmaskering. Christelijk geloof en cultuur*, Zoetermeer 2001.

BEGGIANI, S.J., Theology at the service of mysticism. Method in Pseudo-Dionysius, in: *Theological studies* 57 (1996), 201-223.

BEIERWALTES, W., *Identität und Differenz. Zum Prinzip cusanischen Denkens*, Opladen 1977.

BEIERWALTES, W., BALTHASAR, H.U. VON, HAAS, A., *Grundfragen der Mystik*, Einsiedeln, etc. 2002².

BEKKENKAMP, J., HAARDT, M. DE [EDS], *Begin with body. Corporeality, religion, and gender*, Louvain 1998.

BENZ, H., Nikolaus von Kues: Initiator der Subjektivitätsphilosphie oder Seinsdenker?, in: *Theologie und Philosophie* 73 (1998), 196-224.

BERGER, P.L., LUCKMANN, TH., *The social construction of reality. A treatise in the sociology of knowledge*, New York 1967.

BLOND, PH. [ED.], *Post-secular philosophy. Between philosophy and theology*, London 1998.

BLUMENBERG, H., *Die Legitimität der Neuzeit*, Frankfurt am Main 1988² (1966).

BOCKEN, I., *Waarheid en interpretatie. Perspectieven op het conjecturele denken van Nicolaus Cusanus 1401-1464*, Maastricht 2002.

BOCKEN, I., *De kunst van het verzamelen. Historische inleiding tot de conjecturele hermeneutiek van Nicolaas Cusanus*, Budel 2004.

BOSCH, H. VAN DEN, *Een apologie van het onmogelijke. Een kritische analyse van Mark C. Taylors a/theologie aan de hand van Jacques Derrida en John D. Caputo*, Den Haag 2002.

BROWN, R.F., *The later philosophy of Schelling. The influence of Boehme on the works of 1809-1815*, Lewisburg 1877.

BURKE, P., *The Renaissance*, [Studies in European history], London 1987.

CASSIRER, E., *Das Erkenntnisproblem in der Philosophie und Wissenschaft der neueren Zeit*, Darmstadt 1994 (1922³).

CLAYTON, PH., *The problem of God in modern thought*, Grand Rapids 2000.

DAVIES, O., *A theology of compassion. Metaphysics of difference and the renewal of tradition*, London 2001.

DAVIES, O., TURNER, D., *Silence and the word. Negative theology and incarnation*, Cambridge 2002.

DUINTJER, O., *De vraag naar het transcendentale. Vooral in verband met Heidegger en Kant*, Leiden 1966.

DUPRÉ, L.K., *The other dimension. A search for the meaning of religious attitudes*, New York 1972.
DUPRÉ, L.K., *Transcendent selfhood. The loss and rediscovery of the inner life*, New York 1976.
DUPRÉ, L.K., *De symboliek van het heilige*, Kampen 1991.
DUPRÉ, L.K., *Passage to modernity. An essay in the hermeneutics of nature and culture*, New Haven, etc. 1993.
DUPRÉ, L.K., Cultuur en metafysica, in: *Nexus* 14 (1996), 77-88.
EDWARDS, J., *A treatise concerning religious affections*, New Haven 1959.
EICHER, P., Immanenz oder Transzendenz? Gespräch mit Karl Rahner, in: *Freiburger Zeitschrift für Philosophie und Theologie* 15 (1968), 29-62.
EICHER, P., *Offenbarung, Prinzip neuzeitlicher Theologie*, München 1977.
ELIOT, T.S., *Collected poems 1909-1962*, London 1963.
ERP, S.A.J. VAN, A renaissance of theological aesthetics. Hans Urs von Balthasar's reading of Nicholas of Cusa, in: BOCKEN, I., DUCLOW, D., ERP, S.A.J. VAN, JESPERS, F. [EDS], *On cultural ontology. Religion, philosophy and culture*, [Essays in honor of Wilhelm Dupré], Maastricht 2002, 89-111.
FLASCH, K., *Das Philosophische Denken im Mittelalter. Von Augustin zu Machiavelli*, Stuttgart 1987.
FLASCH, K., *Die Metaphysik des Einen bei Nikolaus von Kues. Problemgeschichtliche Stellung und systematische Bedeutung*, [Studien zur Problemgeschichte der antiken und mittelalterlichen Philosophie VII], Leiden 1973.
FORD, D.F. [ED.], *The modern theologians. An introduction to Christian theology in the twentieth century*, Oxford 1997².
FORD, D.F., *Self and salvation. Being transformed*, Cambridge 1999.
FÜHRER, M.L., Purgation, illumination and perfection in Nicholas of Cusa, in: *The Downside review* 98 (1980), 169-189.
GERTZ, B., *Glaubenswelt als Analogie. Die theologische Analogielehre Erich Przywaras und ihr Ort in der auseinandersetzung um die Analogia fidei*, Düsseldorf 1969.
GÖBEL, W., *Okzidentale Zeit. Die Subjektgeltung des Menschen im Praktischen nach der Entfaltungslogik unserer Geschichte*, Freiburg 1996.
GRESHAKE, G., *Der dreieine Gott. Eine trinitarische Theologie*, Freiburg im Breisgau, etc. 1997.
GUNTON, C., *A brief theology of revelation*, [The 1993 Warfield lectures], Edinburgh 1995.
GUNTON, C., *Intellect and action*, Edinburgh 2000.
GUNTON, C., The God of Jesus Christ, in: *Theology today* 54 (1997), 324-334.
GUNTON, C., *The promise of trinitarian theology*, Edinburgh 1997².
HARVEY, D., *The condition of postmodernity. An enquiry into the origins of cultural change*, Oxford 1990.
HAUBST, R., *Das Bild des Einen und Dreieinen Gottes in der Welt nach Nikolaus von Kues*, Trier 1952.
HAUBST, R., *Die Christologie des Nikolaus von Kues*, Freiburg 1956.
HAUBST, R., *Streifzüge in die cusanische Theologie*, Münster 1991.
HAUBST, R., Nikolaus von Kues und die analogia entis, in: ID., MEUTHEN, E., STALLMACH, J., [HRSG.], *Streifzüge in die cusanische Theologie*, [Buchreihe

der Cusanusgesellschaft, Sonderbeitrag zur Theologie des Cusanus], Münster 1991, 232-242.
HAUERWAS, S., *With the grain of the universe. The church's witness and natural theology*, [The Gifford Lectures delivered at the University of St. Andrews in 2001], London 2002.
HEIDEGGER, M., *Einführung in de Metaphysik*, Tübingen 1987[5].
HINSKE, N., Verschiedenheit und Einheit der transzendentalen Philosophen. Zum Exempel für ein Verhältnis von Problem- und Begriffsgeschichte, in: *Archiv für Begriffsgeschichte* 14 (1970), 41-68.
HIRSCHBERGER, J., Das Prinzip der Inkommensurabilität bei Nikolaus von Kues, in: HAUBST, R. [HRSG.], *Mitteilungen und Forschungsbeiträge der Cusanusgesellschaf, Bd. 11*, Mainz 1975, 39-54.
HOFFMANN, E., *Platonismus und christliche Philosophie*, Zürich 1960.
HOPKINS, G.M., *Poems of Gerard Manley Hopkins*, [Edited with notes by Robert Bridges], London 1918.
T. HUGHES, *Tales from Ovid. Twenty-four passages from the Metamorphoses*, London 1997.
HUIZINGA, J., *Herfsttij der Middeleeuwen. Studie over levens- en gedachtenvormen der veertiende en vijftiende eeuw in Frankrijk en de Nederlanden*, Groningen 1985[18].
HUIZINGA, J., *Homo ludens. Proeve ener bepaling van het spelelement der cultuur*, Amsterdam 1997.
JASPERS, K., *Nikolaus Cusanus*, München 1987 (1964).
JENSON, R.W., The Hauerwas project, in: *Modern theology* 8 (1992), 285-295.
KAISER, A., *Möglichkeiten und Grenzen einer Christologie 'von unten' bei Piet Schoonenberg und dessen Weiterführung mit Blick auf Nikolaus von Kues*, Münster 1992.
KANDLER, K.-H., Die intellektuale Anschauung bei Dietrich von Freiberg und Nikolaus von Kues, in: *Kerygma und Dogma. Zeitschrift für theologische Forschung und kirchliche Lehre* 43 (1997), 2-19.
KASPER, W., *Das Absolute in der Geschichte. Philosophie und Theologie der Geschichte in der Spätphilosophie Schellings*, Mainz 1965.
KIRCHHOFF, J., *Friedrich Wilhelm Joseph von Schelling*, Reinbek 1982.
KOESTLER, A., *The act of creation*, London 1989 (1964).
KUES, N. VON, *Philosophisch theologische Schriften*, [3 Bde., lat.-dt.Studien- und Jubiläumausgabe, hg. und eingef. v. L. Gabriel. übersetzt und kommentiert von D. und W. Dupré], Freiburg 1964-67.
LACUGNA, C.M., *God for us. The Trinity and Christian life*, London 1991.
LASH, N., Ideology, metaphor, and analogy, in: HAUERWAS, S., JONES, L.G. [EDS], *Why narrative? Readings in narrative theology*, Grand Rapids 1989.
LASH, N., *The beginning and the end of 'religion'*, Cambridge 1996.
LEVI, A., *Renaissance and Reformation. The intellectual genesis*, New Haven 2002.
LYOTARD, J.-F., *Le postmoderne expliqué aux enfants. Correspondance 1982-1985*, Paris 1986.
MAAS, F.A., *Vreemd en intiem. Nicolaas van Cusa op zoek naar de verborgen God*, [M.m.v. Inigo Bocken en Stephan van Erp], Zoetermeer 1993.

McFarland, I., The ecstatic God. The Holy Spirit and the constitution of the Trinity, in: *Theology today* 54 (1997), 335-346.
McInerny, R., *Aquinas and analogy*, Washington 1996.
McIntosh, M.A., *Mystical theology*, Oxford 1998.
Meuthen, E., *Nikolaus von Kues. Skizze einer Biographie*, Münster 1964.
Milbank, J., Man as creative and historical being in the theology of Nicholas of Cusa, in: *The Downside review* 97 (1979), 245-257.
Milbank, J., *Theology and social theory. Beyond secular reason*, Oxford 1990.
Milbank, J., *The word made strange. Theology, language, culture*, Oxford 1997.
O'Meara, Th., o.p., *Romantic idealism and Roman Catholicism. Schelling and the theologians*, Notre Dame 1982.
O'Regan, C., *Gnostic return in modernity*, New York 2001.
Petersen, R., Rourke, N.M., *Theological literacy for the twenty-first century*, Grand Rapids 2002.
Pinkard, T., *German philosophy 1760-1860. The legacy of Idealism*, Cambridge 2002.
Przywara, E., s.j., *Analogia Entis. Metaphysik: Ur-Struktur und All-Rhythmus*, Einsiedeln 1962².
Rahner, H., *Der spielende Mensch*, Einsiedeln 1990¹⁰.
Rosenzweig, F., *Das älteste Systemprogramm des deutschen Idealsimus. Ein handschrifter Fund*, Heidelberg 1917.
Santinello, G., *Il pensiero di Nicola Cusano nella sua propetiva estetica*, Padova 1958.
Schelling, F.W.J., *Sämmtliche Werke*, [herausgegeben von K.F.A. Schelling, I. Abtheilung Bde. 1-10; II. Abtheilung Bde. 1-4], Stuttgart, etc. 1856-1861.
Schelling, F.W.J., *Ausgewählte Werke Bde. 1-6*, [Unveränd. reprograf. Nachdr. d. aus d. hs. Nachlass hrsg. Ausg. von 1856 bis 1861], Darmstadt 1980-1990.
Schelling, F.W.J., *Ausgewählte Schriften Bde. 1-6*, Frankfurt am Main 1985.
Schelling, F.W.J., Das älteste Systemprogramm des deutschen Idealismus, in: Sloterdijk, P. [Hrsg.], *Schelling*, [Ausgewählt und vorgestellt von Michaela Boenke], München 1995, 95-97.
Schillebeeckx, E., o.p., *Mensen als verhaal van God*, Baarn 1989.
Schiller, F., *Über die ästhetische Erziehung des Menschen in einer Reihe von Briefen*, Leipzig 1975.
Schleiermacher, F.D.E., *Der christliche Glaube nach den Grundsätzen der evangelischen Kirche im Zusammenhange dargestellt*, [Kritische Gesamtausgabe I. Abt, Bd. 7,1, Hrsg. v. H. Peiter], Berlin 1980 (Berlin 1821-1822).
Schmidt, J., *Die Geschichte des Genie-Gedankens in der deutschen Literatur, Philosophie und Politik. Band 1. Von der Ausklärung bis zum Idealismus*, Darmstadt 1988².
Schneider, G., Gott—Das Nichtandere. Untersuchungen zum metaphysischen Grunde bei Nikolaus von Kues, in: Haubst R. [Hrsg.], *Mitteilungen und Forschungsbeiträge der Cusanus-Gesellschaft 8*, Mainz 1970, 246-254.
Schneider, Th. [Hrsg.], *Handbuch der Dogmatik*, [2 Bde.], Düsseldorf 1995².
Schreiter, R., c.pp.s., *The new catholicity. Theology between the global and the local*, Maryknoll 1997.
Schulz, W., *Der Gott der neuzeitlichen Metaphysik*, Pfullingen 1982⁷.

SCHULZ, W., Einleitung, in: BRANDT, H.D., MÜLLER, P. [HRSG.], *F.W.J. Schelling, System des transzendentalen Idealismus*, Hamburg 1992, IX-XLIV.
SCHULZE, W., *Zahl, Proportion, Analogie. Eine Untersuchung zur Metaphysik und Wissenschaftshaltung des Nikolaus von Kues*, [Buchreihe der Cusanusgesellschaft, Bd. VII, Hrsg. von R. Haubst, E. Meuthen und J Stallmach], Münster 1978.
SCHWÖBEL, CHR. [ED.], *Trinitarian theology today. Essays on divine being and act*, Edinburgh 1995.
SHANKS, A., *God & modernity. A new and better way to do theology*, London 2000.
SIEWERTH, G., *Die Analogie des Seienden*, Einsiedeln 1965.
SLOTERDIJK, P., *Sphären II. Globen*, Frankfurt am Main 1999.
SMITH, J.Z., *Map is not territory. Studies in the history of religions*, Chicago 1978.
SOSKICE, J.M., *Metaphor and religious language*, Oxford 1985.
STAMMBERGER, R.M.W., *On analogy. An essay historical and systematic*, Frankfurt am Main, etc. 1995.
TANNER, K., *Jesus, humanity and the trinity. A brief systematic theology*, Minneapolis 2001.
TAYLOR, CH., *Varieties of religion today. Willliam James revisited*, Cambridge 2002.
THURNER, M., *Gott als das offenbare Geheimnis nach Nikolaus von Kues*, Berlin 2001.
TILLIETTE, X., *Schelling, une philosophie en devenir. I. Le système vivant, 1794-1821; II. La dernière philosophie, 1821-1854*, Paris 1970.
TOULIMIN, S., *Cosmopolis. The hidden agenda of modernity*, New York 1990.
TURNER, D., *Faith seeking*, London 2002.
ULRICH, F., *Gegenwart der Freiheit*, Einsiedeln 1974.
ULRICH, F., *Homo Abyssus. Das Wagnis der Seinsfrage*, [Mit einer Einleitung Martin Bieler], Einsiedeln 1998².
VANHOOZER, K.J., [ED.], *The Cambridge companion to postmodern theology*, Cambridge 2003.
VELTHOVEN, TH. VAN, *Gottesschau und menschliche Kreativität. Studien zur Erkenntnislehre des Nikolaus von Kues*, [Dissertation], Leiden 1977.
VERENE, D.PH., *Philosophy and the return to self-knowledge*, New Haven 1997.
VERWEYEN, H., *Theologie im Zeichen der schwachen Vernunft*, Dusseldorf 2000.
VOLKMANN-SCHLUCK, K.H., *Nicolaus Cusanus. Die Philosophie im übergang vom Mittelalter zur Neuzeit*, Frankfurt am Main 1957.
WARD, G. [ED.], *The Blackwell companion to postmodern theology*, London 2001.
WARD, K., *Religion and revelation. A theology of revelation in the world's religions*, Oxford 1994.
WATTS, P.M., *Nicholas of Cusa. A fifteenth century vision of man*, Leiden 1982.
WAUGH, E., *Brideshead revisited*, Middlesex 1986.
WEBSTER, J., *Barth's ethics of reconciliation*, Cambridge 1995.
WEBSTER, J., *Holiness*, London 2003.
WILLIAMS R., *On Christian theology*, Oxford 2000.
ZIEBERTZ, H.-G., SCHWEITZER, F., HÄRING, H., BROWNIG, D. [EDS], *The human image of God*, Leiden 2001.

INDEX OF NAMES

Aertsen, J. 98-99, 101, 175
Aeschylus 149, 223
Agamben, G. 261
Alberti, L. 175
Albus, M. 140
Allers, R. 77
Allison, H. 47
Alvarez-Gomez, M. 178
Ameriks, K. 202, 204
Anderson, J. 109
Anselm 98, 146, 155, 216
Aristotle 45, 82, 109, 164, 167
Augustine 41, 45, 67-68, 95, 114, 128, 146, 173, 186
Avicenna 217
Avis, P. 22, 42, 243

Baader, F. von 147
Bach, J. 46
Bacon, F. 197, 200
Barth, K. 4, 22, 51-53, 71, 78, 80, 82-83, 88, 91, 108, 111-112, 115-117, 155, 251, 257
Bauckham, R. 29, 265
Baumeister, Th. 46
Baumgarten, A. 46, 78, 203-204, 245
Beardsley, M. 174-175
Beeck, F. van 15, 31, 252
Beek, A. van de 44
Begbie, J. 58
Beierwaltes, W. 178
Belting, H. 46
Benjamin, W. 60
Berger, P. 252
Berkeley, G. 197, 202
Bingen, H. von 46
Biser, E. 19, 103
Blond, Ph. 12, 247-248
Blondel, M. 18-19, 112, 116
Blumenberg, H. 163, 167-169, 179, 224

Bocken, I. 178
Boehme, J. 90, 147, 170
Boethius 173
Boeve, L. 34
Bonaventura 77, 107, 128, 146
Bonnici, J. 81
Bouillard, H. 83
Bowie, A. 202, 204, 207
Bredin, H. 46
Brown, D. 42, 248, 252
Brown, F. 42, 243
Brown, R. 206, 247
Bruno, G. 168, 173, 197
Buchheim, Th. 203
Buckley, J. 148
Bulgakov, S. 107
Bultmann, R. 155
Burckhardt, J. 164
Burke, P. 164-166
Byron, Lord 200

Cajetan 45, 110
Calvin, J. 45
Cano, M. 17
Cassirer, E. 169
Cervantes, M. 172
Chapp, L. 94, 136
Chia, R. 83, 94, 116
Claudel, P. 71
Clayton, Ph. 197, 210
Copernicus, N. 165
Crawford, D. 135, 261
Crockett, C. 42, 48, 214, 261
Cusanus 3, 5-6, 100, 147, 150, 160, **163-194**, 195, 198-199, 211, 216, 218, 231, 233, 236, 239

Daigler, M. 151
Dalferth, I. 15
Damascene, J. 17
Dante 77, 108, 146-147, 173, 220, 258

Davidson, D.   20
Davies, O.   120, 239, 263
De Bruyne, E.   165-166, 178
De Petter, D.   18
De Schrijver, G.   81, 111, 120, 211, 238
Delattre, R.   49
Delrue, M.   58
Descartes, R.   20, 95, 151, 156, 167, 196-198
Dillenberger, J.   38
Disse, J.   103, 244
Dostoievsky, F.   77-78, 172
Drey, J. von   16
Duintjer, O.   99
Dulles, A.   12, 24, 32-33
Dupré, L.   20, 53, 126, 154, 168-170, 197-198, 232
Dyrness, W.   39, 42

Ebeling, G.   17
Eckhart   79, 100, 151, 166, 167, 169, 171-173, 182, 189, 196-199
Eco, U.   138, 175
Edwards, J.   49
Ehrhardt, W.   206
Ehrlich, J.   16
Eibl, H.   77
Eicher, P.   134, 139, 199
Eliot, T.   262
Erasmus, D.   45, 147
Eriugena, J.   100, 173, 182
Erp, S. van   18
Essen, G.   18, 29
Euripides   149

Farley, E.   42
Fénelon, F.   147
Feuerbach, L.   173, 259
Feyaerts, K.   34
Fichte, J.   78, 198, 201-205, 211-212, 226
Ficino, M.   178
Flash, K.   163-164, 178

Ford, D.   12, 246
Foucault, M.   89
Franke, J.   21
Franks, A.   117
Frei, H.   11, 33, 243
Fries, H.   15

Galileo, G.   165
García-Rivera, A.   38, 65
Gardner, L.   74
Gasche, R.   135
Göbel, W.   169
Goethe, J.   77, 78, 134-136, 200, 202, 226
Gombrich, E.   165
Gorringe, T.   247
Green, G.   248-249
Gregory of Nyssa   80
Grenz, S.   21
Grøn, A.   248
Grözinger, A.   60
Gruchy, J. de   45, 65, 257-258
Grünewald, M.   46
Guardini, R.   77
Guerriero, E.   76
Günther, A.   16
Gunton, C.   259

Haas, A.   125
Hamann, J.   146-147, 204
Hammermeister, K.   205, 207, 210
Harries, R.   42
Hart, T.   58
Haubst, R.   169, 178, 184
Hauerwas, S.   30
Hegel, G.   49, 55, 78, 151, 169-170, 195, 198, 201-207, 212, 222, 226, 237
Heidegger, M.   5, 78, 90, 111, 148, 150-151, 160, 235, 238
Heinz, H.   137
Helm, P.   20
Henrici, P.   76, 125
Herder, J.   78

INDEX OF NAMES

Hirschberger, J. 184
Hodgson, P. 252
Hoeps, R. 42, 58-59
Hölderlin, F. 77-78, 150, 202, 205, 207, 214
Holzer, V. 113
Homer 5, 46, 148, 160, 182, 200, 226
Hopkins, G. 41, 44, 67, 146-147
Howes, G. 37
Hughes, T. 1
Huizinga, J. 165
Husserl, E. 78, 217

Irenaeus 146, 256

Jantzen, G. 45, 68
Jaspers, K. 169, 178
Jenson, R. 266
Joest, W. 16
John of the Cross 146, 262
John Paul II 51
Jung, C. 136
Jüngel, E. 44, 65-66, 253

Kaiser, A. 169
Kamitsuka, D. 13, 35
Kant, I. 47-49, 55, 62, 78, 99-100, 134-135, 151, 169, 201-205, 214, 217, 235, 245, 249-250, 261
Kasper, W. 210
Kaufman, G. 248, 250-253
Kay, J. 126
Kearney, R. 189, 248
Keats, J. 200
Kehl, M. 85
Keppler, J. 165
Kerr, F. 88
Kiefer, A. 158
Kierkegaard, S. 54, 127-128, 147
Kirchhoff, J. 205
Klaghofer-Treitler, W. 95-96, 118, 120-121
Knauer, P. 16, 19

Krenski, Th. 76, 81, 87
Küng, H. 44, 64-65, 83, 253
Kuschel, K. 250

Laarhoven, J. van 46
LaCugna, C. 256
Larcher, G. 63
Las Casas, B. de 147
Lash, N. 244
Leahy, B. 126, 141, 154
Leeuw, G. van der 4, 43, 50-54, 56-57, 60
Leibniz, W. von 147, 151, 197
LeRon Shults, F. 37, 123
Lesch, W. 60
Lessing, G. 78, 95, 156, 224
Levi, A. 165
Lévi-Strauss, C. 89
Lindbeck, G. 35
Lochbrunner, M. 82, 84, 101, 126, 147, 154
Lombard, P. 17
Lonergan, B. 19, 21, 31-32
Loyola, I. 79, 172
Lubac, H. de 4, 75, 79-80, 90, 147
Luckmann, Th. 252
Lullus, R. 147, 167
Luther, M. 45, 147, 152, 154-155, 265
Lyotard, J. 61

Maas, F. 42, 60
Mackey, J. 22, 42
Maréchal, J. 111-112, 116
Maritain, J. 49, 55
Marquard, O. 209
Marx, K. 174
Maund, B. 246
Maximus Confessor 79
McInerny, R. 109-110
Mechels, E. 83
Memlinc, H. 177
Meuthen, E. 178
Michelangelo 258

Migliore, D.   28
Milbank, J.   223, 247, 249, 256, 261, 264
Mongrain, K.   81, 87, 115
Moss, D.   74
Mothershill, M.   176
Mul, J. de   207
Munch, E.   239
Murphy, F.   48, 126, 138, 257
Murphy, N.   20,

Newman, J.   147
Nichols, A.   118, 126, 147, 153
Niebuhr, R.   33, 266
Nietzsche, F.   49, 78, 148, 261
Nordhofen, E.   43
Norris, Th.   90
Novalis   78, 202, 205

O'Collins, G.   15, 24
O'Donoghue, N.   104, 126, 150
O'Donovan, O.   256
O'Hanlon, G.   120, 238
O'Meara, Th.   202
O'Regan, C.   196, 221, 239, 265
Oakes, E.   87, 116, 122, 224
Ockegem, J.   177
Ockham   167
Origen   79, 95, 97, 173

Paetzold, H.   206, 209-210
Pannenberg, W.   116
Pascal, B.   77, 146-147
Pattison, G.   42, 239
Paul, J.   78
Péguy, C.   147
Pelikan, J.   43
Petrarca   165
Philip the Chancellor   99
Phillips, D.   22, 243
Picasso, P.   158, 239
Pinkard, T.   201-202
Pius XII   80
Placher, W.   19

Plaga, U.   118
Plato   45, 128, 148-150, 166-167, 177, 189, 226, 233
Plotinus   45, 60, 77, 148-151, 173, 180, 182, 185, 189, 192, 233
Pöltner, G.   101
Proclus   166, 182, 185
Pröpper, Th.   30, 113
Przywara, E.   4, 79, 83, 108, 110-117
Pseudo-Dionysius   45, 99, 146, 149-150, 166, 175, 192

Quash, B.   74, 116
Quine, W.   20

Rahner, K.   19, 21, 29, 38, 62, 84, 112-113, 118, 134
Ratzinger, J.   85
Ricoeur, P.   89
Rilke, R.   78, 224
Roberts, L.   126, 238
Rorty, R.   20
Rosenzweig, F.   207
Roten, J.   81
Rouault, G.   172
Rousselot, P.   18
Ruusbroeck   79, 171

Santinello, G.   178
Santoro-Brienza, L.   46
Scheeben, M.   49
Scheler, M.   78
Schelling, F.W.J.   3, 6, 55, 78, 90, 147, 151, 160, 170, **195-227**, 231-233, 236, 239
Scheurs, N.   15
Schilderman, H.   31
Schillebeeckx, E.   113, 252
Schiller, F.   78, 150, 201-202, 214
Schlegel, F.   78, 202, 205, 208
Schleiermacher, F.   15, 35, 55
Schmid, J.   136
Schmidt, J.   207
Schmidt, P.   42

INDEX OF NAMES

Schneider, G. 178
Schneider, N. 201
Schner, G. 13, 33, 251
Schopenhauer, A. 55, 78, 211
Schreiter, R. 26
Schulze, W. 167, 169, 183
Schüssler Fiorenza, F. 15, 17-19, 21, 23-24, 35
Schwager, R. 19
Schwöbel, C. 22
Scola, A. 83, 87
Scotus 217
Shaftesbury, Earl of 197, 226
Shakespeare, W. 172
Shanks, A. 37
Shelley, M. 200
Shelly, P. 200
Sherry, P. 42, 45, 49, 64, 252, 257
Sidney, Ph. 175
Siewerth, G. 109-110
Sloterdijk, P. 174
Smith, J. 33
Snow, D. 203
Solowjew, V. 146-147
Sophocles 149, 182
Speyr, A. von 4, 71-72, 75, 81-82
Spinoza, B. de 199, 216
Stammberger, R. 109
Steck, C. 138
Steiner, G. 232
Stock, A. 44, 58-59
Suarez, F. 45, 99, 217

Tanner, K. 19
Tatarkiewicz, W. 46, 166-167, 176, 178-179
Tauler, J. 171
Taylor, C. 33
Taylor, M. 61
Thiel, J. 20
Thomas Aquinas 17-18, 45, 99-101, 110-111, 148, 150-151, 171-172, 176, 189, 248-249
Thompson, J. 83, 116

Thurner, M. 169
Tighe, Th. 186
Tillich, P. 4, 35, 43, 50, 53-54, 57-59, 65
Tilliette, X. 206-207
Toulmin, S. 163
Tracy, D. 13-14, 19, 25-28, 168, 248, 250

Ulrich, F. 107, 109-110, 235

Van Eyck, J. 46
VanHoozer, K. 265
Vasari, G. 175
Vaughan, W. 202, 209
Velthoven, Th. van 178
Verene, D. 200, 226
Verweyen, H. 15, 17, 62-63, 113, 211
Viladesau, R. 47, 63-64, 248
Villon, F. 172
Virgil 148, 182
Volkmann-Schluck, K. 178

Wagner, H. 16-18
Waldenfels, H. 15, 18
Wallner, K. 121
Ward, G. 25, 26, 74, 120
Watts, P. 178
Waugh, E. 267
Webster, J. 15, 35, 44, 255-256, 258
Wendel, S. 28
Wenzel van Huyssteen, J. 21, 29-30
Weyden, R. van der 177, 186-187
Wiles, M. 12
Wilkinson, E. 135
Williams, R. 232, 256
Wissink, J. 83
Wolde, E. van 31
Wolterstorff, N. 65, 257

Yandell, K. 26

Zimmy, L. 115